The Black History of the White House

The Black History of the White House

Clarence Lusane

Open Media Series | City Lights Books
San Francisco

Cover design by Pollen, New York
Cover photograph by Frances Benjamin Johnston: White House Easter egg roll, 1898.

The Open Media Series is edited by Greg Ruggiero and archived by the Tamiment Library, New York University.

Library of Congress Cataloging-in-Publication Data

Lusane, Clarence, 1953-
The Black history of the White House / by Clarence Lusane.
p. cm. — (Open media series)
Includes bibliographical references and index.
ISBN 978-0-87286-532-7
1. White House (Washington, D.C.)—History. 2. African Americans—Washington, D.C.—History. 3. African Americans—Washington, D.C.—Social conditions. 4. African Americans—Washington, D.C.—Biography. 5. Presidents—Relations with African Americans—History. 6. Presidents—United States—Racial attitudes—History. 7. Presidents—United States—Staff—History. 8. Slavery—Washington, D.C.—History. 9. United States—Race relations—Political aspects. I. Title.
F204.W5L86 2011
975.3—dc22

2010036925

City Lights Books are published at the City Lights Bookstore, 261 Columbus Avenue, San Francisco, CA 94133.

www.citylights.com

To the Lusane House
(Clarence, Zezeh, Ellington, and Jessica)

To Dr. Ronald W. (Ron) Walters (1938–2010), a friend, mentor, and scholar-activist of the highest order whose life made a substantive difference.

CONTENTS

ILLUSTRATIONS

ACKNOWLEDGMENTS

During the time I was writing this book, Washington, D.C., had one of its worst snowstorms in history. As I waited in an extraordinarily long line at the grocery store, thinking of all the editing and writing I still had to do, a neighbor, who had switched to a much shorter line, beckoned me over. In a relatively short time I had paid for my groceries and was on my way. Her act of kindness likely saved me two hours and allowed me to get back to my desk to keep working. Ultimately, writing is an act of individual discipline, but it takes place in the social world. My neighbor, whom I had never met before and whose name I never knew, and many other unnamed individuals played small and large roles in making this work possible.

As usual, James Steele has always been the brother I never had biologically. He strongly recommended that I take on this project from the very beginning and has always been there whenever I needed him for wisdom, comment, or just a general take on the state of the world (or the NBA). I also want to give a shout to Maurice Jackson, who has kept his eye on this project and sent timely references and notes that fill the seams and crevices of this work. I also thank Clayton LeBouef who provided an important lead in my research on music at the White House.

I have also had the good fortune to be able to count on Darius and Debbie Mans for their helpful insights, caipirinhas, and sage analysis of black politics, U.S. history, and global relations. Debbie was also one of the outside readers I trusted to give me real feedback on the final draft. Others who took this grand task were Wilmer Leon, Keisha Williams, Sylvia Hill, Geoffrey Jacques, and the aforementioned James Steele. Also, I want to express great appreciation to Danny Glover, David Theo Goldberg, Barbara Ransby, and the White House Historical Association.

Greg Ruggiero has more often than not been my repressed brain, creative spirit, and alternate consciousness while writing this book. He has been my indispensable editor. Engaged and passionate, he turned curves into sharp corners, replaced fictions with facts, identified and strengthened weaknesses, and helped to generate reflections. Thank you, Greg.

City Lights Books has been great to work with. Taking a comprehensive approach, the publisher created a Web site, set up speaking engagements, and made every other effort to ensure the success of this project. Demanding when necessary and supportive all the way, City Lights continues to produces books that advance our public discourse and intellectual life. My deep thanks to Stacey and the entire City Lights staff.

Finally, I want to once again acknowledge the support of my family. From D.C. to Detroit to Brazil to New Jersey to Alabama, my family has always been my encouraging and supportive foundation, the embodiment of all that matters. Above all, Zezeh and Ellington provide inexhaustible happiness and pleasure in my daily (non-writing) life.

INTRODUCTION

Black People, White Houses

African Americans and the Promise of the White House

> *I, too, am America*—Langston Hughes, from his poem "I, Too, Sing America"

More than one in four U.S. presidents were involved in human trafficking and slavery. These presidents bought, sold, bred and enslaved black people for profit. Of the twelve presidents who were enslavers, more than half kept people in bondage at the White House. For this reason there is little doubt that the first person of African descent to enter the White House—or the presidential homes used in New York (1788–1790) and Philadelphia (1790–1800) before construction of the White House was complete—was an enslaved person.[1] That person's name and history are lost to obscurity and the tragic anonymity of slavery, which only underscores the jubilation expressed by tens of millions of African Americans—and perhaps billions of other people around the world—220 years later on November 4, 2008, when the people of the United States elected Barack Obama to be the nation's president and commander in chief. His inauguration on January 20, 2009, drew between one and two million people to Washington, D.C., one of the largest gatherings in the history of the city and more than likely the largest presidential inauguration to date.[2] Taking into account the tens of millions around the globe who watched the event live via TV or Internet, it was perhaps the most watched inauguration in world history. It was of great international interest that for the first time in U.S. history, the "first family" in the White House was going to be a black family.

Obama has often stated that he stands on the shoulders of those who came before him. In terms of the White House, this has generally been seen to mean those presidents he admires, such as Abraham Lincoln, Franklin Roosevelt, John Kennedy, and Lyndon Johnson, who all inspired him in his political career. However, he is also standing on the shoulders of the many, many African Americans who were forced to labor for, were employed by, or in some other capacity directly involved with the White House in a wide array of roles, including as slaves, house servants, elected and appointed officials, Secret Service agents, advisers, reporters, lobbyists, artists, musicians, photographers, and family members, not to mention the activists who lobbied and pressured the White House in their struggle for racial and social justice. As the Obama family resides daily in the White House, the narratives of these individuals resonate throughout their home.

The black history of the White House is rich in heroic stories of men, women, and youth who have struggled to make the nation live up to the egalitarian and liberationist principles expressed in its founding documents, including the Declaration of Independence and the U.S. Constitution. For over 200 years African Americans and other people of color were legally disenfranchised and denied basic rights of citizenship, including the right to vote for the person who leads the country from the White House. But despite the oppressive state of racial apartheid that characterized the majority of U.S. history, in the main, as Langston Hughes reminds us, black Americans have always claimed that they too are American.

At the end of the nineteenth century, when Jim Crow segregation and "separate but equal" black codes were aggressively enforced throughout the South, few African Americans were permitted to even visit the White House. As Frances Benjamin Johnston's 1898 photo on the cover of this book indicates, however, black children were allowed to attend the White House's annual Easter egg–rolling ceremony. Permitting black children to integrate with white children on the White House premises one day a year was acceptable, even though such mingling was illegal in many public spaces throughout the South at the time, including libraries and schools.

The Easter egg–rolling tradition had begun on the grounds of the Capitol, but concern over damage to the grounds led to the 1876 Turf Protection Law, which ended the practice at that site. Two years later, President Hayes—who had won the presidency by promising to withdraw federal troops protecting African Americans in the South from whites who opposed black voting and political rights—opened the White House's south lawn for the event. By the time of Johnston's photo, the 1896 *Plessy v. Ferguson* decision legalizing segregation had been implemented, the last of the black politicians elected to Congress would soon be gone by 1901, and accommodationist black leader Booker T. Washington, who was also photographed by Johnston, was on the ascendant.

For many African Americans, the "white" of the White House has meant more than just the building's color; it has symbolized the hue and source of dehumanizing cruelty, domination, and exclusion that has defined the long narrative of whites' relations to people of color in the United States. Well before President Theodore Roosevelt officially designated it the "White House" in October 1901, the premises had been a site of black marginalization and disempowerment, but also of re-

What the White House looked like while human trafficking and enslavement of black people was thriving in Washington, D.C., 1858.

sistance and struggle. Constructed in part by black slave labor, the home and office of the president of the United States has embodied different principles for different people. For whites, whose social privileges and political rights have always been protected by the laws of the land, the White House has symbolized the power of freedom and democracy over monarchy. For blacks, whose history is rooted in slavery and the struggle against white domination, the symbolic power of the White House has shifted along with each president's relation to black citizenship. For many whites and people of color, the White House has symbolized the supremacy of white people both domestically and internationally. U.S. nativists with colonizing and imperialist aspirations understood the symbolism of the White House as a projection of that supremacy on a global scale.

Centuries of slavery, brutally enforced apartheid, and powerful social movements that ended both, are all part of the historical continuum preceding the American people's election of Barack Obama. Few people, black or otherwise, genuinely thought that they would live to see what exists today: a black man commanding the presidency of the United States and a black family running the White House. Despite important advances in public policy and popular attitude since the social movements of the 1950s, '60s and '70s, for the many people of color who lived through the segregation era and experienced the viciousness of racists, the complicity of most of their white neighbors, and the callous disregard and participation of city, state, and national authorities, Obama's election was a moment never imagined. It was never imagined, in part, because of the misleading and unbalanced history we have been taught.

The Struggle over Historical Perspective

> *History is always written wrong, and so always needs to be rewritten.*[3]—George Santayana

U.S. history is taught—and for the most part, learned—through filters. In everything from schoolbooks and movies to oral traditions, historical markers, and museums, we are presented with narratives of the nation's history and evolution. For generations, the dominant stories have validated a view that overly centralizes the experiences, lives, and issues of privileged, white male Americans and silences the voice of others. It has been as though some have an entitlement to historic representation and everyone else does not.

But it is more than a matter of marginalization and silencing. History is not just a series of dates and facts, but more important, involves interpretation, analysis, and point of view. Historic understanding shapes public consciousness, and thus politics and policy decisions, social relations, and access to

African American school children facing the Horatio Greenough statue of George Washington at the U.S. Capitol, circa 1899.

resources and opportunity. The dominant narratives of U.S. history elevate the nation's development through a perspective that reduces the vast scale and consequences of white enslavement of blacks, "Indian removal," violent conquest, genocide, racism, sexism, and class power. The generations of lives, experiences, and voices of marginalized and silenced Americans offer an array of diverse interpretations of U.S. history that have largely gone unheard, unacknowledged, and unrewarded. Without their perspectives, we are presented with an incomplete and incongruent story that is at best a disservice to the historical record and at worst a means of maintaining an unjust status quo.

In education, the field of Black History and other areas of what are generally referred to as Ethnic Studies have attempted to serve as counter-histories, seeking to include the communities and individuals that have too often been written out of the national story. Scholars have attempted not only to correct the record but also to restore a dignity and respect obliterated in official chronicles. These efforts have met with fierce resistance, from the beginning up to the present moment. In spring 2010, conservatives in Arizona not only passed SB 1070, which authorized—in fact, demanded—that law enforcement officers question the immigration status of anyone they deemed suspicious and who looked like they did not belong in the country, but also enacted HB 2281, which bans schools from teaching Ethnic Studies courses. While the former promotes racial profiling, the latter guarantees a continuing ignorance of the social diversity, history, and interests of everyone except white Americans. Framing education about the history of people of color in the worst possible manner, the law states, "Public school pupils should be taught to treat and value each other as individuals and not be taught to resent or hate other races or classes of people."[4] Specifically aimed at Mexican, indigenous, and black studies, the law generated copycat efforts elsewhere, just as attempts to reproduce the anti-immigrant SB 1070 spread to other U.S. states in the expanding culture war over whose history deserves state and political support and promotion.

The challenge of presenting an alternative and more inclusive history of the White House lies not so much in finding the details and facts of other voices, in this instance black voices, but in challenging the long-standing views and dominant discourses that permeate all aspects of our public and popular education. The White House itself is figuratively constructed as a repository of democratic aspirations, high principles, and ethical values. For many Americans, it is an act of unacceptable subversion to criticize the nation's founders, the founding documents, the presidency, the president's house, and other institutions that have come to symbolize the official story of the United States. Understandably, it is uncomfortable to give up long-held and even meaningful beliefs that in many ways build both collective and personal identities. However, partial and distorted knowledge is detrimental, and only through a more diverse voicing of the nation's experience and history, in this case of the White House, can the country—as a people—move forward.

Race, the Presidency, and Grand Crises

> *You never want a serious crisis to go to waste.*[5]—Rahm Emanuel, Barack Obama's White House chief of staff

Even after the celebrations of Obama's historic triumph, achieved with nearly unanimous support from African Americans and the votes of tens of millions of progressives, a nagging question remained: *What would the Obama White House mean for racial progress in the United States?* Will the Obama presidency generate the kind of historic policies that emerged under Franklin Roosevelt and Lyndon Johnson to create greater racial equality, or will Obama's contribution be more symbolic, as Bill Clinton's was? Will having a black president make a difference, and if so, what kind of difference?

United States history has shown that opportunity for sustainable and qualitative social reform, including in the area of race relations, typically arises from a crisis leveraged by massive social and political organizing, i.e., a crisis that threatens the ability of those in power to maintain governability and control. Presidents, and political leaders in general, are captives of the period and circumstances they inherit. Elected leaders have the potential to advance a political and policy agenda, but only within the limits of the social and broader historical constraints of their times. The political status quo is stubborn and, within a system of checks and balances such as exists in the United States, rarely elastic enough to answer civil society's incessant call for change. It is only under extraordinary conditions, such as when the efforts of ordinary citizens are focused on social movements whose demands threaten the elites with crisis, that massive and fundamental social transformation occurs. This trend is particularly pronounced throughout the history of race relations in the United States. In other words, whether Obama will have the opportunity for major advancements in the area of race relations and social equality will depend much more on the evolution of the political balance of forces, the state of the economy, the viability of political and social institutions, and the ideological atmosphere than simply his will (or lack thereof).

The black history of the White House is one in which the institution of the U.S. presidency has, generally speaking, only seriously and qualitatively responded to the nation's unjust racial divide in the face of crisis, when an uncertain future loomed, critical and divisive decisions had to be made, and black and anti-racist resistance were focused, intense, and spreading. Whether the White House response led to progressive social advances, conservative rollback—or both—has been determined by each era's particular factors, the personal predilections of the president in command being only one such element. Presidents Abraham Lincoln, Franklin Roosevelt, and Lyndon Johnson faced crises, arguably, under which the coherence and very existence of the nation itself was at stake. Civil war, economic catastrophe, and urban unrest challenged the legitimacy and power of the state, creating opportunities for radical social proposals that were normally ignored and dismissed.

It is hardly a given that the state's response to crisis will result in progressive democratic change. The Bush White House, for example, responding to the September 11 attacks, instituted antidemocratic, authoritarian, ultraconservative policies that would have been impossible to implement under normal circumstances. These included launching wars in Afghanistan and Iraq; curtailing civil liberties with the harsh USA Patriot Act; violating international human rights conventions with opened-ended detentions, military tribunals, the legal limbo of Guantánamo Bay prison, secret prisons, torture, extraordinary rendition, extrajudicial assassinations, and negligent killing of foreign civilians; and other legally and morally reprehensible actions.

Black Challenges to the White House

There is a long history of both black challenge and black accommodation to the White House. Every point in this country's past has seen black resistance to social injustice, including direct calls to the president for relief from, reparations for, and remediation of institutional racism. The black challenge has taken the form of slave escapes, revolts, underground networks, creation of maroon societies, literacy campaigns, petitions, participation in the Revolution (on both sides) and the Civil War, grassroots Reconstruction efforts, sit-ins, sit-outs, mass mobilizations (and threats thereof), voter registration drives, leadership in massive social movements, campaigns for political office including the offices of president and vice president, and countless other collective and individual counterassaults against white domination and discrimination. All have factored into the policy and political decisions made by U.S. presidents. The squeezing of the president for the juice of justice has been indispensable to black political and social movements in the enduring struggle for equality.

It could not be any other way. Racism and the exercise of white racial hegemony were at the core of the American Revolution and the founding of the nation itself. The establishment of a racial hierarchy was neither unconscious, secondary, an afterthought, nor even what many have called an unfortunate but necessary compromise. Rather than a compromise—implying that both sides gave up something fundamental—it was a surrender by Northern leaders, who set aside their publicly stated antislavery principles and dishonorably granted the South the legally protected business of human trafficking and enslavement of black people, some arguing that abolition was a battle to be fought another day.

As discussed in greater detail in Chapter 1, Southern leaders joined the armed revolutionary movement not so much to fight British domination of the colonies as to protect themselves from the British Crown's foreshadowed intent to liberate blacks from bondage. For the South, the nonnegotiable price of joining the armed revolt was the prolongation of white people's power to buy, sell, breed, and enslave black people in the post-revolution nation.

Perceiving this profound moral and political disjuncture, many free[6] and enslaved blacks joined the war on the side of the British. At the very center of this turbulent mix were the men who would become the first four presidents of the United States—George Washington (1789–1797), John Adams (1797–1801), Thomas Jefferson (1801–1809), and James Madison (1809–1817)—all of whom helped to define the duties, roles, responsibilities, and powers of the presidency itself. Their engagement with the moral and economic questions of slavery and race was complex, and their individual will, private interests, and political courage were as much an influence upon as influenced by social forces and the still gestating processes and structures of state authority. Ultimately, all would fail to rise above the popular racist views of their times and were unwilling and unable to advance egalitarian relations among races. As we will see in Chapters 3 and 4, their vacillations would only postpone the nation's inexorable drive toward civil war and further crises of legitimacy.

Alternative voices, however, would be raised by blacks and others during the Revolutionary period and ever afterward. By all the means at black organizers' disposal, from petitions and direct lobbying to local community organizing and national mass movements, presidents were challenged to live up to their oath of office and the promises of the nation's founding documents. Despite these calls for justice and freedom, until the Civil War, president after president would ratify white people's power to own and traffic blacks by signing laws such as the Fugitive Slave Act of 1793 and Fugitive Slave Act of 1850. James Buchanan (1857–1861), the last president before the Civil War, stated that slavery was "a great political and moral evil" but nonetheless (as president-elect) supported the Supreme Court's 1857 *Dred Scott vs. Sandford* decision, which ruled that no person of African descent could become a citizen of the United States, that blacks had "no rights which the white man was bound to respect, and that the negro [*sic*] might justly and lawfully be reduced to slavery for his benefit."[7] As is discussed in Chapter 5, it would take a horrific civil war and a hesitating but ultimately reformist president to resolve the nation's dilemma by illegalizing slavery.

The reluctance of the pre–Civil War presidents to address and assist the abolition movement only fueled the surging black resistance and directed its outrage at the White House. During the Civil War there was a massive desertion of plantations and work sites by millions of enslaved people—what W. E. B. Du Bois termed a black general strike. Fearing that a Southern victory would maintain the slave system and hoping a Northern win would abolish it, African Americans joined the Southern guerrilla underground and Union Army and fought valiantly to crush the pro-slavery forces.[8] Under pressure from the abolitionist movement, from influential public figures like Frederick Douglass, and simply out of military necessity, President Lincoln eventually permitted blacks to join the armed combat and enlist in the Union Army.

Beyond the military imperatives of winning the war, the Lincoln White House found itself forced to address the black cause; racial issues had become so urgent they could no longer be ignored. The escalating crisis opened up the political space to allow not just piecemeal reforms on human trafficking or another Faustian compromise with politicians representing white enslavers from the South, but the dismantling of the system of slavery once and for all. President Lincoln's personal views on the matter—whether those of a late convert to abolitionism, as argued by historian James M. McPherson, or of an unrepentant defender of the system who was "forced into glory," as historian Lerone Bennett Jr. contends—ultimately became secondary as circumstances demanded he take action on whites' legal right to enslave blacks, a demand that previous presidents had not had to address in a fundamental manner.[9] Although the Emancipation Proclamation, as a strategy against the South, freed only blacks enslaved to Confederate states that were in rebellion at the time, it nevertheless marked the beginning of a series of profound and irrevocable legal and societal shifts away from the barbarity of white domination and toward the democratic equality promised by the American Revolution.

The Lincoln White House resolved the issue of slavery, but not that of racism. Among the other variables that led to the war was the rise of Northern financial interests, which supported the Republican Party and were in competition with the interests of the Southern agricultural-based aristocracy. The push by the Republican Party for "free" labor in an increasingly industrializing nation—meaning a mobile, wage-paid workforce—was not the equivalent of fairness to workers or labor equality between whites and people of color. To advance its agenda and that of its sponsors, the Republican Party needed to break the economic power of the South as well as its dominance in Congress.

In the political openings created by the crisis and the transition of power from Southern interests to Northern ones, the experiment of Reconstruction was launched, wherein state authorities intervened on behalf of newly liberated women, men, and children, addressing the crisis of exclusion with political enfranchisement (for men), economic reparations (through the Freedmen's Bank), and social inclusion (through educational opportunities at all levels).

After the April 14, 1865, assassination of President Lincoln by John Wilkes Booth—the pro-slavery extremist who was impelled to commit the crime by the president's promise of voting rights for blacks—Lincoln's successor, President Andrew Johnson, began almost immediately to roll back the commitments Lincoln had made to black Americans. Republican Party radicals in Congress, led by Thaddeus Stevens, countered the Johnson White House and for nearly nine years pushed through groundbreaking legislation that granted new political rights and protection to blacks.

However, the crisis of the 1876 presidential election, in which a dispute arose over the legality of black votes in Florida, Louisiana, and South Carolina, redrew the political balance of power and once again saw the White House facilitate the subordination of blacks in U.S. society. The Hayes-Tilden Compromise was about more than just an election fiasco; it represented the reemergence of a modernized, post-slavery South that made an accommodation with its Northern counterpart. Once the urgent dispute over economic authority was resolved, there was little motivation on the part of the Republican Party to continue alienating large numbers of whites.

Jim Crow segregation policies and their legal and extralegal enforcement were well in place prior to the 1896 *Plessy v. Ferguson* decision that gave de jure cover to systemic, institutional, and private forms of racism. The Jim Crow presidents, from Rutherford Hayes (1877–1881) to Dwight Eisenhower (1953–1961), did little to support the black challenge to segregation and white domination over U.S. social and economic life. As I discuss in Chapter 5, during this period the White House, with a few notable exceptions, did little to further the cause of full citizenship and equal rights for blacks in America.

Yet the next series of crises would once again see a president—Franklin D. Roosevelt (1933–1945)—confront an issue he would have preferred to keep in the closet. By early 1933, unemployment had grown to 25 percent and more than 4,000 banks had collapsed.[10] The Dust Bowl drought destroyed tens of thousands of farms, rendering more than 500,000 people homeless. Roosevelt desperately launched a number of policies to address these emergencies. Blacks would benefit only partially and often indirectly from his economic rescue policies. Indeed, in some arenas, as more whites' economic and social standing advanced, blacks actually lost ground in one of the most legislatively and policy-generous periods in U.S. history. "The wide array of significant and far-reaching public policies that were shaped and administered during the New Deal and Fair Deal era of the 1930s and 1940s," Ira Katznelson notes in his history-revising book, *When Affirmative Action Was White: An Untold History of Racial Inequality in Twentieth-Century America*, "were crafted and administered in a deeply discriminatory manner."[11]

An equally critical factor was the qualitative transformation of the framework under which U.S. business and much of global capitalism would operate. Keynesian economics, which called for decisive state intervention in managing and policing big business, would result in the opening of political space for working-class prerogatives to emerge. Given the working-class status of most African Americans at the time, they too made some economic and political gains during the period. Progress was more regional than national, however, as the still white-dominated South dug in and refused to budge on the issue of segregation.

Black resistance would not relent either, and soon ballooned into a full-blown uprising with millions of African Americans driving the civil rights campaigns that began to engulf the entire South. In courtrooms, classrooms, and even restrooms, black activists and ordinary people alike challenged the system of white control. The black freedom movement mushroomed, opening new fronts on various levels with wide-ranging tactics and perspectives. The battle streams of civil rights and urban resistance would soon join a mighty river of national turbulence expressing multiple demands upon the nation in general and the White House in particular. Black struggle, antiwar resistance, and a vibrant youth counterculture drove the crises between 1955 and 1974. As discussed in Chapter 7, the political status quo was further destabilized by one president's unexpected refusal to run for reelection, the assassination of a presidential candidate, the resignation of a vice president, the resignation to preempt impeachment of a president, and the installation of both a president and a vice president who had not been elected to the office, all within the span of six years.

The late-term Civil Rights Era presidencies of Dwight Eisenhower (1953–1961), John Kennedy (1961–1963), and Lyndon Johnson (1963–1968) were reluctant to assist the cause of black freedom yet began to champion policies and endorse legislation that attacked Jim Crow. During the four-year period from 1964 to 1968, the black view of the White House became more favorable as presidential pressure helped defeat white opposition to bills that finally broke the back of formal segregation in the South.

Through high rhetoric, low legislation, and symbolic appointments, post-Johnson presidents have been treading water on racial issues since 1968. Richard Nixon (1968–1974), Jimmy Carter (1977–1981), Ronald Reagan (1981–1989), and Bill Clinton (1993–2001) all sustained aggressive attacks on civil rights advances, whereas Gerald Ford (1974–1977), George H. W. Bush (1989–1993), and George W. Bush (2001–2009) engaged in egregious neglect. None proposed legislation that would substantially address the economic and social disparities between whites and people of color, despite symbolism and rhetoric aplenty (e.g., a new national holiday honoring Martin Luther King Jr.; Clinton's Race Initiative; and various cabinet appointments). During this period the White House did not face the type of grand crisis that would have opened the door to major changes advancing equality in politics, education, economics, justice, housing, and labor for people of color in the United States. For most black social justice leaders, activists, and organizers it was a bleak period with little hope on the horizon.

Some pioneering African Americans, rather than looking to the White House for help, decided to run for the White House themselves. These campaigns ran the gamut from the comical to the serious and included women and men, members of major parties and minor parities as well as independent candidates, and ideological tendencies from the far right to the far left and everything in between. As discussed in Chapter 8, each campaign would be a building block for the ones that followed. Then came Obama.

Obama and the Future of Black History

> *I have never been so naïve as to believe that we can get beyond our racial divisions in a single election cycle, or with a single candidacy—particularly a candidacy as imperfect as my own.*[12]—President Barack Obama, March 18, 2008, Philadelphia

Obama may not have been so naïve about the continuation of racism after his election, but many others were. Naïve in some ways, opportunistic in others. While liberal supporters of Obama wishfully believed that his election signified a radical change in American race relations, the anti-Obama right wing took advantage of his election to bruit its "postracial" mantra. Conservative columnist Laura Hollis, writing for *Townhall.com*, stated, "Racism is dead." Writer Shelby Steele, in a post-election *Los Angeles Times* article, asked, "Doesn't a black in the Oval Office put the lie to both black inferiority and white racism? Doesn't it imply a 'post-racial' America?" Conservative media and lobbyists rejoiced in Obama's victory, seeing it as vindication of their decades-old argument that laws passed as a result of the Civil Rights Movement had ended racism in the United States.

Those who make this argument are wrong on many accounts. On the immediate level, they ignore the significance of racial incidents that occurred during the campaigns and the fact that racist incidents actually appeared to escalate after Obama's election. On a deeper level, they fail to acknowledge the perpetuation of institutional racism as it manifests through measurable disparities in job opportunities, career advancement, real estate and housing, education and academic performance, health and access to health care, criminal justice and susceptibility to incarceration, the absence of black history in public education, and lack of black representation in popular media.

President-elect Barack Obama was about to walk out to take the oath of office. Backstage at the U.S. Capitol, he took one last look at his appearance in the mirror.

Despite the victory Obama's election represents, this country is still a long way from realizing the essence and spirit of its founding principles, and thus still a long way from being a genuinely egalitarian and democratic "postracial" society.

Until it is, there's work to do. This book was written in honor of those who have come before, that their stories and efforts may inform and inspire future generations of leaders, organizers, and ordinary people to carry the torch and spread the flame. To that end, this book is narrative driven: more than anything, it is the stories of real people who have challenged the racist dimensions of U.S. power and privilege that convey the history and experience of African Americans and their shifting relationship to the White House. For too many years, their experiences have been ignored, their voices silenced, their history absent from the public classroom. Yet they are an indelible, inextricable part of this country. Their story is our story, and their determined struggle, over generations, to share in the founding promises of equality, life, liberty, and the pursuit of happiness is as much a part of White House history as the stories of the presidents and their families. From the courageous black woman Oney Judge, who escaped enslavement from the first U.S. president, to the regal Michelle LaVaughn Robinson Obama, there has been a black presence in the White House reflecting in one form or another the ongoing struggle for equality and freedom.

In the book's final chapter I attempt to discuss the significance of the Obama White House in the context of black history, and how the crises his presidency faced coming into power may be quite different from the ones he is likely to leave behind. Issues of racial controversy are already manifesting in the first years of his presidency and are likely to escalate as Republican Party strategists attempt to exploit a politics of resentment and fear for electoral gain. This strategy has already unleashed a barrage of racial incidents and a jittery, less than stellar response from the Obama administration. However, it goes without saying that at the time of this writing in 2010, the story of the first black White House is still a work in progress, and what the Obama presidency will do to further extend the nation's founding promises to people of color and others outside the sphere of traditional privilege is still unfolding on a daily basis. Despite the powerful concrete and symbolic victory that the Obama White House represents, one race's privilege, preference, and politics continue to exert undue influence over national civic and private culture. What the first black White House does to level the racial playing field will forever be part of both black history and the nation's history. How far it goes and to what degree it succeeds is still very much up to the actions of ordinary people like you and me.

CHAPTER I

A Declaration of Independence and Racism: Founding Documents, Founding Fathers, and the Preservation of Slavery

Prelude: Oney's White House Story

Oney never knew the year of her birth. Nor did she know what year she successfully escaped to freedom. Befreckled and nearly white in skin color, she was as close to the nation's first genuine national hero as a person could be. During her enslavement she had been a seamstress and waiting maid and had worked indoors rather than out in the field. Although she stated that she never suffered any severe hardships while a slave, the hope of freedom burned incessantly within her. Like tens of thousands of other enslaved people, by seizing her opportunity for freedom she risked living out her life as a permanent fugitive or, if caught, being condemned to brutal physical punishment, execution, or perhaps a life of hard labor as a field slave. But escape she did, and with a determination never to be caught and enslaved again. Ona "Oney" Maria Judge's tremendous courage is perhaps all the more remarkable in that she escaped from the presidential residence of the United States' first president, George Washington, a slave owner.

The building where the first president of the United States lived with his family and the blacks they enslaved, High Street, Philadelphia.

The Revolutionary War general, founding father, and first president of the United States grew up in a slave-owning family, and by the time he was 11 years old he owned his first ten slaves. That number would continue to grow throughout his life as a farmer and planter. He purchased and enslaved more black people and acquired twenty more as a result of his marriage to Martha Custis in 1759. At his death in 1799, he held in slavery more than 300 black men, women, and children. Although he would state in later years that he opposed slavery and wrote in his will that he would free his enslaved upon his and Martha's death, he never took a public stand against the system or, as the nation's leader, called for its abolition.[1]

During the final days of his presidency in 1796, Washington lived with his wife and a group of their slaves in Philadelphia while the White House was being constructed, along with the rest of the capital, on land acquired from Maryland and

Virginia near the Potomac River. Washington's second term in office was to end in 1797, and he had no plans to run for another term. Oney, who served as Martha Washington's personal maid, was rightfully worried that once the Washingtons went back South to Mount Vernon, Virginia, her chances of escaping to freedom would be much slimmer.

As a "dower" slave, Oney was essentially on loan from the estate of Martha's first husband, Daniel Parke Custis, who died in 1757. Dowers were slaves who actually belonged to an estate and could be made available to whomever the estate prescribed for a period of time, usually until the designee's death, and then were passed on to the inheritors of the next generation. In other words, Martha never really owned the slaves, who were legally the property of her deceased husband's descendants. Upon her death, ownership of the dower slaves reverted back to the Custis estate. Since the status of children born into slavery was determined by the status of their mother, Oney's children would also be dower slaves and might never achieve freedom.

Technically, the Washingtons could have granted Oney her freedom, but they would have owed the Custis estate whatever it determined was her monetary value, something George did not want—and perhaps could not afford—to do. Instead, in March 1796, while living at the president's residence in Philadelphia, Martha Washington informed Oney that she was going to be given to Martha's granddaughter as a wedding gift. Oney must have understood that such a transfer would diminish her chances for freedom, and that that her life as a slave would never end unless she took bold action.[2]

Oney bided her time and waited until the summer. As she later told a reporter, "Whilst they were packing up to go to Virginia, I was packing to go," demonstrating the kind of forethought, daring, and planning most slaveholders believed to be beyond their slaves' capacities. Oney went on to say, "I didn't know where; for I knew that if I went back to Virginia, I should never get my liberty. I had friends among the colored people of Philadelphia, had my things carried there beforehand, and left Washington's house while they were eating dinner."[3] One can imagine Martha or George calling for Oney to come and clear the table of dishes, a call that was never to be answered.

Oney was born to an enslaved black mother, Betty, and a white father who had been an indentured servant but eventually won his freedom. Oney's birth likely took place sometime in 1772 or 1773. Like her mother, Oney developed needlework and sewing skills and became very close to Martha, who brought Oney along on shopping trips and other outings.[4] Oney was 17 or 18 when the Washingtons moved to New York in early 1789, bringing her and six other slaves with them. Almost two years later, Washington moved to Philadelphia, the temporary center of government power while the District of Columbia was being constructed. It was from President Washington's Philadelphia residence that Oney made her escape.

It would be logical to surmise that the public attention, honor, and respect that came with being the first president of the United States and leader of the victorious American revolutionary forces would have disposed Washington not to pursue Oney after she escaped. Given that President Washington had both spoken against the evil of slavery and owned hundreds of slaves, one would expect that he would accept the fact that Oney was gone and direct his time and attention to national matters. However, President Washington, like most other white enslavers, considered Oney to be his property, hence he bade others to help him pursue and recapture her.

Like his wife, Martha, President Washington could not understand why Oney would want to run away from them, especially considering how "humanely" they thought they had treated her. According to historian Helen Bryan, the president was reportedly hesitant at first and refused Martha's urging that he advertise for her capture and return.[5] Martha felt that Oney's escape demonstrated an unacceptable unfaithfulness and disloyalty and that slave catchers should be hired to pursue her.[6] Washington felt that publicly pursuing Oney would be unbecoming and settled on having her recaptured in a more surreptitious manner. As the acting president of the United States, George Washington was the most powerful person in the country at the time, and he used his considerable reach in the attempt to capture Oney numerous times.

Oney prepared for her freedom in steps. Before escaping, she first hid clothes and belongings with some of her free black friends in Philadelphia, and when the moment arrived she went to them. Oney left Philadelphia for Portsmouth, New Hampshire, on a ship named *Nancy* captained by John Bolles. Portsmouth was a coastal city and a former center for the importation of slaves. Over time, however, slavery in Portsmouth diminished almost to nonexistence as the Atlantic slave trade vanished, slaves were freed or sold South, and abolitionism grew.

Although New Hampshire did not officially abolish slavery until 1857, by the time Oney arrived, its end was clearly at hand.[7] The 1800 census listed only eight enslaved individuals living in the state. Portsmouth had also become an active area for abolitionism.[8] While Oney found herself protected by blacks and others in the local community there, she was still very much in danger, because her escape to freedom violated national law and the Constitution itself. Under Article 4, Section 2 of the then less than 10-year-old U.S. Constitution,

> No Person held to Service or Labour in one State,

> under the Laws thereof, escaping into another, shall, in Consequence of any Law or Regulation therein, be discharged from such Service or Labour, But shall be delivered up on Claim of the Party to whom such Service or Labour may be due.

The U.S. Constitution's concession to slaveholders, South and North, enforced slavery nationally irrespective of objections to the institution at the state level. For Oney this meant that she could be pursued and captured even in "free" states where slavery had been abolished. White enslavers were further bolstered by the Fugitive Slave Act of 1793, which Washington signed into law—perhaps as Oney and others who were enslaved worked nearby. That law stated:

> any person who shall knowingly and willingly obstruct or hinder such claimant, his agent or attorney in so seizing or arresting such fugitive from labour, or shall rescue such fugitive from such claimant, his agent or attorney when so arrested pursuant to the authority herein given or declared; or shall harbor or conceal such person after notice that he or she was a fugitive from labour, as aforesaid, shall for either of the said offences, forfeit and pay the sum of five hundred dollars.[9]

According to both the U.S. Constitution and the Fugitive Slave Act, Oney and everyone who helped her escape—such as Captain Bolles and the local black community in Philadelphia—were criminals. Under federal law, Oney became a wanted fugitive everywhere in the United States. But Oney and her friends were not the only lawbreakers in this story: So was President Washington.

In 1780, Pennsylvania became the first state to seek an eventual end to slavery with the passage of the symbolically important but substantively weak Gradual Abolition Act.[10] The law's Article X, however, while exempting members of Congress, foreign ministers, and consuls from its stricture against slaveholding, made no such exception for the president.[11] It was a highly complicated law that, among other provisions, stated that domestic slaves held by nonresidents in Pennsylvania had the right to manumission if they stayed in the state continuously for six months. However, if a slave left or was taken out of the state for even one day, the six-month requirement would start all over again once they returned. A 1788 amendment to the law sought to close this loophole by prohibiting slaveholders from deliberately rotating enslaved individuals in and out of the state for the express purpose of averting their eligibility for release. Despite this adjustment to the law, it was difficult to enforce, and Washington, while president, violated it brazenly.

Beginning in 1791, Washington deliberately rotated nine enslaved individuals he had brought with him to Philadelphia, including Oney. That he was fully aware of such violation is demonstrated in an April 12, 1791, letter to his chief secretary, Tobias Lear, expressing his concern about the law. President Washington wrote,

[I]n case it shall be found that any of my Slaves may, or any of them shall attempt their freedom at the expiration of six months, it is my wish and desire that you should send the whole, or such part of them as Mrs. Washington may not chuse [*sic*] to keep, home—for although I do not think they would be benefitted by the change, yet the idea of freedom might be too great a temptation for them to resist. At any rate it might, if they conceived they had a right to it, make them insolent in a State of Slavery. As all except Hercules and Paris are dower negroes, it behooves me to prevent the emancipation of them, otherwise I shall not only loose [*sic*] the use of them, but may have them to pay for. If upon taking good advice it is found expedient to send them back to Virginia, I wish to have it accomplished under the pretext that may deceive both them and the Public.[12]

In unambiguous terms, President Washington clearly sought to circumvent the law. He gives Lear explicit instructions to recycle his slaves without their knowledge in order to maintain a popular public image that he had cultivated as a reluctant and remorseful slave owner. As far back as 1778, Washington had spoken of his desire to be slave-free, in such language as "for Negroes (of whom I every day long more and more to get clear of)" and "to be plain I wish to get quit of Negroes."[13] But his views were mixed, as when he wrote in 1786:

> I can only say that there is not a man living who wishes more sincerely than I do, to see a plan adopted for the abolition of it—but there is only one proper and effectual mode by which it can be accomplished, & that is by Legislative authority: and this, as far as my suffrage will go, shall never be wanting. But when slaves who are happy & content to remain with their present masters, are tampered with & seduced to leave them; when masters are taken at unawar[e]s by these practices; when a conduct of this sort begets discontent on one side and resentment on the other, & when it happens to fall on a man whose purse will not measure with that of the Society, & he looses [*sic*] his property for want of means to defend it—it is oppression in the latter case, & not humanity in any; because it introduces more evils than it can cure.[14]

In a letter dated August 4, 1797, Washington stated that he hoped that the institution would end over time by congressional action: "I wish from my soul that the Legislature of this State [Virginia] could see the policy of a gradual Abolition of Slavery."[15]

However, George Washington also believed that his slaves would not benefit from freedom. The view that blacks were not ready for liberation was a common one among those who publicly condemned the institution but privately profited from their slaves. Whatever may have been the case with his claimed moral aversion to slavery, in action, George Washington did not free a single slave during his lifetime. Instead, he pledged that all of his slaves would be freed upon his and Martha's death. In fact, Martha released all of his slaves and her own before she died in 1803.

Perhaps not privy to George Washington's Hamlet-like dilemmas, at least one of the people kept in bondage by the First Family did not trust the Washingtons' far-off promises for liberation. In 1796, sometime between late May or early June, Oney got away. Unfortunately for her, shortly after arriving in New Hampshire, she was recognized on the streets of Portsmouth by Elizabeth Langdon, the daughter of New Hampshire Senator John Langdon. The Langdons were friends of the Washingtons, and word of Oney's whereabouts got back to the president.

According to researcher Helen Bryan, Martha Washington was extremely eager to re-enslave her reliable maid and pressed George to have her captured.[16] Like every successful escape plot, Oney's not only incurred loss to her owner but undermined the entire system of brutality, coercion, and fear needed to maintain it. From a slaveholder's point of view, inaction on the Washingtons' part would only embolden the field slaves; it wouldn't be prudent to allow a "privileged" house slave to run away without severe consequences. Rather than use the Fugitive Slave Act (which he had signed into law) and patronize the thriving but undignified slave-catcher business, Washington decided to first employ a more secretive approach. Through his treasury secretary, Oliver Wolcott Jr., Washington initially attempted to have New Hampshire Collector of Customs John Whipple detain her and have her shipped back to Virginia. On September 1, 1796, Washington wrote Whipple a note demanding that he "seize her and put her on board a Vessel bound immediately" to either Mount Vernon or Alexandria.[17] He added, "the ingratitude of the girl, who was brought up and treated more like a child than a Servant (and [given] Mrs. Washington's desire to recover her) ought not to escape with impunity if it can be avoided."[18]

The Whipples were an important and well-known family of the Revolution. John's brother William had been one of the original signers of the Declaration of Independence. As with the Langdons, there were personal as well as political ties connecting them to the First Family. According to a letter he wrote to Washington on September 10, 1796, Whipple initially appeared willing to comply with the request. Conscious of the strong antislavery sentiments in the city and of the protective stance of the black community, he could not publicly arrest her. Instead, he secretly arranged to trick her into boarding a ship that would begin her journey back to Mount Vernon.

Whipple's initial ruse was to offer Oney a job and invite her to an interview. She accepted the invitation, and in the course of the interview Whipple clearly sensed what he described as her "thirst for compleat freedom."[19] Because, perhaps, her status as a perpetual fugitive would deny that thirst from ever being completely satisfied, Whipple initially managed to convince her to return to the Washingtons under her two conditions that she would be freed upon their deaths and would at no point be sold or given to someone else. Whipple pledged to help her get her eventual freedom, and Oney seemed ready to return. An intervention by one of Oney's friends, however, made her reconsider the plan, and at the last moment she decided to reject Whipple's offers. As a result, Whipple informed Washington that his only recourse was to send a direct order to the attorney general of New Hampshire to have her apprehended. Whipple also made it clear that the increasingly strong antislavery atmosphere made it extremely difficult for escaped individuals to be captured and returned.

President Washington's response on November 28, 1796, was full of rage at Oney for even proposing such a compromise and railed that her "unfaithfulness" deserved punishment, not rewards.[20] Now more determined than ever, the president turned to his nephew, Burnwell Bassett Jr., and sent him to Portsmouth. Bassett was able to track down Oney and meet with her as well. In what he and Washington surely thought was a grand and honorable gesture, he informed her that if she came back willingly, Washington would grant her freedom back in Virginia. Oney wisely replied, "I am free now and choose to remain so."[21] Rebuffed, Bassett left empty-handed.

After being informed of Oney's intransigence, Washington commanded Bassett to return to Portsmouth and bring her back by force. Before going after Oney a second time, Bassett was entertained by the Langdons at their home in Portsmouth. Perhaps out of guilt for having either intentionally or accidentally let Oney's whereabouts be known, and apparently fearless of breaking the law, they secretly sent a message to Oney while Bassett was dining. As a result of the Langdons' advice, Oney traveled to Greenland, a town about eight miles from Portsmouth, and hid there. Unable to locate her, Bassett once again returned empty-handed. In December 1799, only three months after this last attempt to capture her, Washington died, and Oney was never bothered again. Although Washington designated in his will that all 124 of his legally owned slaves be freed upon his wife's death, two years later on January 1, 1801, Martha Washington decided to grant freedom to all of them and to the one enslaved individual she owned outright. None of the other 153 dower slaves could be freed by the Washingtons without reimbursement to the Custis estate, which Martha was unwilling or unable to make, and they were distributed among Martha's heirs.[22]

Washington's promise to free Oney upon his death was a deception. As a dower slave, Oney could not be granted her freedom by the Washingtons unless they purchased it for her, and there were no instructions in his will to compensate the Custis estate for her release. Faced with the prospect of lifelong slavery, Oney Judge fled the most powerful man in the United States, defied his attempts to trick her back into slavery, and lived out a better life. After her successful attempt became widely known, she was a celebrity of sorts. Her escape from the Washingtons fascinated journalists, writers, and others, but more important, it was an inspiration to the abolition movement and other African Americans who were being enslaved by whites.

Oney lived another fifty years, and though poor, she thrived in ways she could not have under slavery. She learned to read, although teaching literacy to blacks was illegal in many states. Through her talents as a seamstress she became self-employed and, to some degree, independent. She eventually married a sailor, Jack Staines, had three children, and enjoyed the luxury of being active in her community. She died in New Hampshire on February 25, 1848, 75 years old, still a fugitive from the president's house, but *free*.

From Oney Judge's successful escape from slavery to Barack Obama's successful election to the presidency, African Americans' engagement with the White House has been a story of unheard journeys, unheralded struggles, and unacknowledged efforts for full political, economic, and cultural equality and citizenship. The saga of the White House and the politics of the presidents who have occupied it is also the saga of the nation's racial history and struggles. The black history of the White House begins in the pre-revolutionary period during which future occupants of the White House first laid the foundation of what was to become more than two centuries of race-based cruelty, exclusion, and violence.

* * *

> *Well, I think white men were 100 percent of the people that wrote the Constitution, 100 percent of the people that signed the Declaration of Independence, 100 percent of people who died at Gettysburg and Vicksburg. Probably close to 100 percent of the people who died at Normandy. This has been a country built basically by white folks. . . .* —Pat Buchanan on the *Rachel Maddow Show*, July16, 2009

Of course, there never would have been a White House or a United States if the rebellion against Great Britain had failed. The American Revolution, a rebuke to the oppressive regime of England's King George, claimed to be driven by the principle of equality and freedom for all, but in fact embodied all the contradictions of a society destructively divided by race, contradictions that would haunt the nation and the White House for centuries. Buchanan disingenuously and shamelessly ignores the fact that black slave labor and the murderous theft of native lands were the foundation of the U.S. economy. And not only did the labor and land resources of people of color build the economy, but black hands literally built the country's most important national symbols: the U.S. Capitol, the White House, and the city of Washington, D.C., itself.

Despite Pat Buchanan's inaccurate, crude, and brazenly racialized (and gendered) view of the history of the United States, there was a black presence at the writing and signing of the Declaration of Independence, Articles of Confederation, and Constitution. It was a presence of shame manifest in the people of color who accompanied their white enslavers at gatherings where plans to overthrow British rule and create a new nation were formulated. The black personae at these monumental moments of U.S. history included, for example, Richard and Jesse: The former served Thomas Jefferson his tea each evening as he sat and wrote the Declaration of Independence in 1776; the latter rode postilion along Jefferson's journey to the Second Continental Congress. They included Billy Lee, who attended to George Washington's "every need day in and day out for the better part of the general's life" and who served Washington during the deliberations over the Constitution.[23] James Madison, flustered and embarrassed by his enslavement of blacks, chose not to bring any of his slaves to the Constitutional Convention. In spite of his shame and public condemnation of slavery as "evil," President Madison, like many of the early U.S. presidents, died a slave owner.

Despite slavery, African Americans did play a role in the founding of the nation beyond just laboring for the founding fathers and mothers. Blacks were involved in the revolutionary movement as activists and leaders. Historian Douglas Egerton notes that in New York, Joseph Allicocke, a man of mixed race, played such a key role in the Stamp Act riots that he was dubbed a "general" of the Sons of Liberty, a key prewar guerrilla band.[24] Further, Allicocke and other Sons met and planned their revolt at the Queen's Head, a tavern owed by "Black Sam" Fraunces, a mixed-raced Jamaican.[25]

If he really knew his history, Pat Buchanan might have also noted that John Adams himself referred to Christopher "Crispus" Attucks, a fugitive from slavery who was of black and Nantucket Indian heritage, as the first "martyr" of the American Revolution.[26] On March 5, 1770, a crowd of angry colonists gathered near Boston's Old State House after a British sentry hit a boy. After a season of protests against Britain's oppressive tax policies, British soldiers were a familiar and unwanted sight, and some in the crowd began to taunt the soldiers stationed there. Eight soldiers found themselves pelted by snowballs and rocks from a crowd that included Attucks. Outnumbered and nervous, the soldiers fired into the crowd. When the smoke cleared, Attucks, rope maker Samuel Gray, and sailor James Caldwell lay dead or dying, and two others, leather worker Patrick Carr and joiner's apprentice Samuel Maverick, died later. At least six others were wounded. The killings would become infamous as the "Boston Massacre," an incident that helped spark the Revolution.

Attucks, a fugitive from slavery would have been wise to allow others to taunt the British soldiers, whose presence was not only an affront to the sovereignty of the colonies but also an economic drain on the local economy, as soldiers took jobs that the city's underemployed and unemployed, including Attucks, felt they deserved. His sense of injustice, however, drew him out in protest and put him on the front line of a tragic confrontation. Attucks and the others killed by the soldiers were taken to Boston's Faneuil Hall, where they lay in state for three days. They were buried as heroes March 8, and approximately 10,000 people gathered to honor them by following the funeral procession to the Granary Burying Ground, Boston's third-oldest cemetery.

Though he would later become a committed abolitionist and revolutionary, John Adams successfully defended the British soldiers in court and referred to the group that was attacked as a mixture of "saucy boys, negroes and mulattoes, Irish teagues and outlandish jack-tarrs."[27] Thirty years later, Adams would be the new nation's second president, the first to command from the newly built chief executive's residence in the District of Columbia—the building we would come to know as the White House.

The White House was born from the Revolution and embodied all of its triumphs, contradictions, and flaws, particularly those regarding racial relations and power. Understanding the black history of the White House requires an exploration of the racial culture and politics that fundamentally shaped the nation.

Revolution and the Failure to End Slavery

Three central documents emerged that shaped the new nation and defined the principles upon which it was built: the Declaration of Independence, the Articles of Confederation, and the U.S. Constitution. At decisive moments, these writings served to unite and brace the revolutionaries who were committed to supplanting Britain's rule with a new system rooted in principles operative in few other countries at the time, i.e., one in which those residents recognizing the documents' language would be citizens rather than subjects, individuals whose rights would be respected and enshrined in law rather than violated arbitrarily by those in power. Indeed, democratic participation by these citizens would rule rather than absolute religious or monarchical authority.

More than half the population—women, slaves, blacks, indigenous people, and for the most part, men who did not own property—were not recognized in these founding documents and were not granted the same rights as the property-owning white men—many of whom owned hundreds of slaves—who wrote the documents and would soon run the new country.

Despite limitations on inclusion, the passion for collective independence among the people of the thirteen colonies—the two Carolinas, Connecticut, Delaware, Georgia, Maryland, Massachusetts, New Hampshire, New Jersey, New York, Pennsylvania, Rhode Island, and Virginia—grew more intense as they challenged the British crown's policies, impositions, and ultimately, right to rule.

At the core of the colonists' democratic rebellion, however, were the vexing issues of race: the enslavement of nearly 700,000 men, women, and children (whose numbers were growing daily), the ongoing slave trade, and the aggressive displacement of native peoples. In the process of rebellion and nation-building, the American revolutionaries failed to resolve the contradiction between their radical principles and philosophies, on the one hand, and their racist economic, political, and cultural self-interests on the other. Explicit and consistent expressions of repugnance regarding slavery by many of the founders and revolutionary leaders—no doubt genuinely felt in many instances—were offset by the reality of the racialized customs, policies, laws, and hierarchies that were perpetuated and enacted as the nation's governing structure and earliest leaders emerged. This group included the nation's first four presidents: George Washington (1789–1797), John Adams (1797–1801), Thomas Jefferson (1801–1809), and James Madison (1809–1817).

While some of the founding leaders of the United States found themselves ill at ease declaring freedom from British oppression while maintaining the institution of slavery, there were others whose primary motivation for seeking independence from England was to protect slavery from being outlawed by the British. In other words, the conventional narrative that the Founding Fathers and revolutionary leaders were driven only by the noble and enlightened notions of freedom and democracy and simply accommodated themselves to the evil of slavery as a necessary and unavoidable compromise evades a more disturbing analysis. An alternative view argues that a significant driving force behind the American Revolution—certainly not the only one—was a deeply rooted panic that continued ties to England would eventually remove white people's power to enslave blacks. This was certainly the attitude of many Southern leaders and much of the slave-owning class in the key slavery states of Georgia, North Carolina, South Carolina, and Virginia.

In *Slave Nation*, Alfred Blumrosen and Ruth Blumrosen meticulously and persuasively demonstrate the catalytic role of the little-known but highly decisive 1772 *Somerset* decision in England. They state, "The possibility of a British rejection of slavery anywhere in the empire appalled the plantation owners and their representatives because slavery was a necessary underpinning of their prosperity. Slavery was the foundation of the economic and social environment that their leaders represented and protected."[28]

A case can be made that the spark of the American Revolution came in the person of James Somerset. Born in West Africa circa 1740 and captured by slavers in 1749, he was eventually sold to Charles Stewart, paymaster general of the American Board of Customs. Family matters took Stewart—and therefore his slave Somerset—to London in 1769 where they would live for three years. Perhaps it was Somerset's encounters with free and fugitive blacks in London, hearing gut-wrenching British abolitionists' speeches, or simply his own inextinguishable desire for liberation that fanned his courage to rebel, but in any case, on October 1, 1771, Somerset walked away from Stewart's house with the intent never to return to bondage.

Stewart managed to have him tracked down, restrained, and shipped off aboard the vessel *Ann and Mary* with the objective of selling him in Jamaica as a punishment for his escape. Fortunately for Somerset, his cause was adopted by one of the most talented and effective abolitionists in England. Granville Sharp, an activist who in the recent past had successfully helped to emancipate five or six blacks pursuing freedom from their colonial enslavers, employed his steadfast determination to save Somerset.[29] Sharp mobilized a young barrister named Francis Hargrave, who was eager to take the case, and others, including members of London's black community. In the previous emancipations, the Lord Chief Justice of the King's Bench, Lord Mansfield (William Murray), had managed to convince the slave owners involved that it was in their best interest to grant freedom to their slaves rather than have the Court issue a ruling that could have sweeping and disastrous consequences for the whole slave system. It is unknown if the slave owners who preceded Mansfield knew that his beloved grandniece Dido Elizabeth Lindsey was racially mixed, which reportedly fostered his distaste for slavery.

Mansfield had selected himself to oversee the Somerset case. Though he tried repeatedly to persuade Stewart and Captain Knowles of the *Ann and Mary* to do the right thing and let Somerset go, the obdurate pair refused and decided to roll the dice and take their chances with Mansfield's ruling. It was a bad choice for them and the institution from which they profited.

On June 22, 1772, as the colonies were increasingly preparing for war, Lord Mansfield delivered his terse verdict:

> The state of slavery is of such a nature that it is incapable of being introduced on any reason, moral or political; but only by positive law, which preserves its force long after the reasons, occasion, and time itself from whence it was created, is erased from memory: it's so odious, that nothing can be suffered to support it but positive law.[30]

Lord Mansfield concluded, in other words, that nothing existed in English law that sanctioned slavery or could compel Somerset to return to bondage. He continued, in words that would bring celebration to Somerset and hope to the enslaved across the British Empire, including its thirteen American colonies, "Whatever inconveniences, therefore, may follow from the decision, I cannot say this case is allowed by the law of England and therefore the black must be discharged."[31]

This was the first time that the King's Bench Court had issued a ruling that definitively granted freedom to slaves should they choose to seek it in Britain. The "odious" slave system had just been struck a lethal blow in England, liberating 14,000 to 15,000 blacks who had been enslaved there.[32]

The ripple effect was immediate. Transnational black jubilation was broad and swift. So too was the effort by enslaved blacks in the American colonies, who learned of the decision and immediately sought ways to get to England. In Virginia, a slave named Bacchus escaped and was believed headed to Great Britain because he had learned about the Somerset case.[33] The decision was also a catalyst for whites who were opposed to slavery. According to historian John Hope Franklin, the *Somerset* decision directly led to the formation of the Society for Effecting the Abolition of the Slave Trade in 1787.[34]

It would be an understatement to say that celebration of

the decision was not universal. While the ruling did not specifically include the colonies, they were political entities under British rule, hence slave owners in Virginia, North Carolina, South Carolina and Georgia—the four colonies that profited most from slavery—drew the sobering conclusion that the day was likely near when the *Somerset* decision would also apply to them. Preempting the British Crown's abolition of slavery in the colonies became a matter of urgency in the South. Slave owners who perhaps had been hesitant about joining the independence movement now enlisted fully, but their participation came with a price: the perpetuation of slavery. The historical fact is that the American rebellion could not have advanced without a commitment by the revolutionary leadership to continue the institution of slavery after their break from England. Thus deeply conflicting motives—freedom and slavery—drove the white colonists' willingness to risk staging an armed revolution.

It is worth noting that Northern states benefited substantially from slavery even though slave labor on their own soil was minimal in comparison to the South. Shipbuilding, the trade in slaves, and other commercial and financial activities, such as high tariffs and taxes on slave traders, were absolutely essential to the Northern economy in Connecticut, Massachusetts, New York, Rhode Island, New Jersey, and other states. Those industries also generated thousands of jobs for lawyers, clerks, accountants, insurance agents, and the like. Thus Northern leaders were not as much compromised as complicit in perpetuating slavery.

This Faustian bargain would be reflected in the debates and ultimate articulation of the founding documents that would come to define the United States. In each struggle over the tone, content, and purpose of the Declaration of Independence, Articles of Confederation, and Constitution, the issue of slavery was raised and negotiated until leaders of the slave-driven South obtained concessions they considered adequate. While many Northern leaders may have privately found slavery abhorrent, and some even stated so publicly, there was barely an abolitionist word spoken or action taken when it came down to practical matters. The consequences of these decisions would profoundly influence the future course of race and class relations, law, and culture in the United States.

The political life and distribution of power of the nation was shaped by this compromise. For 200 years and beyond, the nation would struggle with a hierarchy of citizenship in which people of color found that freedom had multiple definitions and applications under U.S. law and public policy. The nation's founders could not escape the judgment of history by fudging words in the Declaration, Articles of Confederation, and Constitution; nothing could mask the reality that these iconic documents sanctioned and defended the institution of slavery.

Black radicals from slave revolt leader Nat Turner and human rights advocate Fannie Lou Hamer to the indomitable Harriet Tubman, black power advocate Malcolm X, and many others would reference these texts and the hypocrisy they embodied in their original intent. Conservative defenders of "original intent" obscure the unambiguous willingness of the nation's catalytic leaders to politically and socially continue the disenfranchisement of millions. The Declaration of Independence, Articles of Confederation, and Constitution were as visionary as they were contradictory. They became the building blocks of a divided nation and the White House that would preside over it.

The Declaration of Independence

Perhaps no other document from the era carries as much symbolism as the Declaration of Independence. In 1776, at the

Second Continental Congress in Philadelphia, the throng of rebelling white landowners declared themselves independent of the British crown and, on July 4, 1776, issued the Declaration of Independence. Written primarily by Thomas Jefferson, owner of hundreds of slaves, the Declaration sought to explain to the world the principles and rationale driving the break with England.

By the time of the Second Continental Congress, several colonies had already declared their split from King George, most notably Virginia. As one of the centers of the revolution, Virginia aggressively began to break from British authority and issued its own declaration of why it was necessary to do so. Adopted on June 12, 1776, Virginia's Declaration of Rights was also a declaration in defense of slavery. In its final version it stated, in part,

> That all men are by nature equally free and independent, and have certain inherent rights, of which, when they enter into a state of society, they cannot, by any compact, deprive or divest their posterity; namely, the enjoyment of life and liberty, with the means of acquiring and possessing property, and pursuing and obtaining happiness and safety.[35]

The original draft by George Mason did not include the phrase "when they enter into a state of society," leaving an opening, so felt most delegates to the Virginia Convention, for the document to be interpreted in a way that would assign these inherent rights to people then enslaved. As one delegate later noted, "They saw in the sweeping phraseology of the declaration that its adoption into the fundamental law would immediately emancipate the slave."[36] Realistically, there was little chance of that, however, as those in the powerful slave-owning class wanted total assurance that their interests were safe. The strategic addition of the phrase "when they enter into a state of society" was necessary to blunt any legal challenges to the institution of slavery. The new phrase was understood to be a reference to those outside of the state of society, i.e., those who were enslaved, and therefore they were not by colonial political or legal standards equally free, independent, or in possession of any rights whatsoever. While it was presumed by some that those who were outside would one day enter society, Virginia's Declaration of Rights fundamentally denied rights for enslaved blacks while giving legal and philosophical cover for whites to continue to profit from owning, breeding, and trading blacks.

The language "all men are by nature equally free and independent" was too broad and viewed as too risky legally—especially for delegates representing slave states—to be left standing without qualifiers. As was the case in nearly all the documents that evolved in the revolutionary period, euphemisms and cautious language were employed to mask the patently contradictory and hypocritical nature of the politics. Although the words "slavery" and "slave" never appeared in the final version of this or any other founding document, all parties involved were fully conscious that the institution of slavery was being legally perpetuated.

Thomas Jefferson had a complicated relationship with slavery. While he did advocate legislating the emancipation of slaves in 1769 at the Virginia General Assembly, he was not so opposed to buying, selling, and forcing blacks to labor as slaves that he abstained from doing so himself. Throughout his life he owned hundreds of slaves. When tasked to draft the Declaration of Independence at the Second Continental Congress, Jefferson understood the politics of obfuscation that had been deftly employed in drafting Virginia's political documents. But Jefferson appeared to envision a time when slavery would be abolished and wanted this national declaration to anticipate that period.

On the hot evenings of July, as Thomas Jefferson sat down to pen the words of the document that would truly ignite the Revolutionary War and "dissolve the political bonds" that connected the thirteen rebelling colonies to England, he was surely stressed and perhaps hungry after the long, increasingly hectic and demanding days. As his thoughts swirled over what words to use, he faced two tasks: to mount an argument justifying the armed revolt against King George, and to articulate a vision of a new nation. That vision included a call for participatory democracy, justice, political rights, and full citizenship—all genuinely radical ideas at the time. In the background, careful not to disturb his master's state of concentration, Jefferson's slave Richard quietly brought him his nightly tea. Richard had been born into slavery, and Jefferson brought him along on many of his travels. Perhaps the evening tea is exactly what was needed to facilitate the flow of ideas and words that would become the Declaration of Independence. Perhaps the irony was not lost on either of the two men.[37]

Jefferson's famous opening to the Declaration reflected the highest aspirations of humanity, without even a hint of racial discord. The principles expressed and the language used to articulate them would resonate for centuries and become appropriated by the French Revolution and, paradoxically, the Vietnamese in their own struggle against French colonialism.[38] As noted later, free and enslaved blacks would often quote from the Declaration to advance the antislavery struggle.

Jefferson wrote acutely: "We hold these truths to be self-evident, that all men are created equal, that they are endowed by their Creator with certain unalienable Rights, that among these are Life, Liberty and the pursuit of Happiness."

His literary skills were put to full use in creating a document that had to satisfy competing concerns (pro-slavery vs. antislavery), competing eras (the present vs. the future), and competing temperaments (deliberative vs. brash). His opening phrase, gendered language notwithstanding, was noncategorical. While it did not explicitly include blacks, neither did it explicitly exclude them. It also differed from Virginia's Declaration of Rights, written just one month earlier, in that Jefferson avoided the word "property" to forestall, unsuccessfully as it turned out, any future effort to rely on it as a justification for slavery.[39]

In an early draft of the Declaration, Jefferson included a rather long paragraph that is generally interpreted as antislavery. The rejected clause read:

> He has waged cruel war against human nature itself, violating its most sacred rights of life and liberty in the persons of a distant people who never offended him, captivating and carrying them into slavery in another hemisphere, or to incur miserable death in their transportation thither. This piratical warfare, the opprobrium of infidel powers, is the warfare of the Christian king of Great Britain. Determined to keep open a market where men should be bought and sold, he has prostituted his negative for suppressing every legislative attempt to prohibit or to restrain this execrable commerce; and that this assemblage of horrors might want no fact of distinguished die, he is now exciting those very people to rise in arms among us, and to purchase that liberty of which he has deprived them, by

> murdering the people upon whom he also obtruded them; thus paying off former crimes committed against the liberties of one people, with crimes which he urges them to commit against the lives of another.

According to Jefferson, the clause was rejected "in complaisance to South Carolina and Georgia, who had never attempted to restrain the importation of slaves, and who on the contrary still wished to continue it."[40] Jefferson also blamed his "northern brethren" who were complicit due to their own economic interests in the slave trade through shipping and other means. However, upon closer examination, the proposed clause actually criticized the slave trade—the capture, transportation, and sale of individuals into a life of enslavement—more so than slavery itself. After the sixteenth century, the latter could and did exist without the former. This was low-hanging fruit given that by 1776 nearly all of the colonies had abandoned, severely curtailed, or constrained the slave trade. Elite opposition to the slave trade was framed by interests that were more economic than moral. Blumrosen and Blumrosen contend that the Virginian's opposition to the slave trade dated back to at least 1772 in part due to a surplus of enslaved people caused by a shift in agriculture as a result of soil depletion from tobacco farming.[41] As a consequence, according to historian Gary Wills, excess slaves were being sold for great profit to owners of lands where rice, indigo, and cotton farming were growing.[42] Additionally, historian Egerton believes that Jefferson wished "to relieve his new country—and, more profoundly, himself—of the guilt of importing hundreds of thousands of Africans before taking up arms in the cause of liberty" and to blame England, which at the time had not outlawed the slave trade, for forcing otherwise innocent people into the horror of slavery.[43]

While clearly condemning the "execrable commerce," it is notable that Jefferson never explicitly calls for the complete and immediate abolition of slavery. In fact, he raises the button-pushing issue of slave revolts ("exciting those very people to rise up in arms") in order to mobilize wider support for the Declaration. White fear of slave rebellions was widespread in the colonies. It was rooted in the very real experiences of black uprisings and plots dating back to at least 1663 in Gloucester County, Virginia, where a group of black slaves and white servants was caught planning to achieve their freedom by overthrowing their masters. Scores of plots to revolt were organized in the colonies—including New York, Massachusetts, Connecticut, and New Jersey—in the period prior to the Revolutionary war.[44] In *American Negro Slave Revolts*, Herbert Aptheker describes these revolts in detail, noting that fear of black rebellion was widespread among white enslavers and often spiked into collective panic. An early example of this occurred in South Carolina when it was discovered that fugitive slaves were actively aiding the Yamasee and Lower Creek Indians in their forays against whites in 1727 and 1728.[45] Examples would multiply in the 1800s.

From the onset of slavery, rebellion was common and persistent. Blacks resisted being captured, resisted being transported, and resisted being enslaved. The history of slavery is the history of blacks rebelling against the violent nightmare white enslavers imposed upon them. "The first settlement within the present borders of the United States to contain Negro slaves," writes Aptheker, "was the locale of the first slave revolt."[46] Even prior to the establishment of the thirteen British colonies, in 1526 there was a slave insurrection on what is now the coast of South Carolina in a colony controlled by the Spanish.[47] The settlement consisted of approximately 600 people—500 Spanish and 100 black slaves. When disease ravaged the settlement, several slaves rebelled and fled to shelter with the nearby Indians. The 150 European settlers who survived illness abandoned their settlement for Haiti, leaving the "rebel Negroes with their Indian friends—as the first permanent inhabitants, other than Indians, in what was to be the United States."[48]

In truth, slaves in America did not need external incitement from England or indigenous communities to rise up and strike for freedom. It was the homegrown horrors and atrocities of the U.S. slave system that generated hundreds of slave rebellions from the beginning of slavery to its very final moment.

In any case, the Declaration of Independence, unlike other documents from the revolutionary period, neither expressly sanctioned slavery nor clearly supported its abolition. A generous interpretation is that while permitting whites to continue to enslave blacks, it also foresaw and implied a slavery-free future. Drafted by the individual who would become the nation's third president, it set the template for the long trail of compromise, contradiction, and domination against which generations of blacks would have to struggle in order to achieve the same rights as the country's white founders.

The symbolic power of the Declaration relative to the presidency is perhaps nowhere more poignantly manifest than in the fact that three of the first five presidents died on the Fourth of July—Thomas Jefferson and John Adams on the fiftieth anniversary of the document in 1826 and James Monroe five years later in 1831.[49] But from the historical perspective of blacks alive at that time until slavery's end, the Declaration symbolized the gross inequality of the new nation. Reflecting on the Declaration seventy-six years later, a time when slavery had still not been abolished, Frederick Douglass said, "What, to the American slave, is your Fourth of July? I answer: a day that reveals to him, more than all other days in the year, the gross injustice and cruelty to which he is the constant victim."[50] And to the slaveocracy, writes Aptheker, "the Declaration of Independence became but the mouthings of an irresponsible and dangerous fanatic, a ridiculous and high-sounding concoction of obvious absurdities."[51]

The Articles of Confederation

> *I abhor slavery.*—Henry Laurens, President of the Continental Congress in 1777, during the debate and passage of the Articles of Confederation.[52]

The first effort to create a governing document that would unite the new states culminated in the Articles of Confederation. Written while Continental Congress members were trying desperately to avoid capture by the British, the document failed to establish the authority needed to administer a functional central government. Its weaknesses would ultimately lead to its demise, but its significance for our discussion is that it continued the pro-slavery tilt that had characterized the debates surrounding the Declaration of Independence. Not only did the Articles of Confederation sanction slavery, but they repudiated the *Somerset* decision and foreshadowed the Fugitive Slave Laws and Article 4, Section 2, of the Constitution, stipulating that the federal government had to provide for the return of blacks who had escaped from their owners.

Congress selected a slaveholding lawyer from Pennsylvania, John Dickinson, to draft the Articles. Only a week after the Declaration of Independence was issued, the rebel Congress began to debate Dickinson's draft. Dickinson conceived of a strong central government that would exercise a great deal of authority over the states. Southern leaders reacted immediately and negatively. They believed that any document that did not clearly allow for states to continue the institution of slavery was a threat to their future. North Carolina's Thomas Burke argued for a clause stating "that in all things else each state would exercise all the rights and powers of sovereignty, uncontrolled."[53]

The debate over the Articles lasted for more than a year. In November 1777, the Congress finally adopted a revised version, which it then sent to the states for ratification. The Southerners perpetuated slavery through two components in the Articles: First, through Article II: "Each state retains its sovereignty, freedom, and independence, and every power, jurisdiction, and right, which is not by this Confederation expressly delegated to the United States, in Congress assembled;" and second, through the inclusion of a rule that the Articles could only be amended by unanimous approval by all the states.

While the Articles, up to this point, sheltered the institution of slavery, the document did not address an equally important concern of slaveholders: the phenomenon of slaves freeing themselves by escaping to states where slavery was abolished or only meekly enforced. The *Somerset* nightmare, by which England potentially would free any slave that entered into it, loomed large. This concern was addressed in Article IV, which read as follows:

> The better to secure and perpetuate mutual friendship and intercourse among the people of the different States in this Union, the free inhabitants of each of these States, paupers, vagabonds, and fugitives from justice excepted, shall be entitled to all privileges and immunities of free citizens in the several States . . . and shall enjoy therein all the privileges of trade and commerce, subject to the same duties, im-

> positions, and restrictions as the inhabitants thereof respectively, provided that such restrictions shall not extend so far as to prevent the removal of property imported into any State, to any other State, of which the owner is an inhabitant; provided also that no imposition, duties or restriction shall be laid by any State, on the property of the United States, or either of them.

In a pattern that would repeat itself for centuries, the South argued vigorously for state sovereignty, with particular interest in preventing other states from manifesting their opposition to white Southerners' racial practices. Thus the debate was never purely a philosophical one of states' rights vs. a strong central authority, but rather an ideological one of support or opposition to a particular type and structure of government that legitimated and enforced chattel slavery. In the final version of the Articles, there was no executive branch and no national judiciary, but a continuing concession to the South as its price for participation in the new nation.

"All Other Persons:" The U.S. Constitution and Racial Justice

> *When the architects of our republic wrote the magnificent words of the Constitution and the Declaration of Independence, they were signing a promissory note to which every American was to fall heir. This note was a promise that all men, yes, black men as well as white men, would be guaranteed the unalienable rights of life, liberty, and the pursuit of happiness.*[54]—Martin Luther King Jr.

> *[I]n the United States the slave was a shackled counterbalance to the personal freedoms that defined America. He was written into the Constitution as three-fifths of a man.*[55]—Wynton Marsalis

> *When the Founding Fathers said, 'We the People,' they did not mean us. Our ancestors were considered three-fifths of a person.*[56]—Condoleezza Rice

Worried that the Articles of Confederation were proving inadequate to the task of unifying the new nation, in 1787 James Madison and other reformers called together a Constitutional Convention to amend the Articles. Instead, the fifty-five white men who gathered ended up replacing the Articles with the document that has served as the fundamental instrument defining U.S. federalism, its branches of government, its principles, and the relationship between the federal government and the states.

Under the Articles, the thirteen states functioned as independent entities with only a modicum of authority and respect vested in a central government. Inefficiency and dysfunctionality had led to a growing number of uprisings and class conflicts, most notably Shays' Rebellion—an armed uprising of Revolutionary War veterans, indebted farmers and others who rebelled against high taxes ("rates"), foreclosures, and their loss of their land and livestock. The rebellion started in western Massachusetts on August 29, 1786, and began to spread throughout the state. After months of escalating confrontation, the revolt was finally suppressed in early 1787 by an army funded by a group of men from Boston. In the end, more than 1,000 people were arrested, some of whom were later executed.[57] Shays' Rebellion sent a powerful message to the wealthy that a stronger national government was needed to hold the country together and protect their interests.[58]

The U.S. Constitution put meat on the skeleton of America's infant democracy. It identified and clarified the responsibilities of the different branches of government and their relationship to the states. It made concrete the principles of balance of power and separation of power, both necessary for a system of checks and balances. It (eventually) spelled out a set of rights that few other nations in the world at that time had even considered. It advocated the rule of law and a justice system that would be fair and transparent. It expressed itself as a social contract between the governing and the governed, a principle that would mark democracies in the centuries that would follow. More than any other document, it sought to proclaim to the United States and the world that a genuine new nation was being born in which they would govern themselves by truly democratic principles.

Unfortunately, as with the Declaration of Independence and the Articles of Confederation, the Constitution blatantly neglected to erase the scar of racism from the face of American democracy. Written by wealthy white men, the new Constitution guaranteed them rights it denied to women, enslaved people, and the country's original inhabitants, the indigenous communities. The language of ambiguity would once again triumph as concessions to slaveholders won the day in three key sections of the Constitution. The document reduced blacks, for the purpose of allocating congressional representation, to less than full personhood (Article 1, Section 2); sanctioned the slave trade for another twenty years (Article 1, Section 9); and nationalized slavery with the fugitive slave provision (Article 4, Section 2)—all without once mentioning the words "slave" or "slavery." As the critic Luther Martin noted at the time, "They anxiously sought to avoid the admission of expressions which might be odious in the ears of Americans, although they were willing to admit into their system those things which the expressions signified."[59] Beyond the well-known sections mentioned above, in at least six other sections of the Constitution slavery is protected or referenced. In two other sections, Article 1, Section 8 and Article 4, Section 4, the Constitution asserts the responsibility of the federal government to assist the states in the suppression of "insurrections" and "domestic violence." While these clauses could be interpreted to address class-based uprisings such as that led by Shays and others in Massachusetts only months before the Constitutional Convention, the framers clearly had race-based slave revolts in mind, if not as the central focus. Article 1, Section 2, and Article 1, Section 9, also referred to the apportionment of taxes that took into account the enslaved population. Finally, Article 5 states that Article 1, Section 9, Clauses 1 and 4, referring to the slave trade and direct taxes respectively, were made unamendable.[60]

As Richard Beeman states in *Plain, Honest Men: The Making of the American Constitution*, his brilliant treatise tracing the debates and arguments that ultimately produced the Constitution, "There are no moral heroes to be found in the story of slavery and the making of the American Constitution."[61] In the compromise reached over the issue of allocation of representation in Congress, the Convention delegates agreed that each state would have an equal number of Senators—two—in the U.S. Senate and would have proportional representation in the U.S. House of Representatives based on each state's population. Southern states, for obvious reasons, wanted to include those held in slavery as part of their population figure. Northern states strenuously objected, principally to protect their own power, not to challenge the dehumanized status of those enslaved. Northerners contended that, given that blacks were property, the Southerners might as well include their cows and horses.

The debate was vigorous and lasted for days. The compromised reached by the Convention, perhaps unique in the history of such events, was cloaked in evasive language. Article 1, Section 2.3, stated:

> Representatives and direct taxes shall be apportioned among the several states which may include within this Union, according to their respective numbers, which shall be determined by adding to the whole number of free persons, including those bound to service for a term of years, and excluding Indians not taxed, three fifths of all other persons.

The phrase "all other persons" referenced the nearly 700,000 blacks who were held in slavery throughout the country. While the section did not exclude "free" blacks from being counted as whole persons, the objective of racial exclusion was unambiguous. Madison, one of the mediators of the debate, argued defensively in Federalist Paper No. 54 that Southern states would be constrained by the dual pressure of wanting high numbers for representation purposes and low numbers for tax purposes.[62] He missed the obvious fact that the increased number of representatives gained by the South as a result of the clause would affect decisions on tax policies in ways beneficial to the South.

The impact of this clause was multiple. In the first sense, it perpetuated the disenfranchisement of about 20 percent of the people who resided, worked, died, prayed, and lived in the thirteen colonies at the time. Enslaved blacks and non-taxed Indians—as well as the entire female population and non-property-owning white males—had no electoral or formal political voice in the birthing process of the nation, though all contributed greatly to the revolutionary cause.

Additionally, the three-fifths clause distorted the development of the political system at the national level for decades. The South benefited substantially from this compromise (see Table 1), which resulted in a disproportionately higher number of Southerners in the U.S. House of Representatives. Four states in the North—Connecticut, New Hampshire, Pennsylvania, and Vermont—where the free black population was larger than the enslaved one, gained little. On the other hand, Georgia, South Carolina, and Virginia reaped substantial advantage. Since many politicians used their experience serving in the U.S. House of Representatives to go on to become senators, it meant a disparate impact on the U.S. Senate, the chamber that confirms Supreme Court nominees and cabinet positions. Every nomination to and decision by the U.S. Supreme Court prior to the Civil War Court has to be seen in light of this context. Finally, up until the Civil War, the three-fifths clause also allowed for the South to accumulate a greater number of Electoral College votes, a factor in determining who would win control of the White House. Half of the first sixteen presidents came from the South, including Washington, Jefferson, and Madison.

The Constitution also guaranteed that the supply of enslaved individuals would continue after the Revolution. Article 1, Section 9, states:

> The Migration or Importation of such Persons as any of the States now existing shall think proper to admit, shall not be prohibited by the Congress prior to the Year one thousand eight hundred and eight, but a tax or duty may be imposed on such Importation, not exceeding ten dollars for each Person.

Table 1

The South Benefits from the Three-Fifths Clause, 1790 U.S. Census

	Total Population	Total White Pop.	Total Black Pop.	Free Blacks	Enslaved Blacks	Enslaved Blacks %	Blacks % of Total Pop.
Conn.*	237,946	232,374	5,572	2,808	2,764	50%	2%
Deleware	59,096	46,310	12,786	3,899	8,887	70%	22%
Georgia	82,548	52,886	29,662	398	29,264	99%	36%
Kentucky	73,677	61,133	12,544	114	12,430	99%	17%
Maine	96,540	96,002	538	538	0	0%	1%
Mass.	378,787	373,324	5,463	5,463	0	0%	1%
Maryland	319,728	208,649	111,079	8,043	103,036	93%	35%
N. Carol.	393,751	288,204	105,547	4,975	100,572	95%	27%
N. Hamp.*	141,885	141,097	788	630	158	20%	1%
N. Jersey	184,139	169,954	14,185	2,762	11,423	81%	8%
N. York	340,120	314,142	25,978	4,654	21,324	82%	8%
Penn.*	434,373	424,099	10,274	6,537	3,737	36%	2%
R. Island	68,825	64,470	4,355	3,407	948	22%	6%
S. Carol.	249,073	140,178	108,895	1,801	107,094	98%	44%
Virginia	747,610	442,117	305,493	12,866	292,627	96%	41%
Vermont*	85,539	85,268	271	255	16	6%	>0%
Total	3,893,637	3,140,207	753,430	59,150	694,280		

*States whose free blacks outnumbered those who were enslaved. Source: U.S. Census.

Parsing the language in the Constitution is crucial. Article 1, Section 9, states that Congress shall not prohibit the slave trade prior to 1808, but it does not mandate the abolition of slavery on or after that date. Instead of prohibiting human trafficking, breeding, and ownership, the Article's language in fact gave Southern whites the assurance that there would be nothing in the Constitution to prevent them from perpetuating these practices after 1808.

Despite moves across the colonies to ban or restrain the

slave trade, some Southern delegates to the Convention, in particular South Carolina's Charles Pinckney, argued against any move that would tax either the import or the export of slaves. These delegates were reproved by the aforementioned activist Luther Martin of Maryland, a slaveholder himself, who went on to become one of the most vocal advocates against slavery at the Constitutional Convention and later cofounded the Maryland Society for the Abolition of Slavery. Martin stated that the slave trade "was inconsistent with the principles of the revolution and [it was] dishonorable to the American character to have such a feature in the Constitution."[63] After the Convention, Martin addressed the Maryland legislature as it considered ratification of the Constitution saying, "It must appear to the world absurd and disgraceful, to the last degree, that we should except from the exercise of that power the only branch of commerce which is unjustifiable in its nature, and contrary to the rights of mankind; that on the contrary, we ought to prohibit expressly, in our Constitution, the further importation of slaves."[64]

The Convention also used coded language to defend the slave trade in the Constitution. The enslaved are referred to as "such Persons," and the trade is simply termed "importation." No amount of word play, however, could hide the hideous fact that the framers of the U.S. Constitution were officially giving white people a free pass to enslave black people for at least another twenty years.

Placing a ban on the slave trade in the Constitution would have been important in spite of the efforts unfolding against the trade in the various states. Its critics argued that state legislative action could easily be reversed should the trade become profitable. Foreseen and unforeseen changes—such as the westward expansion of slavery or the invention of new technologies such as the cotton gin, which might make slavery economically viable for decades to come—would sweep away state legislative bans overnight.[65] Only by prohibiting the slave trade in the Constitution could the nation guarantee that short-term opportunities, even twenty years after the writing of the Constitution, would not override a long-term principle.

The third axis of slavery in the Constitution further nationalized the issue by forcing antislavery Northern states to return escaped slaves. This provision superseded the principle of states' rights that the South had so obsessively pursued. While leaders from the main slaveholding states and their Northern counterparts alike fought hard to place limits on the central government's power, when it came to the issue of slavery, the former sought to exploit the national authority and resources of the federal system as much as possible. If the slaveholding states could have the federal government protect their human property, which unlike their other property could and did escape captivity, then the slavery system was on much sounder footing. As we have seen, Article 4, Section 2, of the Constitution states,

> No Person held to Service or Labour in one State, under the Laws thereof, escaping into another, shall, in Consequence of any Law or Regulation therein, be discharged from such Service or Labour, But shall be delivered up on Claim of the Party to whom such Service or Labour may be due.

Beeman notes sadly that not a single voice of opposition was raised to challenge this provision.[66] Given the almost fetish-level priority the Founding Fathers gave to property rights, the return of lost (runaway) property must have seemed a natural right. Article 4, Section 2, was further bolstered by the Fugitive Slave Act of 1793, which was passed by Congress and signed by

President George Washington, the Fugitive Slave Act of 1850, and the slave-catching profession.[67]

On to the White House

George Washington, John Adams, Thomas Jefferson, and James Madison would go on to become the nation's first four presidents. They represented the generation that came of age in the 1770s and 1780s, a time of rebellion, heady transition, and grand crisis. The past was unsustainable, the present was fluid, and the future unknown. The milieu of independent, property-owning white men generated revolutionary ideas that would forge the thirteen independent colonies into one more or less united nation.

However, the American Revolution would not transform the nearly four million individuals who lived there into one people, a just society of equals. When faced with that opportunity, Washington, Adams, Jefferson, and Madison all blanched. The courage they had demonstrated in taking on the British Empire vanished when they were confronted with the entrenchment and obduracy of the slave-owning class. The illusory goal of national unity trumped the morality of undoing slavery and admitting to full citizenship the hundreds of thousands of enslaved blacks and indigenous peoples whose "unalienable rights" to "life, liberty and the pursuit of happiness" were being forcibly denied.

But something much more primary was at work than Northern cowardice and Southern economic and cultural racism. In a fundamental way, the interests of white people in both regions came into alignment: neither political leaders nor popular opinion in the North or the South believed that Blacks or Indians were their equals in body, mind, or spirit. While the country was founded in words that seemed to promise an enlightened society of equals, a deeply rooted and widespread racism, including that of the presidents, would drive generations of barbarous genocide of the indigenous people and the bondage of blacks. For Oney Judge and the other blacks living in the new white-controlled nation, the President's House was not a symbol of newfound freedom but a virtual prison, a place one would risk one's life trying to escape.

CHAPTER 2

The President's House in the Home of the Abolitionist Movement

Prelude: Hercules' White House Story

Hercules was reputed to be one of the best chefs in the nation also a slave who was highly favored by George Washington. He had been Washington's chief cook at Mount Vernon and traveled with him during his presidency to New York and Philadelphia. Washington's step-grandson, G. W. Parke Custis, described Hercules as "a celebrated artiste . . . as highly accomplished a proficient in the culinary art as could be found in the United States."[1]

If there was a hierarchy of slave status, Hercules was certainly at the top. By all accounts, he ran the Washington kitchen with an iron hand, severely punishing those who broke from his discipline or did not carry out their duties with assiduous attention to detail and quality. He was well respected by everyone in the president's household, free or enslaved. Indeed, as he often walked the streets of Philadelphia dressed in some of the finest clothing to be seen in town, he garnered "a formal and respectful bow" from those he met on the street.[2] In one graphic passage, Custis described the way Hercules would dress for his evening promenade, wearing linen of "unexceptionable [*sic*] whiteness and quality, then black silk shorts, ditto waistcoat, ditto

Hercules, cook for George Washington,
one of hundreds of blacks Washington enslaved.

stockings, shoes highly polished, with large buckles covering a considerable part of the foot, blue cloth with velvet collar and bright metal buttons, a long watch-chain dangling from his fob, a cocked-hat and gold-headed cane completed the grand costume of the celebrated dandy."[3] His presence in the president's residence was colorful and uplifting to those around him.

Hercules was able to dress so grandly because he earned considerable extra personal income—estimated between 100 and 200 dollars a year, a tremendous sum at that time—selling leftovers from Washington's kitchen.[4] This was a highly unusual arrangement, because there is very little historic evidence of slaves being permitted to possess funds that their owners could keep themselves. Hercules clearly held a special place in the Washington matrix of slavery. Referred to by the family as "Uncle Harkless"—an honorific title whites saw as a term of endearment but which many blacks viewed as patronizingly insulting—Hercules was perhaps the slave in whom Washington felt the most trust, second to William Lee.

Born around 1750, Lee had been purchased by Washington in 1768 and was with him for thirty years, until Washington died in 1799. Lee was so close to Washington that he can be seen next to him in several famous paintings, including John Trumbull's *George Washington*, painted in London in 1780.[5] Lee rode with and served Washington throughout the Revolutionary War and through both terms of his presidency. Archival documents and letters also indicate that Lee was with Washington continuously while the president was commanding from Philadelphia.[6]

Due to several accidents, Lee became physically disabled and by the age of 38 he was barely able to walk. Although he was given steel braces that helped substantially, Lee's health continued to deteriorate, and in November 1793 Washington wrote to his secretary Tobias Lear to find "a substitute for William."[7] During Washington's second term, Lee was sent back to Mount Vernon, where he took up the relatively non-taxing work of cobbling shoes.

Washington wrote a secret will in July 1799 in an attempt to hide from his wife Martha and other relatives the terms of manumission that he wanted for his slaves. He apparently believed that Martha may not have been as committed as he was to freeing his slaves after his and her death. Completed only a few months before he died, his will stipulated that all of his slaves be freed upon Martha's death, that older slaves be "comfortably cloathed and fed," and that the younger ones be educated into useful occupations.[8] Lee, however, was freed immediately. Though poor and debilitated by alcoholism and ill health, he spent the last decades of his life as a free man, passing away in 1828 at the age of 78.

Surely one of the reasons Washington felt such "generosity" toward Lee was the unyielding loyalty demonstrated by his many years of service and refusal to take advantage of numerous opportunities to escape. Washington had certainly felt such betrayal before, as in the cases of Oney and of Henry "Harry" Washington.

Harry was born free near the Gambia River in West Africa around 1740, and by 1775 Harry was working in the stables of Mount Vernon as one of more than 100 people enslaved to George Washington. Seventeen seventy-five was also the year that Lord Dunmore, on behalf of the English crown, offered freedom to any slave who joined the British forces to quash the revolution, an offer that more than 15,000 blacks accepted. News of the British offer reached Washington's slaves as well. The information seems to have agitated and emboldened Harry in his desire for freedom.

In July 1776, George Washington and the revolutionary leaders declared their independence. One month later, Harry Washington declared his and ran away to join the all-black British regiment known as the Black Pioneers, whose motto was "Liberty to Slaves."[9] Unable to safely stay in the United States after the war, Harry would later join the 3,000 black Loyalists who went to Nova Scotia, Canada, and founded the all-black settlement of Birchtown, the largest free black community in North America at the time.[10]

Even in Canada, however, Harry's freedom was still not totally secure, as Washington initiated means to pursue escaped blacks after the war. According to writer Jill Lepore, it was General Washington who insisted that British ships leaving U.S. waters after the war keep a "Book of Negroes," i.e., a list of blacks onboard the departing ships, so that claims could later be filed against the English by aggrieved slaveholders for the return of those who ran away. Harry kept on the move, however, eventually migrating to Sierra Leone, a state that was founded by a patchwork of indigenous natives; England's "black poor," consisting of Africans, African Americans, and British-born blacks; and Asians.[11] He arrived sometime around 1792 with 1,100 other former African American slaves and lived the rest of his life not far from the Gambia River region where he was born.[12]

Thus his trust of Lee notwithstanding, Washington had a genuine fear that even his most loyal slaves might bolt if given the opportunity. One other factor might also have influenced his relationship with Hercules. Egerton writes that "Washington believed that white blood not only lightened the skin but enlightened the mind, and he preferred 'yellow-skinned' servants within his home."[13] Washington no doubt interpreted "enlightened mind" to mean not only intelligence but also devotion to one's master. Lee was mulatto; Hercules was not.

However, Washington's faith in Hercules was reinforced by an incident in 1791. In spring of that year, when Washington began willfully and consciously to move his slaves back to Virginia to avoid their qualifying for manumission after a continuous six-month stay in Pennsylvania, Hercules was one of the individuals whom Washington slated to return to Mount Vernon. President Washington's assistant, Tobias Lear, conveyed his concern to Washington, warning that "if Hercules should decline the offer which will be made him of going home, it will be a pretty strong proof of his intention to take advantage of the law at the expiration of six months."[14] Unhappy about participating in the chicanery of rotating slaves to prevent their liberation, Lear further added, "You will permit me now, Sir (and I am sure you will pardon me for doing it) to declare, that no consideration should induce me to take these steps to prolong the slavery of a human being, had I not the fullest confidence that they will at some future period be liberated, and the strongest conviction that their situation with you is far preferable to what they would probably obtain in a state of freedom."[15] The spirit of abolitionism was powerful in Philadelphia, not only among the black people trapped in slavery, but also among white people such as Lear. Although Lear, like Washington, had faith in an undetermined post-slavery future, he did little to speed its arrival.

When Hercules discovered that the decision to send him to Virginia was perhaps based on the possibility that he might display some disloyalty and seek freedom in Philadelphia or some other northern city, he expressed shock at the suggestion and volunteered to leave immediately for Mount Vernon. Having convinced Washington of his total loyalty and submission, Hercules was allowed to stay in Philadelphia well beyond the six-month period and traveled at least once on his own to Mount Vernon and returned to Philadelphia. During his time with Washington in Pennsylvania, he never pursued his legal right to be free in that state. Until the very end, that is.

During the final months of Washington's stay in Philadelphia, while at Mt. Vernon, Hercules escaped. Records show that on February 22, 1797, which was Washington's 65th birthday, Hercules absconded according to Mt. Vernon researcher Mary V. Thompson. Exercising his own sense of his rights, to the stunned surprise of his enslaver, he successfully escaped from bondage to the president of the United States. As in Oney's case, the First Family could not understand why Hercules would want to escape from them. They could not fathom the reality that, despite all the material benefits and privileges they had granted him, nothing could deter Hercules from seizing what he wanted most: freedom from slavery.

The loss of Hercules affected George as strongly as the loss of Oney had affected Martha. Historian Fritz Hischfield contends that Hercules' escape to freedom "was considered a minor disaster by the Washington family."[16] Perhaps it had something to do with the strong relationship formed between U.S. presidents and their black cooks. In 1890, President Benjamin Harrison and his wife brought their black cook, Dolly Johnson, in from Indianapolis to replace the White House's French chef Madame Petronard. In President Franklin Roosevelt's White House, Mary Campbell ruled. She had been the cook at the family's home in Hyde Park in New York and came to the president's kitchen—along with her recipes for duck, venison, and terrapin—after Roosevelt's mother died. Vietta Cook, another black chef, played a similar role for the Truman White House. She had worked for the family for thirty-six years and prepared Southern dishes such as fried chicken, candied sweet potatoes, and angel food cake. Zephyr Wright, whom Lyndon Johnson brought with him from Texas, worked for the Johnson family for twenty-seven years.[17] For many presidents, a black-led kitchen at the White House was desirable and necessary and represented their lifetime of experiences of being served by blacks.

One of the most intriguing and trend-setting linkages between black cooks and a U.S. president actually occurred during Hercules' time in Philadelphia: the relationship between Thomas Jefferson and James Hemings. Jefferson paid to have Hemings, a black man Jefferson held enslaved at his Monticello estate, trained for three years as a master chef, including learning to cook exquisite French pastries. During Jefferson's four years in France as a U.S. ambassador (1785 to 1789), Jefferson brought Hemings specifically so that he could learn how to prepare French cuisine. Later, while serving as the nation's first secretary of state from 1790 to 1793 in the Washington administration, Jefferson spent even more time in France with Hemings.

Hemings was later joined by his sister, Sally, who would soon become Jefferson's mistress and later, many believe, bearer of his children.[18] Under French law at the time of Jefferson's ambassadorship, James and Sally could have both claimed their freedom and left Jefferson, but neither did. James first became the chief chef at Jefferson's Champs-Elysées dwellings and then at his residences in Philadelphia and Monticello. In 1793, back in the United States, Hemings decided to seek his liberty. He negotiated a contract with Jefferson that stated, "If the said James shall go with me to Monticello...and shall continue until he shall have taught such persons as I shall place under him for the purpose to be a good cook...he shall be thereupon made free."[19] James trained his brother Peter in the culinary arts and in April 1796 he was freed.

Nowhere is it written that during their common time in Philadelphia, Hercules, the cook for George Washington, and James Hemings, the cook for Thomas Jefferson, were friends. However, as Wilkins points out, at the time there were only 210 slaves in the entire city and it would have been nearly impossible for them not to know each other, even if Washington and Jefferson had not been politically connected.[20] But given that Washington and Jefferson frequently met, and that both Hercules and Hemings were renowned as two of the nation's most famous chefs, their paths probably crossed with some regularity. It is not too much of a stretch to speculate that if they knew each other, the topic of freedom was likely discussed and that James Hemings's manumission one year earlier might have helped fuel Hercules' decision. For sure, Hercules and all of Washington's slaves had been affected by Oney's successful escape the previous summer. A third motivator was the fact that Philadelphia was a center of abolitionist activity and the city's free black community, whose members interacted frequently with their enslaved counterparts, was a full participant in liberation actions, including the Underground Railroad system that helped runaway blacks make it to Canada.

In any case, whether or not a socio-culinary bond existed between black cooks and white presidents, Washington felt deeply motivated to go after Hercules. Believing Hercules to be in Philadelphia, Washington spent months unsuccessfully looking for him there. On March 10, 1797, Washington ordered Lear to "make all the enquiry he can after Hercules, and send him around in the Vessel if he can be discovered and apprehended."[21] Meanwhile, the president's stomach seemed to be growling. Lear writes in his memoir that Washington became so desperate to find a suitable cook for himself and Martha that he broke his vow not to buy any more slaves and sought to buy one who had an excellent reputation as a cook. Washington had written on November 13, 1797, "The running off of my cook has been the most inconvenient thing to this family, and what renders it more disagreeable, is, that I had resolved never to become the master of another slave by purchase, but this resolution I fear I must break."[22]

In the personal battle between refusing to participate in human trafficking or eating well, the latter won out. After returning to Mount Vernon, Washington sought to have his former household steward Frederick Kitt pursue Hercules. On January 10, 1798, he wrote Kitt to seek his help in locating and retrieving Hercules. Continuing to complain about his gastronomical needs and the possibility of buying another black slave, Washington wrote, "If you could accomplish this for me, it would render me an acceptable service as I neither have, nor can get a good Cook to hire, and am disinclined to hold another slave by purchase."[23] Kitt would have no more skill or luck in finding Hercules than had Lear.

Unlike Oney, Hercules was never found. While George and Martha felt disturbed and betrayed by the escape, it was not a sentiment shared by the blacks the Washingtons continued to enslave, including members of Hercules' family whom he had left behind.[24]

When a foreign visitor asked his little daughter if she was sad that her father had gone and left her behind, still enslaved to Washington, she stated with unbridled emotion, "Oh! Sir, I am very glad, because he is free now."[25]

A Home for the President of the United States of America

Although the "White House" is known worldwide as the residence of the U.S. president, its nomenclature has not been consistent. The Philadelphia home in which Presidents George Washington and John Adams lived for most of their terms went by many names, including the Masters-Penn House, the Robert Morris House, the Washington Mansion, the Executive Mansion, the Presidential Mansion, and other names. The first two reflected the names of various owners of the house, while the latter three were popularly used by the local population. However, the label used formally by Washington and Adams was "President's House."[26]

Under Article 1, Section 8, of the Constitution, Congress was empowered to build a federal enclave to "exercise exclusive Legislation in all Cases whatsoever, over such District (not exceeding ten Miles square) as may, by Cession of particular States, and the acceptance of Congress, become the Seat of the Government of the United States, and to exercise like Authority over all Places purchased by the Consent of the Legislature of the State in which the Same shall be, for the Erection of Forts, Magazines, Arsenals, dock-Yards, and other needful Buildings." As it turned out, the president's house was one of those "needful Buildings."

While the Constitution authorized the construction of what would be officially named the "District of Columbia" but referred to as "Washington," it was the Residence Act of 1790 that clarified exactly where the nation's capital and the president's residence were to be constructed. It mandated that "all offices attached to the seat of the government of the United States" would be moved to the capital city no later than the first Monday in December 1800. It also stipulated, under the influence of Washington, that the district "be located as hereafter directed on the river Potomack, at some place between the mouths of the Eastern-Branch [now called the Anacostia] and Connogochegue."[27] Despite the fact that the majority of the white population lived in the North, it would be the South where the new government, including the president's quarters, would be situated. Once again, the ongoing issue of slavery played a key role in that determination.

At the time of the passage of the Residence Act, the seat of the U.S. government was in New York City. During the Revolutionary War, the Constitutional Congress had been displaced on numerous occasions but met often either in Philadelphia, where the Declaration of Independence had been announced and the Constitution written and signed, or in New York. The president's residence was in New York at that time.

Southern states, however, were wary of having the government located in the North where those pesky, aggressive abolitionists were growing in numbers and power. Among Southerners, whispers grew louder that they would not accept a permanent federal district that was in the North. The South-North divide was once again raising its head. Meanwhile, the Pennsylvania delegation argued that the capital should be in Philadelphia, both because of the city's role in the Revolution and because of its stature as a modern, thriving metropolis. As

Pennsylvania was the second-largest state, after Virginia, its wishes could not be ignored without there being serious consequences. Clearly, compromises had to be made.

The most common story told is that there was a decision to separate the issues of the two homes that were needed for the president of the United States—the permanent one that needed to be built and the temporary one to be used in the meantime. New York and Boston both made unsuccessful bids to host the interim residence, losing to Pennsylvania. Choosing Philadelphia as the temporary home quieted the influential Pennsylvania delegates who believed that once the seat of government was established in their great city for ten years, it would not want to leave. The Philadelphia federalists, however, underestimated the distaste that southern political leaders felt toward urban areas and the North in general. The Southerners could tolerate a temporary home for the national government in a state that was kind of north, and given the Southerners' view that states' rights as opposed to an overwhelming national authority would define the political character of the new country a stay in Philadelphia seemed to be a minor threat. But it was unrealistic to believe that they would support long-term placement of the nation's capital in Philadelphia.

The second deal to be struck was that in exchange for the South supporting Alexander Hamilton's proposal, known as the Assumption Act, that would allow the new and somewhat broke national government to assume wartime debts that states had incurred during the Revolutionary War, the national capital itself would be located in the South. Or so the story goes. In this narrative, the Southerners were really open to negotiations and simply drove a hard bargain.

Yet, as historian Garry Wills points out, in reality, the bargain to establish the capital was engineered by three Virginians

—James Madison, Thomas Jefferson, and George Washington—who wanted not only to appease their Southern allies but also ensure that the issue of slavery would be minimized. "The capital *was* purposely embedded in slave territory," argues Wills (emphasis in the original).[28] Just as the South would not have joined the revolution if there had not been a guarantee of protection for slavery, it was certainly not going to accept that the permanent seat of the nation's government be located in an abolitionist stronghold like Philadelphia. Pennsylvania was already leading the nation in the passage of bills that sought to undermine or end slavery. Furthermore, Washington, Madison, and Jefferson all enslaved black people. It would not do for the nation's leader to be in a city or state where protests against slavery were frequent and where legal actions could possibly be taken against him by white abolitionist activists pursuing the freedom of the blacks he enslaved.

Before settling into the friendly culture on land ceded by the two slave states of Virginia and Maryland, the president's residence would be situated first in New York City and then in Philadelphia. And the practice of slave labor in the president's house would travel this road as well.

Washington Moves to Public Housing

As president, George Washington never lived in the city that would one day be named after him. He spent a brief time in New York between 1789 and 1790, then took up temporary residence in Philadelphia from 1790 to 1797.

Washington could and did live away from his wife, Martha, but found it impossible to live away from his slaves. In New York and Philadelphia, he brought with him a number individuals he enslaved, thus establishing a tradition of black slave labor in the president's home that would continue with few exceptions up to the Civil War. All the euphemisms that had been employed in the founding documents to cover up the embarrassment and hypocrisy of slavery could not negate the reality that the first president of the United States was enslaving hundreds of men, women, and children, a reality visible for all to see.

Despite his short stay in New York City, it was really in Philadelphia that Washington's presidency unfolded. Unlike New York, with a ratio of enslaved to free blacks of nearly five to one (21,324 enslaved, 4,654 free), Pennsylvania was one of four states where free blacks (6,537) outnumbered those who were not (3,737).[29] Washington would contribute at least ten additional slaves to the state's numbers. His slave-labor force in Philadelphia over time included six who arrived with him from New York—Moll, Austin, Giles, Paris, Christopher, and the aforementioned Oney—plus Hercules and his son Richmond. Another slave, Joe, who would serve as a horse footman, arrived later. And, of course, William Lee was by his side at least for a short while. Ironically, they would all reside in a city that became the epicenter for early abolitionism and black radicalism.

In Philadelphia, the first presidential residence was a home owned by Robert Morris, one of the richest men in the country at the time. The Market Street house had been built in the late 1760s and was one of the largest in the city. During the Revolutionary War, it had been occupied for a time by General Benedict Arnold until he was forced out due to corruption and other problems. Washington, who was close to the Morris family, was extremely familiar with the property and had even lodged there on many occasions, including during his stay in the city for the Constitutional Convention. Although the city proposed and started to construct a larger residence for the president, Washington would live in the Morris house for nine years (1790–1799) and Adams for one year (1799–1800) until the White House was ready in 1800.[30]

Washington renovated the house, adding a servants' hall and two rooms in an extension of the smokehouse that would house both his servants and the men and women he enslaved. It is this part of the house that would generate passionate controversy over 200 years later.

Abolitionism in Philadelphia

The selection of Pennsylvania to temporarily house the nation's government seems counterintuitive for several reasons. First, it was clearly a concession to the North by the South. Although the permanent home of the federal government was being built in the South, a ten-year commitment was a fairly strong victory for political forces of the North across what was shaping up as a major fault line in American politics between the two regions. Second, while the slavery-enabling Constitution was being written at Independence Hall in Philadelphia, others in the city were igniting new fires against the institution. The Pennsylvania Abolition Society was reorganizing and reasserting itself, and black activists across the city were establishing institutions that would last until this very day. The president's house under both Washington and Adams would attempt to remain aloof from these developments, but nevertheless, the abolitionists' energies would vex presidents for decades to come.

Among whites, the abolitionist movement was rooted in the Quaker religion, whose members had founded Pennsylvania. On April 18, 1688, only six years after the arrival of state founder William Penn, four Quakers—Gerrit Hendricks, Derick op den Graeff, Francis Daniel Pastorius, and Abraham op den Graeff—wrote a letter launching a protest opposing slavery,

Anthony Benezet instructing black children. He was one of the earliest American abolitionists and founded the first anti-slavery society, the Society for the Relief of Free Negroes Unlawfully Held in Bondage.

railing against "the traffic of men-body" and asking "what thing in the world can be done worse towards us, than if men should rob or steal us away, and sell us for slaves to strange countries."[31] This is believed to be the first formal protest by white people against slavery in North America's history.

Historian Maurice Jackson has argued that the Quaker opposition to slavery was rooted in their theological beliefs. First, he contends, Quakers rejected both the notion of "original sin" and the practice of enslaving newborns. Second, they also rejected the notion of "just war" that was used by some to argue that individuals and communities could be taken as part of the booty of war and then enslaved. Linked to that notion, Quakers also preached nonviolence and that no institution was as violent as that of slavery. And third, according to Jackson, Quaker leaders such as Anthony Benezet criticized the institution of slavery on the grounds that it was driven by greed and a lust for money at any cost.[32] For Quakers and others, such values were immoral and ungodly, and fighting to end slavery was not an option but an obligation.

In April 1775, led by Benezet, the Quakers and others formed the Society for the Relief of Free Negroes Unlawfully Held in Bondage. Their activities apparently got under the skin of then General George Washington who, in 1786, wrote a letter supporting a friend and fellow Virginia slaveholder who had to deal with "a vexatious lawsuit respecting a slave of his, which a Society of Quakers in the city (formed for such purposes) have attempted to liberate."[33] The war and the untimely death in 1784 of Benezet, the Society's intellectual and political leader, forced a curtailment of their activities.[34]

The group persevered, however, renaming itself the Pennsylvania Abolition Society in 1787, and pledged to "use such means as are in their power to extend the blessings of freedom to every part of the human race."[35] The group's members achieved a coup when they convinced the ever popular Benjamin Franklin, aged but still energetic, to join the cause. They quickly selected him to become the Abolition Society's president, a position he accepted and held until he died in 1790. Like most of the founding fathers, Franklin had been a slaveholder for many years, but unlike most, he came to see the evil and immorality of the slave system and vigorously spoke out against it in his later years. The Pennsylvania Abolition Society helped to buy freedom for some, provided legal aid to runaways or those who were unlawfully abducted by slave catchers, and promoted pro-abolition legislation. As the Pennsylvania Abolition Society developed, it also formed networks with other abolitionist groups and movements around the world, including groups in Canada and parts of the Caribbean.

Despite its groundbreaking efforts to end slavery, the Pennsylvania Abolition Society had several glaring weaknesses. First, its strategy relied primarily on petitions and legal remedies. The former had propaganda and educational value, but little real-world impact to end slave system. Congress and state legislatures put them on the shelf never to be seen or heard of again. In legal efforts, on the other hand, the Society played a central role in the development of the Gradual Abolition Act (discussed in Chapter 1) and sought other legislative and legal solutions, achieving more than expected given the national and even local social climate. But slavery continued to grow, and other efforts began to overshadow its work, such as those of the American Colonization Society, whose members advocated sending blacks to Africa, or those supporting more radical demands such as slave uprisings or establishing maroon societies. While the Pennsylvania Abolition Society settled for a gradualist policy, others advocated for what writer Richard Newman termed "immediatism"—an immediate end to slavery and the establishment of full equality for African Americans.[36]

Second, and perhaps most telling, the Pennsylvania Abolition Society was segregated and did not allow black members until the 1830s, by which time other integrated or all-black initiatives were well established. The segregationist policy of the Pennsylvania Abolition Society was not that different from that of any other political or social institution of the period. Despite genuinely seeking an end to slavery, its policies reflected the underlying reality that blacks were not seen as equals by even "progressive" whites. The benevolence of the organization might best be seen, then, as more patronizing and moralistic than as part of a political movement for genuine racial equality. That demand would come from the black community itself.

Black Activism Then and Now

At the same time the Constitutional Convention met in Philadelphia to frame the terms of the slavery-permissive U.S. Constitution, the city's black community was actively organizing to abolish slavery. Living in the largest enclave of free blacks in the nation, African Americans in Pennsylvania consolidated and began a concerted push to end slavery and ensconce equal rights and social justice. Movement activity took many forms—speeches, petitions, pamphlets, public gatherings, and the development of black newspapers.

Religious leaders were particularly important in these campaigns. In fall 1787, Methodist convert and former slave Richard Allen, along with Absalom Jones and Peter Williams, knelt down to pray in Philadelphia's St. George Church. The church had recently begun to segregate the increased number of blacks who attended, many of whom came to hear Allen preach. Coordinating segregation, however, became more and more difficult as the black congregation grew. On that particular November Sunday there was confusion regarding exactly where Allen and the others should worship. As the men were kneeling in prayer, church officials first implored them to move and then, when they refused, literally lifted them off their knees and physically removed them from the church.

These churchgoing black men entered separately but left united. Allen's response, with assistance from Jones, was to form the Free African Society and later to found the African Methodist Episcopal Church. Getting thrown out of Philadelphia's St. George Church only served to make the men more defiant never to return. "They were no more plagued with us in the church," said Allen.[37]

The Free African Society was a broad-based network of African Americans that was formed "without regard to religious tenets, provided, the persons lived an orderly and sober life, in order to support one another in sickness, and for the benefit of their widows and fatherless children."[38] It sought to unite the black community—free and enslaved—to fight for justice and to take a stand against racism. Historian Lerone Bennett Jr. referred to it as an "embryonic political cell."[39] Although the group was nondenominational, differences grew between Allen and Jones, and the former left the group in 1789 and established the Bethel African Methodist Episcopal Church in 1794.

By the time President Washington arrived to stay at the president's residence in Philadelphia, he was entering the one area in the new nation where the confluence of militant abolitionism and the struggle for black liberation was at its strongest. Because he did little to abate slavery, he became a target of antislavery campaigners. Pro-abolition Quakers, for example, had met with Washington after he was elected president, lobbying him to end slavery,[40] and in 1797, black Philadelphians petitioned the federal government to prohibit slavery and repeal the 1793 Fugitive Slave Act, which Washington had signed into law in their city.[41] Their efforts were unsuccessful.

Embarrassed by his complicity in the business of human trafficking, Washington apparently made efforts to shield his slaves from public view as much as possible. He was rarely seen with them publicly (except for William Lee, until he was sent to Mount Vernon), and as Washington's tenure went on, visitors noticed a decline in their presence at the president's house. Hundreds of miles from the pro-slavery culture of the South, the first president of the United States must have experienced constant discomfort, possibly accounting for his frequent visits to his sprawling estate in Mount Vernon.

Washington was not the only person shamed by the presence of the black people he kept enslaved in Philadelphia. Over the years, the city of Philadelphia itself quietly erased all historical traces of slavery from the president's residence, or at least attempted to do so.

The Movement to Honor Washington's Enslaved

While ignored by city and national officials, the story of Washington's enslavement of men and women in Philadelphia did not die out in the black community. African Americans there have passed on the stories of that era from generation to generation. But it would take the city's effort to honor another part of its history to trigger contemporary black Philadelphians to organize a movement demanding that the saga of the black people Washington enslaved be included in the city's official history.

In 2002, the National Park Service began its effort to move the Liberty Bell to a new $12.6 million pavilion.[42] The move ignited a firestorm of protests when it was discovered by researcher Edward Lawler Jr., who was doing some digging of his own, that the proposed location for the new pavilion was the exact site where the president's house once stood—the residence where the blacks whom President Washington held enslaved[43] had also lived and toiled.[44] Building on Lawler's research, in 2007 archaeologists uncovered the precise location of the slave quarters. The planned entrance to the pavilion would be situated exactly there, atop the area where Washington's slaves once lived.[45]

The uproar began in January 2002 when Lawler broke the story about the "president's house" in an extensive and detailed article in *The Pennsylvania Magazine of History and Biography.* The article identified the location where Washington quartered the black men and women he enslaved—a part of the residence called the "smokehouse." Dramatically, Lawler noted that the walkway entrance to the Liberty Bell Center was going to be built directly over the place where Washington kept his slaves[46] and that people visiting site would have to walk over the precise spot where black people belonging to the first president of the United States once slept.

Outrage was compounded by the fact that the Liberty Bell itself had been a symbol of the abolitionist movement since 1837, when it became the frontispiece of *Liberty*, a journal published by the New York Anti-Slavery Society.[47] In fact, it was the abolitionists who first began to refer to it as the "Liberty Bell," supplanting its previous title of "State House Bell," and who adopted the militant words inscribed on it: "Proclaim Liberty throughout all the Land unto all the Inhabitants thereof."[48]

Response to Lawler's article was swift. A number of groups formed to challenge the plans of the National Park Service, whose initial reaction to criticism over its omission of the slavery issue was stunningly underwhelming. The National Park Service sought first to minimize the concerns being raised and, when that did not work, to divert them. According to the *Philadelphia Inquirer*, National Park Service officials implied that a focus on slavery would perhaps give undue significance and publicity to the issue, since Washington also had indentured servants and other workers at the house. Some National Park Service officials also suggested that any reference to the people Washington enslaved be displayed at the Deshler-Morris House, another much less prominent National Park Service facility that reportedly receives only around 2,000 visitors a year compared to an estimated 1.2 million annual visitors to the Liberty Bell.[49]

By mid-May 2002, the National Park Service had a change of mind and began to move toward involving scholars, historians, elected officials, and community activists in an effort to determine how best to acknowledge the history of the people Washington enslaved. Park Service officials met with Lawler and another local historian, Charles Brockson, as well as with Representative Bob Brady (D-PA). It also sought input from nationally known historians and academics including the revered John Hope Franklin, the Smithsonian Institution's Faith Ruffin, George Washington University's James Horton, and Spencer Crew, director of Cincinnati's Underground Railroad Museum.[50]

The National Park Service's new attitude was driven by activism on the part of the black community, including a letter-writing campaign led by "Radio Courtroom" host Michael Coard.[51] A group called the Ad-Hoc Historians formed and called for "commemorating the lives of eight enslaved Africans, telling the full and complex history of American freedom."[52]

Events began to move quickly. Congress became involved, and on July 9, 2002, the House Appropriations Committee added an amendment to the $19.7 billion budget bill for the Interior Department (under which National Park Service operates) calling for the Park Service "to appropriately commemorate" those who had been enslaved by Washington in Philadelphia as well as the house itself.[53] The amendment also demanded that the Park Service report on the progress it was making toward fulfilling that obligation by March 2003.[54] By then, it was generally agreed by all the parties that at least a memorial should be constructed. In fall 2003, then-Philadelphia Mayor John Street committed $1.5 million in city funds to the memorial.[55] And Independence National Historic Park, where the Liberty Bell Center is located, raised $4.5 million to pay for the conceptual plan for the memorial. Representatives Chaka Fattah (who played an early role in pushing for the memorial and supporting local initiatives) and Bob Brady announced that the congressional allocation to the project had grown to $3.5 million.[56]

Significantly, the mayor's office and the park formed a committee to oversee the development of the memorial dedicated to the black people President Washington enslaved. Members of the committee represented a broad array of scholars and activists, including:

- Romona Riscoe Benson, interim president and chief executive officer of the African American Museum in Philadelphia;
- Charles L. Blockson, curator of the Charles Blockson Afro-American Collection at Temple University, and a founding member of Generations Unlimited;
- Michael Coard, a founding member of the Avenging the Ancestors Coalition;
- Tanya Hall, executive director of the Philadelphia Multicultural Affairs Congress;
- Edward Lawler Jr., a historian representing the Independence Hall Association;
- Charlene Mires, associate professor of history at Villanova University and editor of the Pennsylvania History Studies Series, representing the Ad-Hoc Historians;
- John Skief, chief administrative officer of the Harambee Institute of Science Technology Charter School;
- Karen Warrington, Representative Bob Brady's director of communications;
- Joyce Wilkerson, Mayor John Street's chief of staff.[57]

Lawler's research not only sparked challenges to the building of the new structure, but also inspired black historians, activists, and political leaders to mobilize numerous community-based groups, including the Ad-Hoc Historians and the Avenging the Ancestors Coalition or ATAC (pronounced "attack"). The group was created to "compel the National Park Service (NPS) and Independence National Historical Park (INHP) to finally agree to the creation of a prominent Slavery Commemoration as a key component of the President's House project."[58] Protests, education campaigns, and negotiations by ATAC were key to winning funds allocated specifically for that purpose from the city and the National Park Service.

Carrying the struggle into the twenty-first century, ATAC also successfully lobbied to ensure that African Americans were employed in the construction of the project. In August 2009, Philadelphia Mayor Michael Nutter announced that 67 percent of the construction jobs through subcontracts were being awarded to minority- and women-owned businesses. In fact, the design of the project itself went to a black-owned architecture firm, Kelly/Maiello Architects & Planners, whose owner made every effort to include other minority firms in the work.

As of mid-2010, a number of issues remained unresolved as the effort to build a replica of the president's house and a memorial to the enslaved people who lived there moved forward. A dispute arose in the committee when historian Edward Lawler criticized three important inaccuracies in the design of the house: "The design incorrectly sited the front of the house, distorted the shape of a much-noted bow window designed by Washington, and placed a commemoration of the house slave quarters in the wrong spot."[59] While not necessarily disagreeing with Lawler, the committee nevertheless went forward without revising the plan. For both legal and practical reasons, they argued that the agreed-upon design was still the best resolution.

ATAC's Michael Coard responded to Lawler and other critics: "There has also been criticism of the placement of the house's slave quarters. But if the quarters were placed exactly where they stood more than 200 years ago, they would almost touch the new Liberty Bell Center, making the quarters impossible to enter and violating the Americans with Disabilities Act."[60] He cautioned that "hyper-technical replication must sometimes give way to practical-minded accessibility" and that "Philadelphia is about to make history with this project. And the designers already made history by envisioning a powerful, important attraction that everyone in America and the world should want to see. But they won't see it if it's not practical."[61]

While the campaign to honor the men and women that Washington enslaved in Philadelphia was successful, a similar campaign has yet to unfold in the nation's capital, where dozens, if not hundreds, of slaves labored for U.S. presidents from James Madison to Zachary Taylor. These black people not only slaved in the White House but actually helped to build it. During the period that Washington and Adams were residing in Philadelphia, the difficult task of building a whole city, including the permanent home of the president, continued.

CHAPTER 3

A White House Built *On* and *With* Slavery

Some view our sable race with scornful eye,
"Their colour is a diabolic dye."
Remember, Christians, Negroes, black as Cain,
May be refin'd, and join th' angelic train.
—Phillis Wheatley, the first black person to be published in the United States[1]

Prelude: Peter's White House Story

Peter, or "Negro Peter" as he was sometimes listed on the payroll, must have been completely exhausted after working all day as a carpenter building the president's house in Washington, D.C., the structure that would one day be called the White House. The winter months are often very cold in Washington, D.C., as wind racing off the Potomac and Anacostia rivers drives the temperature down into single digits, and major snowstorms are not uncommon. Although as a carpenter Peter primarily labored inside, during the icy days of January 1795 the site of the half-built president's residence was certainly a frigid place to work. It was also likely that Peter did not get all the nutrition needed for such labor-intensive work. During the coldest days, he and the others forced to work there were likely underdressed for the weather, and those who contracted a cold or the flu continued to work nevertheless. Suffering the freezing weather, long hours of toil, and meager meals alongside Peter were four other black carpenters—Tom, Ben, Harry, and Daniel—who like Peter were also enslaved.[2]

But these black men may have thought themselves more fortunate than others who were forced to slave in extreme conditions at the various stone quarries in and around Virginia. Those locations have been described as "snake-infested" and "swarmed with mosquitoes," and the labor so arduous that each worker was given "a half-pint of whiskey per day to help them cope."[3] This was spirit-killing work if such there ever was. Enslaved black men were ordered into the quarries from "can't see" to "can't see" to carry out the back-breaking tasks of digging, cutting, lifting, and hauling stone. Tons of the stone from which the U.S. capital is built, and which can still be seen today, got there via the slave labor of black men.

Although enslaved, Peter and the other black carpenters may have also thought themselves more lucky than the men, women, and children they saw each day being held in cages around the city or forced onto the auction block, many of whom were being sent to a life of misery on plantations in the dreaded Southern states of Alabama, Georgia, Mississippi, and Louisiana. Among those in cages or being sold, some were being punished for attempting to escape, learning to read, or being thought to be agitators for freedom. Some had been free but were illegally abducted by slave catchers who destroyed the papers documenting their freedom, and were now selling them off to the highest bidder. The manacles holding these people were heavy, perhaps even rusted from having been exposed to all manner of climates. From the construction site of the president's residence, Peter and the others would have witnessed these events on a daily basis. As writer Walter C. Clephane soberly states, "The District of Columbia became a great slave market."[4]

While forced to work at the construction site, the men would see and hear horrors all around them. An endless parade of shame coursed through the streets as human traffickers transported blacks on horse-drawn carts or ordered shackled men, women, and children into long chain-linked lines on their way to or from the auction block. At Lafayette Square, directly across from where the White House was being built, slave pens stood for all to see. When the pens were full, the city jails were used to hold overflow. In Alexandria, a part of the District until 1846, the firm of Franklin & Armfield became one of the largest dealers of abducted and enslaved people, selling by the 1830s as many as 1,000 black people per year. [5] At Third Street and Pennsylvania, a dozen or so blocks from the White House construction site, the St. Charles Hotel held enslaved people in basement cells. At Seventh Street and Pennsylvania, the most robust and active slave market in the city flourished. At an abode owned by James Birch known as the "Yellow House," hundreds of individuals were treated no better than farm animals. The three-story building was bustling with activity and was considered one of the major East Coast hubs for the buying and selling of black people.

Describing his experience seeing a slave pen in Washington, D.C. in 1835, an English man wrote:

> It is surrounded by a wooden paling fourteen or fifteen feet in height, with the posts outside to prevent escape, and separated from the building by a space too narrow to permit of a free circulation of air. At a small window above, which was unglazed and exposed

Slave pen, Alexandria, Virgina, circa 1863. In 1791, Alexandria was included in the area chosen by George Washington to become the District of Columbia.

alike to the heat of summer and the cold of winter, so trying to the constitution, two or three sable faces appeared looking out wistfully to while away the time and catch a refreshing breeze, the weather being extremely hot. In this wretched hovel all colors except white, both sexes, and all ages, are confined, exposed indiscriminately to the contamination which may be expected in such society and under such seclusion.[6]

Part of the ambient noise in Washington, D.C.'s streets was the constant wails, screams, and cries of the enslaved, their anguish omnipresent. While nearly all whites and a few free blacks were enjoying liberty from British" control and constructing a new city to represent and govern their newfound freedom and democracy, others were brutally forced to live, toil, and die in illiterate misery. So pervasive was the institution of slavery that most, if not all, of the hands that were building the White House were black hands. From their captive position trapped at the bottom of U.S. society, most of these people likely could not envision a time when they could enter the public buildings they were constructing as free and equal citizens, let alone as elected or appointed officials with authority over the inner workings of the nation. Was Peter one of those who believed that his destiny was to die enslaved, or did he imagine a future where he walked in the world as a free man?

As is the case for virtually all the black people who slaved to build the White House, not much is known about Peter's life and family. According to researcher Bob Arnebeck, Peter was likely sent to the District of Columbia by way of South Carolina with his owner, the Irish immigrant James Hoban, about whom a great deal is known.[7]

Born in Desart, Ireland in 1762, James Hoban was living in Charleston, South Carolina, by his early twenties. After meeting President Washington in Charleston during the president's Southern tour in summer 1791, Hoban listened with interest when Washington mentioned the need for builders to help construct the nation's new capital. In 1792, he entered a design contest held to select the best architectural plan for building what would become the permanent residence and official office of all future U.S. presidents. Drawing from his Irish roots, Hoban rendered a plan inspired by Dublin's Leinster House and won the coveted $500 prize.

President Washington then tentatively hired Hoban to oversee the planning and construction of the building, and Hoban attended the groundbreaking ceremony. Washington liked Hoban and later wrote the commission in July 1792 to confirm his hire, stating, "He has been engaged in some of the first buildings in Dublin, appears a master workman, and has a great many hands of his own." By "hands," Washington was likely referring to individuals Hoban was enslaving. Hoban's contributions to the city would go beyond his work on the White House and the Capitol. He would later become the first Superintendent Architect of the Capitol and be elected to the D.C. City Council. Unlike Peter's work, Hoban's has been remembered and honored in both Ireland and the United States.

Hoban and his assistant, Pierce Purcell, traveled to Washington, D.C. and began their work that year. They brought with them a number of the people they kept enslaved, including the carpenters Peter, Tom, Ben, and Harry, who were owned by Hoban, while the carpenter Daniel belonged to Purcell. According to the 1795 payroll records of the commission that oversaw the building of the new city, Peter and Tom were earning wages as much as those paid to the white indentured servants with whom they worked. This included the McCorkill brothers and Peter Smith, all of whom were white and whose contracts were owned by Hoban and Purcell.

In February 1795, Peter worked twenty-one days and earned "six pounds, sixteen shillings, & six pence" at a per diem rate of 6 shillings/6 pence—the same rate being paid Peter Smith, a white servant who was indentured to Purcell. But the money Peter earned he did not get to keep. It went to James Hoban—the man who enslaved him. Hoban and Purcell's enslaved black men appear to be the only ones ever hired as carpenters. George Washington's nephew, William Augustine Washington, had proposed to the commissioners to hire "twelve good Negro carpenters," but they did not take him up on that offer.

From 1793 to 1797—after which they and all other black carpenters were banned from working on the White House—Peter and the others were among the seventeen carpenters that worked at the site and completed a significant amount of the interior carpentry work. Once finished, the White House was projected to be the largest residence in the country.

The black carpenters were banned by the Commissioners as a consequence of a conflict between Hoban and another contractor. By late 1797, a rival Scottish contractor, Collen Williamson, submitted complaints to the commissioners regarding Hoban's use of black carpenters. Among the allegations were that black and Irish carpenters were getting paid too much relative to other carpenters, that Hoban was unfairly profiting from their labor, and that Hoban and Purcell were stealing building materials. Although there was little basis for the charges and it was clear that Williamson was driven by competitive revenge, the commission responded by ordering that "no Negro Carpenters or apprentices be hired at either of the public Buildings and that no Wages be allowed after that day to any white Apprentices without an especial order of the Board," the public buildings meaning the White House and the Capitol.[8]

As the new nation was presenting itself as being guided by the egalitarian principles of democracy, freedom, and justice, the home and office of the nation's president and commander in chief was being built, in part, with the slave labor of black people who were stripped of all rights. As far as the record shows, President Washington, who was in charge of making sure the project was completed, and Secretary of State Thomas Jefferson, who was responsible for the project's implementation, never spoke of or acknowledged this contradiction about the construction of the White House or the work that the black carpenters (and others) were doing.

If Not Slaves, Then Who? Enslaved and Free Labor Builds the Nation's Capital

> *The Federal City is increasing fast in buildings and rising in consequence; and will, no doubt, from the advantages given to it by Nature and its proximity to a rich interior country and the Western Territory, become the emporium of the United States.*[9]—George Washington, December 12, 1793

Enslaved labor built much of early America, particularly in the South. Indeed, almost every major building in every major city constructed in the pre-nineteenth-century era used slave labor in some capacity or was owned by a slaveholder. The list includes Philadelphia's Independence Hall, where both the Declaration of Independence and the U.S. Constitution were drafted, debated, and signed, and Boston's Faneuil Hall, given to the city by Peter Faneuil, who made his fortune in the triangular slave trade.[10] The list also includes the labor involved in the building and maintenance of the palatial plantation homes of George Washington at Mount Vernon, Thomas Jefferson at Monticello, and James Madison at Montpelier. The bodies, bones and muscles of enslaved blacks were used to construct nearly every major structure built in the eighteenth and nineteenth centuries in the United States, but their labor has gone uncelebrated and largely undocumented. That this primary aspect of American labor history has been lost or forgotten does not mitigate the significance of recognizing the role black labor played in constructing the country's original state architecture, buildings and landscapes.

By the latter part of the eighteenth century, in Virginia and Maryland—the two states in which white people enslaved the most blacks—it had become customary for slave owners to hire out some of their blacks when it was profitable for them to do so. In Virginia, the state with the largest number of enslaved by a wide margin, the population of enslaved people had grown from a few hundred at the beginning of the eighteenth century to nearly 300,000 by the end of it. As historian Roger Wilkins notes, "By the time of the Revolution, 40 percent of all Virginians were black," and 96 percent of that population was enslaved.[11] Maryland had more than 100,000 black people enslaved to whites.

When faced with a labor shortage during the early phase of constructing the capital, the order to bring in slave labor was one of the most critical decisions implemented by the commissioners tasked to complete the project. White growers were more than eager to profit from subcontracting out the blacks they enslaved, when it was deemed they were not needed to toil in the fields. Being hired out, however, was not an opportunity for enslaved blacks to earn money for their labor. In nearly all instances, 100 percent of black wages went directly to their white enslavers. If in some rare cases slave workers received money for their work, it was due to the generosity or more likely the motivational intentions of their employer and went beyond what was owed the blacks' enslavers.

Although construction on the nation's capital had begun in 1790, Peter and other enslaved blacks were not ordered to begin work building the White House, the Capitol, and other federal structures until after 1792, because President Washington initially wanted to hire foreign labor to do the job. From the beginning, Washington hoped to bring in German and Scottish immigrants, whom he believed to possess the most talent and discipline for large-scale construction projects. Thomas Jefferson joined him in this belief and ordered the commissioners to investigate the viability of importing Germans workers.

However, outreach by the commissioners had little success in attracting foreign labor.[12]

The original three commissioners—Thomas Johnson, David Stuart, and Daniel Carroll—appointed by Washington on January 24, 1791, to oversee the work had difficulty getting foreign workers to sail to the United States, and at first had to settle for the labor of free and indentured white men.[13] It is possible that free blacks were hired during the first two years of the project, but there is no clear record that that was the case. According to the payroll records of the time, Major Pierre Charles L'Enfant, the chief engineer hired by Washington in March 1791 to initially survey and design the city, had no blacks working for him. However, Washington had also hired Major Andrew Ellicott III to conduct a survey of the area. He in turn employed Benjamin Banneker, an African American writer, astronomer, publisher, and mathematician. Banneker helped to survey the land that became the District of Columbia in 1791. Working under Ellicott, he was instrumental in establishing true north.[14]

The hiring of the Frenchman L'Enfant and later the Irish surveyor James Hoban reflected another grand paradox in the founding of the nation. The aim of the American Revolution was first and foremost to break from England and forge a new nation independent of outside authority, political influence, or foreign culture. Yet it would be noncitizens, non-Americans who would design and build the nation's capital city. And they would bring with them their European ideas and sensibilities. L'Enfant's vision of the city was philosophically linked more to Versailles or Paris than Philadelphia or New York.

Europe's past would continue to shape the United States' future. And not only did the nation's new leaders and founders hire foreigners to plan the city, Washington and Jefferson eagerly sought to bring in foreign, rather than American, workers. It should be remembered that, with few exceptions, that the nation's white founders were initially English by birth, citizenship, and culture. Despite the political break with England, cultural and social orientation and values were still very much framed by their British heritage.

Although they had trouble finding enough workers to begin the construction of the White House and other buildings, neither L'Enfant nor the commissioners used slave labor prior to 1792. The situation was becoming impossible. L'Enfant estimated that he would need more than 500 men to complete the work of building the city. This included carpenters, masons, stonecutters, bricklayers, supervisors, and hundreds of men who would do the challenging physical labor of cutting down trees, hauling lumber and stones, digging the foundation for the building, removing dead animals, and other undesirable tasks. The population of the area ceded by Maryland and Virginia was less than 1,000 people overall. The huge question that loomed before L'Enfant and the commissioners was from where these workers would come.

It was unclear how L'Enfant thought he would meet his labor quota without using slaves as there simply weren't enough free men available for hire. The shortage became a real obstacle to the project. Conflicts grew as L'Enfant resisted working under the commissioners who he considered, as Arnebeck writes, to hold "too narrow a view of the project."[15]

The breaking point came in February 1792 when L'Enfant was fired. Although he had been close to President Washington, he had feuded with the commissioners nearly from the start of the project. The conflicts had already led to the dismissal of his workers in January 1792 because the commissioners felt that L'Enfant was spending too extravagantly on labor. It was only after L'Enfant was gone that they turned to slave labor as a sustainable and cost-effective solution.

According to the commission records, the adjustment in labor policy was driven purely by economics. The commissioners would go back and forth in their assessment of how to get the work done at the cheapest cost, but clearly the use of slave labor was going to be financially beneficial. Those who worked under L'Enfant and Ellicott were paid wages, but after their workers were dismissed, the commissioners wanted to bring in new workers on a piecework basis. This issue would become more complicated once they decided to use enslaved people, because they had to deal with slaveholders as well as the enslaved themselves. In many cases, it would boil down to paying the white owners a yearly fee and paying some of the slaves an additional wage—about thirteen cents a day—as motivation for better quality work. The wages that would go directly to the slaveholders were between $60.00 and $70.00 a year, about $5.00 or so per month. On April 13, 1792, the commissioners met and made the following resolution:

> [T]o hire good labouring negroes by the year, the masters cloathing them well and finding each a blanket, the Commissioners finding them provisions and paying twenty one pounds a year wages. The payment if desired to be made quarterly or half yearly. If the negroes absent themselves a week or more, such time to be deducted.[16]

Two years later, in July 1794, Commissioner Thornton also suggested that the commissioners purchase slaves rather than rent them, to avoid interference from slave owners, and that at the end of five to six years of work, they would be granted their freedom. This strategy would certainly have benefited those who were enslaved and reflected at least a move toward the principles of equality and freedom that were claimed as the basis for the American Revolution. It is unknown if or how the commissioners debated this issue, or whether there was resistance to such a scheme from the area's slaveholders or from Washington and Jefferson, but in any case they decided not to purchase slaves and to continue to hire them from local owners.[17]

"Negroes"—meaning slaves in the vernacular of the times—would begin to work that summer by clearing trees. The land from Capitol Hill to the White House was a jungle of trees that had to be brought down, chopped up, and hauled away before any serious construction could begin. This was manual toil at its toughest and, from the commissioners' vantage, ideally suited to slave labor. The commissioners wanted the "best axe-men" to do the work.

Enslaved black men would also start to work on various dimensions of the president's house. It would take another couple of years before they would also be ordered to labor at the site of the Capitol. Their involvement began on February 11, 1795, and, according to payroll records, ended on May 17, 1801. Overall, for work on the Capitol, 385 payments were made for "Negro hire."[18] Although surviving records indicate how some of the enslaved workers were paid during the 1790–1801 period, it remains unclear who worked in the city and who was sent to the quarries. It's also quite possible that slave labor began on the Capitol earlier than 1795, as it is plausible that work was done without being documented in the commissioners' records.

So exactly what work did enslaved and free blacks do? In addition to cleaning up, black labor was employed in several categories, including cutting stone from the quarries; cutting and sawing trees to create streets; making and laying bricks; hauling materials; and roofing, plastering, painting, and carpentry at the construction sites of the White House and Capitol. The work that white overseers ordered blacks to do evolved over time. The reason the commissioners initially wanted a monthly wage was because they thought they would have no further use for slaves after trees were cut and removed.[19] It took time for them to witness and appreciate the wide variety of tasks that black workers could effectively perform. Seeing the quality of the slaves' work convinced the commissioners to expand use of their labor.

By 1793, it was clear that the commissioners wanted as many enslaved blacks as they could get. They began to place ads in newspapers around the country.[20] In fact, Arnebeck makes the stunning assertion that "[t]he only workers the commissioners seemed comfortable with were slaves."[21] The commissioners provided the slaves with bedding, floor space in a barracks, and meals consisting of cornmeal and either pork or beef.[22] Eventually, a hospital was built for sick slaves and other workers.[23]

As the work progressed, the hiring process became more complicated, with some laborers hired by the year, some by the month, and some by the job. In 1794, for instance, Williams "hired thirty-seven slaves by the year, twenty-six black and white laborers by the month, seven slaves to work with the surveyors, and six to work in the quarries."[24] The use of slave labor embodied a confluence of interests on the part of commissioners, slaveholders, and the enslaved people themselves. In the first place, use of enslaved blacks resolved the issue of labor supply that L'Enfant had been unable to manage. The commissioners had a workforce that was local, available, and except for the occasional few who successfully escaped, manageable. For the region's white growers who had large numbers of enslaved blacks to manage, the timing was nearly perfect. As tobacco farming begin to fade in favor of wheat and other less labor-intensive crops, for long periods of time there was less demand for slave labor than there had been in previous decades. Although slavery was expanding in the deep South, the growth of the cotton industry, the 1808 ban on the foreign importation of slaves, and slavery's expansion westward created new demand for slave labor after the 1820s. At the same time, there was a surplus of slave labor at the end of the eighteenth century in the Maryland-Virginia area. The opportunity to hire out their slaves solved, at least temporarily, the cash flow crisis that many local white growers were experiencing.

Records from the Commission detail which slaveholders in the area hired out their enslaved blacks and list the names of the enslaved themselves. For example, slaveholder William Beall hired out Davy, Frank and Newton. Slaveholder Ignatius Boone hired out Moses, Charles, and Jacob. Slaveholders Elizabeth, Eleanor, Jane, Mary, and Teresa Brent, all sisters, hired out Charles, Davy, Gabriel, Henry, and Nance. Slaveholder Joseph Queen hired out Clem, Moses, and Jess.[25] Slaveholder Edmund Plowden hired out Gerald, Tony, and Jack.[26] In all these instances, the money earned by the slaves went straight to the white owners and was not shared with their black workers.

The enormous task of building the capital city created an economic boom for people living in the area and beyond. It was not only attractive to whites who were looking for jobs and investments, but was also economically enticing to free blacks, enslaved blacks, and white indentured servants from around the country. Employment, investment, and business opportunities grew substantially as the city was being built. By 1795, the city and surrounding areas had grown so much and were populated with so many blacks that Georgetown, then independent of the city, passed regulations forbidding slaves and indentured servants from congregating in groups of more than five. Violators could be punished with thirty-nine lashes and a fine for the person's enslaver.[27]

Stone by Stone, Brick by Brick

While nearly all of the construction work was done by men, there is some evidence that black women were also ordered to labor in the construction process, especially for making bricks. Allen writes that because "it was considered semi-skilled labor, molding bricks was usually the work of female or adolescent slaves, who could mold as many as 5,000 bricks a day."[28] Given that in 1796 the commission placed an order for "[o]ne million of good place bricks," there was no shortage of workers in brickmaking, which probably included a good number of women, and bricklaying, which was probably done by men. In spite of Allen's assertion, it's notable that no record was made in the commissioners' records regarding payments made to women, black or white. It is entirely possible that the black women slaved to make the bricks off-site, on plantations or farms, and that payment for their work was made directly to their white controllers. There is also a speculation that Mrs. Cloe LeClair, the nurse who ran the hospital for the workers for $10 a month, an outstanding salary at the time, was African American.[29]

Moving stone from the quarry to the city was a difficult task. It had to be hauled from the pits to boats, shipped to the city, unloaded—which could take six enslaved men up to two days—then dragged to the construction sites at the Capitol and the White House. To stay on schedule, the commissioners instructed the workers' supervisor, Elisha Williams, "to keep the yearly hirelings at work, from sunrise to sunset, particularly the negroes."[30]

It appears that blacks were not taught how to carve stone, a highly skilled task, but instead were ordered to do the bulk of the digging and excavation. It is certain that black slaves labored at the quarry in Aquia, Virginia. Arnebeck's research indicates that they "tended" to the white and free masons who cut, polished, carved, and set the stone both at the White House and at the Capitol. In August 1795, there were forty-six slaves working with the stone masons at the quarry. And enslaved blacks were likely the ones who did the cleanup work around the quarry. According to surviving payroll records, the blacks known to have slaved there were Jack Fuller, Bob, Alexander, and Moses. It is possible that others who were listed on the payroll—Nias Cooper, Jesse Cooper, Joshua Doing, Jacob Piles, Nimrod Young—were either free or enslaved blacks.

One free black who was involved in the building process was George Planter. According to Allen, Planter owned a boat that was used to transport stone from the quarries. This was likely a highly lucrative enterprise. There is not a lot of other personal information about Planter, but his situation implies that perhaps other free blacks with skills, needed equipment, or other talents worked on building the city as well.

Although there is plenty of historical evidence that blacks were used for making and laying bricks, Arnebeck found only one advertisement for a slave bricklayer in the area newspaper. There is not a lot of direct evidence of the specific role of blacks in the brickwork that went into the White House and the Capitol. It is known, for example, that brickwork contractors Lovering and Lovell wanted and used African Americans in their business.

In addition to the enslaved blacks who were forced to toil in the development and construction of Washington, D.C., a number of free blacks were also involved, including Benjamin Banneker. Although his father and grandfather had been enslaved at various points in their lives, Banneker was born to free parents on November 9, 1731, near Baltimore, Maryland. Banneker's ancestry was unusual for the period. His white grandmother, Mollie Welsh, had been an indentured servant from England who finished her seven years of servitude and bought a farm near the Patapsco River. She eventually saved enough to purchase two slaves. Reportedly, one of those was Banna Ka, later called Banneka and then anglicized to Banneker. Some research has indicated that Banneker's father was an African king who had been stolen off the western coast of Africa. One can only speculate about life on the farm, but apparently it was so harmonious that after several years of prosperity Mollie freed both Banneker and the other enslaved individual. Within a short time, Mollie Welsh and Benjamin Banneker married and eventually raised a family of four children, the oldest a girl named Mary.

As an adult, Mary married a black man who had been captured in Africa just as her father had. However, after he converted, joined the Church of England, and was baptized with the name Robert, he was released from slavery. A free black man, Robert married Mary Banneker and adopted Mary's last name as his own. Mary and Robert Banneker had four children as well, one boy and three girls. They named their boy Benjamin.

Robert displayed the same industrious spirit as his in-laws and soon owned 120 acres of farmland in the area where Benjamin and his sisters would grow up. Mollie took a particular liking to the boy and began to give him special tutoring. She had him study and read the Bible, and later sent him to an integrated school nearby. He became a bookworm. As he grew, his studies expanded to include mathematics and astronomy, and his intellectual talents became known throughout the area. He earned a living farming tobacco.

Benjamin Banneker was sixty years old and living on his farm in Patapsco Valley, Maryland, when he was hired to survey Washington, D.C. He and Major Andrew Ellicott arrived in the area on February 7, 1791, and set up camp. Although he had little experience conducting field surveys, Ellicott needed

Banneker for his knowledge of astronomy. His principal duties included monitoring the instrument known as the astronomical clock and recording and studying the movement of the stars and the sun. Contrary to subsequent rumors, Banneker did not assist in designing the city and there is no evidence that he and L'Enfant had met. However, Banneker played an essential role in laying out the city's boundaries. He was paid $60.00 for approximately three months of work he conducted in 1791.[31]

In March 1791, his efforts were praised in the *Georgetown Weekly Record*, whose editor described Banneker as an "Ethiopian whose abilities as a surveyor and astronomer clearly proved that Mr. Jefferson's concluding that race of men were void of 'mental endowment' was without foundation."[32] The *Record*'s editor was referring to the copious passages in Jefferson's *Notes on the State of Virginia* in which he makes disparaging remarks about the intelligence and characteristics of African Americans. In addition to attacking the quality of the poetry of celebrated black writer Phillis Wheatley (whose poem opens this chapter), Jefferson wrote:

> Comparing them by their faculties of memory, reason, and imagination, it appears to me, that in memory they are equal to the whites; in reason much inferior, as think one could scarcely be found capable of tracing and comprehending the investigations of Euclid; and that in imagination they are dull, tasteless, and anomalous. . . . But never yet could I find that a black had uttered a thought above the level of plain narration; never see even an elementary trait, of painting or sculpture.[33]

Jefferson's bigotry notwithstanding, Banneker made a substantial contribution to the surveying of the nation's capital city.

Phillis Wheatley, the first black woman whose writings were published. Born in Africa circa 1753, abducted and shipped to the American colonies in 1761 where the Wheatley family enslaved her until 1778 when she was legally released.

Banneker later had a famous correspondence with Jefferson, whom he had never met. In a long letter dated August 19, 1791, Banneker chastised Jefferson, then secretary of state, for his views on blacks. He reminded Jefferson of "the injustice of a state of slavery, and in which you had just apprehensions of the horrors of its condition" and quoted Jefferson's renowned opening to the Declaration of Independence: "We hold these truths to be self-evident, that all men are created equal." Banneker's letter argued that Jefferson and all professed Christians had an obligation "to extend their power and influence to the relief of every part of the human race, from whatever burden or oppression they may unjustly labor under." Banneker went on to say:

> I have long been convinced, that if your love for yourselves, and for those inestimable laws, which preserved to you the rights of human nature, was founded on sincerity, you could not but be solicitous, that every individual, of whatever rank or distinction, might with you equally enjoy the blessings thereof; neither could you rest satisfied short of the most active effusion of your exertions, in order to their promotion from any state of degradation, to which the unjustifiable cruelty and barbarism of men may have reduced them.[34]

The twelve-page letter he sent personally to Jefferson was later published in Banneker's *Almanac*. As a black man in the 1790s, Banneker showed great courage—and took great risks—by criticizing Secretary of State Thomas Jefferson in a public manner. Speaking against slavery was illegal in most of the South, and unwise from the perspective of his personal security. Nevertheless, Jefferson responded to Banneker within two weeks. "Nobody wishes more than I do," he wrote in a letter dated August 30, 1791, "to see such proofs as you exhibit, that nature has given to our black brethren, talents equal to those of the other colours of men, & that the appearance of a want of them is owing merely to the degraded condition of their existence both in Africa & America." Jefferson did not address the fact that their "degraded condition" is a direct result of the slavery that had been enshrined in the Constitution. He went on to say, "I can add with truth that nobody wishes more ardently to see a good system commenced for raising the condition both of their body & mind to what it ought to be, as fast as the imbecility of their present existence, and other circumstance which cannot be neglected, will admit." Jefferson was politely deferential to Banneker's criticisms without in any

Benjamin Banneker's Almanac.

way committing to use his authority to assist Banneker and the abolitionist movement.

Banneker's fame continued to grow after his work with Ellicott. From 1792 to 1797, he published a well-received and commercially successful almanac, *Benjamin Banneker's Pennsylvania, Delaware, Maryland, and Virginia Almanack and Ephemeris For the Year of Our Lord. . . .* The popular almanac contained essays, practical information, short stories, poems by Phillis Wheatley, and abolitionist arguments advocating the illegalization of slavery. Each almanac also contained an ephemeris, an astronomical chart that shows the positions of the sun, moon, stars, and planets. Due to deteriorating health, he was forced to suspend his publication after 1797. Banneker died on October 9, 1806, five years after construction of Washington, D.C., was complete and the city officially occupied. In 1980 the U.S. Postal Service celebrated his accomplishments by dedicating a first-class stamp to him in its Black Heritage series.[35]

Little is known about other free blacks who helped build the new city. Among those known to have worked there are Cesar Hall, Isaac Butler, and Jerry (or Jeremiah) Holland. In the records, Hall and Butler are listed as Free Cesar and Free Isaac. They all worked at the White House construction site as laborers. In the records for 1795, Holland was to be paid $8 per month for being considered "the best hand in the department"—a high wage for a black person. However, no records have been found to indicate that he actually got paid that amount. Historical documents indicate that he later worked as a servant for the commissioners in April 1798 and 1800, and lived in a house that was perhaps one that the commissioners built for skilled workers. Unfortunately, payroll records and other data only begin to give a glimpse of the complicated lives these workers led.

In the years leading up to the Civil War, white people's fear of and antagonism toward black folks in Washington, D.C., grew, and in 1835 the city's first race riot erupted. R. Beverly Snow, a free black man, owned a popular restaurant, the Epicurean Eating House, located approximately ten blocks from the White House on the corner of Sixth Street and Pennsylvania. On the night of August 4, Arthur Bowen was accused by the neighbor of his enslaver, Anna Maria Thornton, of having entered her room drunk and carrying an axe.[36] Although Thornton would later state that she perceived no harm from Bowen, and actually tried to defend him, he was eventually arrested. The incident, occurring only four years after the infamous Nat Turner-led slave rebellion in neighboring Virginia, stirred up a mob of white males who took to the streets to get Bowen. They also sought those who were perceived to be spreading abolitionism. When Marines were sent in to protect the jail, the crowd turned their attention to Snow, incited by a rumor he had, in the words of the *Washington Mirror*, "used very indecent and disrespectful language concerning the wives and daughters" of whites.[37]

A lynch mob formed and came after him. In the three days of rioting that followed, many blacks were attacked. Snow escaped, but many others were not as lucky. Snow's bar was trashed, and a number of black businesses, churches, and homes, as well as a black orphanage were attacked, burned, or demolished. The U.S. military finally had to intervene to stop the armed bands of white men who were roving the city hunting for free blacks and abolitionists.[38] In fact, dealing with the lynch mobs ultimately led to the creation of the U.S. National Guard. It also led to a ban on blacks' either selling liquor or owning a commercial business in Washington, D.C.

As it turns out, Francis Scott Key, author of the "Star-Spangled Banner," was the city's district attorney. His role in the whole affair was disreputable. He went after the 18-year-old Bowen and Reuben Crandall, a doctor he accused of sedition for having abolitionist literature, with a vengeance. He sought the death penalty for Bowen that an all-white, all-male jury provided after fifteen minutes of deliberation at his November 1835 trial. However, Thornton wrote a passionate letter to President Jackson to save Bowen, and after granting two reprieves he finally released him—writing "Let the Negro boy John Arthur Bowen be pardoned—effective on July 4, 1836.[39] Despite appealing to the sentiments of white supremacy, Key lost the case against Crandall.

As the *Washington Post* recounts it, Snow left the United States "for a country where a man might live freely: Canada. His troubles had become such a symbol of the unrest that the events of August 1835 would be remembered as 'the Snow Riot.'"[40] Snow thrived in Canada, establishing himself as a successful businessman and owner of several upscale restaurants, including the Tontine Coffee House eatery.[41] While some African Americans chose or were forced to flee the nation's capital, many others would leave their mark on the city. The unacknowledged handiwork of black people would continue to play an important role in constructing the nation's most famous symbols of liberation, freedom, and democracy.

Enslavement and Freedom in the Making of the U.S. Capitol

Adorning the top of the U.S. Capitol building is the statue called *Freedom*. The artwork was designed and executed by Thomas Crawford in 1855–1856. According to the architect of the Capitol, Crawford proposed that the sculpture represent an allegorical figure of "Freedom Triumphant in War and Peace." To Crawford, that meant the figure of a freed slave. He wanted to place a liberty cap on the head of the figure, a symbol of freedom in ancient Greece. However, Secretary of War (and future president of the Confederacy) Jefferson Davis objected and forced Crawford to use a crested Roman helmet instead.

Crawford created *Freedom* at his studio in Rome, Italy. The mammoth statue stands nineteen and a half feet tall and weighs 15,000 pounds. Crawford had completed the piece by 1857 but died before he could personally oversee its installation. *Freedom* was disassembled, packed into six large crates, and shipped to the United States from Italy. After a circuitous journey, the statue finally arrived in Washington, D.C. two years later, in March 1859.[42]

The statue's tribulations were not over. The commissioners had a plaster model of it assembled on the Capitol grounds so it could be viewed by the public prior to the original's final installation. When asked to disassemble the replica, however, the Italian worker who had put it together refused unless he was paid more and guaranteed long-term employment for years into the future. He had faith that his plan would work because he believed he was the only person in the country who could take the model apart in a way that would allow builders to understand how the real one was to be constructed. He was wrong.

To the chagrin of the Italian, a talented iron-worker named Philip Reed intervened. Upon learning of the plot unfolding on the mall, Reed developed an ingenious method to disassemble the model and in the process learn how to put together the real statute. Reed's intervention was decisive in the process of getting *Freedom* correctly installed on the dome of the U.S. Capitol building.

In some accounts, Philip Reed is called Philip Reid and referred to as a slave. In fact, he was enslaved at the time of the episode and was emancipated by the time the statue was placed at the top of the dome on December 2, 1862. Reed had been given his liberty along with the city's other enslaved under the 1862 District of Columbia Emancipation Act. That was not the only significant change in his life. His former owner had spelled his name Reid, but after gaining his freedom, he changed it to Reed—as in "freed," or so speculates Megan Smolenyak Smolenyak, the genealogist who has also uncovered the details of Barack Obama's Irish roots.[43]

Reed had trained for many years at an iron foundry owned by Clark Mills, his former enslaver. Mills described him as "smart in mind, a good workman in a foundry."[44] Reed's skills were so valued that he was paid a wage even during his enslavement period. According to Smolenyak, for Sunday work that he did at the foundry between July 1860 and May 1861, Reed was paid $41.25, money he received on June 6, 1862, seven weeks after he was freed.[45]

Holland believes that Reed's contribution went beyond

simply disassembling the plaster model of *Freedom.* He argues that the anonymous "black master-builder" described in a *New York Tribune* article as having worked together with Clark Mills to assemble *Freedom* "joint to joint, piece by piece, till they blended into the majestic 'Freedom' who to-day lifts her head in the blue clouds above Washington" was Philip Reed.[46] In light of the aforementioned scenario, Holland is likely correct.

* * *

The 1790s were pivotal years not only for the official launch of the nation's new capital, but also for consolidating the hierarchy of race relations that would persist for the next two centuries. Despite the brilliant wording of the Constitution and other revolutionary documents, the nation was born agonizing over the unresolved issue of slavery. Constantly challenging the Founding Fathers' rhetoric and soaring words of liberation and democracy was a rising backlash against their racism—a backlash that would not go away.

The White House would be more or less finished by the date set by President Washington, and at 1:00 p.m. on November 1, 1800, the second president of the United States, John Adams, entered the premises as its first official resident. The labor of Negro Peter and the other enslaved black workers, as well as that of the rest of the multiracial workforce, had completed a home for the nation's highest and most symbolic political office. It would be the site of growing influence and prestige not just for the president and the first family, but for the nation as a whole. With time, the White House would become one of the most famous buildings in Western civilization, an enduring symbol of U.S. power, and forever linked to the American people's internal struggles for freedom, equality, and justice.

After spending his first night there, President John Adams gave a benediction and blessing to his new home, "I pray Heaven bestow the best of the blessings on this house, and on all that shall hereafter inhabit it. May none but honest and wise men ever rule under this roof."[47] He failed to acknowledge the black people whose years of work went into constructing the house.

CHAPTER 4

Burning all Illusions: The White House, Black Slavery, and the Rising Wave of Disunion

Prologue: Paul Jennings's White House Story

The first person to write a memoir of a firsthand experience working in the White House was Paul Jennings, a black man. In 1865, more than half a century after being enslaved by the fourth president of the United States, Jennings published a nineteen-page book titled, *A Colored Man's Reminiscences of James Madison.*[1] Jennings's text was first published two years earlier in the January 1863 issue of *The Historical Magazine, and Notes and Queries Concerning the Antiquities, History, and Biography of America.* Short in length but rich in historical details, Jennings provides critical insights into the lives of free and enslaved blacks in President Madison's White House and beyond.

Father of the U.S. Constitution and the Bill of Rights, James Madison was a towering intellectual figure in the early life of the nation, but not quite as successful as its president. Jennings makes no direct statement on Madison's politics, but he does share personal encounters that are valuable, unique; and notable. Jennings writes about race, war, charity, slavery, and even his presence with the Madisons as the former president took his last breaths. Perhaps no other person was as close to Madison for as long as Paul Jennings, not even Madison's wife, Dolley.

What Jennings does not do in his memoir is discuss his role in one of the most ambitious and daring efforts to free enslaved blacks conceived during the antebellum period. His central involvement in what can perhaps be called the "Great Escape from Washington, D.C." came to light after his death in 1874, and showed a radical side of Jennings that James and Dolley Madison had certainly not witnessed or even suspected, and fortunately for Jennings, not many others had either. His involvement in the clandestine plan to liberate dozens of black people from their white enslavers demonstrates the complicated and multitextured lives that African Americans led during the era of legal slavery. The impact of the great escape and its aftermath had wide-ranging consequences that affected the racial politics of the White House for both Presidents James Polk and Millard Fillmore.

Jennings's articulate and astute observations, as well as his later activism, confute notions that enslaved people were passive and disengaged as they carried out their duties and labor. In fact, as his life experiences show, despite the racist brutality of enslavement and white people's attempt to keep blacks uneducated and illiterate, critical minds were at work. Jennings's story also intimates that the sort of role reversal in which a former slave takes charge and the once high and mighty fall may have occurred to a much greater degree than the records acknowledge. Ironically, it would be Jennings who would take care of his former enslaver—the widow of a U.S. president no less—lending her small amounts of hard-earned money when she had hit bottom and few others were there for her.

Jennings was born into slavery on Madison's farm in 1799. His mother was of mixed African and American Indian heritage

The famous painting of George Washington that was saved from the White House just before the British army sacked and burned it in 1814.

and enslaved to the Madisons; his father was a white man, an English trader.[2] By the age of ten, Jennings was working at the White House as a footman, and when he was older as a valet. He described Washington, D.C. as "a dreary place" that "was always in an awful condition from either mud or dust," and he noted that the East Room of the White House was still unfinished.[3] Jennings continued to serve Madison until the very end. "I was present when he died," Jennings wrote in his memoir.[4]

Madison's presidency is most noted for the launching of an ill-advised war against England. During the course of that war the British invaded and captured Washington, D.C., then sacked and burned the White House on August 24, 1814. The first family and the entire White House staff fled just before the British arrived, and the Madisons, along with Jennings, never returned to the White House during the three years that remained in Madison's presidency. Jennings was not just an eyewitness to history but a participant in events as they unfolded. It is because of Jennings that important details about the British invasion of 1814 are known and that one of the great stories of White House history was exposed as a myth.

The first lady and several servants and slaves were at the White House on the day charging British forces captured a mostly abandoned Washington, D.C. As the frightful word came that the British were near, Dolley ordered an evacuation and told the staff to gather whatever could be preserved. The panicking servants and staff grabbed what they could and fled. She later claimed that she personally saved the famous Gilbert Stuart painting of George Washington, which some consider to be among the White House's most valuable historical objects.[5] While he does not directly accuse Dolley of making the claim, in response to media reports along those lines, Jennings states, "This is totally false. She had no time for doing it."[6] He writes that the French doorkeeper John Susé and the president's gardener Magraw were the ones who "took it down and sent it off on a wagon, with some large silver urns and such other valuables as could be hastily got hold of."[7] This debunking of the Dolley Madison myth happened decades after her death in 1849.

Jennings's version also spotlights his complicated and highly personal relationship with the president's widow. On the one hand, he praises her and holds her in high regard. "She was a remarkably fine woman," he asserts. "She was beloved by everybody in Washington, white and colored."[8] But clearly, not everyone loved her. He also reports a story told him by Sukey, a slave woman traveling with the first family. At one point, Dolley Madison and several servants were separated from James Madison after the White House evacuation. Dolley spent one night at the home of a Mrs. Love, who lived two or three miles across the river from Washington, D.C., and the next night attempted to stay at the home of a different woman. When the woman found out her lodger's identity, she became very upset and screamed at Dolley, "Miss Madison! If that's you, come down and go out! Your husband has got mine out fighting, and d— you, you shan't stay in my house; so get out!"[9] At that time, accentuated by the British occupation of Washington, D.C., disaffection with the war and the Madisons ran high.

Beyond his dubious praises, Jennings had some legitimate grievances toward Dolley Madison. His work for James and then for Dolley kept him away from his beloved wife, Fanny. He had married her in 1822 while she was enslaved, and she was forced to stay on another Virginia plantation. They were unable to live together and were reduced to seeing each other only on late Saturday nights or Sundays.[10] Like married but physically separated slave couples everywhere, Paul engaged in "nightwalking," i.e., the all-night walks that husbands undertook to be with their spouse. It was reported, moreover, that the Madisons treated him less than honorably. Dolley was accused of hiring out Jennings and keeping "the last red cent" of his earnings, leaving him "to get his clothes by presents, night work, or as he might."[11]

His biggest gripe, however, had to be the way she treated his aspiration to be free. In 1841, Dolley had written in her will, "I give to my mulatto man Paul his freedom," leaving the impression that she would not sell Jennings as long as she was alive.[12] Reneging on her self-imposed promise, Dolley sold Jennings for two hundred dollars to Pollard Webb, a Washington, D.C. insurance agent. The low price for someone as valuable and experienced as Jennings may have been because Jennings was in the process of buying his freedom, and the sum may have amounted to the balance that Jennings owed to Madison. In his memoir, Jennings states that he "had years before bought my freedom of her," referring to Dolley.[13] Some have interpreted that statement to mean that he lied to protect her reputation, but more likely it was a poorly worded way of saying that he had—at least in part—been paying her for his freedom at the time he was sold. It would also explain the even lower sum that U.S. Senator Daniel Webster paid to buy Jennings ten months later—$120. Jennings was freed by Webster after negotiating a contract with him on March 19, 1847, with the stipulation that Jennings "agrees to work out the sum [of his purchase price] at $8.00 a month."[14] Jennings paid off Webster as promised and closed out his debt.

In the years following her husband's death, Dolley Madison fell into deep poverty and was largely abandoned by both family members and friends. Few offered help in her state of destitution and despair, but one who did was the enslaved man she had once exploited, Jennings. Clearly in a forgiving mode, he reports that he "occasionally gave her small sums from my own pocket."[15]

For the most part, Jennings never publicly discussed the politics of the White House or what life was like for the blacks whom the president enslaved there. However, Jennings does note that after the British burned the White House and the Capitol, there were efforts to try to move the seat of government to a new location in the North, "but the southern members kept it" in Washington, D.C.[16]

In his memoirs, Jennings avoids any mention of his role in the massive attempted slave escape that shook Washington, D.C. to its slaveholding core in 1848, just one year after he gained his freedom. There were at least three known free black men who were involved in organizing the escape: Paul Jennings, Daniel Bell, and Samuel Edmonson. Bell worked as a butler for a powerful attorney in the city, Joseph Bradley. Edmondson was employed as a blacksmith at the Navy Yard.[17] Jennings's involvement, rooted no doubt in his desire to liberate as many of his people as possible, may have also been driven by the fact that one of the women involved was Mary Ellen Stewart, a black woman who had escaped from Dolley Madison and who was well known to Jennings.[18] In any case, Jennings has been called a "leading plotter" in the escape[19] and is said to have "formed a pack with Daniel Drayton" to execute the plan after meeting him by chance in Baltimore in March 1848.[20]

The week of April 10 was projected to be a busy one in Washington, D.C. Some city leaders were planning to celebrate the recent fall of the French monarchy. In February 1848, King Louis-Philippe abdicated the throne, and shortly thereafter, on February 26, the Second Republic was declared. The era of the French monarchy was over. In the year that Karl Marx published the *Communist Manifesto*, revolutions were occurring in other parts of Europe as well, including Germany, Italy, Hungary, Switzerland, and elsewhere.[21] Many in the United States felt that these revolutions of rural and urban working classes echoed the sentiments and spirit of the American Revolution. Yet most failed to identify their cheering efforts to overthrow oppressive regimes in Europe as being in contradiction with their support of the ever-expanding role of slavery and the racial subjugation of blacks and Native Americans in the United States. In one outrageous statement of obtuseness, slaveholder and slavery-defending Mississippi Senator Henry Foote, speaking about the abdication of the French king, proclaimed that "the age of tyrants and slavery was rapidly drawing to a close."[22]

While the escape was planned long before the dates of the celebration events could have been known (and its exact timing determined by such factors as availability of a large boat), it is notable that Washington, D.C.'s black community—enslaved and free—was simultaneously organizing its own rebellion, highlighting the schism between an avowed love for liberty and its true actualization. In one broad step, black Washington, D.C. was about to secede from white Washington, D.C.

On Saturday evening, April 15, 1848, as parties celebrating French liberty were being held across the city, more than seventy blacks, most enslaved, made their way to the docks where a ship named the *Pearl* was waiting for them. In small groups, they slowly boarded the ship where Captains Edward Sayres and Daniel Drayton were ready and waiting. Sayres was the *Pearl*'s regular captain, and Drayton had been contracted by Washington's Underground Railroad cell to pilot the ship. The plan was to leave late Saturday night, because Sunday was usually a no-work day for most slaves and their white owners would not miss them until it was far too late. Between seventy-four and seventy-seven blacks were on board, representing the "property" of forty-one white enslavers from the area. When the local whites discovered what was happening, it set off what researcher John Paynter called something "approaching a panic."[23]

Unfortunately, two unexpected events foiled the well-planned plot. First, after traveling about 150 miles, the boat ran into bad weather and was forced to anchor at Cornfield Harbor, near the end of the Maryland peninsula. The delay was not welcome, but even under those circumstances the *Pearl* had enough of a head start that a few hours should not have made a difference as long as the escape and its intended route remained undiscovered.

However, a betrayal of epic proportion was unfolding back in Washington, D.C. Although contemporary reports mentioned other individuals, most later researchers believe that Judson Diggs, a free black man, had informed a posse of slave hunters that the escaping blacks were on the *Pearl* and which direction it had headed. Whether it was out of fear, revenge against a woman on the boat who reportedly had jilted him, or for money—all three reasons have been suggested—Diggs's treachery goes down in history as one of the worst betrayals of the antebellum period. Apparently, slave catchers initially believed that the slaves had escaped on foot and were weaving their way north, the exact opposite direction from the way the *Pearl* was headed.[24] Soon, on the information provided by Diggs, a steamboat set out and seized the *Pearl* and everyone on board while the boat was still anchored.

Drayton and Sayres were charged with larceny, and all the black individuals— enslaved and free—were unceremoniously marched through the streets of Washington, D.C. and caged in slave pens. White enslavers and their supporters in Washington, D.C. were so incensed that they wanted to drag Drayton and Sayres out of jail and have them executed on the spot. While a few of the captured blacks were taken back by their owners, most were being prepared to be sold South, where the merciless cruelty of slave breakers was renowned. Of the eleven members of the Bell family that were captured on the *Pearl*, only Mary and her youngest son Thomas were purchased by family and supporters, the rest were bought and re-enslaved. The six Edmonson siblings were all bought, re-enslaved and sent South. "Among those sold were people who were legally free," writes G. Franklin Edwards and Michael R. Winston in an article featured on the White House Historical Society Web site.[25]

The White House of President James Polk found itself in a tight spot, endeavoring to prevent riots from breaking out as news of the white-assisted escape spread. More out of political self-interest—it would have been disastrous to have a race riot in Washington, D.C. during an election year—but his sympathies lying with his fellow white enslavers, President Polk sought to quell the mobs in the streets and reluctantly sent troops to protect the offices of the abolitionist *National Era* newspaper from being destroyed.[26] One ironic link is that in 1845, just two years before Paul Jennings achieved his liberation, Dolley Madison had earned herself a little money by renting him out to President Polk.[27]

Though the escape of 1848 was foiled, it generated a nationwide movement to defend and free both the blacks and the whites who were involved. Abolitionist forces mobilized education campaigns, raised funds, and put together a legal team that included Horace Mann, then a congressman who had succeeded relentless antislavery advocate John Quincy Adams and later became famous as an educator. They also received support from *Uncle Tom's Cabin* author Harriet Beecher Stowe, and a massive effort was mounted to obtain a pardon from President Millard Fillmore.

For their part in the attempted escape, Drayton and Sayres spent four years in prison before receiving an executive pardon from President Fillmore on August 11, 1852. Larceny charges had been dropped, but Sayres was convicted on the charge of illegal importation of slaves.[28] Drayton remained defiant, however, even after being released from prison. Criticizing the racism of slavery, he wrote:

> By my actions, I protested that I did not believe that there was, or could be, any such thing as a right of property in human beings. Nobody in this country will admit, for a moment, that there can be any such thing as property in a white man. The institution of slavery could not last for a day, if the slaves were all white. But I do not see that because their complexions

> are different they are any less men on that account. The doctrine I hold to, and which I desired to preach in a practical way, is the doctrine of Jefferson and Madison, that there cannot be property in man—no, not even in black men.[29]

To reference Madison was a sardonic nod to one of the unacknowledged leaders of the escape attempt, who had been enslaved by the president.

Miraculously, Jennings's involvement went undetected. One report stated that Jennings had originally planned to be on the *Pearl* but had had a change of heart at the last minute when he realized that doing so would violate his contract with Webster—an agreement he was committed to honoring. This account notes that Jennings actually left a letter to Webster stating he was leaving out of a "deep desire to be of help to my poor people."[30] However, as historian Mary Kay Ricks points out, more likely Jennings did not board the *Pearl* because it was unnecessary for a free man to put himself at risk when he could meet the ship almost anywhere it landed. Furthermore, unlike Edmondson and Bell, he did not have family aboard the ship.

Jennings may have gone into hiding after the capture of the *Pearl*. If he did, it was not for long, because he was active in the effort to help those who had been captured. His ability to remain free also indicates that if there was a betrayal, the person or persons involved either did not know of Jennings's involvement or for some unknown reason did not implicate him. Jennings helped to raise money in an attempt to buy and free some of those captured, and thus avoid having them sent South, but the funds raised did not suffice.[31]

Eventually finding work at the Department of the Interior,

Jennings lived to experience the liberation of black people from slavery. He was seventy-five years old when he died in Washington, D.C., in 1874.

Paul Jennings's White House story, in literal and literary forms, is a remarkable one of willpower, honor, sacrifice, courage, activism, and risk in the name of black freedom. His legacy was passed on for generations, and in a noteworthy circle of historic completion, dozens of his descendants returned to the White House for a reunion in August 2009 to honor his role in U.S. history.[32] As part of their visit, they viewed the famous Stuart painting of George Washington. More important, they came to acquaint themselves with the place where their great-great-great-grandfather had lived enslaved by the fourth president of the United States, and to honor his bravery and boldness, along with that of the many undocumented others who, at great personal peril, did all they could to liberate black people from their bondage to white enslavers. In a sense, it was Jennings and the countless others in the underground network—by their rebellions and the actions they took to free the nation from the atrocities of human trafficking and enslavement—who were the true vanguard of Madison's founding vision of a democratic and liberated nation.

The White House Becomes Whiter

> *[T]he city was light and the heavens redden'd with the blaze.*—An eyewitness description of the burning of the White House.[33]

It took three years to rebuild the White House and the other public buildings in Washington, D.C. that had been destroyed by the British invasion. President James Monroe, another Virginian who enslaved dozens of blacks, would formally open the

View from northeast of the damaged White House after the British army looted and burned it on August 24, 1814.

doors of the White House to the public on January 1, 1818. The building had been burnt to a shell, and it required massive work to restore its original structural integrity and appearance. Much of the surviving architecture had to be demolished. For political reasons, however, Monroe and Congress publicly contended that "repair" rather than "reconstruction" was occurring. This deception was facilitated by cheaply substituting timber for bricks "in some of the interior partitions," which would eventually require key parts of the White House to be rebuilt again between 1948 and 1952.[34]

Enslaved black people, in full view of the White House and Congress, continued to toil side by side with free workers to rebuild the nation's capital. It is unclear, however, exactly how many blacks worked on the White House and other D.C. structures that had been damaged by the British attacks. Historian William Seale argues that the growth of capitalism in the United States dramatically changed the nature of the rebuilding compared to the original construction operations. Work done in the 1790s involved many individuals contracting with builder James Hoban, including both free and enslaved blacks. This time, however, instead of one builder dominating, operations opened up to many "manufacturers, merchants, suppliers, contractors, and other businessmen."[35]

Seale estimated that approximately 60 of the 190 men that were hired in the summer of 1817, when the main work was being finished, were enslaved black men who had been rented out by their owners.[36] It is not known exactly what work they performed, nor how many, if any, of the other 130 or so other men were free blacks. It is probably safe to assume that slave labor was also used during the 1815–1816 period, when a great deal of the demolition and trash removal was carried out.

As discussed in Chapter 3, the Capitol, to the east of the burned out White House, also had to be rebuilt. The two sites were linked by the area now known as the national mall, but which then served as a bustling marketplace for human traffickers. From either the legislative or the executive buildings of the U.S. government, one could look out the window any day of the week and see hundreds of poorly dressed, desperate individuals locked in chains, their lamentations and wails impossible to ignore as they were being beaten, forced to march while manacled to others, and sold off on an auction block. That this powerful daily reminder of white people's barbarity toward black people existed in clear sight of advocates for a more inclusive and democratic society surely must have fired the determination of abolitionists in Congress who fought to end, erode, or limit slavery through legislative means. For the most part, they did not get support from the White House while it was in the charge of slave-owning and slavery-enabling presidents.

A New White House Era

The physical reconstruction of the White House also symbolized a transition in the nation's racial politics. Monroe would represent the last generation of Revolutionary War presidents. The debate over slavery's expansion, increasing slave rebellions, and the aggressive abolition movement would force president after president—until Lincoln—to confront the issue, but each would compromise and procrastinate rather than implement a permanent solution. With each passing year, public intolerance of enslavement intensified, driving the country closer and closer to armed conflict.

Of the eleven U.S. presidents between Madison and the beginning of the Civil War, seven enslaved black people—presidents James Monroe, Andrew Jackson, Martin Van Buren, William Henry Harrison, John Tyler, James Knox Polk, and Zachary Taylor—and five of them enslaved blacks at the White House—Monroe, Jackson, Tyler, Polk, and Taylor. Four U.S. presidents during this period—John Quincy Adams, Millard Fillmore, Franklin Pierce, and James Buchanan—did not own slaves either in or outside of the White House, but, as the records show, they did very little as president to end the institution. In the main, rather than undergoing a gradual erosion as many of the founders whimsically hoped, slavery expanded westward, and the political divisions over buying, selling, breeding, and trafficking black people escalated and turned increasingly violent.

In 1812, there were nine slave states and nine "free" states, where slavery was legally abolished but where whites (if they technically lived in other states) were permitted to bring the blacks they enslaved. The "free" states were Connecticut, Massachusetts, New Hampshire, New Jersey, New York, Ohio, Pennsylvania, Rhode Island, and Vermont; the slave states were

Delaware, Georgia, Kentucky, Louisiana, Maryland, North Carolina, South Carolina, Tennessee, and Virginia.

Washington, D.C., then as now, was not a state. Slavery was legal in the city and even so-called free blacks faced severe civil, political, economic, and social restrictions on their freedom. At various times between 1800 and the end of the Civil War, free blacks in D.C. were "legally barred from the streets after 10:00 p.m. . . . required to register and carry a certificate of freedom . . . required to post a $500 bond guaranteed by two white men . . . barred from the Capitol grounds unless present there on business; and . . . barred from owning most types of small businesses."[37]

The effort to keep a balance between free and slave states continued over the next eight years when Indiana (1816) and Illinois (1818) were admitted as free states and Mississippi (1817) and Alabama (1819) entered the union as slave states. But as Thomas Jefferson would belatedly note on April 22, 1820, one month after the Missouri Compromise, this strategy "is a reprieve only, not a final sentence," and "every new irritation will mark [the nation's division] deeper and deeper."[38]

Jefferson despaired at the coming fracture in the country, as competing national interests and agendas headed for an inexorable clash over the issue of slavery. Despite the equality in the number of slave and free states, the agriculturally based South dominated the U.S. Congress, in part due to the exaggerated representation it enjoyed in the U.S. House of Representatives by virtue of the 60 percent of its enslaved blacks who were counted as part of its overall population. Capitalism, however, was in transition, in the United States as in Europe, to an industrial model that necessitated the free movement of labor. Southern agricultural interests based on slave labor served as a fetter on industrial and financial interests elsewhere. Northern political and economic elites increasingly saw the need to break the economic power of the Southern aristocracy, which meant challenging the spread of slavery to the west. The first major battle took place over the admission of Missouri in 1820.

In 1819, when the Missouri territory applied for statehood, Representative James Tallmadge of New York proposed anti-slavery legislation that would prohibit the growth of slavery in Missouri and eventually free the children of Missouri's enslaved black people. A tart debate unfolded that was divided mostly along regional lines' representatives from the North favored the proposal while Southerners adamantly opposed it. Tallmadge's bill passed in the House of Representatives but failed in the Senate. The fight continued, finally producing a compromise in which slavery was prohibited in all territory north of the 36°30' parallel that had been part of the Louisiana Purchase, except for Missouri. At the same time, to continue the balance, Maine was admitted to the union as a free state. Perhaps most important, it was the fight over Missouri that first raised the specter of civil war, as both sides dug in deep for a long and uncompromising battle. The final agreement was, as Jefferson observed, a reprieve, not an end, to the escalating conflict.

President Monroe, as well as former presidents Madison and Jefferson, gave their full support to the inclusion of Missouri as a slave state, hoping against hope that the diffusion of slavery to the west and a movement to export blacks outside the country would help de-escalate the conflict. The diffusion theory argued that the more widely slavery stretched, the more likely its eventual dissolution, as the shortage of slave labor would make the institution financially unfeasible. It was even argued that "slaves would be happier and better fed if they were spread over the West" and that the institution would eventually wither away as its economic necessity disappeared.[39]

President Monroe had a faster solution. A strong supporter of the American Colonization Society (ACS), the main white group advocating that the best solution to the problem of black people was to get rid of them, Monroe sent a ship of former slaves to the African territory that had become Liberia. Originally named the American Society for Colonizing Free People of Color in the United States, the ACS was formed in Washington, D.C., in December 1816 at the Davis Hotel by both antislavery advocates and enslavers.[40] Its members included former presidents Thomas Jefferson, Andrew Jackson, and Millard Fillmore, Supreme Court Justice Roger B. Taney, Congress members Daniel Webster and Stephen Douglas, and "Star Spangled Banner" writer Francis Scott Key, among others. Diplomat, scholar, and enslaver Sen. Henry Clay was the group's president. In 1820, the Colonization Society sent eighty-six free blacks on the ship *Elizabeth* from the Illinois Territory to Liberia, where they would wait more than a year before getting settled on the land. In 1822, the Colonization Society formally established the new country as a site for African Americans freed from slavery, with the wish that eventually all blacks would be sent to Africa.[41]

President Monroe was such an enthusiastic sponsor of the project that in 1824 the country named its capital Monrovia in honor of his efforts. However, his commitment to the expatriation movement was driven more by security and nationalist concerns than by a passion to advance the human rights of blacks. He stated, out of a clear sense of danger, "Unhappily while this class of people exists among us we can never count with certainty on its tranquil submission."[42] Others put the problem in clearer terms. Herbert Aptheker relates that the governor of North Carolina was urged to further the cause of the ACS, because it might "rid us more expeditiously of our greatest pest and danger—the free people of colour."[43]

The president's commitment to black expatriation notwithstanding, the White House continued to support slavery, suppress black civil and political rights, and delay the inevitable. Enslavers including U.S. presidents Van Buren, Tyler, and Polk professed to detest slavery at the same time they continued to hold blacks in bondage, and on key issues related to the institution during their tenure, such as the "gag rule" controversy (discussed later in this chapter) and westward expansion, they failed to live up to their stated convictions. These U.S. presidents were more inclined to attack abolitionism, which Polk termed "fanatical, wicked and dangerous agitation."[44]

On the other hand, presidents Taylor and, in particular, Jackson offered no apologies whatsoever in their staunch defense of slavery and their role in it. Furthermore, both had built reputations as "Indian fighters," but the term is a gross understatement in regard to Jackson. "Jackson was a land speculator, merchant, slave trader, and the most aggressive enemy of the Indians in early American history," wrote Howard Zinn.[45] Known for ruthlessness in battle, Jackson led U.S. forces in several massacres of indigenous peoples, including the Seminoles, whose villages and crops were burned down by his troops. In fact, both Taylor and Jackson had been military leaders in murderous campaigns to remove Native American communities from lands on which they had lived traditionally for generations. Jackson was infamous for his angry, violent character, and the retribution he visited on slaves attempting to run away sometimes led to their disfigurement, disability, or death.[46]

As president, Jackson also led the fight against abolitionists. He referred to them as "monsters" that sought to "stir up amongst the South the horrors of servile war."[47] In 1835, abolitionists flooded South Carolina and other Southern states with antislavery literature. Southern leaders and legislators were outraged and burned stacks of the documents in public squares. In violation of the law, Jackson ordered Postmaster General Amos Kendall to prevent abolitionists from using the mail to spread their propaganda. He also proposed a law that paradoxically would prevent the circulation of antislavery material through the mail but would also publicly identify Southerners who received such mail.[48]

One of Jackson's most notorious acts against African Americans occurred in 1816. A group of 300 black men, women, and children along with about thirty Native Americans took over an abandoned British fort at Apalachicola, Florida, after driving out the Seminoles who had been occupying the fort. Reacting to demands from the Southern press, the United States army was sent in, led by General Andrew Jackson, to take the fort. After a ten-day siege, Jackson's troops blew up an ammunition dump at the fort that killed 270 of those inside. Garcon, the group's leader was captured and eventually hanged.[49] For his contributions to the country, the U.S. Federal Reserve has etched Jackson's image on twenty-dollar bills since 1928.

President Zachary Taylor, who was in the White House only sixteen months before he ate an excessive amount of cherries and milk at a July Fourth celebration and in a few days died of acute gastroenteritis, was a nationalist who supported rapid expansion in the West. When, as a gesture to ease the cumbersome policy of territorial application, Taylor supported allowing potential new states to decide whether they wanted slavery or not, Southerners rebelled at the idea that the carefully calculated balance between slave and free states would be upset, and they threatened to secede. President Taylor countered with the promise that he would use federal troops to hold the union together, the first whiff of the coming conflagration. His death in 1850 eased the tensions, and a (temporary) compromise was worked out. Ultimately, however, the Taylor White House—like that of President Jackson—did nothing to end slavery for those who were already trapped in it.

Most frustrating to antislavery White House watchers were the presidents who did not enslave blacks, railed against the institution, but rolled over in the face of Southern intransigence. Fillmore signed and Pierce enforced the Fugitive Slave Act of 1850. Disappointed in the weak efforts of Northern states to enforce the new law and actually return blacks who had successfully escaped from slavery, Southern legislators included in the 1850 compromise a strengthening of law to increase the role of the federal government in capturing escapees. It also initiated harsher punishments for those who helped them. The law only furthered polarized the country between slavery defenders and abolition advocates.

The most perplexing and frustrating of the presidents regarding race was John Quincy Adams. Although he was the progeny of the second president of the United States and his family had a long history of antislavery politics, during the four years of his presidency (1825–1829) the Adams White House did virtually nothing to address the ongoing misery of the country's enslaved blacks. Instead, his administration focused on large infrastructure and commerce-related issues. Yet, after one relatively unsuccessful term as sixth president of the United States, in 1830 he returned to Congress, and his desk soon became a hub for antislavery proposals, petitions, and policies.

In 1836, amid rising abolitionism and increasing slave uprisings, Southerners in the U.S. House of Representatives managed to pass a "gag rule" that automatically tabled any petition on slavery without consideration. This was actually a milder version of what the hard-liners really wanted—a rule that prevented anti-slavery petitions from being sent in the mail and indeed prevented Congress from dealing with antislavery petitions under any circumstances. Gag-rule proponents argued, incredibly, that petitions against slavery were unconstitutional and even treasonous. Virginia Congressman Henry Wise railed, "Sir, slavery is interwoven with our very political existence, is guaranteed by our Constitution, and its consequences must be borne by our northern brethren as resulting from our system of government, and they cannot attack the system of slavery without attacking the institutions of our country, our safety, and our welfare."[50] This twisted logic conveniently ignored the First Amendment to the Constitution, which unambiguously states, "Congress shall make no law respecting an establishment of religion, or prohibiting the free exercise thereof; or abridging the freedom of speech, or of the press; or the right of the people peaceably to assemble, and *to petition the Government for a redress of grievances.*" (Emphasis added.) Thus by passing the gag rule, it was the U.S. House of Representatives that was actually in violation of the U.S. Constitution.

But legal exactitude was never really the point. It was about defending slavery and the political and economic power derived from it. President Adams opposed the gag rule and for nearly eight years used a succession of creative means to try to override it. While future White House commanders Van Buren, Polk, and Buchanan, with votes in mind, sought accommodation with the rule so as not to alienate Northern opponents or Southern supporters, Representative Adams aggressively introduced petitions at the beginning of every session, leading to long and divisive debates on the issue, the very opposite of what the gag rule sought to achieve. In one especially inventive tactic, Adams started a fight by asking if slaves could present a petition, pointing out that he was asking a question about the petitioners, not the petition itself. He followed that act of defiance by noting that the petition technically would be acceptable, because the presenters were petitioning for slavery *not* to be interfered with in Washington, D.C., and thus it was not a petition calling for interference in slavery as the gag rule stipulated.[51] After five days of debate, a 224 to 18 vote decided that slaves could not submit petitions.[52] It took eight long years for the gag rule to be eliminated, finally, in 1844.

During this period Adams also made headlines due to his involvement in the *Amistad* affair. In July 1839, fifty-three captive blacks led by Cinque (Sengbe Pieh) rose up and seized the ship *Amistad*, which was taking them from Havana, Cuba, to Puerto Principe on another part of the island. They killed the ship's crew and ordered the two surviving Spanish planters, José Ruiz and Pedro Montes, to take them to Africa. However, Ruiz and Montes deceptively sailed up the east coast of the United States, and the vessel was seized by the U.S. Navy and brought to Connecticut. A great deal of legal wrangling ensued involving the United States, Spain, and the planters in Cuba around issues of murder, kidnapping, ownership, and, most fundamentally, whether the abducted Africans should be freed. The case eventually went to the U.S. Supreme Court, and Adams was brought in to present the case for the liberation of the Africans.

In his detailed and wide-ranging presentation before the U.S. Supreme Court, Adams argued that the very arrest and detention of the Africans were illegal acts that amounted to grounds for dismissal of all charges. Employing decisions from the lower courts, letters from Secretary of State John Forsyth, international treaty agreements, and other evidence, he contended that there were no laws broken by the Africans, and that if anyone was guilty of a crime it was Ruiz and Montes, who were "in pursuit of that original unlawful intent of the slave trade" and who "brought the vessel by stratagem into a port of the United States," thus violating the laws of the United States, Great Britain, and Spain. Adams forcefully argued that the "Negroes were free and had a right to assert their liberty" and under that principle alone should be liberated and allowed to be on their way.[53] Eight days later, on March 9, 1841, the Africans won the case, and those who were still alive were set free.

Throughout the crisis, the Van Buren White House acted on behalf of the Spanish government, which favored sending the Africans back to Cuba so as to continue their enslavement. Although the District Court had ordered President Van Buren to send them back to Africa as free individuals, he ordered the U.S. Attorney to appeal the decision. Reportedly, he and Secretary of State Forsyth had drawn up plans to secretly detain the Africans and pass them to the Spanish government if the Africans won their case. It was no wonder that Adams referred to Van Buren as "a northern President with southern principles." They were likely unable to carry out the scheme due to the popular support that the *Amistad* captives had amassed.[54] Adams also accused the Van Buren administration of falsifying legal documents in their effort to win the case.[55]

During this period, the White House continued to exclude black people other than enslaved servants, and soon even that came to an end. According to the history section of the White House Web site,[56] President James Buchanan had only white servants and workers at the White House during his one term as the fifteenth president of the United States. The only bachelor president, he meandered his way through his tenure unable or unwilling to address the multiple crises that were mounting over the expansion of slavery in the western territories, the Fugitive Slave Act, John Brown's insurrection, and the rupture of the Democratic Party to which he belonged.

Poster of Blind Tom.

In fact, President Buchanan's White House is notable for only one groundbreaking racial milestone: it extended the first invitation to a black person to perform on its premises. That summons went to Thomas "Blind Tom" Greene Bethune Wiggins.[57]

Black Entertainment Comes to the White House

The first African American to officially enter the White House who was not a servant or enslaved to the president was the musical genius popularly known as "Blind Tom." Born sightless, from around the age of four he demonstrated astonishing skills, including the ability to reproduce on the piano music that he heard only once. He also came to write many original compositions, sang in a wide variety of languages, and eventually mastered several other instruments. Many of these skills he had achieved by the time he performed at the White House in 1860. He was eleven years old at the time.

Unfortunately, the whites who controlled Wiggins presented him more as a sideshow freak than as the gifted artist he was. Few other nineteenth-century Americans were as misunderstood, misrepresented, and misinterpreted as Wiggins, whose musical brilliance belied white people's narrow perspectives on the intelligence, talent, and creativity of people of color. Wiggins's owners and guardians made enormous profit by marketing him as an oddity rather than as a serious musician. The man's constant practice, rigid determination, innate talent, and gifted ear were ignored in favor of a Barnum & Bailey–like hype that portrayed him as a curiosity almost outside the human race. There is an abundance of evidence, however, indicating that Wiggins must be included among the greatest classical musicians of his or any other era.

Despite pervasive segregation and white society's effort to present music by blacks in the most degrading forms possible, dazzling black musicians and composers emerged, challenging bigoted notions of intelligence and artistic genius. Though well-documented studies demonstrate that African musical traditions crossed the waters and shaped the evolution of spirituals, blues, gospel, ragtime, jazz, and other early black musical genres in the United States, blacks also developed expertise in classical European music.

The United States was home to a significant number of black classical musicians and composers prior to the Civil War. Francis B. "Frank" Johnson (1792–1844) was a composer who also played bugle, cornet, violin and other instruments, and was considered the "first major bandmaster in the U.S." according to Lawrence University professor Dominique-René de Lerma.[58] The details on his early musical training are scant, but by the time he was twenty he was a professional musician in Philadelphia. He wrote more than 300 compositions, and his band was so popular that it toured all over the United States, Canada, and Europe, performing in front of Victoria shortly before she was crowned Queen of England in 1838. It is believed that his band was the first group of African American musicians to tour Europe.

Johnson's work was not devoid of politics. He wrote compositions calling for the end of slavery, such as *The Grave of the Slave*, and in support of Haitian independence. He died at age fifty-two in 1844, leaving a strong legacy of work behind.[59] Two hundred years after his birth, on July 22, 1992, New York Senator Alfonse D'Amato honored Francis B. Johnson in the U.S. Senate with this "Commemoration of a Musical Master":

> Francis Johnson became an incomparable virtuoso violinist, flutist, hornist, natural and keyed (Kent) bugler. He became a master composer, arranger, and orchestrator of music; a music educator and a publisher of music; an accomplished equestrian, impresario, gourmet cook, and an astute businessman. Francis Johnson eked out an illustrious career in music by assuming many musical roles including: coffee-house performer, cavalry trumpeter, circus bandmaster, featured performer at balls and hops, bandmaster for early volunteer firefighters, bandmaster for the 128th Regiment, and more. In 1837 Francis Johnson took the first band of American musicians, the American Minstrels, to Europe where he met up with Johann Strauss and Philippe Musart. When Johnson returned to the States, he introduced America to the music of these two legends. . . . Frank Johnson is best remembered as progenitor of the Nation's music of martial ardor, inventor of cotillions, a pioneer, and one of the

> earliest protagonists of American musical purism. He was a quintessential American musical phenomenon. I ask my colleagues to join me in remembering Francis "Frank" Johnson on the anniversary of his birth and always.[60]

Another important black prewar composer was the teacher and guitarist Justin Holland (1819–1887). Although he was born in the slave state of Virginia, he and his parents were free. At fourteen, after his parents' death, Holland moved to Massachusetts where he would begin studying classical guitar under the tutorship of composer William Shubert. He studied at Oberlin College in Ohio, eventually married, and settled in Cleveland, where he developed a national reputation for guitar composition and arrangement. In his effort to become more fluent in classical guitar, he also became fluent in Spanish, Italian, German, and French.[61]

Holland led not only an active professional life, but an engaged political one as well. He was a leader in the National Negro Convention Movement, which began in the early 1830s and sought to create a national movement for black rights and freedom. Leading activists such as Frederick Douglass were involved.[62] Holland also participated in the Underground Railroad, the clandestine network of people and sites that helped people escape from slavery. The Underground Railroad was very active in Ohio, and many freedom-seeking blacks that had made it there continued northward to Canada. Holland also viewed the struggle for black liberation as an international effort. He was secretary of a group called the Central American Land Company, which for a number of years attempted to buy land in Central America where free blacks could go and set up a colony.[63]

If Johnson, Holland, and other black classical musicians and composers had been invited to perform at the White House, it would have served as an acknowledgment of African Americans' contributions to classical music. However, it was Blind Tom who broke that racial barrier. His promotion as a freak of nature and musical sideshow concealed the fact that he was one of the country's most talented and creative musicians and composers, black or white. Given the racist atmosphere of the times, it is not surprising that the first black musician and composer to perform at the White House—not counting whatever entertainment may have been provided by those who had been enslaved there—was cruelly victimized and exploited.

Blind Tom was a musical prodigy in every sense of the word. There was little expectation that the child, born blind to two enslaved parents on May 25, 1849, would ever be a useful worker. In fact, when his father, Domingo Wiggins, and mother, Charity Greene, were sold to James Bethune, a local enslaver, he was sent with them at no extra cost. Thomas was eight months old at the time and "simply regarded as an encumbrance."[64] Shamelessly self-deluded, Bethune viewed himself as something of a savior and once wrote that slaves were "a class of laborers controlled not by government, for like children, it is too large for government to manage. This class of laborers are [*sic*] incapable of taking care of themselves, so are controlled by individuals who are not only capable of taking care of them but interested in doing so."[65] Bethune sought unconvincingly to present slave owners as nonracists, even antiracists, who were motivated by interests other than profit.

According to Deirdre O'Connell, author of *The Ballad of Blind Tom*:

After arriving at the Bethune Farm, things began to

> change and the toddler began to echo the sounds around him. If a rooster crowed, he made the same noise. If a bird sang, he would pursue it or attack his younger siblings just to hear them scream. . . . By the age of four, Tom could repeat conversations ten minutes in length, but expressed his own needs in whines and tugs. Unless constantly watched, he would escape: to the chicken coop, woods and finally to the piano in his master's house, the sound of each note causing his young body to tremble in ecstasy. After a string of unwelcome visits, General Bethune finally recognized the stirrings of a musical prodigy in the raggedy slave child and installed him in the Big House where he underwent extensive tuition.[66]

Thomas was eventually able to reproduce the difficult and harmonically complex forms of classical music. Within a short time, he was also composing original songs and improvising well beyond the capacity of anyone else in the Bethune household.

Without question, the man was extraordinary. He was playing his own songs by the age of six, and by the time he was eight he was performing publicly and regularly for his enslaver. But it was his performance in October 1857, in a concert hall rented by James Bethune in Columbus, Georgia, that appears to have determined his musical destiny once and for all. Enslaved by Bethune, Thomas received none of the profits made by his music and was forced to perform whether he wanted to or not. Public voyeurism rather than musical appreciation was the marketing tool Bethune used to attract ticket buyers.

Pandering to the racism of whites at that time, Bethune and others who exploited Thomas did so by propagating several enduring myths about him. Geneva Handy Southall spent approximately twenty-five years researching and writing three books about his life in order to refute the racist myths and give him the scholarly treatment he deserves.[67] Among the most popular but untrue stories circulated about Thomas were that he did not train, that he was only popular among curiosity seekers, and that his mother meekly allowed others to exploit him.

Southall and other researchers have disproved these stories. While Thomas certainly possessed an extraordinary amount of inherent artistic talent, he received music lessons most of his life and even traveled with a piano coach. This was in addition to the countless hours of practice he engaged in on a daily basis. Like all great artists, he grew through hard work and was not an empty vessel through which music poured from some mysterious source. Also, despite the carnival-like hype around him, Thomas's skills impressed the professional classical community of the era. His concerts were attended by some of the most serious and best-known classical musicians in the late nineteenth century.

Thomas's parents were often maligned by the media of the time. Southall counters the myths by arguing that Charity regretted having Thomas taken away from her and demonstrates that she had little choice in the matter, even after slavery officially ended.[68]

And despite Bethune's well-constructed tale of benevolence and mercy toward the black people he enslaved, he was a staunch advocate for the perpetuation of black enslavement. In Georgia, the autocratic and aristocratic Bethune was best known as having started *The Corner Store*, the first newspaper in the state to openly and defiantly call for secession.[69] The Bethune family profited from slavery, and the general saw little reason to bring it to an end. His exploitation of Thomas was no different from the labor he appropriated from Domingo, Charity, and the other black men and women he enslaved and forced to work without compensation.

The year 1857, when Thomas began his path to becoming a national and international musical legend, was also the year that the nation's battle over slavery reached a new crescendo. On March 6, 1857, the U.S. Supreme Court issued its long-awaited decision in the case of Dred Scott. Born into slavery in 1799, Scott was eventually bought and enslaved by John Emerson, an army doctor stationed at different times during his career in slave states (Missouri, Louisiana) and free states (Illinois and Wisconsin). In 1846, in Missouri, three years after Emerson died, Scott and his wife, Harriet, filed suit against the widow Irene Sanford for their manumission after she refused their offer to buy their freedom. While the Scotts won in one state court, the Missouri Supreme Court reversed the decision. The Scotts' appeal was accepted by the U.S. Supreme Court and resulted in the infamous seven-to-two decision establishing that black people—whether or not they were slaves—were not protected by the Constitution and could never be citizens of the United States.

It was later discovered that President-elect Buchanan had illegally attempted to influence the Court to rule against Scott. He had furtively communicated with members of the Court to pressure them to use their decision to put a stop to the abolitionists, and he secretly worked with four of the Justices "to guarantee a favorable ruling."[70]

President-elect Buchanan's violation of the "separation of powers" principle was unnecessary. The Supreme Court was dominated by pro-slavery Southerners and their edict not only denied Scott his freedom but issued a sweeping broadside against the abolitionist movement. Chief Justice Roger Taney, speaking for the majority, declared in one infamous passage that African Americans had "no rights which the white man was bound to respect," and that African Americans were not and could not become citizens of the United States. In the Court's interpretation of the Constitution, neither the U.S. Congress nor the president could make or authorize any law that granted freedom to blacks. Thus, the decision vitiated the Ordinance of 1787 and the Missouri Compromise of 1820, both of which had provisions excluding slavery in certain parts of the country and granting manumission and citizenship to some blacks. As "property" of white people, ruled the Court, enslaved blacks had no right to bring suit in federal courts.[71]

While the South celebrated the racist ruling, the decision only intensified the racial crisis and drove a deeper wedge between Northern Democrats, who needed votes from the antislavery North, and Southern Democrats, who were unbending in their defense of enslavement. A party divided could not stand, and the jubilation over the Dred Scott case would soon fade in the face of two new challenges: the newly formed Republican Party and a more important victory for the abolitionist cause.

In June 1860, with the war drums beating more loudly each day, Bethune brought the Blind Tom act to Washington, D.C. Thomas delivered two successful performances—one at a small concert hall and one in a private home for members of an elite wives' club. One of the guests at that event was Harriet Lane, a niece and ward of President Buchanan, who lived at the White House, and as White House hostess she was central to putting together musical performances there for the president.[72] Undoubtedly aware that she was making history, she extended an invitation to Bethune to have his blind eleven-year-old slave perform for her uncle, the fifteenth president of the United States.

A black artist had never been asked to perform at the

White House before, and thus the invitation was a historic milestone. Surprisingly, very little is known about the event, including Thomas's own thoughts on the matter. Indeed, none of the published research even reveals an exact date of the event, although it is clear that it took place sometime between June 9 and June 18, 1860.

To go by a few notes made by some at the performance, the concert was perceived as a strange but satisfying experience by most of those in attendance. According to Virginia Clay-Clopton, who was married to Alabama Senator Clement Claiborne and attended Thomas's performance, Miss Philips and Miss Cohen played a duet together and then one of them volunteered to play with him. Apparently, the young woman attempted to test Thomas's ability to remember the song that she and her partner had just played by skipping one page of the composition. He immediately recognized what she had done and shouted, "You cheat me! You cheat me."[73] Following that incident, Thomas sat down alone at the Chickering grand piano, the finest model of the time, and recited a thirteen-page score followed by a twenty-page score of classical music.[74]

It is unknown what President Buchanan thought of the performance or of Thomas. It is notable that no controversy ensued as a result of having an enslaved black person placed essentially on the same musical level as the other artists who performed at the White House. It seems quite clear that the fact that Thomas was enslaved and considered an oddity served to obviate any problems that might have emerged from fearful whites who would normally strenuously object to any official signs of racial equality, such as having a black "guest" visit the White House.

While there is no record of any political opinions he may have expressed, Thomas would soon be forced to perform at fundraisers for the Southern war effort. When war broke out, Thomas's handlers made sure to keep him out of Northern states. He was also the star of a number of Confederacy fundraisers engineered by Perry Oliver, the manager hired by Bethune to handle the early years of Thomas's career. Thomas, like other blacks, was forced by his white enslavers to sing *Dixie* and entertain the soldiers. O'Connell estimates that these affairs likely raised tens of thousands of dollars.[75]

Far more disturbing was Thomas's ode to the first major military victory of the South over the North, *The Battle of Manassas*, which reproduced the sounds of the battle as Thomas imagined it and became very popular as a cheerleader for the South's pro-slavery cause. Self-servingly, Oliver spread the story that Thomas had independently created the song after listening to him describe the battle, and the composition became a albatross for Thomas for much of the rest of his life.

In 1863, sensing that the South might lose the war, the Bethune family was able to trick Thomas into a long-term contract that would perpetuate their control over his career, and indeed his life, even if slavery were outlawed—a ploy that historian Geneva H. Southall accurately and poetically refers to as Thomas's re-enslavement.[76] The Bethunes' power over Thomas would come to an end in 1887 when the embittered widow (John Bethune having been killed in a railroad accident in 1883) collaborated with Thomas's mother Charity to win legal authority over Thomas. He continued to perform, but by the end of the century his best days were behind him. He died of a stroke on June 14, 1908.

While Thomas was providing beautiful music inside the White House, a discordant political scenario was brewing outside it. Even as President Buchanan was enjoying the magic of Blind Tom's musical prowess, his nation was coming apart

Inauguration of President Lincoln at U.S. Capitol, March 4, 1861.

beneath his feet. In October of the previous year, John Brown had raided the Harpers Ferry military arsenal as a bold first step toward liberating enslaved blacks by force. Brown's plan failed, but his armed assault sent shock waves throughout the country, and his subsequent execution alongside his co-conspirators inflamed the passions of Americans on both sides, as had the *Dred Scott* decision. Buchanan's Democratic Party split between Northern and Southern wings, and three Democrats ran for president under different party labels—Stephen Douglas of the Northern Democratic Party, John C. Breckinridge of the Southern Democratic Party, and John Bell of the Constitutional Union Party—created the electoral space for a victory by the relatively new antislavery Republican Party. Events would reach a crescendo on November 6, 1860 when a relatively unknown, lanky lawyer and former one-term congressman emerged victorious in the fall presidential election. Abraham Lincoln's successful campaign earned 39 percent of the popular vote (virtually none of it from the South) and 180 votes in the Electoral College. The remaining 123 votes in the Electoral College were divided among Lincoln's three opponents. Six weeks later, on December 20, 1860, South Carolina became the first of eleven states to declare its secession from the United States.[77] It was time for war.

CHAPTER 5

The White House Goes to War: Rebellion, Reconstruction and Retrenchment

Prologue: Elizabeth Keckly's White House Story

On the night of April 14, 1865, as President Abraham Lincoln lay dying at Petersen's Boarding House, across from the Ford Theater where he had been shot around 10:30 p.m., Mary Lincoln became increasingly distraught. Sitting next to her husband at the moment he was shot, she faced the terrible prospect of losing him to a brutal assassin's bullet. As she sat with others who were providing security and medical treatment for the president, she desperately needed the personal comfort of a close friend. Three times she sent messengers from Petersen's to retrieve Lizzy, but for some unknown reason the messengers could not find the correct address. Meanwhile, Lizzy had been awakened around 11:00 p.m. with the news of the shooting and immediately sought to make her way to the White House to be with the First Lady. Unable to convince security at the White House to let her in, she returned home unsure if President Lincoln was dead or alive.[1]

Elizabeth Keckly and Mary Lincoln, two powerfully determined and extraordinary women—one black, the other white—forged one of the most unique friendships in American

Elizabeth Keckly, 1861

political history. The former, born into slavery, not only had been able to eventually buy her freedom and start a successful business, but was also an activist who played an important role in aiding less fortunate blacks both during and after the Civil War. In addition, Lizzy, as she was known to the Lincolns, also published a book, *Behind the Scenes or Thirty Years a Slave and Four Years in the White House*, about her experiences in Lincoln's White House, an act that may have strained her relationship with Mary permanently.[2]

Keckly felt heartbroken at being estranged from Mary, her friend of many years. Though their relationship had begun as one between businesswoman and client, it had evolved into a truly warm companionship of deep commitment, shared tragedies, personal sacrifices, and genuine love. In a period when smart, talented, and independent women were scorned, marginalized, and rebuked, Lizzy and Mary pushed back and often prevailed against tremendous odds. They fought fiercely for their rights and dignity against the relentless countervailing forces of their time. That their once close friendship had fallen apart was perhaps less remarkable than the fact that it had existed at all. Equally stunning was that an African American woman had risen to a position of such significance in the White House, and that when President Lincoln was shot, the first person Mary Lincoln sought was Lizzy.

Throughout her life Elizabeth had an astonishing knack for connecting with some of the key historical figures of her time. These encounters were sometimes serendipitous but more often eventuated from her own tenacious engagement with the world and her willingness to challenge the racist and sexist stereotypes of the period.

Elizabeth was born into slavery at Dinwiddie Court-House, Virginia, on January 15, 1818, the only child of two enslaved parents. One of her earliest memories was of being harshly beaten at approximately four years old for not properly taking care of an infant left in her charge. But as she remembers it, the beating seemed to strengthen her character rather than break it.[3] Like countless other enslaved black women and girls, Elizabeth was raped, abused, and impregnated. She gave birth to a son, George, when she was still a teenager. But, as she tells it, she consistently and fiercely fought back in every way she could—though not always successfully—against men who attempted to take advantage of her.[4]

When the white family that enslaved them moved to St. Louis, Elizabeth and her mother were forced to move with them. Indicative of her strong independent character, while enslaved in St. Louis, Elizabeth was able to build a successful dressmaking business by working on her free Sundays and some evenings. She started the enterprise out of an urgent need to raise the money needed to prevent her mother from being sold and sent away from her. The dress business turned out to be an enormous boon. In 1850, the year the Fugitive Slave Act was strengthened, Elizabeth sought to purchase freedom for herself and her son George rather than make a relatively easy escape across the river and be forever on the run and vulnerable to slave catchers. At the time, she was enslaved to Hugh Garland, a prominent St. Louis lawyer and pro-slavery advocate. In January that year, he and his law partner, Lyman D. Norris, had been hired to defend one Mrs. Eliza Irene Emerson against a lawsuit for freedom that had been filed by two blacks she enslaved, Dred and Harriet Scott.[5] In a preview of momentous events to come in her life, Elizabeth was directly linked to the most famous Supreme Court case of the pre–Civil War era.[6]

More out of need to alleviate his own family's severe poverty than from any moral epiphany about her plight, Garland eventually agreed to let Elizabeth buy her freedom from him for $1,200.00, a kingly sum.[7] Although he was ill and likely dying, Garland continued to fight against the Scotts in the Missouri circuit court system. Since Elizabeth had not been able to raise all the money she needed by the time he died in 1854, his brother Armistead and his widow Ann inherited Elizabeth as one of their legal possessions. She persevered, however, and eventually raised the funds with help from friends and clients in St. Louis. On November 13, 1855, she and her son George were emancipated.

While still enslaved to Garland, Elizabeth received a marriage proposal from James Keckly, a man she had meet in Petersburg, Virginia, who had moved to St. Louis. When Garland agreed to her terms, she then accepted Keckly's proposal, and the wedding was held at the Garland home. It was later discovered that James Keckly had misrepresented himself as free, and due to this deception, coupled with his drinking problems, the marriage ended quickly. He disappeared from Elizabeth's life, leaving only his surname behind.[8]

After taking a few years to pay back those who had lent money for her freedom, Elizabeth Keckly decided to move to Washington, D.C., to seek her fortune. Although ambitious and determined to build a better future for her son, she had no way of knowing that she would be engaging some of America's most important historical figures, including abolitionist leaders such as Frederick Douglass, Sojourner Truth, and Reverend Henry Highland Garnet, and, her most pivotal association, Abraham and Mary Lincoln. In Washington, D.C., Keckly also worked at one point for Colonel Robert Lee, one of the two military officers sent to capture John Brown at Harpers Ferry. It was her dressmaking work for his wife that led her to become a dressmaker for Varina Davis, the wife of Mississippi Senator Jefferson

Davis, who would within months resign from the U.S. Senate and become the president of the Confederacy. In January 1861, as Southern congressmembers were leaving town in droves, Varina begged Lizzy to leave Washington, D.C. and come with the family to Mississippi. Varina teased her with the possibility that if the South won the war, she and Jefferson would be coming back to Washington, D.C. to live in the White House as president and first lady. In that scenario, Keckly would come back with them and have a guaranteed job at the White House. This was an enticing opportunity for Keckly.

It was one thing to work for pro-slavery congressmen in the confines of Washington, D.C., but it was quite another to relocate to the deep South and essentially contribute to the war effort on behalf of white enslavers. Alongside her resistance to slavery and her belief that the North would win if war broke out, Lizzy was also shrewd enough to recognize that accepting the offer would likely gain her more clients and possibly even lead to working in the White House, her dream job.[9] Nevertheless, she turned the offer down. As things turned out, though, providence was on her side once again.

In exchange for some emergency work for another client, Margaret McClean, Elizabeth was promised an introduction to Mary Lincoln for the express purpose of securing dressmaking work with the new first lady.[10] McClean kept her word and set up the interview. To Elizabeth's surprise, some of the other prominent socialites in the city had recommended other dressmakers to Mrs. Lincoln. When she went to meet with Mary at the Willard Hotel the day after the inauguration, she found herself waiting in line with several rivals. Even though she was last to meet with the new first lady, Keckly won the job, ironically, because she mentioned that she had worked for Varina Davis, the wife of Lincoln's—and the Union's—greatest enemy.[11]

In the nineteenth century, the relationship between dressmakers and their clients seems to have been akin to the intimacy that sometimes develops between modern hairdressers and their clients. Relations often became so familiar that private information, secrets, and plain old gossip were regularly shared. Whether the women were enslaved or free, the closeness that nevertheless developed between them in these circumstances, generally framed by gaping differences in power and status, provided a safe context where sharing and bonding could and did occur.

And this contact allowed black women like Elizabeth Keckly access to the private spaces where the elite exercise of authority was manifest, discussed, and debated. As her relationship with Mary grew, so did her relationship with President Lincoln. While she never rose to the level of counselor, as Frederick Douglass did—no woman achieved that status, except perhaps Mary—her influence was real, and she played the role of confidante and sounding board on many occasions. Because, as a couple, the Lincolns were very intimate and committed to each other, proximity to the first lady also meant proximity to the president. Mary was his strongest defender in the nation, and he was equally protective of her. Often when Mary and Lizzy were working on an outfit, which was quite frequent, the president would join them or could be found nearby. Over time, he and Mary increasingly felt that they could be candid and unguarded in their conversations around Keckly. As she noted, "Often Mr. and Mrs. Lincoln discussed the relations of Cabinet officers, and gentlemen prominent in politics, in my presence."[12]

Perhaps her most crucial role in the White House was as a stabilizing force for Mrs. Lincoln during several traumatic incidents and throughout the turmoil of the Civil War. The death of the Lincolns' eleven-year-old son, Willie, on February 20, 1862, devastated the Lincolns and left Mary distraught. It took her a year to recover a semblance of her old self. Keckly had been there for her the entire time, from the moment he fell ill with what turned out to be typhoid fever to the end of his life. After his death, Elizabeth was there to help wash and dress his body, and consoled Mary when no one else, including Abraham, could. Keckly could empathize with Mary's profound loss, because her own son, George, had died in the war. Passing for white—blacks were outlawed from signing up at that time—he had enlisted in the military and become one of the war's early casualties. He was killed in the infamous August 10, 1861, Battle of Wilson's Creek in Missouri, where more than 2,500 men died. At the time, Mary had sent Elizabeth a very sympathetic message.[13]

It is important to remember that Elizabeth Keckly was neither a servant nor an employee at the White House, but someone with an independent business relationship that evolved into a close friendship. Her role, while clearly not political, was part of the atmosphere in which the Lincolns endured multiple political and personal crises with few relatives or friends in the mix. That she became a trusted companion to the first lady, and sometimes a sounding board for the president of the United States, is a testament to her social, political, and cultural skills. Given that Mary Lincoln grew up in a slaveholding and pro-Confederacy family, both women must have traversed complex boundaries as their personal friendship deepened.

Quite apart from her connection to the White House, Elizabeth lived an expansive life and was active on many fronts during and after the Civil War. In the early days of the conflict, she was concerned about the large number of so-called "contrabands" who poured into the city as the war disrupted and fractured the slave system. These were enslaved blacks that attempted to free themselves by taking advantage of the chaos

Group of black "contrabands" make it to a Union camp during the Civil War

of war. Although escapees were relatively safe in D.C., in the period before Congress abolished slavery in Washington, D.C. on April 11, 1862, it was uncertain whether the Union would return them to their enslavers even if the North won the war. And certainly if the South won or was able to maintain a secessionist status, it would first and foremost demand that its "contraband" be returned.

As D.C. roiled with all of these economic and political concerns, camps were established to address the needs of these newly free individuals. One camp was constructed on land that would not long after the war become home to Howard University, one of the nation's first colleges for African Americans.

In response to the situation, in 1862 Keckly founded what was initially called the Contraband Association and then, after the war, the Freedmen and Soldiers' Relief Association. To raise funds for the Association, Elizabeth traveled all over the United

States and even to England. She received contributions from all levels of society, from famous and powerful figures like Frederick Douglass, Henry Highland Garnet, and the Lincolns to unknown and struggling individuals such as black waiters.[14]

While Elizabeth had her relatively successful dressmaking business to rely on, Mary Lincoln found herself in dire straits after the assassination of her husband. Circumstances rapidly degenerated for the widowed first lady, never popular with the Washington, D.C. political class and certainly stressed and disoriented by the shocking murder. Foremost among her troubles were mounting debts due to irresponsible and unaffordable spending on dresses and other attire during her time in the White House—debts she had kept from the president. In desperate need of money, in 1867 Mary decided to sell her dresses through a New York distributor. Embarrassed by the situation, she called upon Lizzy to act as her go-between as a way to shield her identity and prevent gossip from possibly leaking out that the former first lady was destitute. In a scenario out of a bad spy movie involving fake names and forged letters, the president's widow and a former slave tried hard to furtively sell the former first lady's dresses, but in the end they mostly lost money.

That episode created an unusual degree of tension in the relationship. However, it was Keckly's publication of her book, *Behind the Scenes, Or, Thirty Years a Slave, and Four Years in the White House*, that brought about a rupture in the friendship. Lizzy did not inform Mary Lincoln that she was working on a book about her experiences at the White House, which of course involved intimate details about her relationship with Mary. The book also included personal letters that the two women had written to each other, which Mary Lincoln claimed had been published without her permission. While the book was generally autobiographical in nature and offered little political discourse, it was deeply personal. Keckly revealed conversations not only between her and the Lincolns but also between President Lincoln and others.

Many critics of the time condemned the book with racist venom. One New York reviewer wrote, "Has the American public no word of protest against the assumption that its literary taste is of low grade as to tolerate the back-stairs gossip of negro [*sic*] servant girls?" A D.C. critic echoed that sentiment, writing, "What family of eminence that employs a negro is safe from such desecration? Where will it end? What family that has a servant may not, in fact, have its peace and happiness destroyed by such treacherous creatures as the Keckly woman?"[15] Overall, it seemed that opposition to the book was due to the fact that a black woman had written it more than to anything else. Breaking the mold of black women as subservient to whites, Elizabeth had stepped into an arena dominated almost exclusively by white men. The idea that a literate black woman could become intimate with the wife and family of the sixteenth president of the United States menaced the racist worldview of many white critics and incited them to attack her and the book.

What with the political climate in Washington, D.C., neglect of her business due to time spent with Mary Lincoln, and the controversy sparked by her book, Keckly's livelihood began to suffer. Her business essentially fell apart, and she no longer held the social influence she had enjoyed during her years of access to the White House. Fortunately, she was able to secure a job teaching at Wilberforce University in Ohio, where from 1892 to 1893 she headed up the Department of Sewing and Domestic Science Arts. When her health began to deteriorate, Elizabeth returned to Washington and spent the rest of her life at the Home for Destitute Women and Children, one of several charitable institutions she had helped to found. It was there, at the age of 89, that Elizabeth Keckly died on May 26, 1907—the end of as full and remarkable an American life as there has ever been.

Harshly criticized when it was first published, Keckly's book had little impact in her time and is still largely unknown today. Most scholars ignore it or give minimum weight to her examination of Lincoln.[16] This is a mistake. It is quite possible that she was the closest black person to him during his presidency. Her read on Lincoln is first person, intimate, and genuinely insightful. And it is impossible to find anyone else who was as much in touch with the first lady as Keckly, perhaps even more so than the Lincolns' son Robert, at various points. While she perhaps broke the unspoken protocol by revealing private communications that had transpired within the White House, she was not there as a servant or staff. She penetrated the inner sanctum as an independent businesswoman and had no obligation to abide by rules meant for those who were White House employees. Her activism also separated her from most other blacks who worked there, many of whom distanced themselves from those who were enslaved, escapees, or poor. Their nonpartisan stance was a necessary part of keeping a good job through changing administrations. Keckly was fiercely clear in her views on race and the policies needed to bring relief to people suffering from the chronic racism of the time. As a black woman who not only survived enslavement but achieved access to multiple levels of U.S. society, her contribution goes beyond the insights she provides on the Lincolns and enriches our understanding of the period's dynamics of race, gender, and class from a vantage point that has often been marginalized, criticized, and dismissed.

A Shaky Emancipation

The two competing stories regarding Abraham Lincoln's signing of the Emancipation Proclamation on January 1, 1863, in many ways reflect the ongoing debate about his legacy in the nation's racial narrative. It is a well-known fact that at the moment Lincoln was about to sign the document, his hand was shaking so much that he postponed the signing. For critics of Lincoln's policies and his views on African Americans, the Civil War, and slavery, his shaking hand reflected his wavering stance on liberating the approximately four million black people whom whites were enslaving at the time. Lincoln's enemies, then and now, contend that his faltering at the signing of a document that in fact *did not* free all of the slaves exposed his real feelings about race relations. Historian Lerone Bennett Jr. argues that "at the last moment, something in him—was it his conscience, his unconscious, or his fear of what he called the evils of sudden emancipation?—revolted, and when he picked up the pen to do it, his arm trembled so violently that he stopped, overcome suddenly by a superstitious feeling."[17] He goes on to say that Lincoln had "compunctions," i.e., regrets and maybe even repulsion at putting his imprimatur on the executive order.[18]

Lincoln proponents, such as historian Doris Kearns Goodwin—and Lincoln himself—offer a more favorable explanation. They state that his hand shook because he had strained it greeting visitors at the White House all day long, as was the traditional New Year's ritual. Reportedly, Lincoln told his old friend Joshua Speed that he paused in signing the Proclamation because he did not want future generations to see any shakiness in his signature. Lincoln stated, "If my hand trembles when I sign this all who examine the document hereafter will say, 'He hesitated.' Yet, I never in my life felt more certain that I was doing right. If my name ever goes into history it will be for this act, and my whole soul is in it."[19]

Lincoln has been the most enigmatic U.S. president, and at the same time the most popular for many African Americans.

It was Lincoln's White House that shattered an unbroken chain of presidential accommodation to the South's racist demands. The Republican Party was established in 1854 with the express purpose of breaking the political and economic power of the South's aristocracy by calling for an end to slavery. It would also seek the black vote.[20] Forged by defectors from the Democratic Party and the Whig Party, and financially backed by the rising industrial and finance sectors of U.S. capitalism, it foreshadowed the coming split in the country. Relatively inexperienced on the national scene but a compelling writer and debater, Lincoln became the new party's standard-bearer. The internal rupture between the Democratic Party's Northern and Southern wings enabled a relatively easy win for the Republican Party in 1860. Lincoln's election victory triggered the inevitable war that had been a long time coming.

There is ample evidence that at critical junctures leading up to the war, not only did Lincoln vacillate regarding how to address the crisis, his sentiments regarding freedom for black people wavered as well. On October 13, 1858, during one of his legendary senate campaign debates with Stephen Douglas, his opponent accused him of seeking "negro equality." Lincoln responded by saying, "I am not, nor ever have been, in favor of bringing about in any way the social and political equality of the white and black races."[21] It is safe to assume that at the moment these thoughts were expressed they genuinely represented Lincoln's feelings regarding race and African Americans. In a sense, Lincoln's stance mirrored that of many who opposed slavery: abolitionist sentiments, even among the most ardent white advocates, often did not include a call for racial equality.

Yet, on another occasion, Lincoln responded to race-baiting by saying, "Let us discard all this quibbling about this man and the other man—this race and that race and the other race being inferior, and therefore they must be placed in an inferior position—disregarding our standard that we have left us. Let us discard all these things, and unite as one people throughout this land, until we shall once more stand up declaring that all men are created equal."[22] These conflicting statements very likely reflect the defensiveness Lincoln must have felt while campaigning for white votes in then Democratic-dominated Illinois and, at the same time, articulating a politics that was more consistent with the progressive dimension of the relatively new Republican Party's stated objectives.

An unanswered historical question is whether Lincoln actually grew more progressive in his views on race and equality. The statements of African Americans who interacted with Lincoln during his presidency would seem to suggest that he did in fact grow in his personal perspective. This is not to say that he fully discarded all of his racist ideas about blacks, but simply that by the time he was assassinated he was not where he had started. We can study his words and the opinions of those who were close to him, but the accumulation of known information still leaves much room for conjecture.

His policies are another matter. The voluminous record on Lincoln makes it relatively easy to track his less than progressive—or perhaps less than courageous—policy tactics as he juggled the various and often contradictory options needed to win a war, save the union, and irrevocably liberate blacks from enslavement. At one point, Lincoln believed that government-sponsored emigration of blacks out of the country was the best solution to the problem of race in the United States. Lincoln had been a public proponent of black emigration from the United States since at least 1852, when, at a eulogy for U.S. diplomat, scholar, and slaveholder Sen. Henry Clay, he stated that if slavery could be eliminated and the slaves returned to "their long-lost fatherland, it will indeed be a glorious consummation."[23] In 1855, he spoke at an American Colonization Society conference.

Once elected president, he did not surrender the idea. Here again, a debate rages. Lerone Bennett Jr. argues that Lincoln had a "White dream" for the United States and that his colonization project was essentially an "ethnic cleansing plan."[24] Writers such as Robert Morgan and Allan Nevins claim that Lincoln supported black colonization until the day he died. Whether due to his belief in cultural, innate, or political differences, these writers assert, Lincoln never embraced the notion of blacks and whites living together.[25] On the other side, scholars such as Michael Vorenberg, Charles Wesley, and Don E. Fehrenbacher have argued that Lincoln's colonization schemes may have been articulated as part of a larger strategy to sell emancipation.[26] According to this theory, Lincoln came to believe, at least until the end of 1862, that only by advocating the expatriation of blacks could he win support from reluctant Northerners and turn the war to save the Union into a war for black liberation.

It is quite possible, of course, that both theories contain elements of truth and are not necessarily in contradiction with each other. At one point in his life Lincoln clearly believed that the races should live apart. Privately, he may never have abandoned this belief. At the same time, he faced the practical reality of ending the war with the nation united. It was a wise and perhaps necessary strategy to advocate black expatriation in order to win support from the North even though it would have been economically impossible to expatriate millions of African Americans.

It is also important to note, similar to the situation that President Obama faces, Lincoln had to balance meeting the concerns of diverse constituencies – northerners who were tiring of the war, radical Republicans who wanted him to move faster on emancipation, African Americans who were fleeing slavery, and even southerners who did not want to leave the Union – with a war that was draining resources, political capital, and morale. It was nearly impossible to force a timetable that could meet all the interests that he had to take into consideration as he necessarily had to reunite the nation.

A Historic Gathering

One of the most significant developments during this period was black political access to the White House, including the first meetings at the White House between a U.S. president and African Americans to discuss policy. Seeking support for his project to relocate blacks to Chiriqui, an area in what is now Panama, Lincoln's Commissioner of Emigration, Rev. James Mitchell, was delegated to bring a group of black leaders to meet with the president.[27] It is telling that this historic meeting was not a discussion about the internal revolution that was under way or the emancipation of millions of black men, women, and children, but rather a hard-line sales pitch for the president's grand plan on black colonization.

On August 14, 1862, as the war raged and emancipation was being secretly planned, Lincoln held a meeting at the White House with five African American ministers. Led by Rev. Edward M. Thomas, head of the Anglo-African Institute for the Encouragement of Industry and Art, the group included John F. Cook, John T. Costin, Cornelius Clark, and Benjamin McCoy. Instead of a thoughtful discussion of a controversial topic—black expatriation and colonization—the meeting turned out to be more of a stern, abusive, and patently racist lecture by Lincoln. A reporter permitted to attend the meeting published an article the next day on the front page of the *New*

York Tribune under the headline "The Colonization of People of African Descent."[28] One of the article's subheadings pinpointed the president's disturbing reasoning for why the races should be apart: "He Holds That the White and Black Races Cannot Dwell Together."[29]

Lincoln explained to the group why separation was desirable:

> You and we are different races. We have between us a broader difference than exists between almost any other two races. Whether it is right or wrong I need not discuss, but this physical difference is a great disadvantage to us both, as I think your race suffer very greatly, many of them by living among us, while ours suffer from your presence. In a word we suffer on each side. If this is admitted, it affords a reason at least why we should be separated.[30]

The president had little interest in hearing the opinions of the black leaders he had assembled at the White House that day. In clarifying the nature of the one-sided meeting, Lincoln dismissively added, "I do not propose to discuss this, but to present it as a fact with which we have to deal."[31] He then seems to hold the entire black race accountable for the Civil War, stating:

> But for your race among us there could not be war, although many men engaged on either side do not care for you one way or the other. Nevertheless, I repeat, without the institution of Slavery and the colored race as a basis, the war could not have an existence.[32]

After calling the example of Liberia a "success" as an example of government-sponsored black expatriation, the president then lectured the group about the value of having blacks relocate closer to the United States in Central America. He did not, perhaps as a tactical measure to keep his options open, specifically tell the group about the Chiriqui plans that were under way. Referring to the region as a country (and denationalizing the group's members whose birth country was the United States), he stated, "The country is a very excellent one for any people, and with great natural resources and advantages, and especially because of the similarity of climate with your native land—thus being suited to your physical condition," and "there is evidence of very rich coal mines."[33]

On the sticky question of whether blacks would be well received, old Abe stated:

> The political affairs in Central America are not in quite as satisfactory condition as I wish. There are contending factions in that quarter; but it is true all the factions are agreed alike on the subject of colonization, and want it, and are more generous than we are here. To your colored race they have no objection. Besides, I would endeavor to have you made equals, and have the best assurance that you should be the equals of the best.[34]

The U.S. president argued, illogically, that he could guarantee equality in a foreign nation over which he had no jurisdiction. Honest Abe was also not so honest on another point. He was wrong about "all factions" agreeing on the subject of black colonization; in fact, all factions, governments, and everyone else vehemently disagreed on Lincoln's plot.

Finally, Lincoln got to the real point of the meeting. He wanted the group (and like-minded blacks, if they could be found) to act as promoters and recruiters for his scheme.

Stroking egos, he argued, "If intelligent colored men, such as are before me, would move in this matter, much might be accomplished. It is exceedingly important that we have men at the beginning capable of thinking as white men, and not those who have been systematically oppressed."[35] President Lincoln wanted the group to find one hundred "tolerably intelligent" men, women, and children as volunteers—although he quickly reduced the number to twenty-five—to start off the project.

As emigration out of the United States had long been a strategy for some black activists, Lincoln's plan resonated with segments of the black community. Unlike the racist rationale undergirding the motives and activities of the American Colonization Society, which sought to get rid of the race problem by getting rid of blacks, African American calls for expatriation were rooted in the ideas of self-determination, racial solidarity, and genuine democratic aspirations.

In 1815, Paul Cuffee of Massachusetts, a free black with some Native American heritage, launched a back-to-Africa movement when he took thirty-eight free blacks to Sierra Leone, a country that had long been a destination for free blacks from England and, after the Revolutionary War, Canada.[36] Even after slavery ended, black leaders such as Martin Delany and Bishop Henry McNeal Turner continued to call for blacks to move to Africa and in some cases did so themselves. Delany was active in national black politics and worked closely with Fredrick Douglass on his newspaper, *North Star*. By the early 1850s, however, Delany broke with Douglass and became a stirring proponent for black emigration to both Africa and South America.

During the Civil War, however, Delany decided to stay in the United States to help the Union defeat the South. In 1865, he met with President Lincoln two months before his assassination to propose building a corps of black men who would help recruit Southern blacks to support Lincoln. After the war, frustrated with the attacks on Reconstruction, Delany again promoted emigration to Liberia.

Active in the African Methodist Episcopal Church and a central figure in Washington, D.C.'s black community, Bishop Turner was appointed by President Lincoln as chaplain to black troops during the Civil War. He later moved to Georgia and ran for political office. After being illegally denied his seat, Bishop Turner grew frustrated with American racism and became a major speaker promoting black emigration to Africa as well as to Canada, where he died in 1915.[37]

One of the strongest movements for black emigration to Africa emerged in Arkansas during the late nineteenth century. On March 10, 1892, about 600 African Americans in central Arkansas participated in an effort to move to Liberia.[38] Thus, when President Lincoln made a pitch for black colonization, it fell on receptive ears in a large part of the black community. Rev. Henry Highland Garnet was one black leader who approved. A longtime proponent of black emigration, he called the president's scheme "the most humane, and merciful movement which this or any other administration has proposed for the benefit of the enslaved," somewhat missing the point that free rather than enslaved blacks were being targeted.[39] Some took to calling the still undetermined destination "Linconia," evoking the naming of Liberia's capital "Monrovia" after President James Monroe.

Returning to the 1862 meeting between Lincoln and the group of black leaders, it appears that some in the delegation mumbled a few "Yes, sirs," and after Lincoln finished his monologue they replied by saying they would get back to him with a response. Reverend Thomas stated that they would consult with other black leaders around the nation to get their opinion on Lincoln's proposal, but he felt optimistic. There is little evidence that Thomas or the other four had much influence over the opinion or politics of the black community. Two days after the meeting, on August 16, Thomas wrote Lincoln confidently, "We were entirely hostile to the movement until all the advantages were so ably brought to our view by you and we believe that our friends and colaborers [*sic*] for our race in those cities [Philadelphia, New York, and Boston] will when the subject is explained by us to them join heartily in sustaining such a movement."[40] Two days later, on August 18, Thomas proposed to Lincoln a national tour of black leaders who would promote his idea to other African Americans.[41]

As it turned out, Thomas's optimism was a bit premature. "Leading colored men" and blacks in general unambiguously and even angrily rejected Lincoln and Thomas's overtures, just as they had for decades rejected the colonization plans of the American Colonization Society and others.

Free blacks saw their future as citizens of the United States and nowhere else. In Philadelphia, in an immediate response, the Statistical Association of the Colored People of Philadelphia met on August 15 and sent a letter to Reverend Thomas condemning Lincoln's presentation and his proposal. Statistical Association President Isaiah C. Wears wrote, "To be asked, after so many years of oppression and wrong have been inflicted in a land and by a people who have been so largely enriched by the black man's toil, to pull up stakes in a civilized and barbarous nation, simple to gratify an unnatural wicked prejudice emanating from slavery, is unreasonable and anti-Christian in the extreme."[42] Addressing Lincoln's assertion that African Americans were the cause of the war, Wears lashed out at the president, stating, "But it is not the Negro that is the cause of the war; it is the unwillingness on the part of the American people to do the race simple justice."[43]

Abolitionist leader Frederick Douglass's response to news of the meeting was hostile and dismissive. He wrote that Lincoln's proposal regarding free blacks "expresses merely the desire to get rid of them and reminds one of the politeness with which a man might try to bow out of his house some troublesome creditor or the witness of some old guilt."[44] He further wrote that "the President of the United States seems to possess an ever increasing passion for making himself appear silly and ridiculous, if nothing worse," and that his remarks were "unusually garrulous, characteristically foggy, remarkably illogical and untimely."[45]

Lincoln moved forward despite opposition from African Americans, radical Republicans, Democrats, Southerners, and even the American Colonization Society, even after the Chiriqui plan fell apart when Nicaragua, Honduras, Panama, and Costa Rica all refused to take part in it. On December 31, 1862, the day before he signed the Emancipation Proclamation, Lincoln approved a contract to send 5,000 volunteer black men, women, and children to an island off the coast of Haiti known as the Île à Vache. The project became a total catastrophe. More than 400 people left the United States on April 6, 1863, and quickly discovered that little preparation had been made for their arrival. After nearly a year of deprivations, illness, death, and little production, the surviving members of the expedition, about 365 people, were brought back to the United States, arriving in Virginia on March 20, 1864. Lincoln's dream of convincing blacks to permanently leave the United States was never heard of again after the incident.[46]

For African Americans, and ultimately the White House, the goal of the Civil War was nothing short of black people's liberation through the illegalization of slavery. For tactical, political, and arguably for personal reasons, Lincoln hesitated, retreated, and then moved forward in pursuit of that goal. His sense of reluctance and caution was demonstrated in his reaction to four key incidents that preceded the Emancipation Proclamation: the Confiscation Act of 1861, the Fremont Declaration, General Order 11, and the Confiscation Act of 1862.

Consistently more radical than the moderate Lincoln, the Republican-controlled Congress passed the first Confiscation Act on August 6, 1861. The Act gave the federal government authority to seize property—including blacks that were enslaved and could be claimed as property—from those in rebellion against the Union, unless they surrendered or ceased such activity within sixty days of the Act's passage. There were several weaknesses to the Act, however, including Lincoln's disinclination to sign and enforce it, the fact that it only applied to those enslaved in territories controlled by the Union, and, most important, the reality that it did not free any of the enslaved—it only "confiscated" them. Wary of frightening the border (and slaveholding) states of Maryland, Delaware, Missouri, and Kentucky, Lincoln opposed the Act and signed it very reluctantly.

As hesitant as Lincoln was about the first Confiscation Act, he was absolutely horrified when on August 31, less than a month later, General John C. Fremont issued an order to free black people enslaved by whites who were in revolt against the Union. The commander of Union forces in Missouri, General Fremont issued his own proclamation, as a war measure, that stated:

> I do hereby extend, and declare established, martial law throughout the State of Missouri. . . . All persons who shall be taken with arms in their hands within

> these lines shall be tried by court-martial, and, if found guilty, will be shot. The property, real and personal, of all persons in the State of Missouri who shall take up arms against the United States, and who shall be directly proven to have taken an active part with their enemies in the field, is declared to be confiscated to the public use; and their slaves, if any they have, are hereby declared free.[47]

Lincoln fumed and immediately rescinded the order.[48] His action would accelerate the ongoing battle between the White House and radical Republicans over how far to go toward ending slavery both for political purposes and to win the war.

The president continued to have trouble with his officers getting ahead of him on the issue of emancipation. Another field officer also sought to use the freeing of slaves as a tactic of war. On May 9, 1862, General David Hunter issued General Order 11, which freed all slaves in Georgia, Florida, and South Carolina. The order stated:

> The three States of Georgia, Florida and South Carolina, comprising the military department of the south, having deliberately declared themselves no longer under the protection of the United States of America, and having taken up arms against the said United States, it becomes a military necessity to declare them under martial law. This was accordingly done on the 25th day of April, 1862. Slavery and martial law in a free country are altogether incompatible; the persons in these three States—Georgia, Florida, and South Carolina—heretofore held as slaves, are therefore declared forever free.[49]

When Lincoln again chastised the general and rescinded the order, Congress responded with a second Confiscation Act. The new bill, passed on July 16, 1862, stated in no uncertain terms that Confederate slave owners who did not surrender within sixty days would have the black people they enslaved permanently freed. The Act excluded those enslaved in the border states of Missouri, Delaware, Tennessee, and Maryland and even, as a result of pressure from Lincoln, sanctioned the return of these states' fugitives from slavery. It also included a provision for voluntary black expatriation. In any case, Lincoln did little to enforce either the first or second Confiscation Acts. And since they were Acts of Congress, they had relatively weak legal standing and could easily be overturned by a more conservative group of legislators.

All of these maneuvers were a prelude to the main event. By July 1862, Lincoln had come to realize that the war could not be won without ending slavery (or at least declaring it abolished). Earlier, on June 19, Congress passed the Territorial Emancipation Act. With Lincoln's signature, the Act abolished slavery in all territories seeking statehood under federal control. This action did *not* free any African Americans in any of the existing states but took a first step by refuting the *Dred Scott* decision's conclusion that the federal government could not regulate slavery in the territories. Congress and the president, at that point, still vacillated on a direct attack on states' rights.

But the real giant step that remained was to issue an order declaring slavery over and done throughout the land. Ultimately, this would not be the Emancipation Proclamation, despite its symbolic power, even though it was the Proclamation that irreversibly pushed the nation to full abolition. Pressure for emancipation was building. On September 7, a mass rally was held in Chicago calling for immediate emancipation of all those enslaved. In an August 19, 1862, editorial, Horace Greeley, editor of the *New York Tribune*, demanded that Lincoln issue an order abolishing slavery immediately and totally. Lincoln's well-known and widely quoted response to Greeley sent chills through the abolition movement. Although Lincoln had already discussed with his cabinet the decision to issue an emancipation proclamation and had decided that he would free black people, he wrote deceptively in a letter to Greeley on August 22, 1862:

> My paramount object in this struggle is to save the Union, and is not either to save or destroy slavery. If I could save the Union without freeing any slave, I would do it, and if I could save it by freeing all the slaves, I would do it; and if I could save it by freeing some and leaving others alone, I would also do that. What I do about slavery and the colored race, I do because I believe it helps to save the Union.[50]

On September 22, 1862, Lincoln issued a Preliminary Emancipation Proclamation that included a line stating that the "effort to colonize persons of African descent . . . will be continued." He gave the forces of the South one hundred days to surrender—with the disturbing provision that they could keep the black people they enslaved—or he would sign the Proclamation on January 1, 1863. They did not.

And so, on the first day of 1863, President Lincoln put his non-shaky signature on the paper that read in part:

> All persons held as slaves within any state, or designated part of a state, the people whereof shall then be in rebellion against the United States, shall be then, thenceforward, and forever, free.

The Proclamation had many shortcomings. It did not free those who were enslaved and already in states in the Union, those who were in Union-held territory in the Confederacy, or those in the border states of Delaware, Kentucky, Maryland, or Missouri. Other areas in West Virginia and Louisiana were also excluded. Additionally, the Proclamation was a presidential order—rather than an Act of Congress or an amendment to the Constitution—that gave it questionable long-term legal standing.

It is also important, however, to acknowledge what it did do. First and foremost, it changed the nature of the war. Political and military leaders from the North and South who were not already there had to come to grips with the reality that liberation of all enslaved blacks—abolition—had become a goal of the war. Few had started off with that assumption. Most Southern leaders had voiced opposition to the Republican Party's plan to stop the expansion of slavery and its probable intent to perhaps in some distant future initiate policies for the institution's gradual abolition. Second, for both free and enslaved blacks, the Proclamation was a powerful organizing and mobilizing tool. For those still in slavery, it inspired tens of thousands to drop their plows and leave the plantation. Legally robust or not, the Proclamation was read as overthrowing the *Dred Scott* decision and the Fugitive Slave Act. Nevertheless, the significance and symbolism of the Emancipation Proclamation has remained the most controversial of all of Lincoln's decisions. It is clear that Lincoln changed and that his antislavery views—long-standing and well documented, though not necessarily based on a commitment to racial equality—evolved into a position of irrevocable abolitionism whether he wished it or not. In the end, he steered the nation to a place that no prior president had dared to go, and the consequences transformed the nation from a legally racist slaveocracy into a new social order.

It is also undeniable that Lincoln's views provoked his assassination. His last public speech, on April 11, 1865, three days before he was assassinated, focused on the postwar issue of reconstructing the nation and on the Louisiana constitution that had been submitted to Congress for approval. Lincoln also addressed the issue of black voting rights, setting himself up for criticism from the left for his racist statement about which blacks he preferred to give the franchise. In those remarks, referring to the proposed Louisiana constitution, Lincoln stated, "It is also unsatisfactory to some that the elective franchise is not given to the colored man. I would myself prefer that it were now conferred on the very intelligent, and on those who serve our cause as soldiers."[51]

According to historian James McPherson, the speech indicated that Lincoln and more radical Republicans in Congress were coming closer to a consensus on how to address this concern, but without doubt some, if not all, African American men were going to become the nation's newest group of voters. At the end of that speech, Lincoln hinted at the direction he was headed in extending rights to blacks, saying, "In the present 'situation' as the phrase goes, it may be my duty to make some new announcement to the people of the South. I am considering, and shall not fail to act, when satisfied that action will be proper."[52] While scholar Lerone Bennett Jr. interprets that remark to be part of Lincoln's evasive language when it came to the rights of African Americans, there was at least one member of the crowd listening that day who believed he had a clear understanding of what the president meant.

John Wilkes Booth, central plotter of a conspiracy to violently bring down the Lincoln administration, was present and is reported to have muttered, "That means nigger citizenship. Now, by God, I'll put him through. That is the last speech he will ever make."[53] And it was. Three days later, Booth, a virulent racist, shot Lincoln in the back of the head at Ford's Theater during the performance of "Our American Cousin."

African Americans and Lincoln's White House

> *Let your motto be Resistance! Resistance! RESISTANCE! No oppressed people have ever secured their liberty without resistance.*[54]—Henry Highland Garnet

Under Lincoln's command, political access to the White House had been extended to the black community for the first time in U.S. history. Among the best-known black leaders who met with Lincoln at the White House were Frederick Douglass and Sojourner Truth, but many lesser-known activists and ordinary African Americans met with him there as well. The significance of these encounters cannot be overstated.

While there is little evidence that black input was the sole determinant in strategic decisions that were made by Lincoln (and presidents that followed him, particularly those in need of black popular support), black views were part of a shifting matrix of considerations in policy construction. While sometimes that meant doing the exact opposite of what African Americans saw as in their interests, the multiracial space that Lincoln opened would be a critical new element in the ongoing struggle for black freedom and equality.

As early as 1829, the emergence of a radical black voice in national public discourse began to appear. September of that year saw the publication of *Walker's Appeal*.[55] The seventy-six-page pamphlet advocated that blacks revolt against their white enslavers and called for nothing short of full liberation and equality for African Americans, enslaved and free.[56] The pamphlet also argued against colonization:

> Let no man of us budge one step, and let slave-holders come to beat us from our country. America is more our country, than it is the whites—we have enriched it with our *blood and tears*. The greatest riches in all America have arisen from our blood and tears: —and will they drive us from our property and homes, which we have earned with our *blood?*[57]

A bounty was put on Walker's head: $10,000 if he were brought in alive, $1,000 if dead. He was found dead at his home nearly one year later in June 1830.

The National Negro Convention movement, which brought together black leaders from around the nation, was another vehicle for challenging the dominant political and racial discourses of the mid to late nineteenth century and for projecting a progressive black perspective in pre–Civil War politics. However, it would be articulate and determined individuals such as Frederick Douglass, Sojourner Truth, Martin Delany, Alexander Crummell, Rev. Bishop Turner, and Rev. Henry Highland Garnet, among others, who would most effectively raise the stakes and agitate the conscience of the nation on the issues of justice, rights for blacks, and the moral atrocity of permitting whites to enslave people of color.

Douglass in particular was a powerful and relentless movement organizer, orator, and writer whose singular voice never yielded to the racist perspectives of the times, whether they were held by hard-core conservatives or sympathetic liberals. Born into slavery in Maryland in 1818, he escaped to the North when he was twenty years old and quickly became a galvanizing force of resistance to the slaveholding South and its Northern allies. His speeches against slavery and for justice for black Americans were riveting and drew massive crowds. Douglass was able to

Frederick Douglass, circa 1855

win supporters across lines of race, class, and gender, from the very poor and marginalized to European kings and queens and American presidents. His visits to the White House were historic, and nearly all were turning points in the relations between African Americans and the U.S. presidency.

By the time of his iconic 1852 Fourth of July speech he was already the most famous black activist in the nation. He had written a best seller in 1845, *Narrative of the Life of Frederick Douglass*, and traveled to Europe to speak on behalf of the rights of African Americans. He played a pivotal role at the 1848 Seneca Falls convention where the American feminist movement was born, and he was the publisher of *North Star*, one of the most important antislavery publications in the country.

On July 5, 1852, in Rochester, New York, Douglass spoke before the Rochester Ladies' Anti-Slavery Society to a crowd of 500 to 600 people in Corinthian Hall. In that speech he articulated the meaning for blacks of the nation's celebration of its independence from England seventy-six years earlier. It was as magnificent a presentation on the morality and politics of race as has ever been delivered in the United States. In that seminal speech, reflecting the collective sentiments of all African Americans, he raises the question, "What to the Slave Is the Fourth of July?" His answer is devastating.

> I answer, a day that reveals to him, more than all other days in the year, the gross injustice and cruelty to which he is the constant victim. To him, your celebration is a sham; your boasted liberty, an unholy license; your national greatness, swelling vanity; your sounds of rejoicing are empty and heartless; your denunciations of tyrants, brass fronted impudence; your shouts of liberty and equality, hollow mockery;

> your prayers and hymns, your sermons and thanksgivings, with all your religious parade, and solemnity, are, to him, mere bombast, fraud, deception, impiety, and hypocrisy—a thin veil to cover up crimes which would disgrace a nation of savages. There is not a nation on the earth guilty of practices, more shocking and bloody, than are the people of these United States, at this very hour."[58]

In the speech, he contrasts "your National Independence" with the reality that he and other African Americans are "not included within the pale of this glorious anniversary. . . . The rich inheritance of justice, liberty, prosperity and independence, bequeathed by your fathers, is shared by you, not by me."[59] Referring to slavery as "the great sin and shame of America," he blasts the hypocrisy of the nation, stating, "Whether we turn to the declarations of the past, or to the professions of the present, the conduct of the nation seems equally hideous and revolting. America is false to the past, false to the present, and solemnly binds herself to be false to the future."[60] Time and time again in his lengthy talk, Douglass returns to the theme of contradictions between hype and reality. Citing a former president, he argues, "You declare, before the world, and are understood by the world to declare, that you 'hold these truths to be self evident, that all men are created equal; and are endowed by their Creator with certain inalienable rights; and that, among these are, life, liberty, and the pursuit of happiness;' and yet, you hold securely, in a bondage which, according to your own Thomas Jefferson, 'is worse than ages of that which your fathers rose in rebellion to oppose,' a seventh part of the inhabitants of your country."[61]

Despite his unyielding critique, he states at the end of the speech that he is hopeful. He believes that there "are forces in operation" fighting for abolition that will "inevitably work the downfall of slavery."[62]

Douglass's relationship to the White House was ongoing and pivotal. He received important appointments from four presidents—secretary of the Santo Domingo Commission (Ulysses S. Grant), U.S. Marshal for the District of Columbia (Rutherford B. Hayes), Recorder of the Deeds for the District of Columbia (James A. Garfield), and Minister-Resident and Consul-General of Haiti (Benjamin Harrison). He turned down an offer from President Andrew Johnson, who, Douglass rightly believed, did not genuinely want fairness and equality for African Americans. With the emergence of Douglass and other national black leaders, never again would the voice of African Americans be silenced in their struggle for liberation, justice, and human rights.

[The negro is] the stomach of the rebellion.[63]
—Frederick Douglass

Although he only met with Lincoln twice (in addition to crashing his second inauguration party), Douglass was the one black leader who clearly had the most access to Lincoln and the most influence on him politically. The two men met on August 10, 1863, and on August 19, 1864, both times at the White House. By 1861, Douglass had emerged as the nation's most prominent black leader. Much debate has emerged regarding his relationship with and views on Lincoln. Douglass was clearly frustrated with Lincoln in the early years of the war and his administration. Speaking against Lincoln's advocacy for black colonization, he stated, as we have seen, that Lincoln seemed bent on making himself appear "silly and ridiculous." He also wrote, "Mr. Lincoln is quite a genuine representative of

"Marching on!"—The Fifty-fifth Massachusetts Colored Regiment singing John Brown's March in the streets of Charleston, February 21, 1865

American prejudice and Negro hatred and far more concerned for the preservation of slavery, and the favor of the Border Slave States, than for any sentiment of magnanimity or principle of justice and humanity."[64]

But Douglass also supported the Civil War and believed from the very beginning that it would result in the liberation of blacks from the nightmare of enslavement to white people. Like Delany, he lobbied Lincoln to include black soldiers in the Union military, and when Lincoln finally relented due to the faltering military efforts of the Union and thus a critical need for more troops, Douglass personally helped recruit and establish the 54th and 55th Regiments of black soldiers.[65] More than 180,000 African Americans would participate as Union soldiers—with 37,000 killed—fighting in 499 combat situations that included thirty-nine major battles.[66] In fact, it was the mistreatment of black soldiers that drove Douglass to seek a meeting with Lincoln. Blacks were not only offered lower pay than white recruits, they were also asked to buy their own uniforms.[67] Injured black soldiers were sent to different treatment facilities than whites and the dead buried in different cemeteries—facts that embittered Harriet Tubman against Lincoln[68] but which drove Douglass to meet with him in person to press for immediate change.

At the August 1863 White House meeting initiated by Douglass, he advocated on behalf of black soldiers: the massacre of black soldiers by the Confederates, equal pay for black soldiers, and fair promotion of black soldiers.[69] From the moment the Union accepted blacks as soldiers, the outraged Confederacy was determined to punish them as harshly as possible. The Confederate secretary of war, James A. Seddon, issued an order early in the war regarding captured black troops, that read, "We ought never to be inconvenienced with such prisoners. . . . Summary execution must therefore be inflicted on those taken."[70] The policy was carried out inconsistently, because some black soldiers were enslaved, some held in prisoner-of-war camps (but never exchanged for white prisoners), and some indeed executed. Black troops were murdered at Milliken's Bend, Louisiana; Jackson, Louisiana; Poison Spring, Arkansas; Olustee, Florida; Petersburg, Virginia; and many other locales, including Fort Pillow, Tennessee, where a notorious massacre took place on April 12, 1864. Led by General Nathan Bedford Forrest—who after the war became the first national leader and founder of the Ku Klux Klan—Confederate troops slaughtered twice as many black troops as they did whites in the captured fort. The massacre even spurred Lincoln to vow retaliation.[71]

As a concession to the racial prejudices of whites in the North, the Union had denied equal pay and fair promotions

White House as it appeared around the time Frederick Douglass went there to meet with President Lincoln.

for black troops. In principle, Lincoln agreed with Douglass on each point, but he demurred when it came to taking political action. Lincoln stated that it was an effort to get black soldiers accepted in the first place, so keeping their pay lower than whites' would help to "smooth the way" for their eventual full inclusion and eligibility for equal pay. He also said he would sign commissions to promote black soldiers given to him by the secretary of war, a weak commitment at best. Finally, Lincoln asserted that retaliation was not the best solution to the targeting and abuse of black soldiers by enemy forces, and went on to say that he thought the conditions for African Americans in the ranks were improving. Following the meeting, however, Lincoln issued an order that the Union would retaliate if black soldiers were massacred or abused. For the most part, Douglass was sympathetic to the president's positions, although he often did not agree with them.[72] He also reports that during a meeting Lincoln said, "Douglass, I hate slavery as much as you do, and I want to see it abolished altogether."[73]

One year later, in August 1864, Douglass met with Lincoln again at the White House. On this occasion, it was Lincoln who had requested the sit-down. The war was faltering and Northern supporters were growing weary; Lincoln was in a fretful mood. According to Douglass, the president told him that he felt "that a peace might be forced upon him which would leave still in slavery all who had not come within our lines."[74] Douglass had been summoned to the White House, he wrote, because Lincoln wanted him to play a central role in distributing information about the Emancipation Proclamation to those who were still enslaved in the Confederate South. Fewer blacks than expected were escaping and crossing Union lines, thus undermining the military dimension of the Proclamation. Most critical for Douglass was his belief that Lincoln had grown since their first meeting, during which the president stated that his top priority was to save the Union with or without ending slavery. However, at their second meeting Douglass sensed "a deeper moral conviction against slavery than I had ever seen before in anything spoken or written by him."[75] He agreed to take on the president's assignment.

Douglass describes what happened at the White House inauguration affair with an almost embarrassing giddiness. As he tells it, he literally crashed through two police officers who, according to Keckly, were under orders to admit no blacks to the event. However, Douglass later discovered that Keckly was mistaken, and no such order had been given.[76] Once inside the White House, he encountered another layer of security preventing him from going farther. While blocked, he protested that the president would want him at the event and implored someone to tell Lincoln that "Fred Douglas is at the door."

In less than a minute word was sent back to let him in. In Douglass's words:

> I could not have been more than ten feet from him when Mr. Lincoln saw me; his countenance lighted up, and he said in a voice which was heard all around; "Here comes my friend Douglass." As I approached him he reached out his hand, gave me a cordial shake, and said: "Douglass, I saw you in the crowd today listening to my inaugural address. There is no man's opinion that I value more than yours; what do you think of it?" I said: "Mr. Lincoln, I cannot stop here to talk with you, as there are thousands waiting to shake you by the hand"; but he said again: "What did you think of it?" I said: "Mr. Lincoln, it was a sacred effort," and then I walked off. "I am glad you liked it," he said.[77]

This was the last time the two men would meet face to face.

According to historian Bennett, Douglass became more mellow in his old age and bought into the post-assassination mythology built up around Lincoln, but he remained overwhelmingly critical of Lincoln and in fact viewed him as a racist.[78] Unable to deny the existence of favorable quotes by Douglass regarding Lincoln, Bennett wants to have it both ways, characterizing the positive quotes as isolated and decontextualized. Bennett's speculations notwithstanding, Douglass seemed entirely genuine when he praised Lincoln as having "conducted the affairs of the nation with singular wisdom, and with absolute fidelity to the great trust confided in him" and considered his assassination a "terrible calamity."[79] It is more likely that Douglass understood Lincoln's limits both as president of the

United States and as a white man constrained by the dominant sensibility of his times, but knew that the steps he took nevertheless led to black liberation from slavery. Douglass best sums up his own complex reading of Lincoln:

> Our faith in him was often taxed and strained to the uttermost, but it never failed . . . when he strangely told us that we were the cause of the war; when he still more strangely told us that we were to leave the land in which we were born; when he refused to employ our arms in defence of the Union; when, after accepting our services as colored soldiers, he refused to retaliate our murder and torture as colored prisoners; when he told us he would save the Union if he could with slavery . . . when we saw all this, and more, we were at times grieved, stunned, and greatly bewildered; but our hearts believed while they ached and bled.[80]

In addition to conferring with Douglass, President Lincoln also met with Sojourner Truth. Born into slavery in Swartekill, New York, in 1797, Isabella Baumfree became one of the nation's foremost advocates for both abolition and women's suffrage. Although an 1827 New York law freed her and all the state's enslaved black people, she had already escaped to another part of the state and was living independently with one of her children. A deeply religious individual, she adopted the name Sojourner Truth in 1843, believing it was sent to her through divine intervention. In an inspired and powerful talk delivered in 1851 at the Women's Convention in Akron, Ohio, known popularly as her "Ain't I a Woman" speech, she linked the struggles for black liberation and women's liberation, an ideological and political leap few took at the time. She stated:

> Well, children, where there is so much racket there must be something out of kilter. I think that 'twixt the negroes of the South and the women at the North, all talking about rights, the white men will be in a fix pretty soon. But what's all this here talking about?
>
> That man over there says that women need to be helped into carriages, and lifted over ditches, and to have the best place everywhere. Nobody ever helps me into carriages, or over mud-puddles, or gives me any best place! And ain't I a woman? Look at me! Look at my arm! I have ploughed and planted, and gathered into barns, and no man could head me! And ain't I a woman? I could work as much and eat as much as a man—when I could get it—and bear the lash as well! And ain't I a woman? I have borne thirteen children, and seen most all sold off to slavery, and when I cried out with my mother's grief, none but Jesus heard me! And ain't I a woman?[81]

By late 1864, Truth had become a great admirer of Lincoln, and that year she traveled from her home in Battle Creek, Michigan, to Washington, D.C. to gain an audience with him. She discovered that she would need someone to arrange the meeting and went to antislavery activist Lucy Colman, who turned to Elizabeth Keckly. Given her fortuitous position relative to the Lincolns, Keckly was able to set up the encounter, which took place in the early morning on October 29, 1864, at the White House. The meeting was thin in substance and more a courtesy call than a substantive discussion about the miserable condition and political future of the country's millions of black people. Nevertheless, Truth writes fondly of the occasion, stating "I must say, and I am proud to say, that I never was treated by

Sojourner Truth and Abraham Lincoln at the White House, October 29, 1864.

any one with more kindness and cordiality than were shown to me by that great and good man, Abraham Lincoln, by the grace of God president of the United States for four years more."[82] She noted that there were "colored persons" among those who were visiting Lincoln, including one black woman who needed help paying her rent.[83] In expressing their mutual admiration for each other she told him that although she had never heard of him prior to his becoming the nation's commander in chief, she considered him "the best president who has ever taken the seat," and he "smilingly replied, 'I had heard of you many times before that.' "[84]

Toward the end of their discussion, he showed her a Bible that had been presented to him as a gift by a group of black people from Baltimore. That moment was captured in a very famous picture of Lincoln and Truth together.

As they ended their time together, Lincoln signed a book

that she had brought with her, writing, "For Aunty Sojourner Truth." For researcher Bennett, Lincoln's calling Truth "Aunty" bolsters his assertion that Lincoln was not only policy-deaf when it came to black interests but harbored personal racist views as well.[85] For Bennett, it does not matter if Lincoln meant it as a term of endearment, which was likely the case. For her part, Truth never complained about the term.

Lincoln and Truth may have also met on other occasions. Lincoln made reference to other times that he had seen her, and it reportedly disturbed him when he discovered that on February 25, 1865, she had gone to the White House but had not been permitted to meet with him. [86] Like Keckly, Truth was interested in the welfare of black refugees from the war who were subsisting in the streets, alleys, and camps of Washington, D.C. On at least one of her trips to Washington, D.C., she sought to address the segregationist policies in the city even after slavery was abolished. She was also active in gathering food and clothing for black soldiers and civilians.

Although she never met with Lincoln personally, Underground Railroad conductor Harriet Tubman also sought to influence the White House. Born into slavery in 1822, she escaped while in her twenties and led approximately twelve successful raids to free enslaved blacks. During the Civil War, she served the Union army as a spy, a nurse, and the commander of a military raid—the first woman to take such a role—in which she and her troops sailed up the Combahee River, destroyed Confederate outposts, and liberated more than 700 black people.[87] Tubman's views on what Lincoln should do to win the war are quoted in an 1862 letter written by white abolitionist Lydia Maria Child. The letter quotes Tubman, who refers to Lincoln as "Master," saying:

Earliest known photo of Harriet Tubman, taken when she was already established as the Moses of her people.[88]

> I'm a poor Negro but this Negro can tell Master Lincoln how to save money and young men. He can do it by setting the Negroes free. Suppose there was an awful big snake down there on the floor. He bites you. Folks all scared, because you may die. You send for doctor to cut the bite; but the snake is rolled up there, and while the doctor is doing it, he bites you again. The doctor cuts out that bite; but while he's doing it, the snake springs up and bites you again, and so he keeps doing it, till you kill him. That's what Master Lincoln ought to know.[89]

Reflecting the views of blacks, free and enslaved, Tubman implored Lincoln to kill slavery once and for all.[90]

Famous, little-known, and unknown African Americans all trekked to the White House to lobby Lincoln during his four-plus years in office. The issues on the table were substantial and often of national importance. Free blacks such as Keckly, and movement leaders such as Douglass and Truth, pioneered African American political access to the White House, and boundaries were redefined as new degrees of inclusion evolved. These encounters, developing in the context of profound national crisis, increased pressure on the reluctant president to see abolition as the only viable resolution. The cumulative impact of the chaos of war, massive escapes from slavery, agitation by abolitionists and free blacks, relentless pressure by Republican radicals, and, yes, the Emancipation Proclamation, all prepared the way for the formal end of slavery and a reconstruction of race relations in the United States. Lincoln walked an uneven, indirect, but successful path toward that end. He may have started his administration as an openly bigoted, colonization-promoting, politically averse, soft antislavery politician, but he evolved, reaching places that no U.S. president before him had dared go, and, it should not be forgotten, it cost him his life. Lincoln, in the end, evolved beyond the limits of his own political experiences and beyond the limits of the dominant political climate of his time.

Ultimately, abolition happened both in spite of and because of Abraham Lincoln. The cautious, hesitant, and vacillating Lincoln finally succumbed to the era-changing, slavery-despising, liberal policy–initiating Lincoln. He challenged the doctrine of states' rights, the political safety valve for the South in insulating slavery from federal intrusion. He initiated political relations with African Americans that had not existed previously. His meetings to discuss (or preach) policy implied a notion of respect for the political intelligence and strategic thinking of (some) black Americans, a posture no previous president had come near. In the end, it was the grand crisis of the Civil War that opened up the possibility of abolishing slavery once and for all, and Lincoln found himself in the position for it to occur on his watch.

Reconstruction, Rise and Fall

Lincoln did not live to see what some have argued was the most racially democratic epoch in U.S. history prior to the civil rights victories of the 1960s and 1970s: the period known as Reconstruction.[91] In that era, constitutional amendments, congressional legislation, and presidential orders sought to give vigor to the policies needed to help the millions of newly freed black men, women, and families integrate successfully into U.S. society. The Freedmen's Bureau—officially titled the Bureau of Refugees, Freedmen, and Abandoned Land—was established by Congress in March 1865 as the main agency charged with addressing the educational, economic, medical, and other needs of Southern blacks. Offices were set up in Alabama, Arkansas, Florida, Georgia, Louisiana, Mississippi, North Carolina, South Carolina, Tennessee, Texas, and Virginia in addition to the Washington, D.C. office.[92] While the Freedmen's Bureau did not distribute land confiscated from the Confederates to the newly freed, an earlier order did. On January 16, 1865, Major General William Tecumseh Sherman issued "Special Order 15," which granted forty acres of arable land apiece to families on the coast of Georgia and the Sea Islands nearby. The families were also given some of the surplus mules that the army held.[93] Access to land would be a key element in the survival and independence of African Americans after the war.

The radical Republicans who held sway in Congress immediately after the war were also able to push through the Thirteenth Amendment (December 6, 1865), which ended slavery; the Fourteenth Amendment (July 9, 1868), which gave the newly emancipated citizenship; and the Fifteenth Amendment (February 3, 1870), which granted voting rights to black men. Congress also passed civil rights acts in 1866 and 1875. The 1866 Civil Rights Act outlawed discrimination in housing, allowed for blacks to make and enforce contracts, legalized black ownership of property, and made it legal for blacks to give testimony in court. These policies and others were essential to initiate repair of the damage that centuries of white-perpetrated enslavement and human trafficking of blacks had wrought.

Actually, the program was carried out in two phases, known as Presidential Reconstruction (1865–1867) and Radical Reconstruction (1867–1877). In the first phase, the White House was seen as the principal driving force in developing, implementing, and enforcing policies that would benefit African Americans. While Lincoln may have demonstrated uncertainty and equivocation, his successor was clear where he stood: on the side of the Southern Confederates. In building what historian Doris Kearns Goodwin called his "team of rivals," in 1864 Lincoln had chosen Tennessee Democrat Andrew Johnson as his vice president.[94] White House doors that were opened to blacks by Lincoln were slammed shut by Johnson. As Frederick Douglass observed, "Whatever Andrew Johnson may be, he certainly is no friend of our race."[95] Johnson, a slaveholder prior to becoming president, acted immediately to restore and perpetuate white racial domination in the South. His personal views on race were hateful; he famously stated in Congress in 1844 that if blacks were given the right to vote it would "place every splay-footed, bandy-shanked, hump-backed, thick-lipped, flat-nosed, woolly-headed, ebon-colored Negro in the country upon an equality with the poor white man."[96]

The seventeenth president of the United States was openly racist, and his list of anti-black actions is long: Johnson failed to intervene when black voters and activists came under attack from white terrorist groups; advocated and gave pardons to unrepentant Confederates; ousted black employees from the Freedmen's Bureau; rescinded Maj. Gen. Sherman's order to give land to blacks; vetoed (re)funding of the Freedmen's Bureau; and vetoed the Civil Rights Act of 1866.

President Johnson did have meetings with black leaders. On February 7, 1866, he held an antagonistic talk with Frederick Douglass and leaders of the Convention of Colored Men. In August 1865, the Convention published a piece in the *New York Times* criticizing Johnson's policies and stating that the president "in his efforts at the reconstruction of the civil government of the States, late in rebellion, left us entirely at the mercy of these subjugated but unconverted rebels, in everything save the privilege of bringing us, our wives and little ones, to the auction block."[97] The meeting was meant to discuss the role of the administration in protecting black voting rights, a subject the president largely dismissed. That gathering and other meetings of African Americans with Johnson were unproductive if not disastrous. After his conversation with Frederick Douglass, Johnson seethed, "Those damned sons of bitches thought they had me in a trap. I know that damned Douglass; he's just like any nigger and he would sooner cut a white man's throat than not."[98]

In response to the racism of the White House, during the second phase of Reconstruction the radicals took over and went to war with President Johnson. On March 2, 1867, Congress overrode Johnson's veto of the Civil Rights Act, and in February 1868, it attempted to try to remove him from office. Offended that he had fired Lincoln's secretary of war, radical Republican Edwin Stanton, in explicit violation of the Tenure of Office Act passed the year before, the House of Representatives voted overwhelmingly, 126 to 47, to impeach Johnson. However, even though a majority of Senators, 35 to 19, voted against the president, under the Constitution it took a two-thirds vote of the Senate to remove him from office. The Senate fell short by one vote. Nevertheless, Johnson was politically weakened for the remainder of his tenure.

Given the radicals in Congress and the hostile political climate toward Johnson, one might have assumed that the Reconstruction agenda would continue. However, within a very short period, not only the White House but Congress would back away from the progressive policies that arose during Reconstruction, and a long period of neglect, compromise, retreat, and outright hostility toward the black community would set in.

CHAPTER 6

James Crow's White House

Prelude: Booker T. Washington's White House Story

> *A century ago, President Theodore Roosevelt's invitation of Booker T. Washington to dine at the White House was taken as an outrage in many quarters.*[1]—John McCain, concession speech, November 4, 2008

> *Parker knocked the assassin down,*
> *And to beat him, he began it;*
> *In order to save the President's life,*
> *Yes, the Negro truly was in it.*—Lena Doolin Mason poem honoring James Benjamin Parker[2]

The year 1901 was a pivotal and traumatic one for the White House. On September 6, Leon Czolgosz, an unemployed factory worker and fervent anarchist from Detroit, stood in front of the twenty-fifth president of the United States at the Pan-American World Fair in Buffalo, New York, lined up with others ostensibly to greet the president. When his turn came, instead of shaking hands, Czolgosz fired two bullets at President William McKinley. One bullet knocked a button off McKinley's jacket, hitting his right breastbone but not penetrating further. The second shot pierced the president's abdomen and struck his liver and pancreas.

Panic ensued. Leaping into action, James Benjamin Parker, a large man who was standing immediately behind him in line, hit Czolgosz hard in the face. Parker's move prevented the assassin from firing a third shot.[3] Czolgosz, who was of Polish heritage, was eventually subdued by Parker and the late-reacting Secret Service and other police assigned to protect McKinley. Reportedly, at least one Secret Service agent was distracted by focusing on Parker, an African American, ignoring Czolgosz and failing to detect the concealed gun he had just fired. Arguably, McKinley may have never been shot if Parker were not being racially profiled during the moment Czolgosz revealed his weapon.

In truth, by preventing Czolgosz from squeezing off a third shot, Parker might have saved McKinley's life. Although the president was seriously injured, competent medical attention should have prevented the wound from being fatal. However, the medical team that worked on McKinley made a number of critical errors and the president died eight days later as result. First, the medical team failed to use an X-ray machine that was available nearby, so they never located or removed the bullet that struck McKinley's stomach. Second, the doctor who performed the surgery to remove the bullet, Matthew Mann, was a gynecologist and an obstetrician who had never worked on a gunshot wound. Lastly, failure to drain the wound properly led to gangrene and infection that eventually killed McKinley. Initially, the president was recovering and expected to live, but he took a turn for the worse a few days later and passed on the morning of September 14, 1901.

James Benjamin Parker became a national hero in the black community overnight. Dozens of newspapers in both the black and white press ran stories about his daring intervention.[4] He was honored with awards, and pieces of the clothes that he wore when the incident happened were reportedly given or sold to strangers. Well over six feet tall, the forty-four-year-old Parker was an imposing figure. Known as "Big Jim," he hailed from Atlanta but was working as a waiter in Buffalo at the time of the assassination.[5]

In this period of American history, racial segregation and lynchings were increasing as white backlash against African Americans gained momentum. The Ku Klux Klan and other white terrorist groups were permitted to flourish. Only five years earlier, the U.S. Supreme Court had ruled in the landmark *Plessy v. Ferguson* case that racial segregation was legal, thereby codifying into national law the "black codes" of exclusion that arose in the South during Reconstruction. George Henry White, a Republican from North Carolina and the only black remaining in the U.S. Congress in 1901, was departing.

Parker's spontaneous but unsuccessful effort to protect the president was held up by many blacks to demonstrate the sacrifices that African Americans were willing to make as citizens even if the nation sought to treat them as second-class and unequal. Parker himself humbly stated, "But I do say that the life of the head of this country is worth more than that of an ordinary citizen and I should have caught the bullets in my body rather than the President should get them. . . . I am a Negro, and am glad that the Ethiopian race has whatever credit comes with what I did. If I did anything, the colored people should get the credit."[6] It is unknown how many other African Americans felt the same way about giving up their life for the president, but it was clear that, Parker's charitable words notwithstanding, black racial pride and American national identity were at that moment in an unhappy marriage.

In official history, however, Parker was excised from the trial and downplayed in the Secret Service account of the assassination. Embarrassed that they had been upstaged, the agency desperately sought to hide the fact that they had failed on the job. Parker was not called to testify in the court that convicted Czolgosz, nor was it even mentioned that he had played a central role in capturing the president's assassin. [7] Before the trial, Secret Service agent Samuel Ireland told the Associated Press, "That colored man was quicker than we. He nearly killed the man."[8] In his testimony at the trial, along with that of Secret Service Agent George Foster, he denied any role for Parker in the event. Foster, who like Ireland had earlier stated that Parker helped capture Czolgosz, said under oath, "I never saw no colored man in the whole fracas."[9] As the *Atlanta Constitution* editorialized, "White men claimed all the credit, and only the names of white men were remembered."[10] There is no record that McKinley was even told about James Benjamin Parker's deed before he perished.

One of the individuals who celebrated Parker's heroics was the then undisputed, though not unchallenged, leader of black America at the time, Booker T. Washington. He included Parker's feats in a number of speeches that he gave in the period immediately following the shooting. According to the *Atlanta Constitution*, at a mass meeting of 5,000 African Americans on September 12, six days after the shooting and two days before McKinley actually died, Washington delivered an address and denounced the murderous action of the "red handed anarchist" and celebrated the fact that a Southern black "had saved President McKinley from death."[11] Ever eager as he was to present African Americans as willing—and sacrificial—patriots, it made sense that he would herald an act that demonstrated that black people were perhaps even more American than most whites. Others may have raised the impolitic question of how many whites were willing to risk taking a bullet for a black leader such as, say, Washington, but he never broached the topic. He would discover rather quickly how much—or how little—impact Parker's risking his life to save the president of the United States would have on the racial consciousness of the nation. Within five weeks of McKinley's murder, Booker T. Washington would be at the center of another racial drama involving the presidency and the White House.

Since his infamous 1895 speech at the Cotton States and International Exposition in Atlanta—which W. E. B. Du Bois dubbed the "Atlanta Compromise"—Booker T. Washington had emerged as the black leader of choice for many whites in America, and for many blacks in America as well. In that speech, part of which was eerily prescient regarding James Benjamin Parker's actions, he stated:

> As we have proved our loyalty to you in the past, in nursing your children, watching by the sick-bed of your mothers and fathers, and often following them with tear-dimmed eyes to their graves, so in the future, in our humble way, we shall stand by you with a devotion that no foreigner can approach, ready to lay down our lives, if need be, in defense of yours, interlacing our industrial, commercial, civil, and religious life with yours in a way that shall make the interests of both races one. In all things that are purely social we can be as separate as the fingers, yet one as the hand in all things essential to mutual progress.[12]

After reassuring his white audience that he fully supported segregation, he went on to critique those African American leaders who did not, or who wanted to rush equality before blacks were ready for it. He elaborated:

> The wisest among my race understand that the agitation of questions of social equality is the extremist folly, and that progress in the enjoyment of all the privileges that will come to us must be the result of severe and constant struggle rather than of artificial forcing. No race that has anything to contribute to the markets of the world is long in any degree ostracized. It is important and right that all privileges of the law be ours, but it is vastly more important that we be prepared for the exercise of these privileges. The opportunity to earn a dollar in a factory just now is worth infinitely more than the opportunity to spend a dollar in an opera-house.[13]

For conservative white political leaders both North and South, and a great deal of the white public, these were the welcome words of accommodation that echoed popular white supremacist sentiments and probably created a few tear-dimmed eyes themselves. By taking this route, Booker T. Washington became both the spokesperson for much of black America and a counsel to presidents, governors, local political officials, business leaders, academics, and other white power brokers. Virtually every major government program or business initiative involving African Americans would go through the Booker T. Washington patronage machine. Few African American leaders have held as much sway over community politics as he did in the twenty years after he delivered that speech. However, there were radical voices in the black community who quickly and strongly opposed its content. Booker T. Washington was harshly criticized by contemporary black leaders such as scholar and activist W. E. B. Du Bois and agitator and journalist William Monroe Trotter. In a lacerating denunciation of Washington in

Booker T. Washington, circa 1895.

his classic book *Souls of Black Folks*, Du Bois called Booker T.'s speech "a complete surrender of the demand for civil and political equality" and argued that he represented "the old attitude of adjustment and submission."[14]

It is thus ironic that it would be Booker T. Washington's visit to the White House that would offend white society and trigger a racist backlash that shut down black access to the White House for decades to follow. McKinley's assassination unexpectedly catapulted his vice president of less than one year into the nation's highest office. Within hours of McKinley's tragic death in September 1901, Theodore Roosevelt was sworn in as twenty-sixth president of the United States, and by the end of the month he was living in the White House.

On October 16, 1901, one month after McKinley's assassination, Roosevelt discovered that Booker T. Washington was going to be in town and invited him and Philip B. Stewart of Colorado to the White House for what was usually called "family supper."[15] Naively, neither Roosevelt nor Washington foresaw any potential issue with the invite. When Roosevelt was governor of New York he had regularly had African Americans over for supper and even occasionally invited them to spend the night.[16] Roosevelt had high regard for Booker T. Washington and patronizingly referred to him as "the most useful, as well as the most distinguished, member of his race in the world."[17]

None of these gestures, however, should be interpreted to mean that President Roosevelt was either progressive or proactive on the issue of racial equality. In fact, he was a quite blatant racist in both word and deed. It was Roosevelt who set the Republican Party on the path to seizing the white South's anti-black vote, which over time evolved into the racially narrow political base that the party represents in contemporary U.S. politics. Roosevelt demeaned blacks in his writings and speeches. Prior to becoming president, he wrote that blacks were the "most utterly under-developed" of the races; that they were "suffering from laziness and shiftlessness"; and that "a perfectly stupid race can never rise to a very high plane; the Negro, for instance, has been kept down as much by lack of intellectual development as by anything else."[18]

Becoming president and commander in chief of the United States did not change his views. Seeking what he thought was perhaps a middle ground between rights and racism, he stated at a Lincoln Day dinner in 1905 that "Civil law can not regulate social practices. Society, as such, is a law unto itself, and will always regulate its own practices and habits. Full recognition of the fundamental fact that all men should stand on an equal footing, as regards civil privileges, in no way interferes with recognition of the further fact that all reflecting men of both races are united in feeling that race purity must be maintained."[19]

Indeed, Roosevelt's firm belief in the superiority of the white race over all others likely fed his delusion that his paternalistic relationship with Booker T. Washington reflected a moral capacity that blacks did not and could not have. His softer form of racism may also have been driven by reciprocating political interests as well. While Roosevelt could claim that he provided black access to the White House (via Booker T. Washington), Washington received patronage positions (via Roosevelt) that he doled out to supporters as a power broker, accruing enough authority to create problems for his black rivals and enemies.

Thus, on the eve of the infamous White House family supper, neither Roosevelt nor Washington was prepared for the level of racist outrage that their dining together would unleash. While the event was certainly not a state dinner—the highest social occasion to which a guest may be formally invited to the White House—it may have been even more egregious to white supremacists, because it lacked the cover of political necessity or obligation. Dining with a black man was a personal choice of the president. In an indication of White House political obtuseness, the next day White House Secretary George Bruce Cortelyou issued a routine press release headlined "Booker T. Washington, of Tuskegee, Alabama, dined with the President last evening."[20] The political and social reaction was immediate, thunderous, and explosive.

Southern newspapers and political leaders unequivocally condemned both President Roosevelt and Booker T. Washington for violating racial boundaries that had been established not only by previous presidents but by the entire edifice of white social propriety. While during the latter half of the nineteenth century the White House had opened its doors to black political leaders such as Frederick Douglass, Sojourner Truth, and others, it was unheard-of that a black person of any standing would be granted the honor of a White House dinner (or any meal), perhaps the most powerful gesture of social equality that could be imagined. That grand gastronomical opportunity clearly had a "whites-only" label on it.

Southern memory was short. In 1798, during the administration of John Adams, Haitian President Toussaint Louverture had sent his representative, Joseph Bunel, to meet with the U.S. president to discuss a trade-related issue. One of the leaders of the 1791 Haitian revolution, Louverture wanted to win support from the United States as the new nation faced French and British threats. He offered to protect U.S. ships that came into the area on trading missions. Adams sought greater influence in the region and agreed to meet Louverture's representative. Bunel, who was mulatto, and his wife, who was black, had dinner with Adams, "the first-ever breaking of bread between an American president and a man [and woman] of color." Southerners and even some Northerners were livid. The Bunels also dined with Adams's secretary of state, Timothy Pickering.[21]

President Roosevelt had clearly misread the praise lavished on Booker T. Washington by whites to mean that he might be an exception to the prevailing social etiquette of white domination.

The viciousness of the attacks and calls for retribution against Roosevelt were unrelenting and offer a hideous portrait of the extent of white animus toward black people. Mississippi Senator James K. Vardaman said that after the dinner, the White House was "so saturated with the odor of the nigger that the rats have taken refuge in the stable."[22] The *Memphis Scimitar* called the dinner "the most damnable outrage which has ever been perpetrated by any citizen of the United States."[23] Former presidential candidate William Jennings Bryan wrote, "It is to be hoped that both of them will upon reflection realize the wisdom of abandoning their purpose to wipe out race lines, if they entertain such a purpose."[24]

The reaction in the black community was a bit different. Perhaps most blacks, if they thought about it at all, viewed the occasion as a mild though irrelevant honor, especially given that the White House was doing nothing to address the rampant acts of terrorism being perpetrated against black communities. There were some who celebrated the event—though not necessarily Booker T. Washington himself—such as activist and black emigration organizer Bishop Henry Turner, who stated paradoxically, "You are about to be the great representative and hero of the Negro race, not withstanding you have been very conservative. I thank you, thank you, thank you."[25] Turner's overdrawn ebullience contrasted with the responses of other black leaders. The radical and longtime Booker T. opponent William Monroe Trotter rebuked the wizard of Tuskegee and called him a hypocrite for supporting social segregation between the races and then going to sup at the White House.[26] For Trotter and other black radicals, Booker T. Washington got his just deserts.

Washington himself appeared both perplexed and traumatized by the controversy. Only a few days after the White House dinner, he dined with Roosevelt once again, this time at Yale University after he and the president both received honorary degrees, an event that sparked no criticism. But he seemed not to understand that dining at the White House was a different issue altogether. Accustomed only to accolades and praise from whites, he was dumbfounded to find himself the target of racial hatred. His role as mediator of all things black was suddenly in jeopardy.

Back at the White House, the president and his staff went into urgent damage-control mode. The White House first sought to deny that the event had taken place at all, contradicting its own press release that had reported the exact opposite. Further confusing matters, some White House staffers spread rumors that there had been a luncheon rather than a dinner, though it seems the difference would matter little to hard-core white supremacists. The press was also told that the Roosevelt women, the president's wife and daughters, absolutely had not been part of a dinner with a black man—failing to mention that Washington had just sat next to Roosevelt's daughter Alice as they all dined together at the Yale supper.

Though Booker T. was not invited back to the White House, Roosevelt continued to work and consult with him, but more often behind closed doors or through intermediaries. And despite the public backlash from the supper scandal, Roosevelt would still call upon Washington to edit parts of his speeches that addressed racial concerns and later accepted an invitation to serve as a trustee at Washington's Tuskegee Institute.[27]

Although the controversy eventually died down, its impact shaped White House politics for decades. No black person would be invited to dinner at the White House again for nearly thirty years. Ironically, that would occur during the presidency of Theodore Roosevelt's distant relative, Franklin D. Roosevelt. The whites-only eating policy remained unbreached until 1929. Early that year, Herbert Hoover's wife, Lou, faced a dilemma involving the holding of her traditional tea at the White House for the wives of congressional members. She had to decide whether to invite Jessie Williams De Priest, the wife of Rep. Oscar De Priest, who had become the first African American elected to Congress in the twentieth century with his 1928 victory in Illinois. With the Booker T. Washington–Theodore Roosevelt dinner still echoing, to invite her to sit down with white Southern women would have undoubtedly infuriated white Southern leaders and voters. But not to invite her would insult not only the De Priests but the black community as a whole, as well as many whites outside of the South. A tactically brilliant though racially cautious solution was found. Lou decided to have four sets of teas, the last of which, on June 19, 1929, would include Jessie De Priest and congressional wives whom she had consulted who did not object to having tea with an African American. She was still sharply criticized for that gesture, some Southern legislatures passing resolutions "condemning certain social policies of the administration in entertaining Negroes in the White House on a parity with white ladies."[28]

The Washington-Roosevelt incident signaled the full and complete lockout of millions of blacks from the nation's official political channels. If the president of the United States could be attacked for merely having supper with an accommodating black leader and then be seen to distance himself from that leader publicly, clearly other strategies were necessary to move issues of racial justice forward. Soon, thanks to Du Bois and other progressive blacks, the Niagara Movement would evolve into the National Association for the Advancement of Colored People. Some African Americans would embrace socialism, and the Garvey movement would emerge as well. The real legacy of the Booker T. Washington dinner has been that it catalyzed a new and more radical path for the black movement for freedom.

One final mockery redounded from the affair. On October 17, 1901, the day after the Washington dinner fiasco, Roosevelt issued an order officially naming the president's residence "the White House."[29]

Jim Crow in the White House (and Congress)

> *Any black man who votes for the present Republican Party out of gratitude . . . is born a fool. Equally no*

> *Negro Democrat can for a moment forget that his party depends primarily on the lynching, mobbing, disfranchising South. Toward any Third Party advocates the intelligent Negro must be receptive. . . .*[30]— W. E. B. Du Bois

The White House dinner controversy, however dramatic, should not have been unexpected. It occurred in the period following Reconstruction, when white Americans broadly and often forcefully suppressed the rights of Americans of color. The White House was not immune to the social, cultural, and political dictates of the period, and the growth of segregation went hand in hand with the political aspirations, agendas, and strategies of each of the White House occupants from Andrew Johnson to Dwight Eisenhower, with a few notable exceptions along the way. While a number of presidents expressed personal feelings of opposition to Jim Crow and the oppression of blacks, none used the power of the office to substantially confront Southern segregation and advance black rights. Indeed, many of the presidents during this period did all they could to perpetuate the racial power structure that kept whites at the top and everyone else on the bottom. For decades, the White House felt whiter than ever to most African Americans, Asian Americans, Latinos, Native Americans, and other racially marginalized groups.

Racial politics at the White House, however, were more complicated than at the regional or state level. Unlike local and state seats of government, the White House had to project its leadership over the entire nation, which included not only a growing and organized black electorate but also progressives and radicals who were brown, red, white, and yellow and who were increasingly organizing for racial justice and equality. In addition, as the United States's role in the global arena grew, particularly after World War I, foreign policy considerations had to be taken into account. Racial issues had manifested in the struggle to create the League of Nations and were critical to the objectives and themes of the United Nations. The Cold War would be particularly challenging to the segregationists and those who accommodated them, as the Soviets and newly independent African and Caribbean nations would point to the audacious racial hypocrisy of the South to undermine the U.S. claim to be the world's leading democracy.

The official naming of the president's home "the White House" in 1901 coincided with the domestic and global perception of the residence as a symbol of a racially constructed nation in deep conflict with both its founding call and frequent international exhortations for freedom and democracy.

The era began with the murder of Reconstruction. Critically ill and on its deathbed for years, it received its death blow with the Hayes-Tilden Compromise of 1876, which determined who would control the White House after that year's presidential election. As soon as Southern white leaders were able to return to power they began to institute "black codes" that segregated blacks and whites. These legalisms were enforced with coercive brutality inflicted on black communities by terrorist organizations like the Ku Klux Klan, Red Shirts, White League, Southern Cross, Knights of the White Camellia, and other groups driven by notions of white supremacy and hatred for people of color. However Lincoln may have equivocated in addressing the needs of African Americans, his successors in the White House demonstrated scarcely any courage in challenging the multiple levels of institutional racism that had run rampant in the nation from the day it was founded. Following Andrew Johnson, who openly fought to advance mechanisms of white domination to

Black woman working in the White House kitchen, circa 1892.

pre–Civil War levels, and down the line, the White House illustrated racial regression rather than racial progress.

With African Americans freed from slavery but denied equality, black agitation and resistance grew in response to pervasive hostility, exclusion and abuse from white society. Black organizations such as the National Convention of Colored Men and the National Association for the Advancement of Colored People (NAACP) built countrywide networks of activists who along with thousands of local groups organized and mobilized to overthrow systems of segregation. A central focus of the black community was the call for federal intervention to end lynching, a call that repeatedly fell on deaf ears. The movement for racial equality was also strengthened, for a time, by the presence of African Americans in the U.S. Congress. Nearly two dozen blacks served in Congress from the end of the Civil War to the turn of the twentieth century.

Black workers continued to staff the White House as

butlers, maids, and cooks and in other noninfluential service capacities. Like Paul Jennings and Elizabeth Keckly, some of these individuals went on to tell their stories in memoirs and other literature. While most of their writing was nonpolitical, it was not necessarily nonpartisan. Generations of butlers and maids were passing on their experiences and insights, providing voices of authenticity and alternative points of view on the history of their era. By the end of the segregation era, the White House would also have its first African American in an executive staff position.

Black musical presence at the White House also became more frequent and more diverse. For most black artists—from opera performers to classical musicians and gospel singers—the White House created opportunities to perform before dignitaries, world leaders, and others that did not exist outside of its doors. For some blacks, the only venue that gave them a chance to perform before prestigious audiences was the White House.

But these "advances" were nothing compared to the nightmare most black families experienced during the era. Overall, it was a time characterized by white disenfranchisement of black people, the introduction and enforcement of black codes and segregation, and terrorism from mob violence, lynching, organized groups, and corrupt law enforcement. President after president of the United States mostly ignored these developments and their impact on black families and communities. While the White House itself sometimes became the only site of non-discrimination in the city of Washington, in the main, it reflected all of the racial tensions, contradictions, and struggles of the segregationist period.

The Pre-Plessy Presidents

Andrew Johnson began a long line of U.S. presidents whose

tenure in the White House reinforced rather than combated the re-imposition of near slave-like conditions on African Americans in the South. Black sharecropping, for example, in which black laborers were given a share of the crop they produced on white-owned land in lieu of wages, generally kept them in perpetual debt and unable to advance economically. Black families were forced to continue to work without pay for generations.[31] Even worse conditions were not uncommon, from convict leasing to outright abduction and enslavement. Douglas A. Blackmon's book *Slavery By Another Name, The Re-Enslavement of Black Americans from the Civil War to World War II* documents these cases and demonstrates how whites were able to re-enslave blacks well into the twentieth century.

> On July 31, 1903, a letter to President Theodore Roosevelt arrived at the White House from Carrie Kinsey, a barely literate African American woman in Bainbridge, Georgia. Her fourteen-year-old brother, James Robinson, had been abducted a year earlier and sold to a plantation. Local police would take no interest. "Mr. Prassident," wrote Mrs. Kinsey, struggling to overcome the illiteracy of her world. "They wont let me have him. . . . He hase not don nothing for them to have him in chanes so I rite to you for your help." Like the vast majority of such pleas, her letter was slipped into a small rectangular folder at the Department of Justice and tagged with a reference number, in this case 12007.4 No further action was ever recorded. Her letter lies today in the National Archives.
>
> A world in which the seizure and sale of a black man—even a black child—was viewed as neither criminal nor extraordinary had reemerged.[32]

W. E. B. Du Bois notes that the sharecropping system and convict-leasing system were interrelated, and that both amounted to the re-enslavement of African Americans. He argues that they are "the direct children of slavery, and to all intents and purposes are slavery itself."[33] He goes to state, "The South believed in slave labor, and was thoroughly convinced that free Negroes would not work steadily or effectively. The whites were determined after the war, therefore, to restore slavery in everything but in name."[34] Du Bois's description of the conditions of convict-leasing is chilling:

> The innocent were made bad, the bad worse; women were outraged and children tainted; whipping and torture were in vogue, and the death rate from cruelty, exposure, and the overwork rose to large percentages. . . . The prisoners often had scarcely any clothing, they were fed on a scanty diet of corn bread and fat meat, and worked twelve or more hours a day. After work each must do his own cooking.[35]

The battle between a radical Congress and a conservative White House would not endure. Due to partisan political interests, presidential politics, lack of popular support, and perhaps exhaustion, by the time of the disputed 1876 election between Republican Rutherford B. Hayes and Democrat Samuel Tilden, black support in Congress had waned. Progressive, combative, and powerful legislators such as Thaddeus Stevens and Charles Sumner were gone or going.

Controversy over the black votes cast in Florida, South Carolina, and Louisiana sent the decision over the election to Congress. A bipartisan commission of fifteen representatives, senators, and Supreme Court members voted eight to seven to give the White House to Hayes, the infamous "Hayes-Tilden

Compromise," with the understanding that he would implement the Democrats' anti-black agenda. By then, to a great degree, it did not matter much who won the presidency: Tilden, who clearly wanted to stop all progressive legislation and policies that favored African Americans, or Hayes, who quickly demonstrated his willingness to cast aside blacks within weeks of gaining the office. Congress's refusal to provide troop funding, and Hayes's order in the spring of 1877 to pull out the last of the troops that had been sent to the South to protect the right to vote for African Americans, merely symbolized the ongoing retrenchment of Southern racist domination that the White Houses of Andrew Johnson and Ulysses Grant, who both supported the restoration of political rights to the Confederates, had allowed to develop.[36]

Despite pre-presidential histories of support for abolition and black civil and voting rights by some presidents, including Republicans James A. Garfield, Chester A. Arthur, and Benjamin H. Harrison, once in the White House, they showed virtually no courage in challenging the forces of white domination. Little was gained and much was lost during the administrations of Garfield, Arthur, Harrison, and Democrat Grover Cleveland. Garfield's 199 days in office, a term cut short by an assassin's bullets, accomplished nothing to advance the racial equality agenda. In his March 4, 1881, inauguration speech, Garfield spoke strong words of support for educational inclusion and black civil and political rights stating:

> The elevation of the negro [*sic*] race from slavery to the full rights of citizenship is the most important political change we have known since the adoption of the Constitution of 1787. . . . There was no middle ground for the negro race between slavery and equal

African American school children and teacher, studying leaves out of doors, circa 1899.

> citizenship. There can be no permanent disfranchised peasantry in the United States. Freedom can never yield its fullness of blessings so long as the law or its administration places the smallest obstacle in the pathway of any virtuous citizen. . . . The nation itself is responsible for the extension of the suffrage, and is under special obligations to aid in removing the illiteracy which it has added to the voting population. For the North and South alike there is but one remedy. All the constitutional power of the nation and of the States and all the volunteer forces of the people should be surrendered to meet this danger by the savory influence of universal education.[37]

Denial of education to blacks had been brutally enforced in the South during the era of slavery.

After the war, white views on black education did not change quickly. In his book *Black Reconstruction in America: 1660–1880*, W. E. B. Du Bois writes:

> It was soon after the war that a white member of Johnson's restored Louisiana legislature passed one of the schools set up by the Freedmen's Bureau in New Orleans. The grounds were filled with children. He stopped and looked intently, and then asked, "Is this a school?" "Yes," was the reply. "What, for niggers?" "Evidently." He threw up his hands. "Well, well," he said, " I have seen many an absurdity in my lifetime, *but this is the climax*."[38]

However, in his brief time at the White House, President Garfield defended states' rights and thus abdicated any responsibility to address the increasing acts of terrorism by whites against black communities. Garfield's commitment to an antiracist agenda was also suspect, given that he had once confided privately that he had "a strong feeling of repugnance when I think of the negro [*sic*] being made our political equal and I would be glad if they could be colonized, sent to heaven, or got rid of in any decent way."[39]

After Garfield had been sent to heaven or elsewhere by his assassin, he was replaced by Chester Arthur, who simply avoided the issue. Frederick Douglass states that when he learned that Arthur was going to be Garfield's vice president, he "felt the hand of death" upon himself.[40] President Garfield's command of the White House was mostly inconsequential relative to black interests. However, it was on his watch in 1883 that the Supreme Court made its appalling decision that the Civil Rights Act of 1875 (outlawing discrimination in public accommodations) was unconstitutional. Arthur meekly informed Congress that he would support remedial civil rights legislation to address the decision, but no such legislation was ever drafted or passed.[41] Congress did not pass another civil rights bill until 1957.

Frustrated with the Republicans' pace of reform and facing an economic crisis, the country elected the first Democrat to the White House since the period before Lincoln. Grover Cleveland (1885–1889, 1893–1897), who uniquely would lose his reelection and then win again in the next election, represented a transitional moment in the relationship between African Americans and the White House, and African Americans and the nation. In 1895, during Cleveland's second term in office, the fearless and determined warrior Frederick Douglas passed, and within months Booker T. Washington rose to power, propelled by his aforementioned "Atlanta Compromise" speech. Cleveland attended the Atlanta Cotton States and International Exposition and heard Washington's delivery. He met with Washington right after the speech and later sent him a letter stating, "Your words cannot fail to delight and encourage all who wish well for your race; and if our colored fellow-citizens do not from your utterances gather new hope and form new determination to gain every valuable advantage offered them by their citizenship, it will be strange indeed."[42]

The blame-the-victim philosophy of Cleveland (and Washington) mixed comfortably with the former's states' rights approach. As historian Rayford Logan points out, President Cleveland "undoubtedly believed . . . that the Southern question should be handled by Southerners."[43] His hands-off approach, of course, left the black community vulnerable to every nefarious strategy, evil scheme, and murderous plot to reassert white control. And, fittingly, it was during Cleveland's tenure that the Supreme Court ruled in *Plessy v. Ferguson* that segregation was

The first black senator and representatives—in the 41st and 42nd Congress of the United States.

legal under the spurious "separate but equal" premise, thereby giving Constitutional sanction for state-sponsored apartheid for the next six decades. The black community, however, would not concede the battle so easily.

One source of opposition came from inside the government. Following the Civil War, black leadership expanded beyond civil and political rights activists like Sojourner Truth and Frederick Douglass to elected and appointed officials, including those who were elected to Congress. From 1870 to 1901, twenty-two blacks, all Republicans, served in the U.S. Senate and U.S. House of Representatives.[44] Many of them were newly freed, but all were articulate and educated on the issues confronting the black community and the nation. Among the group were "seven lawyers, three ministers, one banker, one publisher, two school teachers, and three college presidents."[45] As advocates of black civil rights, benefits for black veterans, halting

Klan violence, advance of educational opportunities, and black land rights, they served as an oppositional voice to the conservative racial politics of the White House. Fittingly, the first black Senator in U.S. history, Mississippi's Hiram Rhodes was elected in 1870 to finish out the term of the former president of the Confederacy, Jefferson Davis.

Ultimately, however, black legislators were unable to have much collective impact on either Congress or the White House. Unlike the contemporary Congressional Black Caucus, they did not and could not form a strong bloc in Congress. After the 1870s, the number of black members in each Congress declined significantly and often boiled down to one or two members. Lacking seniority, they were not positioned to do anything more than challenge legislation, often alone. All were from the South and faced strong antagonism from whites—and at least five of the African Americans who were elected during the period were prevented from being seated. Many of them served only two years. The longest tenure, nine years, was served by Rep. Joseph Hayne Rainey (SC, 1870–1879); South Carolina elected the most with eight, followed by North Carolina (four), Alabama and Mississippi (three each), Florida (two), and Georgia and Virginia (one each).

Following the purge of black voters with disenfranchisement strategies such as "grandfather clauses" and literacy tests, and of elected officials through intimidation, election fraud, and violence, it would be over 100 years in most of these states before another African American would be elected. In 1901, Rep. George White was the lone African American congressmember, and in his final speech before the House of Representatives on January 29, he prophetically stated, "This, Mr. Chairman, is perhaps the negroes' [*sic*] temporary farewell to the American Congress, but let me say, Phoenix-like he will rise up someday and come again. These parting words are in behalf of an outraged, heartbroken, bruised and bleeding people, but God fearing people, faithful, industrious, loyal people . . . rising people full of potential."[46] By the time Rep. White departed, one issue had arisen that would shape black politics for at least the next half century: lynching.[47]

Racism Continues to Hang Around: Jim Crow Presidents and the Anti-Lynching Campaigns

Charles Lynch was a Virginian justice of the peace during the Revolutionary War. He was also a Quaker. During the war he punished those who were loyal to the British with imprisonment and worse, including acts of punishment outside the law. After the war, when some of those who had been mistreated by Lynch's rulings sought to bring suit, the Virginia legislature passed a special law exonerating and pardoning him for any excessive activities or lawbreaking he had committed.[48] Given his Quaker background and the heroic role of Quakers in helping escaped slaves and free blacks, it is ironic that the term employed for extrajudicial retribution meted out by mobs or hate groups was derived from his name.

Lynching African Americans and others became the ultimate act of racial domination by whites who were frightened by the social, political, and economic changes posed by an emancipated black population. Hangings, shootings, decapitations, drownings, and beatings were carried out against black men, women, and even children as violence became the key means for the reinstatement of white power. Victims were often publicly tortured, mutilated, and burned, their body parts taken as souvenirs by members of the crowd. The barbaric gatherings sometimes took on a festival atmosphere, occasionally announced in advance, and entire white families would often attend. Photos of the dead victims were made into postcards.[49]

Naturally, the black community demanded federal action against lynchings and the local and state officials who did nothing to intervene. From the end of Reconstruction to well into the twentieth century, white mobs murdered more than 4,700 blacks and other people. Virtually no perpetrators were held accountable, as in many cases local and state law enforcement officials watched or participated in the atrocities.

The movement against lynchings lasted for decades, and one of its most outspoken leaders was journalist and activist Ida B. Wells. Seventy-one years before Rosa Parks refused to give up her bus seat to a white individual and sparked the 1955 bus boycott that brought down segregation in transportation, Ida B. Wells launched and initially won a lawsuit against a Tennessee train company that forcefully removed her from a whites-only area on one of the company's trains. Her lower-court victory was reversed by the Tennessee Supreme Court. Already active in the struggle for equality, she joined the campaign against lynching after her friend Tom Moss and his two business partners, Will Stewart and Calvin McDowell, were killed in 1882 by a racist mob incensed by the success of their grocery business. Born two months before the signing of the Emancipation Proclamation, Wells became a fierce leader who constantly faced danger as she campaigned for justice. Wells worked with and sometimes fought against the famous black leaders of the period, including Frederick Douglass, W. E. B. Du Bois, Marcus Garvey, and Booker T. Washington. She was one of the cofounders of the Niagara Movement/National Association for the Advancement of Colored People (NAACP) but later fell out with Du Bois and the organization due to disagreements over strategy.

The gun-packing Wells chronicled the incidents of lynchings that occurred in the years and decades after the murder of Moss and his partners. She demonstrated, significantly, that the apologists who claimed that black men had provoked these attacks by raping or harming white women were wrong, and she exposed the lies behind those rationalizations. In 1893 Ida Wells, Frederick Douglass, educator Irvine Garland Penn, and lawyer and publisher (and Wells's future husband) Ferdinand L. Barnett published a blistering critique of U.S. race relations in response to the exclusion of African Americans from the World's Columbian Exposition in Chicago. They contended, correctly, that the deliberate exclusion of blacks—except for an exhibit featuring "Aunt Jemima" pancakes and other insulting displays—from the Exposition mirrored the status of blacks in the country. In her article in the pamphlet, Wells graphically and empirically documents the rise in lynchings from 1882 to the time of the Exposition. She demonstrates that the incidents grew in numbers and became more brutal and barbaric over time. She also notes that black women were among those killed, citing murders in Jackson, Tennessee; Rayville, Louisiana; and Hollendale, Mississippi.[50]

In 1898, Wells led a delegation from Chicago that met with President McKinley after the black postmaster of Lake City, South Carolina, was killed by a mob enraged by the prospect of an African American commanding such a high public rank. Postmaster Frazier B. Baker had been appointed by McKinley in Fall 1897 and was under attack from the moment he took office. On February 22, 1898, an armed mob of more than 100 white people burned down the local post office and attacked Baker's home. The mob shot into the house, killing Baker and his three-year-old daughter. The Baker family was only one of many to be assaulted by racist violence in that era.

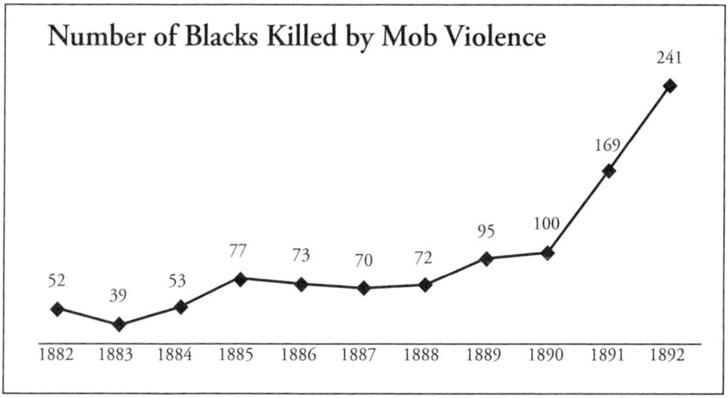

Wells had campaigned for McKinley in the 1896 election and had recently been elected chairperson of the Anti-Lynching Bureau of the National African Council. She felt an obligation to meet directly with the president to demand that a federal investigation be launched into the killing of the Bakers and others. President McKinley promised that he would do something, but once again there was no follow-up from the White House.[51]

McKinley also failed to intervene in or investigate two significant race riots that occurred during his presidency. On election day, November 8, 1898, in Phoenix, South Carolina, whites disgruntled about the prospect of black voters asserting their voting rights attacked African Americans and other whites who supported them. On that date and in several days to follow more than a dozen people were killed, homes were vandalized, and a number of African Americans were publicly whipped. On November 11, 1898, Robert "Red" Tolbert, a member of a prominent white South Carolina Republican clan whose family were leaders in promoting the black vote met with President McKinley in Washington, D.C. He asked for a federal investigation into the riot and for more protection for black voters in the South. Meanwhile, in Wilmington, North Carolina, on November 10, 1898, white Democrats violently took back the local government. They forced all Republican officeholders, including the mayor and the multi-racial city council, to resign from office and had Democrats in place by the end of the day. In the days that followed, dozens of African Americans were killed and many others forced to flee the area. An appeal was made to the McKinley administration to intervene. In both the Phoenix and Wilmington cases, McKinley failed to act, come to the defense of fellow black and white Republicans, or even allow federal investigations of the incidents.[52]

Lynchings would continue well into the twentieth century. According to the Society of American Historians, there were ninety-seven reported in 1908, eighty-three in 1919, thirty in 1926, and twenty-eight in 1933 involving the killing of mostly African Americans but also whites, Latinos, Jews, and others.[53] Like Wells, Du Bois recognized that these murders were not fundamentally caused by any criminality on the part of blacks. There was "one thing that the white South feared more than Negro dishonesty, ignorance, and incompetency," wrote Du Bois, "and that was Negro honesty, knowledge, and efficiency."[54]

Many organizations from the black community and beyond campaigned and mobilized against lynching for decades. Among the key groups involved were the NAACP, National Association of Colored Women (NACW), Council for Interracial Cooperation (CIC), and the Association of Southern Women for the Prevention of Lynching (ASWPL). These organizations relentlessly lobbied the White House and Congress to address the issue. While progressive and liberal members of Congress proposed legislation, from the White House came empty symbols, calculated silence, or condemnation of anti-lynching activists. In 1911, in Livermore, Kentucky, a black man was snatched from the local jail, taken to the opera house, and hanged from the ceiling. Town residents paid an admission to be allowed to shoot the body as it hung. Those in orchestra seats could shoot as many as six shots while those in the cheaper gallery seats only got one shot. The NAACP sent an emergency message to President William Howard Taft to urge Congress to respond to this and other lynching atrocities. Taft never answered.[55]

More than 200 anti-lynching bills were introduced in Congress, most never receiving a vote or serious debate. In January 1922, the House of Representatives passed the Dyer Anti-Lynching Bill, which would have made lynching and officials' failure to prevent it a federal crime, but it died in the U.S. Senate under the unyielding threat of a Southern filibuster. Supported by the NAACP, it was introduced in subsequent Congresses but never garnered sufficient support. In 1935, the Costigan-Wagner Anti-Lynching Bill also passed in the House but did not receive support from President Roosevelt, and it too was killed by the filibuster menace. If passed, the new law would have punished sheriffs who failed to protect their prisoners. In a final effort to establish legislation, the Wagner–Van Nuys Bill was passed by the House in 1938, but after a thirty-day filibuster by Southern Senators, it was tabled by a fifty-eight to twenty-two vote and was never revived. In essence, white lawmakers were granting immunity to white people to commit hate crimes, murder, and terrorism against black communities.

Plessy provided a convenient cover for presidents to either avoid direct confrontation with the South over systemic racial injustice perpetrated by whites, or even to give succor to Southern racism under the aegis of constitutional authority. While some U.S. presidents spoke in favor of anti-lynching legislation, not a single one made it a priority or decisively pushed for the passage of any of the bills that were offered. In line with their overall stance on Jim Crow, passing the issue on to the next White House became the preferred and implemented strategy.

In his 1903 State of the Union address, President Theodore Roosevelt addressed the issue of lynching, but instead of holding whites accountable, he blamed black men. "The greatest existing cause of lynching," said Roosevelt, "is the perpetration, especially by black men, of the hideous crime of rape—the most abominable in all the category of crimes, even worse than murder. Mobs frequently avenge the commission of this crime by themselves torturing to death the man committing it; thus avenging in bestial fashion a bestial deed, and reducing themselves to a level with the criminal."[56]

His successor, Taft, condemned lynching but only called for better law enforcement and, like Roosevelt, did not speak of the issue in the South.[57] President Taft backpedaled, however, when it came to making any kind of serious intervention, stating, "It is not the disposition or within the province of the Federal Government to interfere with the regulation by the Southern States of their domestic affairs."[58]

During World War I, Germany raised the issue of lynching to embarrass the United States, thus forcing the Wilson White House to release a statement of condemnation in response.[59] On October 26, 1921, the twenty-ninth President of the United States Warren G. Harding became the first sitting president to deliver a speech against lynching while in the deep South—Birmingham, Alabama.[60] He also weakly supported the Dyer Antilynching Bill, although he thought it was unconstitutional and did very little to promote its passage.[61]

During the election of 1912, W. E. B. Du Bois broke with the history of black support for the Republican nominee by

Still from the pro-KKK film, Birth of a Nation.

endorsing Democrat Woodrow Wilson, but along with other black leaders would eventually break with him over his lack of support for antidiscrimination policies. Wilson issued a statement supporting black voting rights, and it won him approximately 5 to 7 percent of the African American vote. Progressive on international affairs, Wilson's positions on human equality however, were hardly enlightened. He referred to blacks as an "ignorant and inferior race."

In a clear manifestation of that mentality, on February 18, 1915, Wilson screened the first film ever shown in the White House, the vehmently racist *Birth of a Nation*. The film was based on Thomas Dixon's *The Clansman,* a novel and play that portrays the "knights" of the Klu Klux Klan as heroes. Dixon was a former schoolmate of Wilson's and through his relationship with Wilson arranged for the screening at the White House.

Wilson is reported to have commented that the film was "like writing history with lightning. And my only regret is that it is all so terribly true," a statement Wilson later vehemently denied making. However, as *Birth of a Nation* researcher Melvyn Stokes points out, whether or not Wilson made the statement, the film undeniably reflected his sensibilities and even directly quoted his earlier writings praising the Ku Klux Klan.[62] It should also be noted that the bloody months of 1919, when whites attacked blacks in more than two dozen U.S. cities—what James Weldon Johnson called "Red Summer"—occurred on Wilson's watch.

His successor, William G. Harding, whose presidency was cut short when he died after a little more than two years in office, had earlier spoken out against lynching but as president railed against social equality between the races. Continuing the behavior of Wilson and Harding, Calvin Coolidge also refused to intervene and stop white atrocities against African American communities, citing the protection of states' rights in the Constitution.

As part of its anti-lynching campaign, the NAACP circulated an August 13, 1930, letter from thirty-first President of the United States Herbert Hoover in which he stated, "Every decent citizen must condemn the lynching evil as an undermining of the very essence of justice and democracy."[63] Hoover, however, was unwilling to do much else. His unresponsive attitude toward black interests drove blacks to switch to the Democratic Party. Considered one of the worst presidents in U.S. history, Hoover allowed the party's Southern white wing to enforce segregation.

During this period, one of the bitterest battles to be waged between the black community and the White House broke out over President Hoover's 1930 nomination of John Parker to the Supreme Court. During Parker's 1920 gubernatorial campaign he was reported to have said, "The participation of the Negro in politics is a source of evil and danger to both races."[64] The effort to stop Parker from reaching the Supreme Court became one of the signature struggles for the NAACP. It also represented a shift in the organization's tactics: for the first time the NAACP launched a campaign that sought to engage every branch of the federal government—an assertion of the very African Americans rights of citizenship that were being denied at the local and state levels. After intense lobbying and mobilization by the NAACP and the American Federation of Labor, which objected to his views on labor, Parker's nomination was rejected on May 21, 1930 in a forty-one to thirty-nine vote in the Senate.

The Franklin D. Roosevelt administration is often cited as the one bright light in the long dark history of White House collusion with the forces of white racism. And it is true that the Roosevelt White House, principally due to the activities of Eleanor Roosevelt, broke a number of political and social taboos on interracial socializing at the White House.

On the issue of lynching, little progress was made. Franklin Roosevelt initially refused to address the issue in an effort to keep the support of white Southerners. He told the NAACP, "I did not choose the tools with which I must work. Had I been permitted to choose then I would have selected quite different ones. But I've got to get legislation passed by Congress to save America. The Southerners by reason of the seniority rule in Congress are chairmen or occupy strategic places on most of the Senate and House committees. If I come out for the anti-lynching bill now, they will block every bill I ask Congress to pass to keep America from collapsing. I just can't take that risk."[65]

On December 6, 1933, President Roosevelt finally moved to speak against lynching—not in response to the ongoing mob killings of African Americans, however, but as a reaction to California Governor James Rolph's celebration of the lynching of two whites in San Jose. Roosevelt's comments marked the end of his anti-lynching efforts. He did not support legislation in Congress nor did he use his link to millions of Americans with his radio broadcasts to raise the issue.[66] During this dark period in our nation's history, black families lived in a lawless society in which the menace of white terror and mob violence went unaddressed by officials on every level of authority, from the local sheriff's office to the White House. In the South and beyond, hate crimes against blacks were being committed with impunity.

During the Roosevelt era, jazz singer Billie Holiday recorded "Strange Fruit," her haunting cry against lynching, and released the song on her own record label. Despite death threats, she sang the song in cities around the country. The song opens with the following lines:

Southern trees bear a strange fruit,
Blood on the leaves and blood at the root,
Black bodies swinging in the Southern breeze,
Strange fruit hanging from the poplar trees.

Beyond the lynching issue, the reputed progressive nature of the Roosevelt years are cited as a time of black political awakening when black voters abandoned the Republican Party for the Democratic Party. While President Roosevelt did not create any policy initiatives intended specifically to assist the black community, it is argued that blacks benefited from the overall policies that generated hundreds of thousands of jobs during the Great Depression and, for the first time, created a safety net for millions of Americans who were unemployed, veterans, or aged. Many profound changes occurred as a result of the multiple crises President Roosevelt faced during the Depression and World War II. Unfortunately, upon closer examination, documentation clearly shows that not only did President Roosevelt's most famous projects not benefit black people, but they created harmful precedents that still resonate in the black community today.

The most astute and searing critique of the impact of Roosevelt's policies on the black community is found in the research of political scientist Ira Katznelson. In his pivotal and legend-shattering book, *When Affirmative Action Was White: An Untold History of Racial Inequality in Twentieth-Century America*, he details the means by which legislators in the South ensured that Roosevelt and congressional Democrats instituted the new policies in a manner that privileged whites. Katznelson soberly writes, "The wide array of significant and far-reaching public policies that were shaped and administered during the New Deal and Fair Deal era of the 1930s and 1940s were crafted and administered in a deeply discriminatory manner."[67] The impact on black workers and black veterans was devastating.

Although they had fewer numbers than other regions, because of seniority and other mechanisms, Southern legislators dominated the power centers of the U.S. Congress.[68] They were determined that any legislation to address the nation's economic crisis would not touch the structure of racial control that existed in the South or benefit African Americans.

To achieve these objectives, Katznelson notes, three strategies were employed that were accepted by Roosevelt and congressional Democrats. First, the Southerners were able to exclude categories of work where most blacks were employed, such as farm workers and maids, "from the legislation that created modern unions, from laws that set minimum wages and regulated the hours of work, and from Social Security until the 1950s."[69] In the 1930s, approximately 85 percent of black women worked either in agriculture or in domestic household service. Earning from $2.00 to $5.00 for seventy-hour work-weeks, they were truly "the most exploited group of workers in the country."[70] Although Roosevelt's Committee on Economic Security strongly and clearly recommended that no categories of work be excluded from the proposed Social Security legislation, Congress wrote in the exclusions anyway, and in August 1935 Roosevelt signed the bill. At the time, 65 percent of blacks fell outside of the program nationally, and 70 to 80 percent or more in the South, where the majority of African Americans lived.[71]

Second, the White House and Democrats allowed the programs to be supervised by local and state officials. This basically guaranteed that any loopholes to antidiscrimination would be fully exploited. And third, no antidiscrimination amendments were allowed or attached to any of the legislation.

Event though Roosevelt's signature programs failed to address the needs of most of the black community, the fact that it addressed the needs of some was a giant leap forward and helped define his presidency as a transition in the political life of African Americans. Between the 1910s and the end of World War II, close to four million blacks left the South and migrated North.[72] In cities like Detroit, Chicago, Philadelphia, and elsewhere, newly arriving blacks found a more receptive and open Democratic Party that eagerly wanted their votes and were willing to advocate policies and use political patronage toward that end. In addition, civil rights and human rights activism on the part of Eleanor Roosevelt cast a favorable light on an administration that did very little for the black community. Although Democrats from the South continued to be the principal obstacle to black political and social inclusion there, Republicans in the North had abdicated their responsibility to meet the interests of blacks and working people. For these reasons, for many in the black community a shift to the Democratic Party seemed warranted and logical.

In 1932, Roosevelt received just 23 percent of the black vote. By 1936, that number skyrocketed to 71 percent.[73] More important, in 1932 the percent of blacks who identified themselves as Democrats was in single digits; by 1936 the number grew to 44 percent. By the time Roosevelt's successor, Harry Truman, was elected president in 1948, 56 percent of blacks identified themselves as Democrats, and the numbers continued to increase.[74]

The anti-lynching campaign continued, and in September 1946, activist, actor, and internationally renowned human rights activist Paul Robeson led a delegation to meet with President Truman and urge that he take federal action.[75] Robeson also charged that President Truman's program for African development would mean "new slavery" for millions of Africans. Although Truman rebuffed Robeson's group, one year later the Truman White House circulated a report, *To Secure These Rights*, that advocated national civil rights reforms, including making lynching a federal crime.[76]

It was not until 1968 that the first federal anti-lynching law was passed as part of the Civil Rights Act. On June 13, 2005, the U.S. Senate officially apologized for its failure to enact anti-lynching bills. A *New York Times* article published the following day reported:

> The resolution is the first time that members of Congress, who have apologized to Japanese-Americans for their internment in World War II and to Hawaiians for the overthrow of their kingdom, have apologized to African-Americans for any reason, proponents of the measure said.

> "The Senate failed you and your ancestors and our nation," Senator Mary L. Landrieu of Louisiana, chief Democratic sponsor of the resolution, said at a luncheon attended by 200 family members and descendants of victims. They included 100 relatives of Anthony Crawford, as well as a 91-year-old man believed to be the only known survivor of an attempted lynching.
>
> He is James Cameron, who in 1930, as a 16-year-old shoeshine boy in Marion, Ind., was accused with two friends of murdering a white man and raping a white woman. His friends were killed. But as Mr. Cameron felt a noose being slipped around his neck, a man in the crowd stepped forward to proclaim Mr. Cameron's innocence.[77]

Though state-allowed and mob-driven lynchings have disappeared, symbols of lynchings still pack a powerful emotional punch as racial threats. Conservative and anti–civil rights Justice Clarence Thomas memorably used the term "high-tech lynching" to describe his opponents' actions during his combative nomination battle in 1991. As the *Boston Globe* reported in 2007, nooses or pictures of nooses as acts of hate have appeared as late as 2007 on campuses, work sites, and other places from Boston, New York, Pennsylvania, and Jena, Louisiana. Even more recently, in early 2010 a noose appeared in the library of the University of California at San Diego.[78] It is clear that as long as racial discrimination and hate exists, the symbolic power of lynching will as well. The *Boston Globe* notes correctly, "Lynching is not a footnote to American history, but integral to the text."[79]

Jubilee Singers between 1870 and 1880

Blacks Entertainers at the Pre-1960s White House

Following Blind Tom, the White House also increased the variety of black entertainers it invited to perform there. From classical musicians to gospel singers, black performers appeared before the presidents and their guests and family. While some presidents preferred only white entertainers, many sought a variety of musicians and singers to perform before foreign dignitaries.

Gospel and spiritual groups were perennial favorites at the White House in the nineteenth and early twentieth century. The first spiritual ensemble to be invited was the Fisk Jubilee Singers, who performed slave songs as well as spirituals. The name Jubilee was a reference to the year of jubilee as described in the twenty-fifth chapter of the Book of Leviticus—the year in which all those enslaved are set free. The group started as a project to raise money for Fisk University, which was established in 1866 as a school open to students of all races. Many of the Jubilee Singers had been formerly enslaved. The group toured both the United States and Europe and performed before kings and queens.

In 1872, the Jubilee Singers performed at the World Peace Festival in Boston and on March 5 of that year entertained President Grant at the White House. Despite the fame they had achieved, the group temporarily disbanded in 1878 due to exhaustion and a grueling travel schedule, but eventually reunited and continued to tour and perform. During the Bush administration, in 2008, the contemporary Fisk Jubilee Singers were selected as a recipient of the 2008 National Medal of Arts, the nation's highest honor for artists and patrons of the arts. The group continues to tour and perform today.[80] Although traditional black music was popular with presidents, it was not the only genre in which African Americans excelled.

As far back as 1878, African Americans were performing opera and classical music at the White House. While African American political leaders would find themselves more and more excluded as the century moved toward its conclusions, black entertainers would become a norm of sort at White House functions. One leader would serve as a sort of bridge between the two. In addition to his ceaseless activism and journalism, not to mention holding a number of political offices, Frederick Douglass was also a dedicated violinist. But it was Douglass's grandson who became a professional violinist with a successful career that included performing at the White House. There is a rich and long history of virtuoso black violinists in the United States dating back to the central role that the instrument held during the slave era. At the same time, free blacks were also learning to play expertly, including Philadelphia's Francis Johnson (1792–1844) and Newark's Peter O'Fake (1820–1884).[81]

Joseph Henry Douglass was born in 1869. Besides the training he received from his grandfather, he was educated at the

Frederick Douglass with his grandson, Joseph Henry Douglass, the violinist.

Boston Conservatory. He traveled and toured in Europe and later taught at Howard University. When not busy writing, lecturing or traveling, Frederick Douglass gave lessons to his grandson, and the two often played Schubert together in the music room at Douglass's Cedar Hill home in southeast Washington. Frederick Douglass reportedly paid $1,000 for a violin while visiting Germany, and later gave the instrument as a gift to grandson Joseph Henry.[82] According to Kenneth B. Morris Jr., great-great-great-grandson of Frederick Douglass, Joseph Henry was the only grandchild ever photographed with his grandfather.[83]

For a time, Joseph Henry Douglass worked as Chief of the Office of Inter-Agency Liaison of the National Institute of Mental Health, but left to pursue a life of music.[84] In September 1889, in the early days of his career, he played with the legendary James Reese Europe in Washington, D.C. James Reese Europe was the musician who would be credited with bringing early forms of jazz to Europe during World War I. He was a lieutenant in the all-black 369th Infantry Regiment—better known as the "Harlem Hellfighter"—and director of the regiment's marching band. The September 26 concert was reportedly the first time a solo was played on the saxophone by an African American and African American woman, Elsie Hoffman.[85]

For thirty years Douglass played across the globe and the United States, including, reportedly, every black education institution in the country.[86] He was often accompanied by his wife, Fannie Howard Douglass, who played piano. In 1914, he became one of the first violinists, black or otherwise, to record for the Victor Talking Machine Company, the leading phonograph producer at the time, but the recordings were never released.[87] He played for both President McKinley and President Taft.[88] Unfortunately, there is no detailed account of either concert. Despite having performed at the White House and in Europe, Joseph Henry Douglass, like virtually all black classical musicians, was forced to play in segregated venues for all of his public performing career in the United States.[89]

African Americans in the opera world faced similar discrimination. Opera star Marie Selika Williams performed in the Green Room for President Hayes and his wife Lucy Webb Hayes on November 13, 1878, just two years after she first appeared in concert.[90] Her performance included Verdi's "Ernani, involami," Thomas Moore's "The Last Rose of Summer," Harrison Millard's "Ave Maria," and Richard Mulder's "Staccato Polka," according to researcher Deborah McNally.[91] First Lady Lucy Hayes was so impressed that she attended her concert fundraiser at St. Luke's Protestant Episcopal Church the next year in Washington, D.C.[92] A mark of the event's importance was the presence of Frederick Douglass, who introduced Williams. She also had a connection with the First Family, which, like Williams, originally hailed from Ohio. She later toured Europe and performed before Queen Victoria. As with other black opera artists of the period, the racism of white society denied her the opportunity to perform in the formal opera world in the United States, thus her career remained limited.

Some black classical and opera stars, such as Sissieretta Jones, performed numerous times at the White House. Jones (born Matilda Jones), performed for Presidents Harrison, Cleveland, McKinley, and Theodore Roosevelt.[93] Favorably compared to Italian opera diva Adelina Patti, she acquired the nickname "Black Patti," which she disliked but used to her advantage. At her 1882 performance in the White House Blue Room before President Harrison, she sang "Swanee River" and the cavatina from Meyerbeer's *Robert le diable.* Like Marie Selika Williams, she also toured Europe, South America, the Caribbean, Australia, India, and parts of Africa, where there were more opportunities for a black American opera singer than at home. She built a review and a troupe called the "Black Patti Troubadours" that performed all over the United States. The Troubadours, unfortunately, made the most money performing "coon shows," i.e., acting out white stereotypes of blacks, although she ended the show with selections from operas and spirituals.[94]

No other black opera performers were invited to the White House until the Franklin D. Roosevelt administration decades later. Eleanor Roosevelt opened up the White House to a large number of black artists from different genres. Her most famous public act to support a black artist against discrimination occurred in 1939 when she helped arrange for opera star Marian Anderson to perform at the Lincoln Memorial in Washington, D.C., after she had been turned down from performing at Constitution Hall, which was owned by the Daughters of the American Revolution.

Marian Anderson, 1940.

The first lady was familiar with Anderson from her performance in the Monroe Room on the second floor of the White House in February 1936. The Daughters of the American Revolution had a whites-only policy, and they had rejected Anderson once before in 1935. They again refused to let her perform, and the Lincoln Memorial became the alternative site. Her performance was magnificent and an embarrassment for the Daughters of the American Revolution—as was the First Lady's resignation from the organization.

Racist attacks on Anderson continued. Later that year, along with the North Carolina Spiritual Singers, Anderson gave a command performance at the White House before the king and queen of England. As historian Elise Kirk reports, a pro-segregationist Miami Democrat wrote in ire, "It is an insult to the British King and Queen who are caucasians [*sic*] to present a negro [*sic*] vocalist for their entertainment. Do you want to engender racial hatred which might lead to serious consequences in the entire South?" The first lady's assistant, Edith Helm, replied with a somewhat racially stereotyped justification: "Mrs. Roosevelt asks me to acknowledge your telegram and to tell you that she is trying to give the King and Queen a picture of all American music. As the colored people are outstanding in a musical way, Mrs. Roosevelt feels that they should be presented with the others who will appear here."[95]

Anderson was not the first black opera singer to come to the Roosevelt White House. On February 9, 1934, the young soprano Lillian Evanti of Washington, D.C., performed for the Roosevelts at the White House. According to Kirk, she was the "first black to appear with an organized European opera company, the Nice Opera, in 1926."[96] She was followed the next year by soprano Dorothy Maynor, who was described as having a "soaring bell-like voice," and baritone Todd Duncan, who would sing at the White House on three more occasions after mesmerizing the president with his presentation of Cecil Cohen's "Death of an Old Seaman."

Soprano Leontyne Price performed repeatedly at the White House during the Johnson, Reagan, and Carter administrations. On July 4, 1964, Price and composer Aaron Copland became the first artists to receive the Presidential Medal of Freedom, which had been created in 1963 by President Kennedy to honor distinguished Americans in the fields of science, business, journalism, and theology as well as the arts.[97] Price's most politically significant performance was at the historic dinner that followed the signing of the peace accord between Egypt's Anwar Sadat and Israel's Menachem Begin. It had been agreed that each country, Egypt, Israel, and the United States, would choose an artist to perform at what was the largest White House dinner in history. Begin choose virtuoso violinists Itzhak Perlman and Pinchas Zukerman; Sadat picked an Egyptian trio (guitar, tabla, and organ); and Carter selected Price. She sang the aria "Pace, pace, mio Dio" from Verdi's opera *La forza del destino*.[98]

Another great opera artist to appear at the White House was Metropolitan Opera diva Grace Bumbry. Born in St. Louis in 1937, she rose to fame in the late 1950s and early 1960s with a series of sensational performances. When a segregated local conservatory refused to honor a scholarship she had won allowing her to attend classes, she decided to audition for Arthur Godfrey's popular "Talent Scouts" program, a performance that moved the host to tears and took place on the same day the Supreme Court announced the decision to ban segregated education.[99] At twenty-three, Grace Bumbry made her operatic debut at the Paris Opera Theater, one of the most prestigious and frightening stages to perform on, even for seasoned artists. The international press deemed it an unmitigated success. However, it was her role as Venus in a production of *Tannhäuser* that catapulted her to everlasting fame. Wieland Wagner, grandson of legendary composer Richard Wagner, organized the production and cast her as "the first black opera singer to appear at Bayreuth [Germany], the world's most revered shrine to the great composer and his art."[100] While the opera was still in rehearsal, many critics and fans called the casting a cultural disgrace and worse. Bumbry's stellar performance, however, destroyed all criticism with the opening show; she received a thirty-minute standing ovation and forty-two curtain calls.

Bumbry was invited to the White House twice. Her first appearance came during the Kennedy administration in response to a direct invitation from First Lady Jacqueline Kennedy. She returned in the 1980s when President Ronald Reagan, whose musical tastes were more country-western than classical, invited her to perform for the Chinese premier. In December 2009, President Obama awarded Bumbry a Kennedy Center honor.[101]

Black Staffers at the White House: Butlers and Maids

By the turn of the twentieth century, several generations of African Americans had worked at the White House. Similar to Paul Jennings and Elizabeth Keckly before them, some black staffers wrote memoirs and autobiographies.

From 1933 to 1955, Alonzo Fields was butler, chief butler, and eventually maître d'hôtel, for the White House during the administrations of Hoover, Roosevelt, Truman, and Eisenhower. He had initially wanted to be a professional singer but was unable to fulfill that ambition. Fields also had training in domestic and household skills, however, that led to a chance to work for the Hoovers. His social and personal talents allowed him to stay and rise in the household structure of the White House. Fields captured all of his experiences and reflections in his book, *My 21 Years at the White House*.[102]

Fields was originally from the all-black town of Lyles Station, Indiana. His father, a general store owner, headed an all-black brass band. Alonzo learned to play many brass instruments and was reputed to have "a beautiful singing voice."[103] Unable to afford the musical education needed to make it as a concert singer, Fields, under the pressure of family responsibilities, joined the White House staff as a butler in 1931.

One of the many requirements of working at the White House was discretion—staff could not publicly discuss the things they saw and heard while at work. Fields respected that obligation, but secretly keep a diary recording his experiences in private code. He also saved mementos and souvenirs, including White House menus and special invitations. Many of the documents and other items he collected he later donated to the Truman Library after he retired.

Fields' job as chief butler entailed being "responsible for keeping track of all White House tablecloths, napkins, silverware, glassware, and china. Also, he made menu suggestions to the first lady for important state dinners, receptions, teas, and family dinners. He supervised the chefs and servers. . . . He had to learn what would and would not please each president and his family."[104] Often the job was extremely personal, such as when he served breakfast to President Hoover.[105] He also reminded his staff that their work was historically significant. He told them, "Boys, remember that we are helping to make history. We have a small part, perhaps a menial part, but they can't do much here without us. They've got to eat, you know."[106]

Among the individuals he encountered over the years were Winston Churchill, England's Princess Elizabeth, Thomas Alva Edison, and John D. Rockefeller as well as cabinet members, senators, representatives, Supreme Court justices, and governors. Black leaders such as educator and diplomat Ralph Bunche, radical Paul Robeson, and educator Mary McCleod Bethune, also visited the White House during Fields's tenure.[107] Similar to the fictional butler James Stevens in *The Remains of the Day*, Fields served the Roosevelts and Trumans through turbulent times including wars, presidents' deaths, the Great Depression, the attack on Pearl Harbor, and the massive protests and mobilizations of the Civil Rights Movement.

Fields also provides insight into the racial politics of the White House. Few outside the White House, for example, were aware of the segregation that existed within it. According to Fields, prior to the Roosevelts, "even in the White House we had separate dining rooms. They had a Black and a White kitchen for the servants, yet they were working all together, all the time. But to me that shouldn't have been—not in the White House of all places. The White House should have been taking the lead on that." Eleanor Roosevelt had a simple solution to the problem: she fired all the white staffers, "so all the help was colored, and there was only one dining room."[108] Fields seemed to like the Roosevelts most, although like many African Americans at the time, he was critical of the fact that Roosevelt would not speak out strongly against lynching until two whites were killed in California.[109]

He says that Hoover told his cabinet, "I had my colored brethren in last night after dinner for a talk. . . . With our convention due soon, I wanted to talk to them about the related conditions of the races on employment and the Depression. . . . I told them that as their people are representative of 10 percent of our citizens, I couldn't see why they couldn't take a share in equal proportions in contributions to the nation."[110] Hoover, he claims, thought that long-term racial inequality would be harmful to the nation.

On Truman, he notes that the president was rebuked by the Soviet Union's Joseph Stalin when they met in Germany, with the latter asking, "Why are you so interested in the Poles when you have American citizens who are not getting their voting rights?" An infuriated Truman later stated, "I'll never go anywhere to meet anybody again until we get these situations cleared up because I will never have anyone throw that up in my face again, that I'm far more interested in other people's voting rights than I am in the people in my nation."[111] Fields retired shortly after Eisenhower came to the White House in 1953.

Tenures of White House servant staff have tended to be long, spanning multiple administrations. John Ficklin served at the White House for more than forty-three years and worked for nine U.S. presidents. He first came to work for Franklin Roosevelt in 1940 and stayed until Ronald Reagan's administration, retiring in 1983. *Jet* magazine noted that he had been called the "soul of the White House."[112] Like Fields, he worked as a butler and supervisor during his career.[113] Over the years, nine members of the Ficklin family worked at the White House, including John's brothers Charles and Samuel. Eugene Allen, who worked as a pantryman, butler, and maître d'hôtel, worked at the White House from the Truman administration until 1986, leaving during Reagan's second term. Staff careers are long in part due to the collegiality among the workers. Allen stated, "I had a good relationship with all the butlers. You know, it's closer than your relatives, because you work so close together. You see them every day. You eat together, you work together. It's every day."[114]

Butlers were not the only workers to write their stories—so did the maids. In 1961, Lillian Rogers Parks published her memoir, *My Thirty Years Backstairs at the White House.*[115] The book, written with author Frances Spatz Leighton, was actually the story not only of her own work life as a seamstress and maid in the White House from Hoover to Eisenhower, but also of the experiences of her mother, Maggie Rogers, who worked there from Taft years into the Roosevelt era. Maggie Rogers regularly took her daughter with her to work, and, like Alonzo Fields and other staffers, wrote of her experiences both from notes and from memory. She encouraged Parks to write a book about their unique observations. Rogers rose to become the first black maid to work on the presidential floor of the White House.

As the *New York Times* wrote, the book was quite tame although extremely popular when it came out. It was on the *New York Times* best-seller list for twenty-six weeks. In 1979, Parks's book led to a nine-part NBC mini-series. Reportedly, the book's popularity was so far-reaching that incoming First Lady Jacqueline Kennedy made all the staff sign nondisclosure agreements stipulating that they would not write about their experiences at the White House once they left. Unfortunately, the person put in charge of getting the signatures, Jacqueline's white secretary Mary Gallagher, conveniently did not sign one herself and in 1969 published a book about her White House life, titled *My Boss.*[116]

Perhaps for reasons of discretion, *My Thirty Years* provides only minimum insight into the racial politics of the various presidents. The Roosevelts, particularly Eleanor, come across as the most consistent about racial equality inside the White House. When Eleanor's mother-in-law came to visit the White House and criticized her "for using colored help instead of white help," she reportedly responded, "You run your house and I'll run mine."

Despite the writings that later appeared after their leaving the White House, the household staff members were meant to be seen and not heard, and, under no circumstances were they to demonstrate partisan politics. For more than 150 years, the White House had never employed a black person in any position outside the servant staff. Things were finally about to change.

Morrow, Eisenhower, and the Power of Symbolism

Black political engagement with the White House was hampered by the fact that the only African Americans on the presidential payroll were household staff. It was not until 1955 that the first African American—E. Frederic Morrow—was officially employed as a presidential aide. As always with such racial firsts, the question is raised of whether or not having a black face in a high place necessarily constitutes genuine racial progress. Symbolism aside, black appointments are defined by the substance of the position, the use of the position by the individual involved, and the social and political context within which the position must operate to effectively address the consensus concerns of

Civil rights leaders, 1958. From left to right: Lester Granger, Dr. Martin Luther King, Jr, E. Frederic Morrow (White House Staff), President Eisenhower, Asa Phillip Randolph, William Rogers (Attorney General), Rocco Siciliano (White House Staff), Roy Wilkins.

the black community. These concerns are generally not only racial but also center on broader issues of economic fairness, political inclusion, social justice, human rights, and other areas of life and society. While expectations are often high that a black person who becomes a first will deliver the maximum change possible, experience has shown that ultimately it is the nuts and bolts of organizing, politicking, negotiating, educating, mobilizing, and bringing as much pressure to bear as possible that leads to substantial transformation. The degree to which the breakthrough is an authentic reflection of these processes, rather than an appeasement or ploy to deflect criticism, determines whether real progress occurs. While Dwight D. Eisenhower appointed E. Frederic Morrow to be the first African American to hold an executive position on the president's White House staff, he also sought to do as little as possible to advance civil rights during his two terms in office, and Morrow, despite his personal aims, could do very little to change that fact.

On July 10, 1955, the White House officially announced that Morrow had been appointed to serve as a top aide to Eisenhower.[117] He brought with him high qualifications, including a law degree from Rutgers University Law School. In black politics, he had served a stint as field secretary for the NAACP. In most ways, however, Morrow's politics were more party oriented than racial. As a committed Republican who had had to endure twenty years of Democratic administrations, he eagerly took a leave of absence from his public affairs position at CBS to work on Eisenhower's 1952 campaign. In that period, when the black vote was wavering between the two major parties, it would not have been unusual for an African American to work for a Republican presidential candidate. Morrow apparently labored hard enough to be recognized by the campaign's leadership, particularly Sherman Adams, who became Eisenhower's chief of staff. After the election, Adams not only promised Morrow a White House job but, somewhat irresponsibly, it seems, recommended that he quit his CBS position in the interim and move to Washington, D.C.

Morrow naively took Adams' suggestion and then waited. And waited and waited. After six months of putting him off, presidential adviser Bernard Shanley finally told Morrow that there was no job for him, and offered no explanation as to why. As it turned out, not everyone on Eisenhower's staff was as racially enlightened as Adams. One aide, Wilton B. Persons, an Alabama native and staunch segregationist, had threatened to lead a walkout of presidential staff, particularly of white women staffers, if Morrow—or any black person—was given such a high-level position.[118] The threat worked, and Morrow was forced to seek employment elsewhere. He finally landed a position at the Commerce Department as a business adviser.

More than two years later, in July 1955, he did get a call and was officially appointed administrative officer for special projects, a purposely vague title referring to equally vague work. Morrow himself called the job "just plain housekeeping."[119] Reflective of the deliberate ambiguity of the position and the president's own hesitancy, Morrow was not officially sworn in to the position until January 27, 1959, at a ceremony the president usually attended, but Eisenhower did not go. Thus, seven years after the election, and heading towards the end of Eisenhower's second term, Morrow made history.

Although Morrow took the stance that he was not there specifically to address civil rights, i.e., he did not want to be the "black man in the White House," in fact, he was. He was often sent to speak to black groups or be present at state functions to demonstrate the diversity of the administration and the advanced state of black progress.

As times changed and his tenure wore on, Morrow grew more militant regarding racial issues. His own civil rights concerns lead him to continually advocate for the administration to address the explosive state of race relations of the 1950s. He sent memos to Adams requesting that the president speak out about the murder of Emmett Till in Mississippi in 1955.[120] He suggested that the White House invite a dozen black leaders to the White House for a conversation about the nation's civil rights issues.[121] In February 1956, as the Montgomery Bus Boycott was becoming more intense and violent, its leaders increasingly under attack, Morrow asked to go to Alabama to unofficially represent the administration and talk to the movement's organizers. All of these requests were politely but unambiguously rejected. Like almost every other administration before it, the

White House made it clear that appeasing Southern whites took priority over any substantial action regarding rights and protection for the black community.

All the while, Morrow was Jim Crowed at the White House and, like the White House's black servant staff, in the city of Washington as well. Initially none of the White House secretaries were willing to work for him. That only changed when a woman volunteer agreed to work for him as an expression of her religious practice of nondiscrimination. It became an unspoken policy that women would only enter his office in twos. Life was not much better outside the walls of the White House. Washington, D.C. was segregated at the time, so Morrow's historic appointment notwithstanding, he lived, ate, and moved around only within strictly racially determined divisions of the city.

After Eisenhower was reelected with 47 percent of the black vote, his administration seemed satisfied that its do-nothing strategy on civil rights had paid off, despite the fact that racial tensions were escalating by the hour. In June 1957, Morrow fired off yet another memo to Sherman Adams, stating truthfully that black leaders were being "ignored, snubbed, and belittled by the president and his staff."[122] Morrow strongly suggested that Eisenhower meet with Montgomery Bus Boycott leader Martin Luther King, labor leader A. Philip Randolph, and NAACP head Roy Wilkins all together. Adams agreed, and a meeting was set up for later that fall. However, the school integration crisis in Little Rock postponed the gathering as Eisenhower gave preference to meeting with Arkansas Governor Orval Faubus. Rather than sit down with those who could have provided a progressive insight and a peaceful solution to the conflagration, Eisenhower choose to meet with the person who was the chief obstacle to a resolution.

Finally, on June 23, 1958, after almost a year of delays, the Morrow-initiated meeting occurred, with Lester Granger of the National Urban League added to the group. It was the first presidential sit-down with black leaders since Eisenhower was elected president in 1952. The meeting lasted less than an hour and consisted mostly of Randolph reading a nine-point list of recommendations. The participants felt that the president had listened civilly and indicated some sympathy for their cause.

Following the meeting, there is no indication that Eisenhower made any change in his cautious, hesitant, publicity-concerned, Southern-favoring approach to civil rights. There were changes for Morrow, however. For a short time he was reluctantly moved to a position as an assistant to Arthur Lawson, the president's speechwriter, and later he was named White House Officer for Special Projects, which seemed little different from his original position except that this time he was explicitly tasked to work only on White House policy and politics regarding civil rights. The surreal nature of his tenure was further amplified when his nemesis, Wilton Persons, replaced the man who was nearly his only supporter, Adams, as White House chief of staff. Before either of them assumed their new positions, Persons at one point had told Morrow never to approach him with anything involving civil rights, because, being from Alabama, he had experienced personal conflicts within his family due to "the administration and its stand on civil rights."[123] In other words, even the mildest of efforts by Eisenhower regarding civil rights was so offensive to the Persons clan that any discussion on the issue was a non-starter for him. If Morrow had been marginalized before, now he was completely shut out.

As if he did not have enough troubles, a few months later he tried to convince baseball great Jackie Robinson that he should not participate in a youth march being organized by Harry Belafonte, A. Philip Randolph, and others in Washington, D.C.'s radical black network. In the post–Little Rock atmosphere, the integrated march was set to forcefully criticize the woefully poor efforts of state and federal integration policies. The attempt to pressure Robinson backfired when Robinson went to the media with the threat, and Morrow came under severe criticism from the black community. Up to that point, despite Eisenhower's tepid policies and weak responses, Morrow had generally been given a pass by African Americans, a kind of credit card for being the first, but now it had cashed out. The walls were caving in on Morrow.

On occasion Morrow would publicly speak out against racism in brutally frank terms, such as when he admonished the Republican Women's Conference for its segregationist policy prohibiting black women from joining the organization. However, he rarely criticized the administration's nonfunctional civil rights policy in any public manner. In fact, one of his key responsibilities was to sell White House policy without qualification to an understandably and increasingly skeptical black public. The banality of his position was brought home full force when he gave a speech honoring Eisenhower at the 1960 Republican National Convention during which he thanked him for "bringing equality to all" and ludicrously added, "No man has done more to bring the truth about real democracy to the world than Dwight David Eisenhower."[124]

Although is it unknown if Morrow would have continued working in the White House if Nixon had won, with John F. Kennedy's victory the question was moot. At that point, Morrow had little utility for the Republican Party, which would soon turn Eisenhower's conciliation to Southern white racism into its principal strategy. The sea change in which black voters shifted to the Democratic Party, and the growing, increasingly militant black movement of the 1960s and 1970s, also marginalized Morrow. The first black person in U.S. history to work in the White House in a position of power soon faded into obscurity.

CHAPTER 7

The 1960s and the Crisis of Power: The White House and Black Mobilization

Prologue: Abraham Bolden's White House Story

The black struggle for freedom and equality reached new heights and intensity in the 1960s and early 1970s. As activist Stokely Carmichael noted, the desire was for black power because "With power, the masses could make or participate in making the decisions which govern their destinies, and thus create basic change in their day-to-day lives."[1] Black activists and the black community targeted racism on all fronts; no area of society in which discrimination and bigotry existed was immune. The direct-action politics of the decade was launched on February 1, 1960, when four students from North Carolina Agricultural and Technical State University sat in at a Woolworth's lunch counter in Greensboro, North Carolina, that refused to serve blacks. Within five years, the call for "black power" was a national cry of the black community. By the end of the 1960s and early 1970s, radical and revolutionary black organizations such as the Black Panther Party, Revolutionary Action Movement (RAM), and League of Revolutionary Black Workers were calling for the establishment of a socialist United States where racism would no longer exist nor its resurgence be tolerated. Black nationalist organizations and movements such as the Nation of Islam (NOI), Congress of African People, United Slaves (US), and many local groups were demanding black control of black communities. Civil rights leaders were shifting from protest strategies to electoral ones, taking advantage of the hard-won Voting Rights Act of 1965.

The government responded to these developments, on the one hand, with brutal repression and murderous attacks: local, state, and federal law enforcement collaborated to kill, jail, and marginalize black leaders and activists. On the other hand, the state was also forced to open up opportunities to African Americans, Latinos, women, and others who would no longer accept second-class status.

It was within this context that even state institutions with a long history of racial insulation and white control were obligated to become more inclusive. The Secret Service would become one of them.

President John F. Kennedy called Abraham Bolden the "Jackie Robinson" of the service.[2] In June 1961, after one year with the agency, Bolden became the first African American Secret Service agent to be assigned to the White House detail directly responsible for the protection of the president. President Kennedy had personally requested him to consider the assignment, and he accepted. By the end of June 1966, Bolden was no longer at the White House, no longer with the Secret Service, and on his way to prison.

In his riveting memoir, *The Echo from Dealey Plaza: The True Story of the First African American on the White House Secret Service Detail and His Quest for Justice After the Assassination of JFK,* Bolden weaves a tale of institutional racism, government cover-up, political intrigue, criminal frame-up, and eventually, personal enlightenment. He graphically chronicles not only the overt racial insults and bigotry on the part of many of his colleagues and supervisors in the Secret Service, but also the lack of professionalism and prejudice by White House agents that may have enabled Kennedy's assassination. Bolden's very vocal and public critique of the president's assassination sparked a chain of events that culminated in his being charged with a felony, fired from the Service, railroaded by a conspiring judge, and eventually incarcerated for three years, including some time spent in a facility for the criminally insane. More than forty years after those incidents, Bolden continues to seek justice for his persecution by government officials who he believes sought to neutralize and discredit his explosive accusations.

And he might just find that vindication, given new research into the Kennedy assassination focusing on nearly four million pages of documents released under the Freedom of Information Act and the 1992 President John F. Kennedy Assassination Records Collection Act. Declassified documents from the Warren Commission, House Select Committee on Assassinations (HSCA), and Assassinations Records Review Board all support Bolden's claim that an aborted plot to assassinate on Kennedy in Chicago was a significant threat.[3] Recent detailed research by Lamar Waldron and Thom Hartmann appears to verify at least part of Bolden's story.[4] In addition, a lawsuit filed by black Secret Service agents initiated in 2000 charging racism on the part of the agency demonstrates that bigotry and discrimination continued long after Bolden was dismissed. Bolden was both the first of many black agents to work in the Secret Service and the first of many to experience racist harassment within the elite agency.

One of the great historic presidential ironies is that President Lincoln formally authorized the creation of the Secret Service on the day of his assassination, April 14, 1865.[5] The Secret Service began to operate on July 5, 1865, with the mission to investigate counterfeiting of U.S. currency, a major problem at the time carried out by defeated Confederates, the Ku Klux Klan, professional and petty criminals, and others. In 1883, it was formally established as part of the Department of Treasury. After September 11, 2001, the Secret Service was brought under the Department of Homeland Security.[6]

It wasn't until the 1901 assassination of President McKinley that the agency was given responsibility for full-time protection of the president. Before then, U.S. presidents were more or less on their own. By 1960, when Bolden was hired, protective services had grown to cover the president-elect, the president, the vice president–elect, the vice president, and their immediate families. It also continued its original work of going after those who committed fraud against the U.S. government and counterfeiters.

For the first nearly 100 years of its existence, the Secret Service, like most of the federal intelligence and law enforcement organizations, had only employed white people. Yet, in an era when the U.S. government felt unavoidable domestic and international pressure to address the country's pervasive racial inequities, and with a new president who understood the rapidly shifting calculations of race and political power, the time for change had come.

The passion and courage of the sit-ins of 1960 were embedded and expanded into the determination and bravery of the "freedom rides" during spring 1961. Although the Supreme Court's 1960 decision in *Boynton v. Virginia* had outlawed segregation in interstate travel, there was little enforcement of the policy by officials in the South. Committed to integrating interstate transportation, the Congress of Racial Equality (CORE) launched a series of bus rides of blacks and whites from the North to the deep South virtually challenging the Ku Klux Klan and other racists to attempt to stop them. The goal, whether successful in reaching their destination of New Orleans or not, was to force the nation, Congress, and the White House to acknowledge the shame of segregation and its brutal enforcement. The riders were arrested and harassed along the way, and in Alabama and Mississippi, groups of white people savagely beat them with baseball bats, iron pipes, and steel chains. Even a Department of Justice official, John Seigenthaler, who was sent personally by Attorney General Robert Kennedy, was brutally beaten and left unconscious in the street. The new president, who delivered stirring words supporting equality and integration in speeches, weakly called for a "cooling-off" period and refused to intervene until the well-publicized viciousness of the assaults on the riders was too disturbing to ignore.[7]

The Kennedys preferred to work behind the scenes rather than publicly denounce Southern officials' refusal to carry out their sworn responsibilities. Eventually, by the end of May, the Kennedy White House made a deal with Mississippi Governor Ross Barnett that it would not send federal troops if Mississippi's state troopers and National Guard provided protection.[8] The deal also allowed for the freedom riders to be arrested once they reached Jackson, Mississippi, which they were. Many were sent to the horrific Parchman Penitentiary, more a modern-day plantation than a prison. The racial crisis was escalating.

Against this background, two weeks later, on June 6, 1961, the first black Secret Service agent appointed to White House duty, i.e., responsible for protecting the president and the First Family, went to work. Bolden was looking forward to a long career in the Secret Service and was overjoyed by the opportunity. It was hard for him to imagine how this appointment, one in which Kennedy himself was proud and boastful, could go so sour so quickly. But it did.

In 1957, Bolden, a former music teacher, started his career in law enforcement in St. Louis by working for the Pinkerton Detective Agency (infamous for its strike-breaking work in the late nineteenth and early twentieth century), and rose to become its first black detective. That position would lead to his next job as an Illinois state trooper the following year. In those days, state troopers would work with the local or nearest Secret Service office to provide security if the president or any other high-ranking officials were going to be in the area. Bolden's path to making history was gradually unfolding.

In 1960, while state troops were teamed with the Secret Service to provide security for then-candidate Kennedy, Bolden asked one of the agents if there were any blacks in the Secret Service. The agent, Fred Backstrom, said that he was not sure there were, but he was sure that the Secret Service was expanding and looking for new agents. He later sent Bolden an application, and by the end of October he was on the job in the Chicago office. Bolden states that there was another black or mixed-raced agent in the Secret Service that he worked with once. However, that agent strenuously denied that he was black, according to Bolden, telling him, "Don't call me a Negro. I'm no Negro. I'm Puerto Rican, so don't ever call me a Negro again!"[9] This agent clearly had issues, and his relationship with Bolden remained strained throughout their time together in the Service. Bolden also had to deal with racist antics in his Chicago office. One agent routinely told "colored boy" jokes to menace him, and although he complained, his supervisors took no action.[10]

Bolden's path to the White House began next to a toilet. In April 1961, when the president came to visit Chicago, Bolden had been assigned to guard a basement restroom reserved exclusively for Kennedy. At one point, Kennedy's entourage came down to the area and the president spotted Bolden. After being told his name and learning that he was a Secret Service agent and not a local police officer, the president struck up a conversation. Kennedy asked, "Has there ever been a Negro agent on the Secret Service White House detail, Mr. Bolden?" Bolden replied, "Not to my acknowledge Mr. President." Kennedy then asked, "Would you like to be the first?" Unhesitatingly, Bolden stated, "Yes, sir, Mr. President."[11]

Soon thereafter Bolden received an invitation for a thirty-day routine training at the White House. In Washington, D.C., Bolden quickly found himself in a racial vise. In his relatively brief time at the White House, he noted a significant number of racist incidents by other Secret Service agents, mostly directed at him. After only four days on the job, on June 9, 1961, someone left him a racist caricature in the Secret Service manual that he had been studying. Other offensive behavior included regular use of the word "nigger" by white agents.

The Secret Service official in charge of the day shift, Harvey Henderson, was particularly hateful. On one occasion Henderson told Bolden in front of a room full of fellow agents, "You were born a nigger, and when you die, you'll still be a nigger. You will always be nothing but a nigger. So act like one."[12]

Bolden was also forced to live in Jim Crow housing while traveling. He found out that he would be segregated on a trip to West Palm Beach, Florida. A memo stated that Woody's South Wind Motel "would not accept a colored agent at this motel but that he could find housing at a first-class colored motel at Riviera Beach, Florida."[13] He also felt very uncomfortable professionally because some agents expressed ire toward Kennedy because of his civil rights agenda, some referring to him as "that nigger-lover," and Bolden felt that they were compromised in their willingness or capacity to protect the president, some going as far to say, according to Bolden, that "they'd take no action to protect him" if he were targeted by gunfire.[14]

Kennedy himself appeared to take a liking to Bolden in their few encounters at the White House and at the Kennedy family compound in Hyannis Port, Massachusetts. Kennedy's Jackie Robinson reference was made when the president happily introduced him to his press secretary, Pierre Salinger and his secretary, Evelyn Lincoln. President Kennedy also introduced Bolden to his brother, Attorney General Robert Kennedy, who congratulated him on the appointment and even tried to recruit him to join the FBI, which was then under the jurisdiction of the Justice Department.[15]

Whatever the Kennedys might have felt about having a black Secret Service agent on detail in the White House, the atmosphere of bigotry and the personal pressure on Bolden was too much to bear, and he decided to return to the Chicago office rather than apply for a relocation within the president's detail. Approximately one month after arriving at the White House, Bolden was already on his way home. This would turn out to be a significant turning point for him. His hope to return to a normal life and continue in his career without the issues he had confronted in Washington, D.C. would be short-lived.

Two years later, in 1963, the nation experienced even more intense turmoil as the battle over black rights continued to dominate national politics. Across the entire country voices were calling for equality and inclusion for black people. A dramatic turning point in civil rights and U.S. history occurred when, on August 28, 1963, Martin Luther King Jr. electrified the nation with his magnificent "I Have a Dream" speech at the Lincoln Memorial in Washington, D.C., in front of 250,000 people, the largest demonstration in the nation's capital up to that point. Under the theme of "Jobs and Freedom," the rally was organized by the so-called "big six" of the Civil Rights Movement—A. Philip Randolph (Brotherhood of Sleeping Car Porters); Whitney Young (National Urban League); Roy Wilkins (NAACP); James Farmer (Congress of Racial Equality); John Lewis, (Student Nonviolent Coordinating Committee); and Martin Luther King Jr. (Southern Christian Leadership Conference). Held 100 years after the signing of the Emancipation Proclamation and one day after the tragic death of black historian, author, and radical leader W. E. B. Du Bois, it was the prophetic high point of the civil rights era, soon to be eclipsed by the black power movement, the urban rebellions of the mid to late 1960s, and a shift in focus to electoral politics.

White reaction against extending civil rights to black people was aggressive and violent. Whites in the South constantly threatened, frequently attacked, and sometimes murdered civil rights organizers. In a particularly brutal case, earlier in 1963 the black community in Birmingham, Alabama, had been terrorized by the police, the Ku Klux Klan, and organized mobs that attacked men, women, children, and the leaders of the local movement. On May 2, 600 children marched for civil rights in Birmingham. Local white authorities attacked them with police dogs and fire hoses and arrested hundreds. The situation became even more barbaric when on Sunday morning, September 15, members of the Klu Klux Klan planted a bomb at the Sixteenth Street Baptist Church. The timed explosion was one of the worst terrorist atrocities of the period, and killed four young black girls—Denise McNair, eleven years old; Addie Mae Collins, fourteen; Cynthia Wesley, fourteen; and Carol Robertson, fourteen.[16] The bombing was followed by acts of arson and shootings in other parts of the city during which racist whites killed two more black children.[17]

Across the region these types of attacks were common,

occurring on a daily basis. The KKK was active in every state in the South, as were other racist groups and individuals prepared to kill anyone who dared to challenged the region's white supremacy power structure.

Murder was also on the mind of some of those who opposed Kennedy. Documents released in 1992 reveal that the FBI had discovered a plot to assassinate Kennedy during an Army-Navy football game that the president planned to attend in Chicago in early November 1963. The FBI informed the Secret Service in Chicago, and an investigation was launched. Kennedy ended up canceling the trip, although it remains unclear whether or not this was due to security concerns. Meanwhile, reportedly the group of two to four Cuban suspects somehow got away without being arrested.[18] Bolden became frustrated at the way the office had handled the case and let his feelings be known. An additional plot to kill Kennedy was discovered in Tampa, Florida, and again an investigation was begun.[19] On November 22, 1963, Kennedy was shot and killed in Dallas. Information about both the Chicago and the Tampa plots would be hidden from investigators in the period immediately after the assassination.

Bolden had been aware of the earlier plots and felt they were directly relevant to the investigation of President Kennedy's murder. He also wanted investigators to know that some Secret Service agents had behaved in a compromised manner that may have contributed to the security failure—through their unprofessional drinking and partying while on duty or their open antagonism toward the president. Undeterred after his superiors in Chicago discouraged him from pursuing the matter further, he decided to independently report what he knew to the Warren Commission, the body established by Congress to officially investigate the assassination.

Bolden seriously misjudged the forces lined up against him. Although he had not made direct contact with the Commission yet, he had planned to secretly give testimony while in Washington, D.C. for a training; however, he was arrested on the first day of training and charged with discussing taking a bribe from one of his former arrestees. This felony charge would lead to his eventual conviction and dismissal from the agency, and, of course, prevented him from testifying before the Warren Commission.

When at the end of his trial the jury appeared that it was deadlocked, Judge J. Sam Perry, incredibly, informed the jurors that Bolden was guilty. He stated, "Ladies and gentlemen of the jury, I will now exercise a prerogative that I have as a judge that I seldom exercise. I will express to you and comment upon the evidence. In my opinion, the evidence sustains a verdict of guilty on counts one, two, and three of the indictment. Now, with that in mind, ladies and gentlemen, you may now retire and reconsider the evidence in light of this court's instructions."[20]

Judge Perry's highly prejudicial intervention and other improprieties failed to work. One lone juror continued to hold out against the other eleven who had voted guilty, and eventually a mistrial was declared. Stunningly, the second trial was assigned to the same judge, and this time the jury came back with a conviction. On June 29, 1966, two U.S. marshals arrived at Bolden's home. He was taken first to Cook County jail and then transferred to the Terre Haute prison. He would spend three years there, at Fort Leavenworth, and at other facilities before being released on parole on September 25, 1969.

Over time, Bolden's charge of a frame-up became increasingly credible. There were two main witnesses against him. One was Frank Jones, whom Bolden had once arrested in a counterfeiting case. The other was Joseph Spagnoli, who later recanted his story. It also appeared that one of the U.S. attorneys, Richard T. Sikes, knew that Spagnoli's story was false, because he had put him up to it.[21]

There is more than one way to interpret Bolden's experiences. At one level, Bolden's tribulations could have been the consequence of an agency's embarrassment at being unable to faithfully execute the mission with which it was tasked: to protect the president of the United States at all costs. Assertions from an agent that incompetence and bigotry were factors in the Secret Service's actions would have had a ring of authenticity and needed to be quashed at all costs. Given the agency was still all white and that many of the agents held openly racist views, railroading Bolden would have been simple. Willfully making false accusations to discredit and destroy outspoken blacks was part of the U.S. government's covert COINTELPRO (counterintelligence) operations during the 1960s, and taking Bolden out of play in this manner would have been consistent with the policies of the times.

This is all the more likely given that Bolden's information, unbeknownst to him, was entangled in much larger international intrigues emanating from the White House. In what was termed "Operation AmWorld," President Kennedy and his brother, the U.S. attorney general, had formed covert plans for the overthrow of the Castro government, to take place on December 1, 1963. For close to forty years, Operation AmWorld had been kept secret from the media, the public, Bolden, and, most directly, from multiple Congressional investigations (and the Warren Commission) that have been conducted into the Kennedy assassination. In a September 30, 1963, memo titled "Plan for a Coup in Cuba," written by Army Secretary Cyrus Vance, the Kennedy brothers had laid out plans for Cuban President Fidel Castro and his brother Raúl to be "neutralized" in a "palace coup." The coup leaders would then present themselves as a provisional government and declare martial law. The provisional government would also, if needed, "request" military assistance from the United States, justifying a U.S. invasion. The coup was to be lead by Juan Almeida, a hero of the revolution and then Commander of the Cuban Army, who was in communication with the Kennedys. Hartmann reports that Fidel Castro only discovered Almeida's role almost thirty years later. Almeida briefly disappeared, then returned to public life, and his death on September 11, 2008, was a national day of mourning and honor. His dealings with the Kennedys, according to historian Thom Hartmann, have never been made public in Cuba.[22]

Bolden had no way of knowing that exposing the Chicago assassination attempt would have likely triggered an investigation that would have led to uncovering the Kennedys' covert plans to overthrow Castro. The existence of Operation AmWorld was revealed for the first time in 1999, disclosed in the millions of pages of newly declassified documents released under the President John F. Kennedy Assassination Records Collection Act.[23] Lamar Waldron, Thom Hartmann, and other researchers have argued that due to the need to keep Operation AmWorld secret, given its potential for escalating the Cold War or generating another missile crisis, Bolden became a sacrificed pawn. His story of Cuban assassins in Chicago was linked to international issues too politically volatile to be made public.

"The files released after Congress passed the JFK Act unanimously in 1992 show the massive amount of information that had been withheld from at least five Congressional investigations," write Lamar Waldron and Thom Hartmann.[24] "Even worse, the Final Report of the JFK Board created by Congress shows that crucial files about attempts against JFK—the cases Bolden worked on—were destroyed by the Secret Service in

1995. And, a report by the government oversight group OMB Watch says that "well over one million CIA records" related to JFK's era remain unreleased, perhaps until the mandatory release date of 2017."[25]

It is difficult not to conclude that race played a major role in what happened to Bolden, the lone black man in an all-white agency. This likely made it easier for his colleagues to avoid offering him support and assistance. Indeed, what has happened to other black Secret Service agents after Bolden only strengthens his story of racism and conspiracy within the agency.

In 2000, the group Black Agents of the Secret Service (BASS), which grew to represent more than 250 black agents, filed a class action lawsuit on behalf of ten of them accusing the agency of racism. They declared that the Secret Service has "discriminated against African-American Special Agents, from at least January 1974 forward, in its personnel policies, practices, and procedures."[26] In 2004, after four years of delays by the Secret Service and the Bush administration, Black Agents of the Secret Service filed a Writ of Mandamus in the U.S. Court of Appeals for the District of Columbia Circuit to force the court to expedite their case. They contended that the Bush administration had purposely allowed the case to languish.[27] With the Writ, the group asked the federal appeals court to intercede and compel the federal district court to take action. They alleged that "the Bush Administration and the Secret Service have used the judicial process to prevent a discussion of this case on its merits," including not calling a "single witness" or producing "a single document." "The refusal to address the merits of the Black Agents' case is shameful," said BASS president and Special Agent Reginald G. Moore. He stated further, "For the future of the Secret Service, we must have a hearing on the merits of more than 20 years of racial discrimination and a remedy that dissolves the 'Good Ol' Boy' network, which has worked so often to disadvantage black agents."[28]

A plaintiff in the case, Moore had worked on President Clinton's security detail as well as that of Presidents Carter, George H. W. Bush, and Ford.[29] Moore claims that he had been passed over to head the Service's Joint Operation Center, for which he had been the acting head, and which oversees security for the White House. The position was given to a white agent who had never even been on a presidential protection detail or ever worked at the Joint Operations Center. In other instances, Moore states that positions that he applied for were given to less-qualified relatives of Service directors. Camilla Simms, another plaintiff, spoke of a racially hostile atmosphere that was also beset by problematic gender bias. After she complained about the defacing of a picture of a black woman by several white agents on a calendar that was given out to all agents, she was ostracized.[30]

The 2004 Writ of Mandamus pleading states:

> Over four years have passed since the government filed its motion to dismiss and the Petitioners filed their motion for class certification. Petitioners have waited patiently, but they are suffering prejudice. They have not been allowed to depose any fact witnesses, analyze any personnel databases, or conduct any discovery whatsoever. In the meanwhile, the Secret Service admits that it has not in the past and will not in the future preserve electronic mail evidence relevant to the present action. Petitioners have no way to determine if the Secret Service is complying with its responsibility to preserve other documents relevant to the case.[31]

One factor complicating the case is that Black Agents of

the Secret Service contend, with more than a little evidence, that the original judge in the case has a substantial conflict of interest. In a long footnote in the Writ, it was stated:

> In a July 13, 2000 Order, Judge Richard Roberts disclosed to the parties that he was personal friends with then Treasury Undersecretary James Johnson, who had supervised the United States Secret Service for the Department of Treasury during much of the relevant time period. Judge Roberts disclosed that he and Johnson had discussed the case as it had been reported by the *Washington Post* one morning over breakfast. In addition, Judge Roberts disclosed that as a Department of Justice attorney he served on the "Church Arson Task Force," co-chaired by Undersecretary Johnson. As a result, he was exposed to the "Good Ol' Boy Roundup" investigation which had documented organized racism by Agents in the Justice and Treasury law enforcement bureaus, including the Secret Service. At that time, Judge Roberts deemed recusal (stepping down from the case) inappropriate because there was no indication that he would be required to assess then Undersecretary Johnson's credibility and that the Roundup allegations were a small part of Petitioners' complaint. Four years later, the facts have changed substantially.
>
> Through Freedom of Information Requests, witness interviews, and other investigative techniques, Petitioners have learned more about the Roundups and Undersecretary Johnson's role in the subsequent investigation. Petitioners believe that Treasury Undersecretary James Johnson will be a key witness and that the

> "Good Ol' Boy Roundups" will be a significant part of this case. Thus, Judge Roberts will be required to assess Undersecretary Johnson's credibility and to rule on matters concerning the Roundup investigation.[32]

After years of delay, Roberts suddenly acquired a work ethic and reacted quickly to the Writ. On October 24, 2004, within two days of its filing, he ruled that "despite the [agents'] compelling allegations of discrimination within the Secret Service," the class action part of the suit should be dismissed on technical grounds because all the agents had not, as required, completely exhausted all necessary federal administrative channels before bringing the case into federal court.[33] Roberts contended that the agents had bypassed the internal processes for settling their disputes. Unsurprisingly, Roberts did not address the conflict-of-interest allegation raised by the Black Agents group.

While Roberts's ruling was a setback, it did not prevent Black Agents of the Secret Service from refiling the class action suit after going through all the administration steps and still finding no relief. In addition, individual claims would continue. Despite the filing of the case in 2000 and the unfavorable attention it brought to the Secret Service, overt racism continued to be a problem within the agency. In 2008, once some records were finally released, it was revealed that from 2003 through 2005, during the Bush administration, at least ten email messages contained racist jokes and messages. Remarkably, these messages were sent or forwarded from Secret Service supervisors. One email, referring to an assassination attempt on black leader Reverend Jesse Jackson, stated that if a missile hit a plane on which he was flying, it "certainly wouldn't be a great loss and it probably wouldn't be an accident either."[34] Another email made a joke about lynching.

The high rank of the Secret Service officials sending these emails demonstrated that the hostility was not a matter of isolated improprieties of entry-level employees, but rather institutional racism being perpetuated by agency leadership. One email dated October 9, 2003, that referred to a "Harlem Spelling Bee" and ridiculed black speaking styles was sent by Thomas Grupski, then assistant director for protective operations and later promoted to head the Office of Government Liaison and Public Affairs. Another racially inappropriate email about interracial sex, dated February 2003, was sent by Donald White—then head of the Presidential Protective Detail—to Kurt Douglass, the agent in charge of the Secret Service office in Cincinnati.[35]

In April 2008, a noose was left in a room used by a black instructor at the James J. Rowley Training Center in Beltsville, Maryland, where the Secret Service trains. A white agent admitted to leaving the rope and was put on administrative leave. The first response by the Secret Service was to state, "There has been no indication of racial intent on the part of the employee who has claimed responsibility."[36] Although the rope was found and reported on April 16, it took the agency's Office of Professional Responsibility eight more days to begin a formal investigation.[37] As *Newsweek* reported, the agency first debated whether the noose was even a noose or just a hanging rope.[38]

The emails came to light because a different judge in the case brought by the Black Agents group, Magistrate Judge Deborah A. Robinson, proved much more aggressive than her predecessor in pushing the Secret Service to give up files relevant to the case. She strongly criticized the agency for destroying records, deleting emails, failing to produce documents, and needlessly dragging out the case. On three occasions she admonished the agency and the Bush administration. The agency had been able to get away with stonewalling the case for so long because the Bush Justice Department had allowed it to.

The carefully cultivated and protected image of the Secret Service as a model of impeccable service and selfless professionalism was further shattered by a notorious security breakdown during the first year of the Obama administration. On November 24, 2009, at the first official state dinner hosted by the Obamas for Indian Prime Minister Manmohan Singh, the supposedly super-tight, multilayered, impenetrable circle of security around the White House and the president was brazenly breached by a publicity-seeking couple, Tareq and Michaele Salahi, and Carlos Allen, who entered with the official Indian delegation. Without an official invitation, all three were able to get into the event and even shake hands with President Obama and other top administration officials. Before the dinner was officially over, the Salahis had left and began posting pictures of themselves at the White House on the Internet.

While it is doubtful that a similar black couple would have been able to talk their way through White House security—the fact that both as a candidate and as a U.S. president Obama had reportedly received more death threats than any president in history, in part because of his race, underscores the seriousness of the security failure.[39]

Bolden has surely been watching these developments with some sense of vindication. His persecution by the agency and then the judicial system was a toxic mix of race and politics at the White House. From Kennedy to George W. Bush, and perhaps beyond, the White House has allowed racist behavior and discrimination to run rampant within the agency charged with protecting the president.

After the pioneering appointments of E. Frederic Morrow by Eisenhower and Bolden by Kennedy, black faces in high places became more frequent at the White House. Soon there would be other presidential aides, with significantly more visibility and authority than Morrow or Bolden. The 1960s would also bring black cabinet appointments, beginning with a trickle and then becoming normal. In fact, as a consequence of black activism, even conservative presidents felt an obligation to bring some racial diversity to their cabinets. The White House would also start to swing as it had never done before, as the sweet sound of black jazz musicians began to flow at 1600 Pennsylvania Avenue.

The 1960s and 1970s: The White House, the Modern Black Freedom Movement, and Averting Crisis

> *Time is on the side of the oppressed today, it's against the oppressor. Truth is on the side of the oppressed today, it's against the oppressor. You don't need anything else.*—Malcolm X, 1965

> *In this country American means white. Everybody else has to hyphenate.*— Toni Morrison

The 1960s would be a challenging time for the White House on many levels, particularly in racial politics. Racial and ethnic barriers (as well as gender, age, religion, disability, and sexual orientation) were being pushed and broken at a dizzying pace. Millions were mobilizing in the streets, suites, and other sites to become involved in their communities and in the political structures that made decisions affecting their lives. Trade unions found new life after decades of retreat following the organizing advances of the 1930s. Young people fought the White House over the Vietnam War and its other foreign and domestic policies. The 1960s were a time of turmoil not only in the United States but around the world as workers' movements in Europe and liberation movements in Africa, Asia, the Caribbean, and Latin American directly confronted centuries-old power structures.

Under John Kennedy, Lyndon Johnson, Richard Nixon, and Gerald Ford, the White House would be relentlessly confronted by the black community. On multiple fronts, black organizations, churches, and social movements mobilized to fight back against racial inequality at every level of daily life. With powerful leadership, black people of all ages used protest marches, civil disobedience, and relentless lobbying to open up space for landmark reforms in the area of racial justice and civil rights. The black freedom struggle was creating a culture of resistance that spread through church networks, the media, and the popular music of the time.

What historian C. Vann Woodward has called the "Second Reconstruction" came about because substantial change was the only way to prevent widespread civil unrest and revolt.[40] Power brokers in the White House, Congress, and Supreme Court passed reforms that had been rejected or ignored for decades. In nearly every area of U.S. society, African Americans, Latinos, Asians, and other groups historically oppressed and marginalized by whites were making breakthroughs by organizing. These accomplishments, however, were overwhelmingly driven from the bottom up rather than top-down organizing strategies. Wide-ranging social movements were applying relentless pressure on a historically white-dominated system to transform or risk continued disruption, rebellion, or even destruction. Those in power in the areas of public policy, business, academics, sports, and entertainment were forced to get involved, and their concessions were for the most part due to the mobilization of millions of activists and the radicalizing atmosphere of the period. It is also important to note that these changes were profoundly uneven. While the two coasts and large urban areas in the Midwest made changes relatively rapidly, in the South and many small communities around the country change was difficult and slow, and white backlash was stern and often violent.

And, once in place, newly gained reforms were often immediately endangered, either from passivity and timidity in their enforcement or from determined attack. Democratic administrations gave strong rhetorical support to defending the gains of the period while offering little support when they came under assault, and sometimes distancing themselves from black legislators, civil rights leadership, and other progressives. Republicans, using supposedly race-neutral frames, sought to roll back or stall any advances in racial equity and social justice.

The White House was not immune to the transformations and turbulence occurring across the country. From the liberal and progressive candidates who ran for office to the newly diverse staff at the White House to the opening for a more inclusive cultural life, 1600 Pennsylvania Avenue was forced to change with the times. And militant black advocates who went to the White House to meet with the president during this period, such as Martin Luther King Jr., A. Philip Randolph, and John Lewis, came with support from millions of African Americans who were working at the local level to bring more justice, fairness, democracy, and equality into U.S. social, cultural, economic, and political life.

For the twenty years from the mid-1950s to the mid-1970s, liberal, centrist, and even conservative presidents made accommodations with a vibrant black movement whose demands pushed the white-dominated political system to places it never could have imagined. And whether it was protests outside the White House or negotiations inside the White House, it was clear, in the words of 1960s soul singer Sam Cooke, that *change gonna come.*

Following the generally unresponsive Dwight Eisenhower administration, the 1960 victory of John F. Kennedy over the anti–civil rights agenda of Richard Nixon energized the black community. Although Kennedy's politics were mostly moderate on domestic policy (and hawkish on foreign policy), they were also pragmatic, and he recognized early on that black rights were an issue that could no longer be ignored. The increasing urbanization of African Americans put significant stress on the Democratic Party not only to address the civil rights issues that were being raised by the black community in cities like Newark, Detroit, Chicago, Philadelphia, and elsewhere, but also to support the voting and political rights of blacks in the South. Blacks outside the South identified with Southern blacks, not least because many were only a generation or two removed from the region, and the overwhelming majority still had family and friends there. Even for those who did not, the sense of shared pain and destiny was acute, and support for ending legal segregation was nearly universal.

Kennedy's words tended to carry more impact than his policies. During his campaign he gave personal support to the Civil Rights Movement by calling Coretta Scott King after Martin Luther King Jr. and others were arrested attempting to desegregate Rich's department store in Atlanta in October 1960, only a few weeks before the election. While the Nixon campaign declined E. Frederic Morrow's suggestion that the candidate send a telegram, the Kennedys were deftly manipulating the situation. Robert negotiated behind the scenes to have King released, always wary of losing white Southern votes, as John placed the now famous call to Coretta (which Robert initially vigorously opposed). Most analysts believe that the black vote was decisive in Kennedy's winning the White House, one of the narrowest election victories in U.S. history. As researcher Christopher Booker notes, Kennedy won Illinois by only 9,000 votes in a state with 250,000 black voters, and South Carolina by only 10,000 votes in a state with 40,000 black voters.[41] Overall, Kennedy won 49.7 percent of the vote compared to Nixon's 49.6 percent.

However, except for a number of low-level appointments and two Executive Orders that reinforced the need for anti-discrimination policies throughout the federal system and, in a limited way, desegregated public housing, it is difficult to identify any substantive effort on the part of Kennedy regarding civil rights. On March 6, 1961, he issued Executive Order 10925, which required that federal contractors take "affirmative action to ensure that applicants are employed, and that employees are treated during employment, without regard to their race, creed, color, or national origin." Besides being the first federal document to use the words "affirmative action," the Order also established the President's Committee on Equal Employment Opportunity, a tepid step that later evolved into the Equal Employment Opportunity Commission (EEOC). Executive Order 11063, issued on November 20, 1962, addressed discrimination in housing but only applied to new housing or construction directly financed by the federal government. And this was issued after the 1962 midterm Congressional elections, protecting the president and the Democrats against any backlash from white voters.

Meanwhile the president's brother, Attorney General Robert Kennedy, spent a great deal of time looking for communist infiltration of the Civil Rights Movement. During this period J. Edgar Hoover's FBI, under Robert Kennedy's Justice Department, extensively monitored King and other civil rights leaders.

Alerted by FBI wiretaps, on June 22, 1963, the president took King for a walk in the Rose Garden to ask him to dismiss two suspected communists on his staff—fundraiser and voter mobilizer Jack O'Dell and strategist Stanley Levinson.[42] When King told O'Dell about the encounter later (and his speculation that maybe Kennedy was being wiretapped himself, accounting for why the talk took place in the Rose Garden), O'Dell's understandable response was "Hoover can kiss my ass!"[43] O'Dell and King were convinced that the real aim was to limit the power and success of the movement, and that authorities hoped to accomplish that by getting rid of two of King's most trusted and effective advisers.

Keeping pace with the times, Kennedy regularly met with civil rights leaders. In most instances, they left empty-handed. They sought a strong push from the White House to work with Congress toward forging civil rights legislation, rather than to address civil rights concerns by just churning out Executive Orders, which could be easily overturned by future administrations. Kennedy supported the movement's voting rights campaigns for obvious reasons—putting more black voters on the rolls as they were switching to the Democratic Party was a no-brainer—but tended to oppose demonstrations and rallies. He tried to prevent, then co-opt, the August 1963 March on Washington. According to Thomas Reeves, the Kennedys were prepared to pull the plug on the microphones if they deemed the speeches too radical.[44] However, on the more serious black rights controversies of his presidency, from the freedom rides to the 1963 murder of Medgar Evers in Mississippi, the Kennedy administration was mostly absent. On June 11, after extreme provocation and the death of many activists, Kennedy announced that he would push Congress to pass a civil rights bill.[45]

But the crisis only grew. The intensity of movement for black equality in the South mushroomed and spread to the North and West. Kennedy and Johnson initially considered Martin Luther King a radical. Within a few short years, however, King seemed conservative compared to the Black Panthers, Malcolm X, Fannie Lou Hamer, Muhammad Ali, Abby Lincoln, Tommie Smith, John Carlos, Stokely Carmichael, Max Roach, H. Rap Brown, and other militant and revolutionary black voices of the period. These pioneering black women and men were not asking something from power; they were emanating power itself. From the smallest community group to internationally linked organizations, the radicalizing atmosphere of the period challenged the legitimacy of the state and the male, white-dominated system of power that enforced the status quo.

The Student Non-Violent Coordinating Committee (SNCC), which had been one of the key organizations on the front lines in the South, eventually evolved to being no longer just students, nor non-violent, centrally coordinated, or merely a committee. The organization came out against the Vietnam War long before many white student groups and based its opposition on a critique of capitalism, racism, and imperialism. In addition to the civil rights and black power movements, other people of color, women, peace, labor, and even seniors were making demands on the system that could not be fully ignored, marginalized, or repressed—all strategies that had been employed with some degree of success in the past but were no longer viable. Black Panthers, White Panthers, Gray Panthers, and their supporters would not retreat in the face of state refusal to respond.

Many of the most passionate and confrontational demonstrations concerned the war in Vietnam. U.S. support for the French in the late 1950s dramatically escalated under Dem-

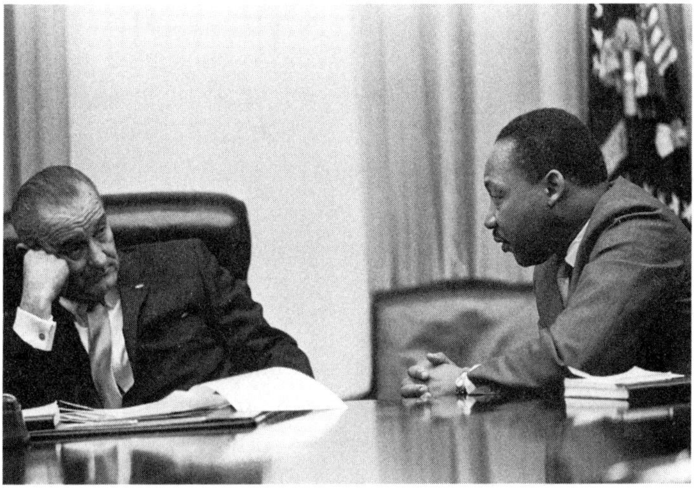

Martin Luther King Jr. meets with President Lyndon B. Johnson in the White House Cabinet Room, March 18, 1966.

ocratic and Republican administrations alike in the 1960s. The antiwar movement was overwhelmingly dominated by young, white, student activists. But African Americans were also involved. Conservatives, who did not necessarily support civil rights, charged that foreign policy should not be on the agenda of those fighting for civil rights, a racist assertion that reduced black politics to the narrow confines of national and local race issues.

From the very beginning, young black activists had opposed the war on numerous grounds. Some argued that is made little sense to fight for a democracy abroad that did not exist at home. Others contended that they had no disagreement with the Vietnamese and saw little reason to join the military to fight them. Those who were ideologically more to the left actually identified with the Vietnamese, supported socialism, and actively encouraged a U.S. defeat. A number of young activists who refused to be drafted left the country, went underground, or went to jail for years. SNCC had been one of the first organizations, black or white, to come out against the war. In a statement issued in 1966, it wrote, "We are in sympathy with, and support, the men in this country who are willing to respond to a military draft which would compel them to contribute their lives to United States aggression in Vietnam in the name of the 'freedom' we find so false in this country."[46] SNCC member Michael Simmons was one of those activists who refused to serve in the war. Initially active in Philadelphia, he built support there for the 1965 Selma, Alabama march, then he moved to the South to work with SNCC. He was one of the authors of SNCC's "Black Consciousness" paper and helped draft the SNCC statement against the war in 1966. For his own principled refusal to be inducted into the military and go to Vietnam, Simmons spent two and a half years in prison.

The early sacrifices of young blacks were not in vain: the antiwar movement grew, and some older leaders of the Civil Rights Movement joined their opposition. Eventually, even the more moderate elements of the black movement came to oppose the war. King's speech, "A Time to Break Silence," on April 4, 1967, exactly one year before his assassination, asserted that no line should be drawn between domestic policy and foreign policy, and that injustice should be fought wherever it exists. The speech was a turning point for the Johnson White House. In that speech, delivered at the historic Riverside Church in New York City, King stated that it was "incandescently clear that no one who has any concern for the integrity and life of America today can ignore the present war. If America's soul becomes totally poisoned, part of the autopsy must read Vietnam. It can never be saved so long as it destroys the deepest hopes of men the world over."[47]

Civil rights march from Selma to Montgomery, Alabama in 1965.

Intervention and reform became the most reasonable and necessary responses to the crisis by Congress, the Supreme Court, and the White House. Reacting to the pressure from below, Johnson's White House signed and celebrated the key civil rights legislative victories of the era, including the Civil Rights Act (1964), Voting Rights Act (1965), and Fair Housing Act (1968). Martin Luther King Jr. and other civil rights leaders would stand next to President Johnson in the White House again and again as he officially put his signature on these historic documents.

A number of high-level appointments would also occur under Johnson, the two most striking being the naming of the first black Supreme Court justice, Thurgood Marshall (whom the Kennedys had considered too radical), in 1967, and of Robert Weaver, the first black Cabinet member, as Secretary of the Department of Housing and Urban Development in 1966. For the first time, black women also received high-level appointments, including Patricia Harris as ambassador to Luxembourg (1965) and Constance Baker Motley to a federal judgeship (1966).

The legislation and the appointments grew out of a very painful, difficult struggle that saw state power employing both carrots and sticks as it attempted to resolve a crisis of legitimacy and authority without making fundamental or systemic changes. Much the way Lincoln and Franklin Roosevelt had, President Johnson faced cataclysmic internal disorder for which the state was unprepared. Urban rebellions in every year from 1964 to 1968 signaled the transformation of the major cities from enclaves of white power to contested sites of racial conflict involving educational, cultural, housing, employment, and criminal justice concerns. Radical theorist James Boggs argued that the city had become the black man's land, a reconfigured zone where blackness could contend effectively and forcefully with white power.[48]

In the end, due to widespread animosity toward the war, widespread urban rebellions in 1967 and 1968, loss of his base in the South, and the looming possibility of tens of thousands of low-income people pouring into D.C. and setting up camp, on March 31, 1968, Johnson announced that he would not seek reelection. The assassination of King four days later and then Robert Kennedy on June 5 not only spelled the end of Johnson's "Great Society" effort, but opened the door for a law-and-order Republican to succeed him. Though embarrassingly defeated by Kennedy in 1960, in part due to his ambiguous stance on civil rights, Richard Nixon and the Republican Party retooled their strategy and overtly went after the white Southern vote.

Republican president Richard Nixon would come to be called the most "anti-Negro" president since Woodrow Wilson. The black community's long list of grievances against Nixon[49] included the unsuccessful Supreme Court nominations of two anti–civil rights judges, Clement Haynsworth Jr. and G. Harrold Carswell; support for tax-exemption for whites-only private schools; and foot-dragging on school desegregation. Nixon opposed not only school desegregation but also the 1972 Equal Education Opportunities Act that sought to provide resources and support for black education without busing or desegregation.[50]

The Nixon years saw a continuation of the repressive, illegal, and debilitating covert attacks by the FBI and other federal law enforcement and intelligence agencies against major organizations in the black movement. The Black Panther Party, Republic of New Africa, Revolutionary Action Movement, black student organizations, black press, and many black power groups were infiltrated, destabilized and nearly destroyed. Civil rights organizations were also harassed and under surveillance. From 1956 to1971, the FBI launched its COINTELPRO campaign against the Communist Party, other left and socialist groups, and eventually a wide range of organizations and movements that arose in the 1960s seeking justice and inclusion. Although since its inception the FBI had used covert and illegal operations to try to destroy or neutralize black organizations, such as Garvey's Universal Negro Improvement Association, the level of intensity, coordination, systemic disruption and unconstitutional behavior reached its peak in the 1960s. The formal implementation of the program against the black movement began in mid-1967. In an August 25, 1967 memo from FBI headquarters to its offices around the country, Director J. Edgar Hoover noted, "The purpose of this new counterintelligence endeavor is to expose, disrupt, misdirect, discredit, or otherwise neutralize the activities of black nationalist, hate-type organizations and groupings, their leaderships, spokesmen, membership, and supporters, and to counter their propensity for violence and civil disorder."[51] With vigor and enthusiasm, the FBI manipulated black groups to fight each other, set up assassinations and false arrests, spread deadly rumors, and fostered violence all in violation of due process, civil rights, and other constitutional protections. The program formally ended in 1971 when the FBI admitted its role in abusing the rights of those who were legally dissenting. Researchers Ward Churchill and Jim Vander Wall argue that the strategies, tactics, and maneuvers continued though under different names.[52]

Nixon's foreign policy was also controversial and unpopular. He continued and dramatically escalated the Vietnam War, spreading it to Cambodia and Laos. His secretary of state, Henry Kissinger, lied and misled the public on countless occasions and is still seen as a war criminal by many people around the world. Nixon also sided with the oppressive apartheid regime in South Africa.

The paranoid Nixon saw adversaries on all fronts—among the media, students, the military, elected officials, and grassroots political organizations. To identify and presumably strike back at these opponents, Nixon created an "enemies list." Though it is doubtful that he was the first president to do so, perhaps he was the only one who actually wrote it down. Among the African Americans on the list were all twelve black Democratic Representatives (excluding Republican Sen. Edward Brooke), comedian Bill Cosby, the Black Panthers, the Southern Christian Leadership Conference, journalist Carl Rowan, social critic Dick Gregory, former Nixon aide Clifford Alexander Jr., former ambassador Patricia Harris, and civil rights activist Bayard Rustin.

His relationship with the Congressional Black Caucus, formed in 1969, was particularly acrimonious. In 1970 the Black Caucus requested a meeting with the president to discuss issues relevant to the black community. The administration refused to meet despite repeated requests. To demonstrate their ire at the situation, all members of the Black Caucus except Brooke boycotted Nixon's 1971 State of the Union address. Finally realizing the political seriousness of the squabble, Nixon consented to a meeting on March 25, 1971. At that meeting the Black Caucus presented him with sixty policy recommendations that had been culled from the work of a task force of "academicians, economists, lawyers, and civil rights activists" and 400 position papers. Although the meeting was cordial and the Black Caucus was able to articulate at length on the importance of implementing the recommendations, Nixon simply ignored the suggestions, and his relationship with the Caucus remained antagonistic through the remainder of his time in office.[53]

Nixon's long-lasting contribution to racial politics is the "Southern strategy." As the Republicans watched black voters increasingly switch to the Democratic Party, it dawned upon them that they could exploit the racial tensions in the South by positioning themselves as the party of whites. The Nixon campaign of 1968 developed a number of themes that were racially coded to appeal to whites in the region (and nationally) who felt threatened by the successes of the black freedom movement.

The Southern strategy called for opposition to busing and open housing, emphasized "law and order," supported public aid for private schools, advocated for states' rights, and gave succor to other thinly coded policies and proposals that signaled to whites that an anti-black agenda was on the way. As future Reagan strategist and Republican Party chairman Lee Atwater once stated, "You start out in 1954 by saying, 'Nigger, nigger, nigger.' By 1968 you can't say 'nigger.' . . . So you say stuff like forced busing, states' rights."[54] Nixon's campaign focused on those issues as well as "law and order" and "cutting taxes," all of which were seen through a racial lens.

The architect of the plan was political strategist Kevin Phillips, who described the strategy explicitly in his 1979 book *The Emerging Republican Majority*.[55] As reported by the *New York Times* in 1970, Phillips stated bluntly, "From now on, the Republicans are never going to get more than 10 to 20 percent of the Negro vote and they don't need any more than that . . . but Republicans would be shortsighted if they weakened enforcement of the Voting Rights Act. The more Negroes who register as Democrats in the South, the sooner the Negrophobe whites will quit the Democrats and become Republicans. That's where the votes are. Without that prodding from the blacks, the whites will backslide into their old comfortable arrangement with the local Democrats."[56]

The strategy worked and within a decade, whites in the South were solidly Republican. Even the election of two Southern Democrats, Jimmy Carter in 1976 and Bill Clinton in 1992 and 1996, did not yield a majority of white voters from the region (or nationally) for either candidate. As he lay dying from brain cancer, Atwater apologized for the tactics he had used throughout his career, particularly those employed to defeat Michael Dukakis in 1984. In 2005, Republican National Committee chairman Ken Mehlman, in a talk before the NAACP, apologized for the party's use of race as a wedge issue, saying that it was a "wrong" strategy.[57]

Ironically, it was Nixon who first instituted the federal polices now known as affirmative action. In 1969, Nixon appointed Arthur Fletcher as Assistant Secretary of Wage and Labor Standards at the Department of Labor. Fletcher, an old-school, moderate black Republican, devised what was called the "Philadelphia Plan," a program that pushed for more employment and business opportunities for African Americans and other minorities in the construction industry, i.e., an affirmative action program. This effort was a part of Nixon's push for black capitalism, an effort he championed as "black power." Fletcher would later work for the White House during the Ford, Reagan, and George H. W. Bush administrations.

Given Nixon's overall anti-black agenda, policies, and covert programs, it is fitting that he was brought down by a black security guard. On the evening of June 17, 1972, Frank Wills was working as an $80.00-a-week security guard in the Watergate Building in Washington, D.C. The many swank offices located there included the headquarters of the Democratic National Committee. When he noticed that duct tape had been put over the lock of one of the doors, and then saw later that it had been removed, he knew something was wrong. He called the police, and they discovered five burglars—Bernard Baker, Virgilio Gonzales, James McCord, Eugenio Martinez, and Frank Sturgis—who had been trying to place secret wiretaps in the office on behalf of Nixon's reelection campaign. While Nixon may or may not have known about the burglary beforehand, tape recordings from the White House reveal that he was involved in the illegal effort to cover up the administration's complicity in the crime.

Although he was seen as a hero in the black community, as it turned out, Wills's future would not be bright. While the *Washington Post* reporters who covered the news story, Carl Bernstein and Bob Woodward, went on to make millions from the books, movies, documentaries, and papers they produced, Wills had a difficult time finding work and fell into deep poverty. (He played himself in the film version of their book, *All the President's Men*.) Although Nixon was permitted to resign without facing criminal charges, Wills was arrested on a shoplifting charge and spent a year in jail. He moved back to Georgia and died nearly penniless on September 27, 2000.

Gerald Ford's presidency was unremarkable on almost every level. A telling detail of his legacy as a footnote to history, he was the only chief executive to serve who had not been elected either president or vice president. It is a testimony to his lack of political import that he is most remembered and, in many cases, reviled for his pardon of Nixon shortly after the president resigned in disgrace. While he was more prone to meet with black leaders than Nixon, he essentially continued his predecessor's agenda of opposing busing, rejected race-based remedies for improving black attendance in higher education, and supported a states' rights approach to most policy issues.

Although much of the country was tilting right as a backlash against the revolts of the sixties, Nixon's dishonorable resignation opened the door for a Democratic victory in 1976. Jimmy Carter became the deep South's first Democrat to win the White House in generations. The peanut farmer and nuclear engineer from Georgia received strong endorsements from the civil rights elite based in Atlanta—Andrew Young, Coretta Scott King, and Martin King Sr.—as well as from Jesse Jackson, NAACP Chairman Benjamin Hooks, and National Urban League President Vernon Jordan. Having grown up in a community that consisted of twenty-three black families and two white families, one of which was the Carters, Jimmy was comfortable around African Americans in ways that nearly all previous presidents were not. But that incubator embodied the unequal status endemic to the South; in Carter's neighborhood blacks always deferred to whites.

Carter's White House appointed a number of African Americans to highly visible high-ranking positions. They included Andrew Young as ambassador to the United Nations, Patricia Roberts Harris as Secretary of Housing and Urban Development, Eleanor Holmes Norton as head of the EEOC, and Clifford Alexander as Secretary of the Army. The Young appointment ended in disaster when, in August 1979, it was exposed that contrary to administration policy, he had met secretly with the Palestine Liberation Organization's chief UN representative Zehdi Terzi earlier that year on July 26. Carter had a formal agreement with Israel that no unauthorized or unplanned meetings should take place between U.S. officials and the PLO. Young compounded the situation by initially stating that the encounter had been an accident but later revealing that it had indeed been planned. Although black leaders almost universally supported Young and endorsed the United States meeting with the PLO, Carter did not hesitate to ask for his resignation. Young had gotten into trouble earlier in his tenure for stating that Cuba was a "stabilizing" factor in the civil war that was unfolding in Angola during that time, a war in which the U.S. government backed the other side. Although Carter's foreign policy doctrine gave emphasis to human rights, he and Secretary of State Zbigniew Brzezinski held to Cold War politics when it came to African policies.

To help address his black and female constituencies, President Carter hired Louis Martin as a special assistant. He was instrumental in the black appointments noted above and helped Carter navigate the racial waters of Washington, D.C. Martin coordinated the symbolic dimensions of the White House's outreach to black America, including Carter's visits to black organizations, photo opportunities between the president and blacks, and other efforts.

During Carter's tenure, perhaps the most significant policy issue for the nation's racial politics was the *Bakke* decision. When Allan Bakke was turned down for admission to the University of California at Davis Medical School, he charged "reverse" discrimination. Bakke claimed that he had been discriminated against as a white person because the school had admitted, through a special task force program, African Americans who on average had lower test scores and lower grade point averages than he did. He failed to mention that about 20 percent of whites that had been admitted to the school also scored lower than Bakke had, and that there were a number of blacks who were turned down for admission through the task force program. Rather than focus on what was more likely age discrimination—Bakke was thirty-two at the time he applied and had been turned down by twelve other medical schools—he decided to present himself as a victim of racism. On October 12, 1977, the case that many considered the most significant affecting education since *Brown v. Board of Education*, went before the U.S. Supreme Court.

At the Carter White House, chaos ensued. Without a strong and clear stance from the president, staffers presented conflicting positions. Carter sought a middle ground by opposing quotas but supporting remedies that would increase the number of blacks and other minorities in medical schools. In the end, the Supreme Court decision, announced on June 28, 1978, was a mixed bag of conclusions. In a five-to-four vote, the Court ruled that a special admission program through the task force process was "unlawful," and it directed that Bakke be admitted to the school. However, also on a five-to-four vote, the Court ruled that race could remain a consideration in the admissions process. Four Justices (Burger, Rehnquist, Stevens, and Steward) found the program illegal on statutory grounds, while Powell argued its unlawfulness for constitutional reasons. Thurgood Marshall, the first and only black on the Court, wrote a seething dissent contending that the decision meant the country had "come full circle" and comparing it to the 1896 *Plessy v. Ferguson* ruling.[58] The Congressional Black Caucus, civil rights leaders, and black academics severely criticized the decision as a step backward and the opening salvo of a series of attacks on affirmative action. Although the decision came fairly close to what President Carter wanted, he lost both black and white support because of the White House's poor handling of public discourse.

Carter would only last one term. Although his lackadaisical approach to civil rights concerns lost him some black votes, it was his handling of the Iranian hostage crisis that conveyed an image of weakness and lack of resolve. When militant Iranian students took hostages at the U.S. embassy in Tehran on November 4, 1979, Carter was unable to win their freedom before election day, and he paid the cost. The crisis was an opening for the Republican Party to reassert a force-driven foreign policy and ratchet up Cold War tensions. Representing a sea change in both domestic and foreign affairs, the next occupant of the White House was Republican victor Ronald Reagan.

The Reagan Reversal and Beyond

Reagan's White House represented a true turning point in black history. On every single issue of concern to the black community and every step that had been taken forward, the new administration was pushing back. As global demand for an immediate end to the racist apartheid system in South Africa grew, the Reagan administration issued its policy of "constructive engagement," i.e., limiting criticism of the regime's murderous behavior while supplying white South Africa the resources to perpetuate its domination of the black population. Reagan had opposed *all* the key civil rights bills of the 1960s, including the Civil Rights Act, Voting Rights Act, Fair Housing Act, and affirmative action across the board.

Reagan also sought to bring an end to the influence of

the civil rights leadership network. Unlike the presidents that had recently preceded him, he brought in his own network of conservative black activists to challenge the black members of congress and civil rights leaders for the political ears, eyes, and heart of the black community. This included academics Thomas Sowell, Glenn Loury, Walter Williams, Robert Woodson, Shelby Steele, and Stephen Carter; journalists Juan Williams and Armstrong Williams; and government staffers Alan Keyes, Clarence Thomas, Clarence Pendleton, and William Keyes. None of these individuals had a broad, or in most cases even narrow constituency among African Americans, or any ties to the civil rights community. A key distinction between them and previous black Republican and conservative African Americans who served or worked with Republican presidents is that they were vehemently anti–civil rights, anti-welfare, and antigovernment. They were generally unknown until given prominence during the Reagan era by media that preferred controversy over history and context. As scholar Leon Newton notes, Reagan deliberately worked to foster a "change of public discourse regarding race and politics as it affects the lives of African Americans."[59]

In December 1980, a few weeks after Reagan won the election, a number of these black conservatives met in San Francisco—one of the most Democratic cities in the nation—to set an agenda for seizing the initiative in black politics. All of the traditional conservative scripts were rolled out as they railed against the government-dependent politics of African American leaders. These black Reaganites missed the irony that outside the pool of white conservatives, they were unable to raise any resources or generate support for their anti–civil rights cause on their own. Yet it was their very blackness that was being traded on. While they steadfastly claim that they wanted to be seen as individuals and not as racial beings, they had no value to their white conservative sponsors beyond being black.[60]

Reagan's black appointments reflected the scarcity of qualified far-right black conservatives for key positions in his administration. His only black cabinet appointment was the politically moderate Samuel Pierce as Secretary of Housing and Urban Development, and reportedly Reagan often forgot his name, although that may have been due to the onset of his Alzheimer's disease, which grew worse during his presidency.

Colin L. Powell was appointed by Ronald Reagan as White House National Security Advisor, launching his long career, during which he was often in conflict with more far-right conservatives inside and outside the Republican Party. Pierce and Powell represented the moderate conservatism of the blacks appointed by the Reagan White House. Others, such as State Department minor bureaucrat Alan Keyes, Reagan's chair of the U.S. Civil Rights Commission Clarence Pendleton, and EEOC head Clarence Thomas, led the ideological war against civil rights and civil rights leaders.

Reagan's vigorous anti-black agenda did not go unchallenged. In 1984, only days after Reagan's reelection, the black-led Free South Africa Movement (FSAM) was born that launched a year-long political mobilization against Reagan's collaborationist policies toward the Apartheid regime. FSAM employed a dual nationwide campaign that included civil disobedience at the South African embassy in Washington, D.C. and consulates around the country, and lobbying black and progressive members of Congress to impose sanctions against South Africa. With support from celebrities to grassroots activists, public opinion turned against Reagan and he suffered his only foreign policy defeat when in October 1986, Congress overrode Reagan's veto and passed the Comprehensive Anti-

Apartheid Act that banned trade and investment in South Africa. The movement, led by FSAM, had successfully shifted the debate from anti-communism to a debate regarding racism against South Africa's black majority.

George H. W. Bush softened but essentially carried forward Reagan's agenda. He falsely promised a "kindler, gentler" administration but attacked the civil rights agenda with budget cuts and tepid law enforcement of civil rights. He left three marks that stand out in White House racial politics: the Willie Horton campaign advertisement, the selection of Clarence Thomas for the U.S. Supreme Court, and the war on drugs.

Bush's opponent in the 1988 campaign turned out to be more the convicted murderer and rapist William Horton than Massachusetts Governor Michael Dukakis. Horton had escaped from a Massachusetts prison furlough program in June 1986 and a year later brutally and repeatedly raped a white woman after beating and tying up her fiancé in Maryland. He was eventually caught and sentenced to life in prison without the possibility of parole in Maryland. Although the furlough program had started under Dukakis's Republican predecessor, Governor Francis W. Sargent, in 1972, he maintained and strongly defended the program. Republicans saw a racial opening, and after focus groups demonstrated that the Horton story could turn even Democrats to vote for Bush, it became a central issue in the race. Both the formal Bush campaign and groups that supported it began to air commercials featuring Horton—even calling him "Willie" rather than "William," which the Bush campaign preferred in an effort to make Horton sound even blacker—and the inept Dukakis never recovered. Bush tapped white fear of blacks to win the White House.

After the venerable Thurgood Marshall, the first and only black Supreme Court Justice up to that point in history, announced his retirement in July 1991, Bush nominated Clarence Thomas as his replacement. Supremely unqualified, having only served one year as a federal judge on the D.C. Circuit Court of Appeals, Thomas had never argued before the Supreme Court and had no legal writings of note. Bush cynically counted on the reluctance of an all-white U.S. Senate to deny a black candidate and on the predictable division among African Americans. He was correct on both counts. Thomas held the most extreme conservative view possible and was chosen to satisfy Bush's right-wing anti-abortion, antigovernment, pro-corporate, anti–affirmative action, and anti–civil rights base. His nomination generated the most intense mobilization of African Americans around a Supreme Court nominee since the case of Judge Parker in the 1920s. However, support for Thomas by some prominent liberal African Americans, including poet Maya Angelou, civil rights leader Rev. Joseph Lowry, and NAACP board chair Margaret Bush Wilson, created enough space for some white Democrats to feel that they could support Thomas's nomination.

Despite Anita Hill's credible charges of sexual harassment which surfaced during the nomination process and were later verified by the *Washington Post* and other media sources, as well as irrefutable evidence of Thomas's extremist views, which he sought to deny and obfuscate during the hearings, he was confirmed to the Court by a Senate vote of fifty-two to forty-eight on October 15, 1991, the narrowest margin in over 100 years (forty-one Republicans and eleven Democrats voted yes; forty-six Democrats and two Republicans voted no).[61] Since that time he has been the most consistent far-right voice on the U.S. Supreme Court.

As president, Bush also escalated a war against drug users and traffickers. The explosion of crack cocaine use and marketing was exploited by the administration and its allies in Congress to institute a series of new federal laws that harshly and disproportionately punished users, small-time dealers, and petty criminals. Laws that sent people away permanently, such as the "Three-Strikes-and-You're-Out" law, tended to fill the jails and prisons without substantially denting the use or sale of illegal narcotics. Two-thirds of the antidrug budget focused on law enforcement, while only one-third addressed prevention and treatment. To sell this program, the drug threat was racialized by pervasive images of black users and young black men dealing drugs.[62]

The impact of those discriminatory policies is felt today. As Human Rights Watch researcher James Fellner sadly notes, "Among black defendants convicted of drug offenses, 71 percent received sentences to incarceration in contrast to 63 percent of convicted white drug offenders. Human Rights Watch's analysis of prison admission data for 2003 revealed that relative to population, blacks are 10.1 times more likely than whites to be sent to prison for drug offenses."[63] Drug policies account for the grossly disproportionate incarceration of African Americans. According to the U.S. Department of Justice, Bureau of Justice Statistics' report *Prison Inmates at Midyear 2007*:

> The custody incarceration rate for black males was 4,618 per 100,000. Hispanic males were incarcerated at a rate of 1,747 per 100,000. Compared to the estimated numbers of black, white, and Hispanic males in the U.S. resident population, black males (6 times) and Hispanic males (a little more than 2 times) were more likely to be held in custody than white males. At midyear 2007 the estimated incarceration rate of white males was 773 per 100,000.[64]

Due to his implementation of tax increases after he had sworn to oppose them, and his halfhearted response to the 1992 uprising in Los Angeles following the not guilty verdict in the Rodney King beating trial, Bush's support from conservatives and moderates eroded. The upstart candidacy of H. Ross Perot and the skilled campaign of Bill Clinton cost Bush his reelection and brought another Southern Democratic governor to the White House.

Clinton appointed five black Cabinet members during his first term—Commerce Secretary Ron Brown, Agriculture Secretary Mike Espy, Labor Secretary Alexis Herman, Energy Secretary Hazel R. O'Leary, and Veteran Affairs Secretary Jesse Brown—and enjoyed widespread support by blacks. He was called "our first black president" by Nobel Prize–winning author Toni Morrison. She went on to write, "Clinton displays almost every trope of blackness: single-parent household, born poor, working-class, saxophone-playing, McDonald's-and-junk-food-loving boy from Arkansas."[65] Naturally, Clinton relished his cozy relationship with the black community. Yet a number of critical policy moves by Clinton generated high opposition among blacks, most notably the North American Free Trade Agreement (NAFTA), the 1994 Crime Bill, and welfare reform. All these initiatives had begun under the previous Bush administration, and there had been hope that Clinton would end them. NAFTA was strongly opposed by all the traditional constituencies of the Democratic Party: organized labor, blacks, Latinos, women, and human rights activists. They feared correctly that the legislation would drive jobs out of the country, disproportionately benefit large corporations, destroy what was left of the domestic textile industry, and hurt minority employment. Clinton was only able to pass the bill by building a coalition of moderate and conservative Republican legislators and some Democrats.

Another wedge issue that Clinton bought into was crime. In 1994, still in the midst of hysteria about crack cocaine and narco-terrorism, Congress debated the passage of the most sweeping reform in federal crime policy in generations. The legislation included more than fifty new death-penalty provisions, harsher penalties for a wide range of crimes, and essentially an abandonment of the notion of rehabilitation. Clinton was again forced to build a conservative-to-moderate coalition of Republicans and Democrats to pass the bill. During this same period, the controversy emerged over the Reagan-era relationship between the CIA-backed Contras—the murderous band of rebels who were fighting the Sandinista government in Nicaragua—and Latin American drug dealers who trafficked cocaine to America's inner cities. Research by Pultizer Prize–winning journalist Gary Webb documented that for the better part of a decade, a California-based drug ring sold tons of cocaine to Los Angeles street gangs and funneled millions in drug profits to the CIA-backed Contras.[66] Webb's revelation that high-level U.S. officials knowingly allowed massive amounts of drugs and money to change hands at the expense of poor inner-city neighborhoods, mostly communities of color, set off an explosive controversy that rocked Washington. Declassified government documents and testimony conclusively proved that the CIA had secret dealings with the Justice Department from 1982 to 1995 that permitted the agency to avoid reporting cases of drug trafficking by its agents and assets.[67] Many black commentators further believed that the CIA and the U.S. government deliberately allowed drugs into the cities to subvert black militancy there.

Since the days of Reagan's racist "welfare queen" stereotypes, conservatives had been calling for an end to the Aid to Families with Dependent Children (AFDC) program, decrying what they called government-bred dependency on the part of the undeserving poor. In seeking moderate votes, the Clinton campaign highlighted welfare reform as a policy goal. After the Republican victory in Congress in 1994, conservatives passed a radical reform bill that Clinton signed despite massive opposition from black communities. Congressional Black Caucus members, divided on many of these issues, were not able to prevent any of these initiatives from becoming law.

Another milestone occurred during Clinton's term: the elevation of Ron Brown as the first African American chair of the Democratic Party. Brown, a moderate, helped maintain the administration's centrist posture and was crucial to Clinton's successful reelection in 1996. African Americans had strongly supported Clinton in both his presidential campaigns: he won 82 percent of the black vote in 1992, and 84 percent in1996.[68] But in neither election did Clinton win the majority of the white vote.

The White House "Race Initiative" was Clinton's major thrust into racial politics. The project was launched in June 1997 with goals "to articulate the President's vision of racial reconciliation" and "to promote a constructive dialogue" about race. President Clinton conducted a series of town hall meetings around the country and established an advisory board chaired by historian John Hope Franklin. The initiative was all talk, and no new programs were developed as a result of it.

The racially sophisticated Clinton was followed by the racially clueless George W. Bush. Although former vice president Al Gore had won the popular vote by 50,999,897 to 50,456,002, former Texas governor Bush won control of the White House with a Supreme Court vote of five to four in what became one of the most disputed elections in the nation's history. The African American community felt especially aggrieved, because so many

Condoleezza Rice, March 1, 2005

votes cast by African Americans in Florida were not counted, suppressed with shady methods by the state's Republican Party. The fact that Bush's brother, Jeb Bush, was governor of Florida at the time—and that Florida secretary of state Katherine Harris headed up George Bush's campaign in the state—fed the sense of electoral fraud and collusion.

As president, Bush mostly evaded the issue, primarily because he had very little to say beyond conservative clichés and bromides. When asked about his civil rights record two years after being in office, he began with a vague reference to Secretary of State Colin Powell and National Security Advisor Condoleezza Rice, and then his voice began to trail off. Perhaps he suddenly realized the foolishness of equating two appointments with a civil rights policy agenda. Perhaps not. Powell and Rice were sometimes sent to speak to black audiences or respond when a racial situation arose, such as when Rice was sent to talk to blacks after the Hurricane Katrina crisis. There were points of conflicts between the two; for instance, Powell wanted to attend the United Nations World Conference Against Racism in Durban, South Africa, while Rice opposed U.S. participation almost from the beginning of the Bush administration. Powell was also a strong, longtime supporter of affirmative action, while Rice was less so.

The politically moderate Colin Powell was never really welcome in the West Wing, intimidating to Bush and anathema to Cheney, but Condoleezza Rice would rise to become an integral force among the president's innermost circle. While Powell's role diminished daily until he was finally pushed out at the end of the president's first term, Rice's position grew stronger as she was promoted from National Security Advisor to Secretary of State. Certainly, no other African American woman has held such a high staff position, and only one other woman, former secretary of state Madeleine Albright, achieved the same power and reach.

Rice's personal closeness to Bush was well known (she once accidentally referred to Bush as "my husband" while speaking at a dinner hosted by *New York Times* bureau chief Philip Taubman[69]) and likely protected her from blame for an embarrassing series of intelligence failures on her watch as National Security Advisor—from missing all the signals that Al Qaeda was preparing to attack the United States to leading the false charge that Saddam Hussein possessed weapons of mass destruction—that would have led to the firing of most anyone else. She served as Bush's brain on foreign affairs in many instances and personally tutored him during his campaign for president in 2000. Ultimately, her alliance with the administration's neoconservatives during Bush's first term, moderated during the second when their discredited policies had obviously failed and their influence waned, left her a poor legacy overall.

However, on domestic and race issues, Rice did not represent the politics of the far right, where many contemporary black Republicans have chosen to situate themselves. During an interview with the *Washington Times*, she once described slavery and the role it played in the founding of this country as a national "birth defect."

"Black Americans were a founding population," she said. "Africans and Europeans came here and founded this country together—Europeans by choice and Africans in chains. That's not a very pretty reality of our founding." As a result, Rice told the paper's editors and reporters, "descendants of slaves did not get much of a head start, and I think you continue to see some of the effects of that. That particular birth defect makes it hard for us to confront it, hard for us to talk about it, and hard for us to realize that it has continuing relevance for who we are today."[70]

Not only has she been soft on affirmative action, but she appears to be agnostic on abortion—calling herself at times "mildly pro-choice"[71]—and libertarian on other social issues that are dear to the Republican Party's right wing. Perhaps most galling to the political right, she does not vilify the Civil Rights Movement or bash race-related concerns. This would explain, in part, her relatively low profile in Republican circles after a brief attempt to encourage her to run for president in 2008. Nearly all modern-day black Republicans serve the conservative movement's purposes by their willingness to use their race to attack efforts at antiracism, something Rice has been hesitant to do.

There were few blacks among Bush's higher staff and very, very few African American women. Indeed, a number of high-ranking conservative black women were brought in by Rice, including some of her former students, such as Jendayi Frazer and former Rice coauthor Kiron K. Skinner. Frazer worked with Rice for the National Security Council and later became ambassador to South Africa. Skinner is a noted and admiring writer about Ronald Reagan and at this writing is a Fellow at the Hoover Institution at Stanford University, where Rice once served as provost. In the main, however, Rice spent her days working with older, conservative, old-school white males. By all evidence, Cheney and Rumsfeld demonstrated little tolerance or respect for anyone they did not consider their equal, a category that certainly included Rice. However, her strong relationship with the president shielded her from the worst aggression and allowed her to survive the vicious internal politics of the administration.

It is notable that McCain never seriously considered Rice as a vice presidential running mate, instead choosing the ill-prepared, ignorant, and vapid Alaska governor Sarah Palin. While he selected Palin with the thought that she could help bring the party's far-right base along, he also may have rejected Rice for expressing early on a racial sympathy for Obama's campaign. She has never revealed whom she voted for, but she joined millions of other African Americans who gushed with emotion after his victory.[72]

In July 2010, in a demonstration that she has not lost touch with black culture as some have argued, Rice performed with "Queen of Soul" Aretha Franklin in a fund-raising concert for a program to increase arts awareness among urban children. Rice is an accomplished classical pianist who plays regularly with a chamber music group in Washington and has performed publicly with revered cellist Yo-Yo Ma. Her concert with Aretha Franklin, held at Philadelphia's Mann Music Center, included classical pieces, patriotic songs, and Franklin standards such as "Respect" and "I Say a Little Prayer." Franklin was a strong supporter of Obama during the 2008 campaign and almost stole the show at his inauguration when she performed with a much talked-about matching coat and hat. Both Rice and Franklin agreed that educational budget cuts have disproportionately targeted music programs and the arts.[73]

In the end, Rice held the most powerful political position ever achieved by an African American woman in the United States. She wielded real political authority that went far beyond the symbolism of high office. Ultimately, however, that position did not translate into policy or political benefits for U.S. black communities, other communities of color, working people, or women in any significant manner. Although her tasks did not include domestic issues, she bears a responsibility, along with Powell, for defending and advancing the administration's deleterious policies overall.

Beyond Powell and Rice, there were few other African Americans visible in Bush's inner circle or his staff at the White House. One individual was Claude Allen, who held the highly important position of Assistant to the President for Domestic Policy. The job required coordinating the president's domestic policy agenda.

According to the *Washington Post*, Allen earned $161,000 annually, the highest salary paid in the White House, the same amount that was paid to Karl Rove, Andrew Card, and Stephen Hadley, among others. After graduating from college, he had gone to work for far-right Senator Jesse Helms (R-NC). He later worked as Secretary of Health and Human Resources for Virginia governor James S. Gilmore III (R) in the late 1990s. Before coming to the White House in 2005, he had been deputy secretary at the U.S. Department of Health and Human Services for the administration. He also became a protégé of Supreme Court Justice Clarence Thomas when the latter was a judge on the U.S. Court of Appeals for the D.C. Circuit. Cut from the same radical-right political mold as Clarence Thomas, he was nominated to the Fourth Circuit Court of Appeals, which covers Maryland, Virginia, West Virginia, South Carolina, and North Carolina. Like Thomas, he had no judicial experience or any significant writings. He was rated partially unqualified by the American Bar Association. Bush later withdrew his nomination in the face of fierce opposition from the NAACP, People for the American Way, and a number of feminist groups. In January 2005, Bush brought him to the White House. As domestic policy chief, he helped develop Bush's position on a wide range of labor, health, housing, education, and other issues, always from a hard conservative posture. He pushed for abstinence-based sex education and called for expanding the No Child Left Behind program.

A year after coming to the White House, Allen suddenly and inexplicably resigned. At first, the White House stated that he was leaving to spend more time with his family. In fact, Allen was in legal trouble. Despite his $161,000 salary, he had been caught stealing about $5,000 in what the police called a "refund scheme" at the retail stores Target and Hecht's. Allegedly, Allen would purchase an item, leave the store and put it in his car, return to the store, get the same item off the shelf, and ask for a refund on his credit card.[74] Like most contemporary black conservatives, Allen was sharply critical of liberals for what he considered their lack of moral consistency and dismissal of family values.

A crisis provides an opportunity to bring about change, though such opportunities are not always seized. In terms of race politics and black history, Bush's defining moment was his response to the Hurricane Katrina crisis. Despite warnings that the storm would be devastating, almost no one in the administration, including President Bush, acted on the situation with appropriate urgency. While the administration seemed incapable of getting help to the city, tens of thousands of media and private services descended upon New Orleans to offer aid and make the plight of the people there known to the world. What appeared to be a callous disregard for thousands of people—disproportionately black and poor—clinched African American opinion toward Bush. That, and the consistent rejection of Bush's Iraq War by black Americans, left him with one of the lowest, if not the lowest, ranking of any president by African Americans. In one controversial poll conducted by NBC and the *Wall Street Journal* in 2005, Bush's approval rating among African Americans had dropped to 2 percent. Although there was criticism that the survey only interviewed 89 blacks out of 809 interviewees, most experts still agreed that approval was under 15 percent, a historic low by any measure.[75]

While African Americans for the most part found it difficult to penetrate the White House as policy shapers, there would be other avenues though which a black presence would be felt. Although many genres of black music had been performed at the White House, significantly, perhaps the single most original and deeply rooted form of black creative expression was absent from the home of the president for more than the first sixty years of its existence: jazz. As music and as political opportunity, jazz in the White House would become another prism through which the nation's racial politics would manifest.

Jazz in the (White) House

> *There's probably no better example of democracy than a jazz ensemble—individual freedom, but with responsibility to the group.*[76]—First Lady Michelle Obama

Freedom is a word that is the foundation of our country.[77]—Duke Ellington

Duke Ellington has a White House story. On his seventieth birthday, April 29, 1969, his long career at the top of the jazz world was celebrated by President Richard Nixon with a dinner at the White House. At that event, Ellington was presented the Presidential Medal of Freedom, the highest award given by the United States to a citizen. After more than seven decades of evolution and global impact, jazz and one of its grand masters were finally getting their due. Ellington biographer John Edward Hasse referred to the event as "the capstone of his career."[78]

Ellington's relationship to the White House dated back to the Roosevelts. As early as February 16, 1934, Ellington had offered to play for President Franklin Roosevelt's White House in a time when Eleanor Roosevelt was actively expanding the number and range of performances at the residence, including many black artists. However, Ellington and a number of other famous acts, such as the Andrews Sisters and Igor Stravinsky, were turned down, primarily due to scheduling issues.[79]

Presidents Truman, Eisenhower, and Johnson had encounters with Ellington as well. On September 29, 1950, he met with Truman at the White House to personally present him with a copy of a musical piece he had written, titled "Harlem," and a portion of his Toscanini-commissioned manuscript, "Portrait of New York Suite."[80] He admired the fact that Truman—albeit under pressure—had desegregated the military. Ellington planned to premiere his "Harlem" piece in January 1951 for a NAACP fundraiser at New York's Metropolitan Opera House. Later, in November 1950, in a letter to Truman, he noted that the proceeds from the upcoming concert "will be used to help fight for your civil rights program—to stamp out segregation, discrimination, bigotry and a variety of intolerances in our own American society."[81]

Truman's civil rights program was more mirage than reality, so it is not clear if Ellington was being kind or naïve. He was also recognized by Eisenhower, although it is unknown if he held the same opinion of him that Louis Armstrong did. In response to the president's mishandling the school integration crisis at Central High School in Little Rock, Armstrong famously stated, "The way they are treating my people in the South, the Government can go to hell. The president has no guts."[82] In 1960 the State Department sponsored a tour to the Congo in which Armstrong participated. Only months later, the CIA and Belgian intelligence played a covert role in the assassination of the Congo's progressive, anticolonial president Patrice Lumumba on January 17, 1961.[83]

At age sixty-six, Ellington gave his first concert at the White House, on June 14, 1965, for the "White House Festival of the Arts." Ellington's performance was neither overtly political nor entirely neutral. He played his "Impressions of the Far East," which reflected his travels to spread the music and a positive image of African Americans around the world, and his epic musical narrative of black history "Black, Brown, and Beige."[84] In 1966, President Lyndon Johnson presented Ellington with the Congressional Gold Medal. This award is given by Congress and delivered by the president to those who have achieved excellence and outstanding achievement in their field, or performed an outstanding service to the nation.

By the 1960s, jazz had been a worldwide phenomenon for decades. Nearly every corner of the globe had a jazz culture and paid homage to what many considered America's most original musical contribution to world culture. Born in America's black segregated communities around the beginning of the twentieth century, it spread to every corner of the nation, evolving local varieties and innovations as it went. Around the world, jazz was seen as embodying the principles of democracy in its harmonious reconciliation between the collective and the individual.[85] In Hitler's Germany, it galvanized young people to rebel against Nazism. In South Africa, anti-apartheid activists used jazz to challenge the racist white regime. In Brazil, it was appropriated by a rising middle class in the form of Bossa Nova. In Cuba, jazz remained popular both before and after the 1959 revolution. In India, it symbolized modernity and became the rage of the upper classes.[86]

Cold War and Hot Jazz

For millions around the world, jazz was heard on a regular basis through "Voice of America," the U.S. propaganda radio station that was broadcast to 100 million people in dozens of countries by the mid-1960s, including, illegally, into Eastern Europe. And for many, the mellifluous voice of Willis Conover was *the* voice of America. Beginning in January 1955, his "Music USA" broadcasts were heard one hour a day, seven days a week, 365 days a year. While he consciously sought not to engage in extreme pro-American cant, Conover was labeled "one of the country's greatest foreign policy tools," and he did believe in the Cold War objectives of U.S. foreign policy through several administrations.[87] He felt that his show and what he considered the politics of the music were linked. In reference to non-Americans he said, "They love jazz because they love freedom."[88] His show would last for more than four decades before coming to an end in 1996.[89]

The global popularity of jazz and the democratic impulse that it was perceived to express were of such significance that in 1955, the year the Montgomery Bus Boycott began, President

Eisenhower's State Department, in collaboration with black congressman Adam Clayton Powell, initiated a program of diplomacy that sent American jazz musicians around the world. Powell had a personal link to jazz, because at the time he was married to pianist Hazel Scott. Fearful of Soviet inroads into the newly independent African countries and the consolidation of Eastern European states into the Soviet sphere, with a green light from the White House the State Department, and Powell sought to enlist jazz artists in the rapidly intensifying Cold War. It should be noted that jazz's sordid and disreputable reputation in certain circles, and the fact that it was seen as black music, generated opposition to the program from Southern members of Congress.

The "Jazz Ambassadors" program sought to use cultural diplomacy—what political scientist Louis Nye calls "soft power," or "the ability to affect others to obtain the outcomes one wants through attraction rather than coercion"—in the service of a post–World War II global agenda. The strategy was to challenge Soviet efforts to expand its international positioning even as the United States was making its own efforts in that direction.[90] The State Department's Jazz Ambassadors program was conceived by the U.S. government to use what Ellington called America's "classic music" in an effort to reposition through cultural means (along with the standard economic, political, and military aggression) the hegemonic aspirations of the United States.

In a period in which the United States was on the defensive against charges of racism in international forums from soon-to-be independent African nations, liberation movements, leftist camps, and even globally conscious and active African Americans, the state-sponsored promotion of jazz was seen as a buffer against such accusations. Using a recognized black, American-born music genre made world famous by its black, Latin, and white performers, U.S. strategists applied a two-pronged approach of soft and hard power efforts. The bands of Dizzy Gillespie and David Brubeck were two of the earlier ambassadors. Like many who came after them, they did not propagate rigid pro-American hype, maintaining a critical voice when it came to the nation's racial situation. At the same time, they more or less adhered to a liberal realist view, accepting the notion of American exceptionalism and the superiority of its democratic model. And although none were fervently anticommunist, they were sometimes guilty of framing their experience in such terminology, such as when Gillespie wired Eisenhower after his tour, writing, "Our trip through the Middle East proved conclusively that our interracial group was powerfully effective against red propaganda."[91]

Ellington was also one of the ambassadors. Between September 1963, two weeks after the March on Washington, and the beginning of 1974, when his health began to seriously deteriorate, he and the band traveled around the world on behalf of the State Department, including gigs in the Middle East, Soviet Union, Africa, South America, South Asia, and Eastern Europe.[92] He was most active during the Nixon years, coinciding with the president's foreign policy initiatives toward the Soviet Union. Politically, scholar Penny Von Eschen argues, Ellington "appears to have been not only a patriot but a sincere believer in the American Cold War mission of promoting the superiority of American democracy."[93] At the same time, Ellington was profoundly sensitive to African Americans' image and status in U.S. society although that sensitivity was filtered through a privileged, middle-class framework and life experience. Relative to the normative politics of U.S. foreign policy and the administrations through which he worked, he represented a progressive perspective, and central to his notion of democracy was a politics of antiracism.

However, just as black politics became more radical in the mid-1960s and 1970s, so did the jazz world. A new generation of jazz musicians and critics deemed Ellington's views too conciliatory and passive in the face of the racism of the times. Long-simmering tensions between more radical blacks—led by black nationalism–oriented jazz musicians and activists such as Max Roach, Abby Lincoln, Albert Ayler, Eric Dolphy, the Chicago Art Ensemble, Charles Mingus, and Ornette Coleman, and black critics Amiri Baraka and A. B. Spellman—and moderate-conservative blacks and whites in the U.S. jazz world finally exploded, as charges of racism in access to clubs, payment for performances, critical exposure, radio play, and other areas were expressed. Fundamentally, the issue was over who owned the music and what it represented in terms of American racial politics.

Towering above the fray was musically pioneering, genre-shattering John Coltrane who was mostly, though not completely, nonpolitical and helped to take jazz in a new direction. Many in the "free jazz" movement viewed Ellington and Armstrong as antiquated or even "sellouts" and "Uncle Toms," contrasting their own liberated sounds with what they considered the musical shackles of the style played by Ellington and musicians prior to the 1960s. They denounced the U.S. government as imperialist and the country as hopelessly and permanently racist.[94] Needless to say, the black nationalist and Pan-Africanist wing of jazz was not invited to participate in the Jazz Ambassadors program or, for that matter, jazz concerts at the White House.

Despite a century of showcasing all types of musical performances and despite the State Department's jazz tours, it would take until 1962 before jazz was actually heard in the White House.[95] And perhaps predictably, the premier performance was not by an African American group. On November 19, 1962, jazz made its maiden appearance at the White House and, according to the *New York Times*, shook "the crystal chandeliers of the stately old East Room."[96] Alto and soprano saxophonist Paul Winter and his sextet, an all-white group, made history by giving the first jazz mini-concert in the White House, at a children's party organized by Jacqueline Kennedy. Earlier in the year Winter's group had toured Latin America as part of the Jazz Ambassadors program.

Soon, however, black jazz artists would become frequent visitors. The opening of the White House to black jazz musicians was an emotional moment for some. Bess Abell, who was Lyndon Johnson's White House social secretary, vividly remembers a state dinner at which Sarah Vaughan sang but then, after dinner, disappeared. She stated, "I found her in this office, which had been turned over to her as a dressing room, and she was sobbing. And I said, 'Mrs. Vaughan, what's wrong? What can I do?' And she said, 'There's nothing wrong. This is the most wonderful day of my life. When I first came to Washington, I couldn't get a hotel room, and tonight, I danced with the president.'"[97]

In the Johnson's dancing White House, jazz found perhaps an unexpected reception, given Johnson's conservative Texas background. Many musicians received an invitation to perform. Stan Getz and Gerry Mulligan were only two of the veteran jazz artists who came to the White House. Indeed, a number of jazz groups were tasked to perform for royalty from around the world during the Johnson years. The Dave Brubeck band played for Jordan's King Hussein, guitarist Charlie Byrd played for the King and Queen of Nepal, flutist Herbie Mann performed for Great Britain's Princess Alexandra, and the North Texas State University Lab jazz band jammed for the King of Thailand.[98]

For Ellington, the Nixon event was certainly enhanced by the fact that his journey to being honored at the White House could be traced back to his father's own White House story. In 1899, the year Ellington was born and decades before the cultural rise of Harlem, Washington was seen by some as "the undisputed center of Negro civilization" due to its large and active black middle class.[99] However, few black men found work outside of manual labor or personal service, including Ellington's father, James Edward. Over a number of years, he worked as a "coachman (1898, 1901), driver (1899, 1900), butler (1903–4, 1906–7, 1909–17), caretaker (1918–19), Navy Yard employee (1920)," as well as caterer and eventually worker at the Government Printing Office.[100] James—also known as "J.E."—sought desperately to provide for his family, which meant he worked a number of jobs at the same time. One of those outside jobs included occasional butler work at the White House during the Harding administration.[101]

Despite the tremendous hope he held for his son's future, it is doubtful that James could imagine that one day the White House would hold a celebration of his son as one of the greatest jazz artists of all time. James had severe reservations about Duke making a career of jazz, especially as he had married relatively young and had started a family. Nevertheless, the younger Ellington prevailed and went on not only to join the jazz community, but to become one of its all-time leading lights.

During the ceremony, President Richard Nixon remarked on Ellington's parental legacy at the White House:

> To all of our guests here this evening, I think you would be interested to know that many years ago, the father of our guest of honor, in this very room, serving as one of the butlers in this White House, helped

> to serve state dinners. Tonight, in honoring his son, I was trying to think of something that would be appropriate, something that has not been more adequately said, I think very well, by the music that we have heard. We have tried to convey our affection for Duke Ellington through that music, and later on in the East Room, when I will make the first presentation in this administration of the Medal of Freedom to Duke Ellington, I will have more to say in more extended remarks about what this day means to us and what it means to this House. But in this room, at this time, for these special guests, it occurred to me that the most appropriate thing for me to say would be this: I, and many others here, have been guests at state dinners. I have been here when an emperor has been toasted. I have been here when we have raised our glasses to a king, to a queen, to presidents, and to prime ministers. But in studying the history of all of the great dinners held in this room, never before has a Duke been toasted. So tonight I ask you all to rise and join me in raising our glasses to the greatest Duke of them all, Duke Ellington.[102]

The genesis and fanfare of the Ellington tribute had political undertones. In 1960, Nixon had received 32 percent of the black vote; in 1968, that number had dropped to 15 percent.[103] In a period when the Republican Party actually cared about winning black votes, some actions had to be taken, even if symbolic and in contradiction to the larger strategy unfolding. In that context, Leonard Garment, a counsel to President Nixon, suggested to the president after his inaugural in early 1969 that he celebrate Duke's upcoming seventieth birthday with a grand dinner and award him the Medal of Freedom. Reflecting on the jazz throng in attendance and Nixon's unpopularity with African Americans, Garment noted, "This was not exactly a crowd of Nixon fans."[104] Garment was a jazz enthusiast and amateur musician who had played clarinet with Woody Herman. Garmet along with Willis Conover and several others made the arrangements for Ellington's grand White House celebration.[105] And it was a good thing because Nixon's notion of jazz was somewhat suspect—he wanted to include Guy Lombardo. The affair was attended by numerous jazz luminaries, among them Count Basie, Dizzy Gillespie, Benny Goodman, Billy Taylor, and Mahalia Jackson.[106] President Nixon played "Happy Birthday" to Ellington on the piano. In turn, Ellington composed a melody on the spot dedicated to Nixon's wife Pat.[107]

Following the Nixon years, black jazz musicians would continue to be invited to White House events under both Democratic and Republican presidents. On June 18, 1978, the White House celebrated the twenty-fifth anniversary of the renowned Newport Jazz Festival. Jimmy Carter and hundreds of guests listened to a galaxy of jazz stars, with performances by Eubie Blake, Ornette Coleman, Mary Lou Williams, Stan Getz, Dizzy Gillespie, Lionel Hampton, Herbie Hancock, Joe Jones, Katherine Handy Lewis, Max Roach, Sonny Rollins, Cecil Taylor, and Clark Terry. In the audience with the Carters and guests were Billy Taylor, Gerry Mulligan, John Lewis, and Charles Mingus, among others.[108] Carter stated, "[I]f there ever was an indigenous art form, one that is peculiar to the United States and represents what we are as a country, I would say it is jazz."[109]

Republican and jazz vibraphone player Lionel Hampton also played for the Reagans. He noted the class and cultural difference between the two administrations, saying, "During the

Carter party we had a barbecue. At this one we have caviar."[110] In addition to Hampton, many other jazz luminaries appeared before Reagan. These included Art Blakey, Chick Corea, Stan Getz, Dizzy Gillespie, Roy Haynes, and George Shearing. Reagan made his most important impact on jazz, however, not by having musicians play at the White House but by making budget cuts at the National Endowment for the Arts (NEA) and by supporting conservative attacks on the arts. In fact, Reagan initially sought to wipe out the agency altogether. He only relented when a special task force on the arts, which included conservatives Adolph Coors and Charlton Heston, recommended otherwise.[111] More broadly, the Republican Party and conservatives argued that the government should not be involved in supporting art. This campaign continued at the George H. W. Bush White House, where, records show, the White House held no jazz performances.

While Bush's White House ignored jazz, it was a subject of discussion and policy in the U.S. Congress, principally due to the relentless efforts of jazz enthusiast Rep. John Conyers (D-MI). Conyers, who was also instrumental in the passage of the Martin Luther King Jr. National Holiday bill in 1983, proposed House Concurrent Resolution 57, which declared jazz a "national treasure."[112] It was passed by the House of Representatives on September 23, 1987, and by the Senate on December 4, 1987. As a Congressional Resolution, rather than a bill, it did not require a presidential signature or approval.

During the presidential campaign of 1992, Bill Clinton demonstrated his jazz credentials when he went on the popular *Arsenio Hall Show* and played the saxophone with the show's band. On June 18, 1993, the White House set up a large tent and kicked off the "In Performance at the White House" series with a rousing evening of jazz by some its greatest performers, including trumpeters Clark Terry and Red Rodney, saxophonists Illinois Jacquet and Joe Henderson, pianists Dorothy Donegan and John Lewis, and singers Rosemary Clooney and Joe Williams. The event, subtitled, "A Salute to the Newport Jazz Festival," was the first major musical event for the Clintons.[113]

In September 1998, Jazz at Lincoln Center and the Thelonious Monk Institute put together a workshop on jazz and a concert at Clinton's White House. The event occurred as the Republican-controlled Congress was moving to impeach and try Clinton on charges related to the Monica Lewinsky sex scandal. While talking to a reporter at the event, he seemed to make an oblique reference to it when, in response to a question about the relationship between art and democracy, Clinton replied, "Art is part of our better selves. So much of public life is destructive nowadays. Things like this allow us to show our better side, not the dark, evil part of ourselves."[114]

Wynton Marsalis, who helped to revive jazz in the United States through his efforts at Lincoln Center in New York, and Marian McPartland hosted about 100 U.S. and foreign guests including the president and First Lady, Czech President Vaclav Havel; Secretary of State Madeleine Albright; Rep. John Conyers, and NEA Chairman William J. Ivey; saxophonists Wayne Shorter and Illinois Jacquet; bassist Ron Carter; Institute of Jazz Studies head Dan Morgenstern; and jazz and social critic Stanley Crouch. Speeches and lectures were given by Bill Clinton, Hillary Clinton, Havel, Marsalis, McPartland, and two jazz educators, Billy Taylor and David Baker. Havel reminisced about "how jazz had been a symbol of freedom in Czechoslovakia, how first the Nazis, then the Communists, had driven the music underground" and remarked, "Music is the enemy of totalitarianism."[115]

Jazz was also performed at the White House during the

Eli Yamin, Todd Williams, Stephen Massey, Sean Jones, First Lady Michelle Obama, Wynton Marsalis, Artistic Director, Jazz at Lincoln Center, Branford Marsalis, Jason Marsalis, Ellis Marsalis, Delfaeyo Marsalis at the White House, June 2009.

George W. Bush administration on a number of occasions. In 2004, in recognition of the NEA Jazz Masters program, a concert took place in the White House's East Room with a jazz trio consisting of Billy Taylor (piano), Chico Hamilton (drums), and James Moody (saxophone). Also performing was Other Jazz and a New Generation, jazz students that included Eldar Djangirov, pianist; Philip Kuehn, bassist; Caley Monahon-Ward, violinist; Matt Marantz, saxophonist; and Crystal Torres, vocalist. At the event, Bush stated, "These performers and many others carried forward the tradition of black music in our country. We take great pride in this heritage. We're grateful to every musician who keeps that heritage so rich and so vital today."[116] In March 2007, the Thelonious Monk Institute of Jazz, celebrating its twentieth anniversary, provided a jazz showcase at the White

House featuring Herbie Hancock, Anita Baker, Wayne Shorter, Nnenna Freelon, Clark Terry, Lisa Henry, and Bobby Watson, among others.

Although Capitol Hill Republicans continued to attack what they perceived to be liberal dominance in the arts and levied budget cuts on the NEA, National Endowment for the Humanities, and the Smithsonian Institution, the environment was not completely hostile to jazz. On August 18, 2003, Bush signed Public Law 108-72, which among other things endorsed jazz, commended the Smithsonian Institution's National Museum of American History for establishing a "Jazz Appreciation Month," and urged "musicians, schools, colleges, libraries, concert halls, museums, radio and television stations, and other organizations to develop programs that explore, perpetuate, and honor jazz as a national and world treasure."[117]

The Obamas are big jazz fans as well. In his first year in office, a large number of jazz musicians visited the White House. In June 2009, the Obamas brought 150 talented young jazz musicians to rehearse, participate in a workshop, and perform before the first family. The jazz-playing Marsalis family—father Ellis and sons Branford, Wynton, Delfeayo and Jason—also attended the event. Other jazz artists included Cuban trumpeter Paquito D'Rivera and Washington, D.C.–based saxophonist and Washington Jazz Arts Institute Director Davey Yarborough. Michelle Obama, her mother, and her daughters attended the event. She stated that she wanted her daughters to be "aware of all kinds of music other than hip hop."[118]

The program was part of a series of arts education activities held at the White House that included other music genres and other art forms. In commenting on the occasion and linking the music to politics, Michelle Obama stated, "There's probably no better example of democracy than a jazz ensemble—individual freedom, but with responsibility to the group."[119] She also discussed the relationship between America's "classic music" and America's presidential resident. She stated,

> Today's event exemplifies what I think the White House, the People's House, should be about. This is a place to honor America's past, celebrate its present and create its future. And that's why all of you are here today. It's about you, the future. And what better example of this . . . than jazz, America's indigenous art form. . . . It's essential that we preserve, develop and expand this treasured art form for our future generations by recognizing and elevating the importance of our jazz education programs in every single school across America.[120]

CHAPTER 8

Black Challenges to the White House: The Campaigns to Make the White House Black

Prelude: Marcus Garvey's Black House Story

Barack Obama was not America's first black president. Well, at least not in the broader realm of black politics and popular culture. There has been at least one claim to a presidency that sought to create a black alternative to the all-white, anti-black system which for centuries had brutally denied black people their rights in the United States. This effort appropriated the mantle, if not the structure, of government in its effort to put forth an alternative to the racist system that repressed and excluded African Americans from all venues of social, economic, cultural, and political power.

In 1920, at its New York convention, the Universal Negro Improvement Association/African Communities League (UNIA), headed by Marcus Mosiah Garvey, took several steps in declaring its—and black America—independence from the United States. It adopted a constitution and a "Declaration of the Rights of the Negro Race." The Declaration is a long and detailed list of grievances, from segregation and lynching to land seizures and taxation without representation, regarding the treatment of African Americans and other black people around the world.[1]

Marcus Garvey, August 5, 1924

The Declaration also designates a flag with the colors red, black, and green—red for the blood that African-descent people have shed, black for the people, and green for the land that will be the basis for freedom—as the official symbol of the League, and an anthem, "Ethiopia, Thou Land of Our Fathers" for the global black community. Reflecting the organization's goal of returning to a free Africa, the anthem says, in part, "Advance, advance to victory, Let Africa be free; Advance to meet the foe, with the might Of the red, the black and the green."[2]

Garvey spoke of the political frustration felt by millions of African Americans. He stated compellingly to the 20,000 gathered, "We are unable to elect a leader to the White House, but we intend to have a Black House in Washington where one of our race will serve us four years."[3] He announced that Dr. J. W. H. Eason had been elected president of Black America. Garvey himself was proclaimed the "Provisional President of Africa."

Given the events of the previous year, it was understandable why the League would feel that it had little choice but to seek other options outside the U.S. political system as it existed. Dubbed the "Red Summer" by National Association for the Advancement of Colored People (NAACP) leader James Weldon Johnson, in 1919 there were more than twenty-five deadly race riots around the United States in which white mobs attacked blacks. In Longview, Texas white people invaded a black community and burned homes, flogged a black school principle, and forced some blacks to leave town.

In Washington, D.C. one week later, U.S. marines, sailors, and soldiers killed several blacks after rumors of black men assaulting white women circulated. One of the worst riots occurred in Chicago, a city whose black population had doubled over the preceding ten years. For thirteen days, mobs of whites and blacks attacked each other before order was finally restored. The casualty list was extensive: 15 whites and 23 blacks were killed, and 178 whites and 342 blacks were seriously injured officially. Over 1,000 were made homeless. Most experts assume that the numbers were really much higher. These disturbances were just the prelude. Over the rest of the summer, racial disorder burst out in Omaha, Nebraska; Elaine, Texas; Lexington, Kentucky; Knoxville, Tennessee; and elsewhere.[4] The heroic exploits of many black soldiers in World War I were eviscerated as they became targets of racist mobs across the country. Some were attacked and killed while in uniform.[5]

As the riots demonstrated, white hostility to black progress had intensified in many parts of the country. The nation was experiencing rapid change. Industrialization was opening up opportunities for jobs in the North that could not be filled by either the white population or, due to new laws, a restricted immigrant influx. At the same time, racism was driving tens of thousands of black families out of the South. New black communities were sprouting from Chicago to New York and everywhere in-between. By some estimates, nearly 500,000 African Americans migrated North during the war years between 1916 and 1918.[6]

Another factor was the more assertive attitude of a black generation that had been to war for the nation and was much less tolerant of racial abuse. Almost 400,000 blacks served in the military in some capacity during the war, including 140,000 black soldiers that went to France. All of these factors drove many whites to violence in attempt to subjugate blacks and prevent progress.

But black resistance also grew. One response was the emergence of the NAACP in 1909 and its mobilizations and education campaigns against inequality and abuse perpetrated by whites. Another was Cyril Briggs' socialist-oriented, Harlem-based African Blood Brotherhood.[7] And still another was Garvey's Universal Negro Improvement Association/African Communities League (UNIA). Garvey had originally come to the United States from Jamaica in 1916, seeking support for his Industrial Farm and Institute and hoping to get guidance from and to work with Booker T. Washington. However, Washington had died a year earlier and Garvey found himself left to his own political devices.[8]

Garvey's U.S.-based League was created in 1917 with the expressed purpose of uniting people of African descent around the world. Within a relatively short period, he built the organization into dozens of chapters across the United States and eventually into several thousand chapters around the world. The League's base constituency was working-class African Americans and black immigrants from the Caribbean and Africa. In the United States, many of his supporters were African

Americans who had left the South after World War I looking for a better life up North but only found more racism and denial of opportunity.

Despite the popularity of Garvey's movement, he found himself in conflict with many in the black community. In the racially difficult period of the late teens and early 1920s, Garvey and his League would grow to clash with scholar and NAACP activist W. E. B. Du Bois and other black leaders over objectives, strategy and personality differences. Differences arose that were not only political but also personal. Garvey's dark skin was a source of ridicule, and Du Bois's elitist appetites were mocked.

On September 24, after the convention, Garvey went to Washington, D.C. to meet with supporters and others to inform them about the results of the New York gathering and that they now had a black president. Garvey was in a feisty and combative mood, and opened the discussion with a warning to the D.C. crowd. He started saying,

> I have appeared here more than once—many times—and it would appear that every time I speak to you, you hear me and you go away forgetting all I say. I trust you are not going to forget what I say tonight: otherwise I better not come back to Washington. I will leave Washington out and we will redeem the great cause, I suppose, without Washington.[9]

Garvey's remarks seem to indicate that the D.C. chapter or network was not as engaged as other parts of the country, and clearly members of the audience had not attended the convention. However, Washington was deemed too important to ignore, so he personally came to speak to the group. Noting the importance of the League's global effort, he continued:

> [The] political apportionment of the world means for the people in this age who fail to find a place for themselves, such a people is doomed forever. That is why I waste the time and make the opportunity to come to Washington so often, to speak to you and to make you understand what we are endeavoring to do in other parts of the world. In New York, in Philadelphia, in Boston, in the great eastern states, we have already rolled up an organization of over a million and a half men and women in these United States of America, and the cry is the slogan of AFRICA FOR THE AFRICANS.[10]

By all indications, Garvey's claim of a million and a half members was correct. By 1920, the League had more than 1,100 chapters or divisions in the United States and around the world including in more than forty countries. Among the nations were Costa Rica, Cuba, Ecuador, India, Liberia, Nigeria, Panama, South Africa, and Venezuela.

After Garvey describes the broad objectives of the movement, he asks those in attendance for their solidarity:

> We are asking you to lend your sympathy and your moral and financial and physical support to the building of Africa and the making of Africa a great republic. Make it a first-class nation, a first-rate power, and when Africa becomes a first-rate power, if you live in Georgia, if you live in Mississippi, if you live in Texas, as a black man I will dare them to lynch you, because you are an African citizen and you will have a great army and a great navy to protect your rights. In concluding I want you to realize this: I am not talking

> for an untried organization. I am here representing an organization that is a power in the world. The Universal Negro Improvement Association is the only movement among Negroes now that is striking fear in the breast of the nations of the world.[11]

Garvey went on to announce that the convention had created its own government but not just for African Americans, but for Africans and people of African descent globally. Garvey proudly states,

> Washington, I say to you, 'awake, awake because the world of Negroes around you is asserting itself to throw off the yoke of the white man of 300 years.' We, in the convention of August, have elected leaders, and on the first of November we will send into the District of Columbia the first Negro ever elected by the Negroes of the United States of America to lead them. In August we elected the Hon. J. W. H. Eason as the leader of the 15,000,000 Negroes of America. Eason has proved to be one of the ablest men of the race, and we will send him up here in November to occupy the Black House of Washington. And around him we will have men who will be able to rank in the Diplomatic Circle, just as at the French Embassy they have men. As Provisional President of Africa I hope, also, in a few months, to have a Minister Plenipotentiary as an ambassador in Washington. We are going to have representatives of the Negro in Washington, but after November we are going to have a minister plenipotentiary and ambassador in England, Germany, France, and Italy to protect the rights of the Negro.[12]

There is little known about J. W. H. Eason's background other than he was a minister of a church in New Orleans. In an address given in Chicago on September 30, 1919, he stated, "[T]he Universal Negro Improvement Association and African Communities League has [*sic*] come into existence for the express purpose, primarily, of uniting all the black folks throughout the world, that we, in turn, might see to it that all wickedness and all discrimination, and all segregation, and all wrongs be forever banished from the earth."[13] Speaking in universal terms, he argued "there is no African Negro, there is no East Indian Negro, there is no French Negro, there is no German Negro, and there is no American Negro; but there is just simply one Negro the world over.[14] At this meeting he also announced his candidacy for "presidency of the African Republic."[15] It is unclear if the "presidency of the African Republic" refers to the position that Garvey would eventually obtain as president of the African world, which Eason competed with him for and lost, or if Eason is referring to the position of president of black America. Before finishing his talk, Eason took a personal and political swipe at Garvey's adversaries stating, "If the white folks hire DuBois [*sic*] and Moton . . . did not do what those white folks told them to do, they would cut off their beard [*sic*]. But we have decided that they have served their day and generation."[16]

Eason never made it to the Black House. And the Black House itself was never established. Eason's tenure as president and member of the Garvey movement did not turn out well. Within two years of being selected Black America's president, he had a falling out with the League, and, like President Andrew Johnson in 1868, was impeached. Unlike Johnson, he was removed from office and became one of Garvey's most bitter foes. Eason was actually set to testify against Garvey at his trial on mail fraud charges. However, before that could happen he was gunned down in New Orleans on January 1, 1923. Two of Garvey's associates, Fred Dyer and William Shakespeare, who Eason reportedly identified with his dying words, were charged and convicted of the murder but were acquitted on appeal.[17] There were rumors, certainly spread by government intelligence and his black opponents, that Garvey had somehow been involved. There was no concrete evidence, however, to support the allegation.[18]

At that point the organization was in profound turmoil. Garvey had created the Black Star Steamship Line to purchase ships to transport people to Africa and other areas. Much of the funding had been raised through mail solicitations. Long seeking a case against Garvey, the federal government finally charged him and UNIA with mail fraud related to the sale of Black Star Line stock. By 1921, the company was having massive financial and accountability difficulties and was forced to close down although three ships had been purchased. This crisis provided an opening for Garvey's foes, which were numerous. Using perjured witnesses and information from informants, as well as eager support from most of the black leadership, Garvey was convicted on the charge.

Garvey's conviction was not the first time that mail fraud charges had been used to repress a surging black political movement. At the end of the nineteenth century, a movement arose to win pensions for those who had been formerly enslaved. The National Ex-Slave Mutual Relief, Bounty, and Pension Association was founded in 1894 and led by Callie House, a Nashville-based laundress and other black activists.[19]

She was inspired by a pamphlet entitled, *Freedmen's Pension Bill: A Plea for American Freedmen* promoting passage of a bill introduced by Rep. William J. Connell in Congress in 1890.

Modeled after the pension bill that paid veterans of the Civil War, the bill proposed inclusion of every black person alive before 1861 who had been enslaved, with older individuals receiving slightly more than their younger counterparts.[20] Other versions of the bill would appear in later years.

House deeply believed in the cause. In her first letter to the membership after being elected Secretary in 1898, she wrote that it was "but a question of time when those of our race who have borne the burden and heat of the day, will receive some recompense for honest labor performed during the dark and bitter days of slavery."[21] The Association held conventions, organized local chapters, and lobbied Congress. It was financed by member dues that, importantly, were paid mostly by mail.

One objective of the Ex-Slave Association was to send a petition to Congress in support of a pension bill with the names of every ex-slave in the United States. In 1899, the number of living ex-slaves constituted about 21 percent of all African Americans. At the local level, the Association provided aid to the elderly and infirm, and helped with burial services.

The movement grew despite fierce hostility from much of the black elite. While Frederick Douglass, before his death in 1895, endorsed the idea, other black leaders, elected officials, and newspaper publishers opposed the legislation and the movement for pensions. The three black Representatives in Congress at the time the legislation was introduced—Henry P. Cheatham (R-NC), Thomas E. Miller (R-SC), and John Mercer Langston (R-VA)—sought to focus their energies on education and voting rights for African Americans, efforts that were painfully unsuccessful. Both W. E. B. Du Bois and Booker T. Washington, who agreed on little between them, rejected the struggle for reparations in the form of pensions.

It was estimated that the movement expanded to over

300,000 thousand and ominously drew the attention of several U.S. government agencies. According to researcher Mary Francis Berry, "the Justice Department and the Post Office Department, at the behest of the Pension Bureau decided to declare war on the Association."[22] In the mid-to-late 19th century, the Post Office Department had accumulated enormous and arguably unconstitutional authority to stop the mail service of individuals or organizations it deemed engaged in fraudulent activities. Furthermore, decisions by the Post Office Department were not reviewable or subject to appeal to a higher authority.[23]

During the presidency of William McKinley, in 1898 the Pension Department convinced the Post Office Department to send letters to House and other Association officers denying them use of the mails because the Association was supposedly engaging in fraudulent activities. Signed by acting Assistant Attorney General Harrison Barrett, he warned that House and the others could face a maximum $1,000 fine or up to three years in prison or both if they continued their activities. It was clear, however, that Barrett, the Post Office and the Pension Bureau were not concerned about illegalities, but the advance of a radical black movement that was challenging white power. The real agenda of the government was expressed in the words of Pension Bureau Inspector W. L. Reid who wrote to his superiors that the efforts of the ex-slave pension movement "is setting the negroes wild, robbing them of their money and making anarchists of them" and will lead to "some very serious questions to settle in connection with the control of the race."[24]

The U.S. Post Office's attacks and stalled congressional legislation were successful in eroding the movement's efforts. Undeterred, however, House changed tactics and initiated a lawsuit campaign to sue the Treasury Department for $68,073,388.99 in cotton taxes traceable to slave labor in Texas. The suit was thrown out in 1915 and one year later the Postmaster General A. S. Burleson indicted House and other Association leaders on mail fraud accusing them of collecting money from ex-slaves under the false claim that pensions were forthcoming. Although the government's case did not include a single named victim and was generally weak, an all-white, all-male jury found House guilty, and she would spend nearly a year, from November 1917 to August 1918, in the Jefferson City, Missouri penitentiary. Upon her release, she went back to working as a laundress and was never active again in the reparations effort. The pension movement and the Association more or less died when House and the others went to prison, and House herself passed on June 6, 1928.

What happened to Garvey was not the beginning of government-coordinated attacks on black activists using dubious laws and questionable authority. It was the continuation of a disturbing pattern of official repression against peaceful and lawful social movements who organized to confront injustices perpetrated by the white-dominated system.

With Garvey in and out of prison or on trial, diminished popular support and membership, internal strife, relentless attacks by other black leaders, and wide criticism over Garvey's June 1922 meeting with Ku Klux Klan Imperial Wizard Edward M. Clarke, the movement was experiencing escalating problems.

It must also be noted that whatever internal conflicts existed within the Garvey movement, there was a concerted effort on the part of U.S. federal law enforcement agencies and local authorities to destroy his organization and that of other black radical groups. Even though he was an anti-communist, U.S. authorities saw Garvey and his movement as part of the "New Negro Crowd" of militants in the late teens and early 1920s who they believed were being influenced by the Communist Party. Garvey's international reach through his newspaper,

Negro World, was seen as inspired, if not funded and controlled, by Bolsheviks. As early as September 1919, the U.S. Justice Department was seeking a way to deport Garvey.[25] By 1923, the Garvey organization was thoroughly infiltrated with black agents and the federal government was manipulating the conflicts between the League and its black rivals.[26] Indeed, the very first black agent, James Wormley Jones, to be hired by the Bureau of Investigation (BOI), the precursor to the FBI, was brought on explicitly to infiltrate Garvey's movement. At least four other agents would soon be working to covertly subvert other militant groups with the expressed purpose of devastating their operations and their leadership.

The Bureau of Investigation was run by an ambitious and ruthless federal employee named J. Edgar Hoover, who would stop at nothing to root out and annihilate communists and any blacks influenced by them. The Post Office's Translation Bureau, working with the Bureau of Investigation, was brought in to stop the spread of Garvey's *Negro World* whose great crime was that it sought "to instill into the minds of the negroes [*sic*] of this and other countries that they have been greatly wronged and oppressed by the white races and that they can only hope for relief and redress through concerted and aggressive action on their part."[27]

The combined efforts of the federal government and Garvey's political adversaries, internal conflicts, and mass black opposition to emigration ultimately brought down Garvey and his dream of black repatriation to Africa and of a Black House in the United States. Garvey was sent to prison in February 1925. However, after two years, in 1927, President Coolidge commuted his sentence and he was deported to Jamaica. He continued to be active there and later in London where he relocated in 1935. He died in London on June 10, 1940.

Black Presidential Aspirations: Political and Cultural Challenges to the White House

> *I've seen levels of compliance with the civil rights bill and changes that have been most surprising. So, on the basis of this, I think we may be able to get a Negro president in less than 40 years. I would think that this could come in 25 years or less.*[28]—Rev. Martin Luther King Jr. in an interview with the BBC in 1964 while on his way to Oslo, Norway to receive the Nobel Peace Prize.

By the 1960s, black activists not only wanted to meet with the president, they wanted to be the president. Within both major parties as well as through third parties and independent runs, African Americans sought to use the vehicle of a presidential or vice-presidential campaign to raise issues important to the black community, put pressure on the major party candidates to address black concerns, or expose the political system as hopelessly racist, sexist, anti-working class, and geared to the demands of an economic and political elite. These efforts were limited by the reality that the overwhelming majority of whites (and perhaps other minorities) was not willing to vote for a black candidate for president. Indeed, until the Jesse Jackson campaigns in the 1980s, neither were most African Americans. And since most black elected officials and civil rights leaders practiced leverage politics, i.e., whereby black votes are traded for policy favors, they were reluctant to support a candidate that could not win.

Black presidential campaigns flowed from two political streams. In the two major political parties, procedural or formal objection to a black candidate no longer existed by the early 1960s. The struggles led by activists such as Mississippi's Fannie Lou Hamer had torn down barriers to black participation inside of the Democratic Party and people of color were able to achieve more leadership roles in the party. And although the overwhelming majority of blacks had switched to the Democratic Party, there was still a black presence inside of the Republican Party. Both parties, however, for all practical purposes were still overwhelmingly white-only in terms of holding statewide and national offices. The Civil Rights Movement rightfully targeted black voting rights as a central objective of the struggle, and many died fighting for that cause. It would take the passage of the 1965 Voting Rights Act, and a willingness to enforce it to change the racial dynamics of U.S. elections.

As a consequence, by 1971, in the U.S. House of Representatives, there were thirteen African Americans, enough to form the Congressional Black Caucus. Most were from major urban areas in the North. There were none from the deep South until 1973 when Andrew Young was elected from Atlanta. In other parts of the region where there were significant numbers of black voters, obstacles to voting, party participation, independent candidacies, and outright violence diluted black voting strength to nearly nil. Even after the passage of the 1965 Voting Rights Act, it would take another almost twenty years for the fruit of that struggle to produce forty or so House members, many from the South. Some breakthroughs would happen in the North. The first black person to be elected to the U.S. Senate after a century of absence was Massachusetts Republican Edward Brooke, in 1966, a moderate politician from a liberal state who served for two terms. Brooke refused to join the Congressional Black Caucus, though he often fought against the conservative and anti-civil rights policies of Nixon.

For aspiring black presidential candidates, white attempts to suppress and dilute the impact of black voting was only the beginning of the problems. Candidacies run on money, media, and mobilization. Fundraising for the White House has historically been a big-money process. Despite an extremely complex regime of rules that have existed over the years, there has been little debate that corporate and elite funds dominate the fundraising process. That pool of funding, naturally, has been situated with white and generally moderate-to-conservative candidates with many corporate donors giving to both parties. These doors were closed to genuine liberal candidates not to mention more progressive and radical ones.

Many, though not all, media access issues flowed from a lack of funding. Without long financial resources, candidates cannot buy media time, hire media consultants, or convince big-audience media that they are viable. When you add in the race dynamic and the prevailing view that a black presidential candidate hasn't a ghost of a chance, it is not surprising that few, including most African Americans, were aware of most of the black candidates who have ran for president. Without this awareness, it becomes almost impossible to mobilize the millions that would be needed to offset the other issues. In the pre-Internet era, direct communication was costly, labor-intensive, and time-consuming. In today's world of instant email, text messaging, and Facebook, it is hard to imagine that voters rarely heard from candidates unless they were directly pivotal to their election chances.

Despite all these issues, black presidential candidates running in the major parties' primaries and caucuses made a number of important contributions that in the long run were pivotal to the campaign and election of the first black president of the United States, Barack Obama. While none obviously won the nomination, they laid the groundwork in some critical ways that opened the door for his victory in 2008.

In the Mainstream: Black Democratic and Republican Candidates

Shirley Chisholm

The most important though under-acknowledged pioneer of a serious run for the presidency by an African American was Representative Shirley Anita St. Hill Chisholm (NY-D) who ran for president in 1972. Ahead of her time, she challenged the prevailing notions of gender, race, and, due to her Caribbean background, ethnic stereotypes. Chisholm had been a teacher prior to becoming involved in politics, winning a seat in the New York State Assembly in 1964. She initially made history by being the first black woman to be elected to Congress when she won in Brooklyn's Twelfth Congressional District in 1968. In her first speech before the House of Representatives on March 26, 1969, she began by pointing out the contradiction between millions being spent on defense by Nixon and the social needs of the nation, "Mr. Speaker, on the same day President Nixon announced he had decided the United States will not be safe unless we start to build a defense system against missiles, the Headstart program in the District of Columbia was cut back for lack of money."[29]

After asserting that she was not a pacifist, she sharply objected to the war priorities of the Nixon administration and famously vowed:

> to vote "No" on every money bill that comes to the floor or this House that provides any funds for the Department of Defense. Any bill whatsoever, until the time comes when our values and priorities have been turned right side up again, until the monstrous waste and the shocking profits in the defense budget

Congresswoman Shirley Chisholm announcing her candidacy for presidential nomination, January 25, 1972.

> have been eliminated and our country starts to use its strength, its tremendous resources, for people and peace, not for profits and war.[30]

In January 1972, Chisholm audaciously declared herself a candidate for the Democratic Party presidential nomination. In her declaration, she stated, "I stand before you today as a candidate for the Democratic nomination for the presidency of the United States. I am not the candidate of black America, although I am black and proud. I am not the candidate of the women's movement of this country, although I am equally proud of that. I am not the candidate of any political bosses or special interests. I am the candidate of the people."[31]

Dismissed by many as a whimsical run, she received scant support from women's organizations, black groups or prominent individuals. A multitude of variables existed that harmed her effort, including committed black political support for George McGovern or Hubert Humphrey, inability to raise funds, and lack of a national base. But nearly all of these issues could be linked into perceptions regarding her race and gender, as well as her ideologically progressive views. Virtually unknown outside of New York and black political circles, Chisholm had little chance to win white votes, particularly those of men. While she did win endorsements from some women's groups, such as the National Organization of Women, most did not support her. And there were some black men who felt it was an affront that a black woman should run for president before a black male. She did receive the endorsement of the Black Panther Party, and when she was pressured to reject their support, she refused to do so.[32] Despite all the forces against her, Chisholm opened the door and made the contemporary notion of a black person running for president normal. She campaigned in twelve states and won more than 400,000 votes, and had 151 delegate votes at the National Democratic Convention.[33] She won the New Jersey primary with 66.9 percent of the vote, and 23 percent of the vote in Massachusetts.[34]

In reflecting back on her campaign, she wrote, "I ran because someone had to do it first. In this country everybody is supposed to be able to run for President, but that's never been really true. I ran *because* most people think the country is not ready for a black candidate, not ready for a woman candidate."[35] Referring to herself as "unbought" and "unbossed," the title of her book on her campaign, she was a genuine groundbreaker.[36]

Jesse Jackson

I want to offer the highest and the best service in our

> *highest and most sensitive job, the job that has the most capacity to bring justice in our land, mitigate misery in the world and bring peace on earth—the office of president. Only in America is such a dream possible.*[37]
> —Jackson's announcement speech for his 1988 run for the Democratic nomination, October 10, 1987.

In Democratic Party politics, Shirley Chisholm was followed by the high-energy and certainly much more popular campaigns of Reverend Jesse Jackson in 1984 and 1988. Jackson ran in an era when defeat of Ronald Reagan and George H. W. Bush were paramount among mainstream Democrats, including black Americans. The Reagan administration on both foreign and domestic policy represented a setback for people of color, women, peace activists, working and poor people, and pretty much anyone who sought economic and social fairness in the 1980s America. Rather than challenge the conservatism of Reagan, many Democrats believed that moving toward the political center was the best strategy for defeating his bid for a second term.

Despite massive opposition from the black political elite that in 1984 was mostly committed to Walter Mondale (who eventually became the nominee) for a first-timer, Jackson ran a credible campaign and won 3.5 million votes in the primaries, electrifying the progressive wing of the party's base. Jackson won about18 percent of the total and five primaries and caucuses, including Louisiana, the District of Columbia, South Carolina, and Virginia. Jackson raised issues of democracy and inclusion within the Democratic Party as the campaign quickly realized the challenges it faced from the party elite and the structure of U.S. politics. His platform included support for D.C. statehood, curtailing the Defense budget, ending Reagan's tax cuts, sanctions against the Apartheid government in South Africa, nuclear disarmament, universal health care, and other popular progressive demands.

Jackson was also at the center of the National Rainbow Coalition, a dominant force in the progressive wing of the party. The Rainbow Coalition was comprised of progressive civil rights, labor, women, peace, environmental, and human rights activists from across the racial spectrum. With Jackson's relative success in 1984, a number of elected officials also participated in and joined the organization including individuals like California's Rep. Maxine Waters. In fact, the sudden interest in Jackson's possibilities left many progressives feeling squeezed out of prominent roles in the organization.

Jackson returned to the trail in 1988 with more experience, skill, support, and capacities. In fact, he started off as the frontrunner, and even appeared to be headed toward victory after winning the all-important Michigan caucus. He captured almost seven million votes and won primary contests in Alabama, Washington, D.C., Georgia, Louisiana, Mississippi, Puerto Rico and Virginia and four caucuses in Delaware, Michigan, South Carolina and Vermont. One direct consequence of Jackson's challenges was that Ron Brown, an African American, became chairman of the Democratic Party in 1989, a first for a major party.

Yet, however legitimate he may have come across to black communities and some in the civil rights, ethnic rights, labor, environmental, women's, human rights, and other social change movements, for much of the rest of the country, he was still viewed as a black candidate with a black agenda. Regardless of how much Jackson and the campaign addressed other issues—from workers' rights to foreign policy—he could never escape his civil rights past (and present). This meant that even within the narrow confines of the Democratic primaries, he could not win enough non-black votes to defeat the relatively unknown and hapless governor of Massachusetts, Michael Dukakis.

Jackson's campaigns for the White House were pivotal, however, in providing rule changes that would benefit Obama in 2008. After the 1984 primary season, when he had some leverage over how peaceful and cooperative the Democratic National Convention would turn out, Jackson argued that winner-take-all primaries and caucuses were patently unfair. He was able to win rule changes that allowed for proportional distribution of delegates for those candidates who won 15 percent or more of the vote. This important rule change was so critical to Obama's campaign that it is difficult to see how he would have won without it. As discussed in Chapter 9, although Hillary Clinton was winning big states in the primaries, Obama was still gathering delegates because he was coming in a close second. That, in addition to the small and Republican-oriented states that he was winning that the Clinton and other Democrats abandoned, were his numerical keys to victory. The Obamas owe that strategic opening to Jackson.

The major impact of the Jackson campaign was to invigorate the progressive wing of the Democratic Party and to inject a more progressive discourse into the national political debate. Liberals in the party were cowed by Reagan's popularity and were reluctant to promote a progressive agenda. For African Americans, Jackson represented the most significant challenge to the party's racial politics since the days of Fannie Lou Hamer and the Mississippi Democratic Party in the 1960s. He mobilized millions who would later be the basis for victory for local and state candidates around the nation. And just as Obama would do two decades later, he motivated countless young and old to become involved in electoral politics and community activism.

Jackson, however, undercut a potential future run and the

establishment of a formal progressive element in Democratic politics by demobilizing the National Rainbow Coalition after the 1988 race. At a turbulent meeting at the Democratic National Convention following the nomination of Dukakis, Jackson told his followers that they needed to fold into the Democratic Party structure for the campaign, support the party's candidate, and not act independently. That fateful decision pushed away many activists who were wary of Dukakis and the Democrats, and politically fractured the Rainbow Coalition.[38] The Rainbow was eventually merged into Jackson's Chicago-based organization Operation PUSH. Jackson teased with the idea of running again, but then ultimately decided not to run in 1992.

Doug Wilder

Many of the more popular Democrats, perhaps including Jackson, felt that President George H. W. Bush was in too strong a position to be defeated and declined to enter the race. This left the door open for some lesser known candidates to run, candidates such as Arkansas Governor Bill Clinton and Virginia Governor L. Douglas Wilder. On September 13, 1991, during the middle of his term as Virginia governor, Wilder, the first African American elected to that position declared himself a candidate.

Wilder's victory in Virginia, in November 1989, perhaps foreshadowed his presidential hopes. Leading Republican J. Marshall Coleman by fifteen points two weeks before the election, Wilder only won by 6,854 votes out of nearly two million cast, less than 0.37 of one percent.[39] In New York that same year, African American candidate David Dinkins had been leading by 18 percent but only won the mayor's race by 2 percentage points.[40] The gap between pre-election polls and election-day reality has been called by some political scientists the "Bradley effect" in reference to the experience of Tom Bradley in California in 1982. Former Los Angeles mayor Bradley, who is African American, ran for governor and according to polls was likely to win. However, on election day he lost a close race. Post-election analysis seemed to demonstrate that many white voters were hesitant to tell pollsters that they would not vote for an African American candidate, but on election day that is exactly what happened, i.e., the "Bradley effect." These elections stood out because Bradley, Wilder, and Dinkins were all moderate, race-neutral candidates. By 2008, however, it was believed that both more whites were willing to vote for a black candidate and that polling sophistication was better able to account for respondents who lied.

In a basically traditional announcement speech where he put himself forward as a savior of sort, Wilder stated:

> In seeking the Presidency, I recognize that I am the longest of long shots. I may not win. I may not get but a few votes. But I would not be doing my job as Governor—indeed, I would not deserve to be who I am—if I failed to step forward at this critical juncture in our nation's history. For if we fail to heal this nation in 1992, it may not be healed in my lifetime. If we fail to put this country on a sound fiscal posture in 1992, then order may not be restored in my lifetime. If elected, I pledge to all of you that I will do everything in my power to heal the growing divisions among us; to restore economic vitality...so that more people can enter the middle class...and to secure peace around the world through American economic and military strength.[41]

Neither in his speech nor in the abbreviated campaign did Wilder focus on race or issues of special concern to the black community. Only once did he address the issue stating, "Washington seems to have lost the passion to fight the deterioration in race relations in this nation."[42] Wilder's moderation on race concerns was not surprising given his affiliation with the centrist Democratic Leadership Council (DLC) at the time. The Council arose as a rival to Jackson's National Rainbow Coalition. In fact, there were suspicions in the Jackson camp that Wilder's long-shot bid was to reposition another African American to vie for black votes. Those fears were reinforced by the celebration of Wilder's run as a blow to Jackson's political future by the *Boston Globe*'s Robert Jordan, who wrote, "We may be seeing the sun beginning to set on the 'Jesse Jackson era.'"[43]

Washington Post reporter Juan Williams, a conservative black writer who was often critical of Jackson, rejoiced at Wilder's bid. Referring rather ridiculously to Wilder as the most important "black American politician of the 20th century," Williams opined, "It is not just that Wilder is an alternative to the best-known black spokesman, Jesse Jackson: his success is a rebuke to Jackson's 1980s political vision of Blacks as America's victims."[44]

Besides missing the point that Wilder's success was largely driven by the black voters that Jackson's campaigns generated, Williams' flawed assertion of him as an alternative collapsed rather quickly. Wilder ran a very poor campaign, raised little money, and garnered very few endorsements of note. Four months after jumping in, on January 8, 1992, before a single primary or caucus, Wilder jumped out.

Although Jackson bowed out in November 1991, he became a part of the winning politics for candidate Bill Clinton. In May 1992 interview with the *Washington Post*, rap artist Sistah Souljah discussed the uprising in Los Angeles after the exoneration of four white Los Angeles police officers in the beating of black motorist Rodney King. She stated, among other remarks, "If Black people kill Black people every day, why not have a week and kill White people."[45] The statement was pulled out of the context of the overall interview and incorrectly promoted to say that she advocated murdering whites. Few critics noted that she was a widely respected youth organizer and active on a wide range of issues. In June, based on her activism, Souljah was invited to participate in Jackson's National Rainbow Coalition conference in Washington, D.C. So was Democratic Party's presumptive nominee Bill Clinton. Jackson was holding the gathering to strengthen his and the Rainbow Coalitions ability to influence the platform and strategy of the Democratic Party in the fall elections. To burnish his conservative credentials as he sought votes from the political center, Clinton decided to use the event to not only criticize Souljah but to also chastise Jackson for inviting her to the conference. At the time, Clinton was trailing in the polls behind President George H. W. Bush and independent upstart, Ross Perot. In his talk, Clinton compared Souljah to white supremacist and former Klan leader David Duke. Jackson was blindsided. Clinton's strategy of distancing himself from Jackson and the progressive wing of the party, and presenting himself as a centrist to win moderate white voters was successful enough to win him the nomination.[46]

Al Sharpton

In 2004, New York's Reverend Al Sharpton ran in the Democratic primaries. Like Jackson, he also tried to position himself not as a black candidate, but one representing a broad range of constituencies. He told CNN, "I'm not running an African-American campaign. We're running a broad-based campaign that includes African-Americans and Latinos and gays and lesbians and laborers and others."[47] Sharpton built his reputation as a rabble-rouser in New York politics taking strong stands on a number of racial and non-racial issues and incidents. He morphed, however, into a respected and savvy political insider in Democratic politics. And he was seen by many, including himself, as the heir to the Jackson throne. Lacking Jackson's reach and connections, but more willing to engage others as equals, Sharpton was taken seriously when he decided to enter the race although he had no chance of actually winning.

Although he won no states (but nearly 400,000 votes) and came in far behind, his high quality performances at the debates during the two months he campaigned were well-informed and quick-witted. The debates went a long way in shedding the image of him as a confrontational extremist and racial rebel that the media had built over the years—an image that Sharpton himself helped create. Nevertheless, few people watched the debates or read campaign literature—not that those would have been decisive anyway—so the old Sharpton image remained for many Democratic voters. And even those who agreed with what Sharpton had to say and with his policy proposals had little doubt that if he miraculously made it through the primaries and Convention and emerged as the nominee, that the Democrats would go down in a historic defeat. To his credit, Sharpton was aware of these politics and used them to his advantage as he attempted to leverage a progressive and pro-civil rights agenda.

Since the 2008 election, Sharpton has emerged as Obama's favored black leader, having visited the White House at least five times by mid-2010. He has been described as the president's "go-to man" when it comes to responding to black politicians, media personalities, and civil rights leaders who are critical of the administration's policies as they relate to the black community.

From issues ranging from civil rights to agricultural policy, Sharpton has provided the administration space to present its point-of-view primarily on his radio show, and debated black opinion-makers such as black talk show host and activist Tavis Smiley, who is a harsh critic of Obama and now Sharpton. Smiley said it was hard for Sharpton "to speak truth to power about the suffering of black people on the one hand, and then to be running in and out of the Oval Office and trying to run the president's agenda or express White House talking points."[48] Sharpton argued in response, "The president does not need to get out there and do what we should be doing," and there should not be a double standard where African American leaders "expect more from a black president" than from a white one.[49]

While Smiley, Rev. Jesse Jackson and others have fumed at what they believe has been a poor response by the Obama administration to black concerns, Sharpton and other black leaders, such as NAACP President Benjamin Jealous, National Urban League President Marc Morial, and Harvard's Charles Ogletree have met with Obama on a number of occasions including a snowy February 10, 2010 meeting with Sharpton, Morial, and Jealous regarding the economy.[50] Smiley criticized that gathering for not focusing more strongly on a black agenda. He and Sharpton continued to clash publicly on several radio shows. Sharpton refused to participate in Smiley's March 20, 2010 "We Count! The Black Agenda is the American Agenda" symposium that included Jackson, scholars Michael Eric Dyson, Michael Fauntroy, Cornel West, and Ron Walters, economist Julianne Malveaux, and Minister Louis Farrakhan among others. Sharpton viewed it as an Obama-bashing session and a diversion from addressing a real program for change.[51] Sharpton has directly engaged with the White House even partnering with former Republican House Speaker Newt Gingrich on the issue of education access for minority youth as part of a Obama-supported initiative, the Education Equality Project.[52]

Carol Moseley-Braun

Former Senator Carol Moseley-Braun (D-IL) announced that she also was running for the 2004 Democratic presidential nomination. She stated, "I'm in this race to ensure that the American dream finally gets extended to all Americans without regard to race, color, or gender."[53]

Some felt that she was convinced to join the race to be a spoiler to stop Sharpton getting a monopoly on black votes. However, she was still relatively unknown despite having been an U.S. senator, the first African American woman to achieve that position. She left office after one term, a tenure wrought with controversy and generally seen as a disappointment. One high point of her time in Congress was her challenge to Senator Jesse Helms, one of the Senate's most anti-civil rights legislators. Unafraid to be brazenly racist, sexist, and homophobic, Helms was one of the institution's most powerful members. In his 1990 campaign for reelection, he ran the infamous "white hands" advertisement against African American Henry Gantt, which showed a pair of white hands crumbling a rejection notice for a job that had been given to an unqualified person of color.[54] A states'-rights advocate and segregationist until the day he died, Helms' defense of racist Southern habits went unchecked by his Senate colleagues until he ran into Moseley-Braun. In July 1993, Helms proposed an Amendment to the National Service Act that would have renewed the patent for the logo of the United Daughters of the Confederacy (UDC). Helms described the group as "24,000 ladies" who work as unpaid volunteers at veterans' hospitals. In fact, it is an organization that seeks to preserve, defend, and even make-up Confederate culture and history. It protects a manufactured image of an idyllic pre-Civil War white South that minimizes or denies the brutality and racism of slavery, an objective Helms embraced.[55] Moseley went to war with Helms over the issue and after a fiery speech on the Senate floor, a number of Senators including some from the South and Republican colleagues of Helms changed their vote and the legislation was defeated.

Similar to Chisholm many years earlier, there was also a hope that she would garner support from women's organizations and voters given that she was the only woman in the race. Given her lack of popular support, inability to raise funds, and media snipes, she dropped out of the race early.

Alan Keyes

On the Republican side, political nuisance and far-right extremist Alan Keyes, who more often than not has bordered on the fanatical, has run three times, in 1996, 2000, and 2008, for the Republican nomination. He left the GOP campaign in March 2008 to run for the nomination under the banner of the Lancaster, Pennsylvania-based ultra-conservative Constitution Party, which he lost finally running as an independent. His campaign themes have remained unchanged: an end to all abortion rights, elimination of the income tax, opposition to gay rights, and anti-socialism and other far-right positions. In an almost comical fashion, he generated a barely hidden contempt from other Republican candidates who, unlike Democrats, felt a need to tolerate his sideshow. His participation in debates always generated a tension not as much due to race—although despite his pathological opposition to civil rights and racial justice, he complained that he was being slighted because of it—but because his views were outside that of the main party candidates who needed to try to both appeal to the highly motivated right wing of the party, but also moderate and independent voters. Most—well some—understood they could not win a national election with only the party's right wing. Keyes, on the other hand, most clearly and aggressively sought support from the far right end of his party's base. The results were fairly predictable. He won little support and was more an embarrassment than anything else. Like many black Republican candidates, he wanted to be seen both as non-racial and still get special credit for his insights into blackness.

Keyes's extremism seems to be boundless. As a youth, he was defending the Vietnam War long after even most hawks had given it up. Although he holds a Ph.D. from Harvard, he has failed at nearly every endeavor, from hosting television or radio shows to running for countless offices. His angry denunciations of everyone that disagrees with him often take on a personal dimension.

During a 2004 interview, Keyes launched into a tirade against gays. Mary Cheney's name came up. She is an active Republican and the openly gay daughter of former Vice President Dick Cheney. Keyes said that she, like other gays and lesbians, was a "selfish hedonist." In this instance Keyes would later prove that he was no hypocrite. Sometime later when his daughter Maya announced that she was a lesbian—and had liberal views—he and his wife Jocelyn kicked her out of the house, both referring to her as a "liberal queer." This was after Maya had delayed her entrance into Brown University to work on his 2004 Senate campaign although she disagreed with virtually every position he articulated except for abortion. Even more disturbing, if possible, after his slur against Mary Cheney, Keyes also volunteered—unprovoked and while his daughter was sitting there—"if my daughter were a lesbian, I'd look at her and say, 'That is a relationship that is based on selfish hedonism.' I would also tell my daughter that it's a sin and she needs to pray to the Lord God to help her deal with that sin." At the time, Keyes actually did know that Maya was a lesbian, but, as she noted in an interview, as long as she was quiet about it, she got along okay with her parents. Keyes's family values went out the window after Maya came out and he fired her from her job in his political organization and refused to pay for her tuition.[56]

The always furious Keyes holds the distinction of being the last candidate to run against Barack Obama before he ran for president. In the 2004 Illinois Senate race, Keyes parachuted in at the last moment after all of the Illinois Republican hopefuls dropped or felled out of the race. His farcical campaign is only notable for the historic margin of defeat—73 percent to 37 percent—that he suffered. Obama won 90 percent of the black vote, 70 percent of the white vote, 75 percent of the independents, and even 40 percent of the Republican vote.[57] The campaign did make history in that it was the first time that two major party candidates running against each other for the U.S. Senate were black, although Keyes was hardly celebrating that fact. He declared during the campaign, with some insider knowledge no one else had, that "Jesus would not vote for Obama," and he refused to call and congratulate him on the win.[58] Since the 2008 campaign, Keyes has been one of the leaders of the so-called "birther" movement that questions the citizenship of Obama. Keyes and others ludicrously claim that Obama was born outside of the United States, either in Kenya or Indonesia, and that his Hawaiian birth certificate is a forgery, and, therefore not legally qualified to be president. The grand conspiracy that they weave is knee-deep in racist and nativist assumptions that involve multiple governments, major media, political leaders, and even law enforcement and intelligence agencies, and is further spread by the Fox News network and faux "journalists" like Rush Limbaugh, Glenn Beck, and Lou Dobbs. He has also argued that Obama is a socialist and Marxist "on the verge of outright dictatorship." [59]

Outsiders: Independents, Third Parties, and the Fringe

A key difference between the mainstream candidates and the third party/independent aspirants is that the latter are mainly unconstrained by the prospects of winning and from the prevailing political status quo. They are also free from the politics of running in the primaries and caucuses, and then, after losing, free from pledging support to the candidate who did win even if there is a fundamental difference in values and views.

Black Third Party and independent candidates for presidents have been numerous. This includes comedian Dick Gregory, former Black Panther Eldridge Cleaver, National Alliance Party activist Lenora Fulani and Dennis Serrette, jazz musician Dizzy Gillespie, Ohio activist Ron Daniels, and candidates from the Workers World Party, Socialist Workers Party, and other small parties. These candidates were not running to exert leverage necessarily on the major parties but to carve out a political space for alternative and more radical voices in presidential politics. While they were marginal to non-existent for most whites in America, they did resonate with some, though few black Americans voted for them. Some campaigns were more whimsical than serious, but all raised critically relevant issues and concerns.

In terms of tone, popular receptivity, and impact there is also a sharp political dividing line between those who ran in the 1960s and 70s and those who came later. In the earlier period, the campaigns took place when the Black Liberation Movement was at a height, a movement that had dissipated by the end of the 1970s. While the Civil Rights Movement found itself in what has often been called a "crisis of victory" in the mid-1960s after achieving many of its goals, the Black Power Movement spread from East to West to Midwest. Not satisfied with civil rights legislation that gave formal equality but did not change the fundamental power relationship between blacks and whites, more urban-based activists demanded black control of the institutions in the black community, including schools, stores, businesses, cultural activities, political inclusion, and other sites where whites dominated. Candidates for political office in this era were much more likely to have come from an activist background, and even if they did not, they felt an accountability that was not always present in their successors.

These candidates, perhaps more than anything, help to expose the narrow political range that the two major parties offer to Americans. It is nearly impossible for third party and independents, black or otherwise, impoverished or wealthy, to break through the barriers that have narrowed the political arena to a very few. From ballot access to media exposure to fundraising, these candidates are at a fatal disadvantage. Regardless, of the odds, they ran.

Dizzy Gillespie

The first campaign in this era came from jazz-activist John Birks "Dizzy" Gillespie in 1964. With escalating protests against the Vietnam War, turmoil following the assassination of John Kennedy, the emergence of radical black voices within the jazz community, and his own history as a musical outsider, it was not all that illogical that Dizzy would be interested in the 1964 presidential race.

As a jazz trumpeter, Gillespie was known for the rapid chord changes he and Charlie Parker played during the bebop era. In 1963 and 1964, in his short-lived presidential campaign, he sought to bring changes in the way the country was run. Beginning somewhat as a joke, the campaign grew as Dizzy's supporters began to organize support for him. They formed an organization called the John Birks Society. This was a clear rebuke to the John Birch Society, the ultra-conservative, anti-government, anti-United Nations group that supported Rep. Barry Goldwater and other right-wing politicians and movements during its heyday in the 1960s. The John Birks Society, on the other hand, was a free-spirit network of jazz fans and civil libertarians.

They initially began to circulate a petition to get Gillespie on the California ballot. The petition stated, "We, the undersigned, hereby petition the Secretary of State of California to place the name of John Birks "Dizzy" Gillespie as an independent candidate for the Presidency of the United States."[60] Although people from about twenty-five states had demonstrated interest in supporting the campaign, it was later decided to conduct a write-in effort focused on California. The whole idea was initiated and grew from the efforts of jazz critic Ralph Gleason and his wife Jeanne, who managed the campaign.

Gillespie stated that he was running "to take advantage of the votes and publicity I'd receive and to promote change. It wasn't just a publicity stunt. I made campaign speeches and mobilized people."[61] He was also critical of the current state of political affairs where, when it came to racial justice, presidents and public officials "were dillydallying about protecting blacks in the exercise of their civil and human rights and carrying on secret wars against people around the world."[62] To demonstrate his concerns beyond just the black community, he chose Native American Ramona Crowell of the Sioux tribe to be his running mate for vice president.

Dizzy promised that his closest advisors would be comprised of jazz and music luminaries, including Dick Gregory, who would later make a presidential run himself. Gregory sent a note of support that read, "I am sure you know that Diz has my vote but I would like to make one suggestion . . . How about

Miles Davis for Secretary of State? With best wishes, Dick Gregory."[63] Rather than "secretaries" he would have "ministers" including drummer Max Roach as Minister of Defense, bassist Charles Mingus as Minister of Peace, Malcolm X as Attorney General, composer Duke Ellington as Minister of State, pianist Mary Lou Williams as Ambassador to the Vatican, Louis Armstrong as Minister of Agriculture, and singer Ray Charles would be in charge of the Library of Congress. Other positions were to go to Ella Fitzgerald, Peggy Lee, Carmen McRae, Woody Herman, and Count Basie.

Dizzy's campaign raised many issues. His platform included "the need to eliminate racism in music, and all other fields." He wanted Africa and the developing world to be treated fairer. As he noted in his autobiography, he began to wear African clothing signaling that his "candidacy meant a more progressive outlook toward Africa and the "third world." He also wanted to abolish the FBI, and have the anti-democratic Senate Internal Security Committee "investigate everything under white sheets." He also called for total disarmament, free health care, and free education. He developed a stump speech that opened with, "When I am elected President of the United States, my first executive order will be to change the name of the White House to the Blues House."[64] On the more serious side, money raised through sales of buttons and other materials went to civil rights organizations such as the Congress of Racial Equality and the Southern Christian Leadership Conference.

As the campaign picked up some steam, Dizzy states that there was some pressure for him to withdraw. There was some fear that although he had no chance of winning, he could be a spoiler especially in a key state such as California. And his popularity was certainly a wild card. He thought about pulling out, however, as he evaluated the leverage that he was accumulating, he decided he would wait until after the Democratic National Convention that was being held in Atlantic City in August 24–27, and review the plank in the Democrats platform that related to civil rights.[65] Presumably, if he thought it insufficient, he would not withdraw and directly try to pull votes from Johnson.

The 1964 Democratic National Convention was marked by a controversy over the seating of the Mississippi delegation. The Mississippi Freedom Democratic Party (MFDP) was an affiliate group formed in Mississippi to challenge the legitimacy of the all-white delegation that was being sent to the Convention. Comprised of both whites and blacks, the MFDP contended that the racially segregated election in Mississippi was undemocratic and that those elected should not be seated. MFDP leader Fannie Lou Hamer's riveting testimony before the credentials committee on live television exposed a mass audience to the oppressive and brutal conditions that African Americans and poor people endured in the South. She graphically described how she was arrested and savagely beaten for trying to organize black communities to register and vote.[66] She states that Alabama State Highway Patrol ordered two black prisoners to beat her, "I was beat by the first Negro until he was exhausted."[67] She laments, "I question America, is this America, the land of the free and the home of the brave where we have to sleep with our telephones off the hooks because our lives be threatened daily because we want to live as decent human beings in America?"[68]

After a fierce fight that threatened not only the Convention but Johnson's election chances depending on what decision was made, a negotiation was worked out between the party leaders and civil rights leaders including SCLC's Martin Luther King Jr., NAACP's Roy Wilkins, and Bayard Rustin. It was agreed that the Mississippi Freedom Democratic Party would get two delegate seats; the all-white delegation would be required to pledge to support the party ticket; and from that point forward, delegations to the national convention would have to be selected in a non-discriminatory manner. The decision left many Mississippi Freedom Democratic Party activists disenchanted.[69]

Though mostly forgotten in the United States, in 2004, the legacy of the campaign was highlighted in a play in London titled, *Vote Dizzy!*. It was produced by American actor Jack Brooder and ran for a brief period around the time of the 2004 November election.[70]

Any future runs by Gillespie were forestalled after he adopted the Baha'i faith. According to Gillespie, the religion forbids its adherents from seeking political office because they believe that "to aspire to any political office in this age is below our station."[71]

Eldridge Cleaver

In 1968, two of the most familiar names of the era, Eldridge Cleaver and Dick Gregory, ran what were mirror campaigns. Cleaver ran as the candidate for the Peace and Freedom Party (PFP), an organization that promoted itself as:

> committed to socialism, democracy, ecology, feminism and racial equality. We represent the working class, those without capital in a capitalist society. We organize toward a world where cooperation replaces competition, a world where all people are well fed, clothed and housed; where all women and men have equal status; where all individuals may freely endeavour to fulfil their own talents and desires; a world of freedom and peace where every community retains its cultural integrity and lives with all others in harmony.

Eldridge Cleaver, Minister of Information for the Black Panther Party and presidential candidate for the Peace and Freedom Party speaking at the Woods-Brown Outdoor Theatre, American University, October 18, 1968.

The harmony was somewhat broken in 1968 when after the party's Ann Arbor convention selected Cleaver for its nominee, a group broke from the PFP and formed the Freedom and Peace Party and selected Dick Gregory as their presidential candidate. Thus both Dick Gregory and Eldridge Cleaver ran as president on competing tickets with almost identical platforms.

Already popular in the San Francisco Bay area due to his articles in *Ramparts* magazine, Cleaver achieved national fame with his 1968 book *Soul on Ice*, an essentially biographical track of his violent life of crime spiced with black liberation theorizing and rage at whites and women. The book became a bestseller. He argued, "Black people in North America have always been plagued by a dual status. We were both slave and Christian, we were both free and segregated, we are both integrated and colonized. . . . Yesterday we were black and oppressed; today our blackness is a tool for our liberation."[72] His writings not only attracted the white left but also the newly formed Black Panther Party.

Formed in October 1966 in Oakland, California, and originally called the Black Panther Party for Self-Defense, the Panthers recruited Cleaver to become their Minister of Information. The Black Panther Party was a complex organization whose members ranged politically from socialists to black nationalists to anti-ideological radical reformers. Founded and led initially by Huey Newton, Bobby Seale, David Hilliard, and a few others, it sought to first defend the black community from the abusive activities of the Oakland Police force, abuses that were common in many black communities around the United States. When Newton discovered that under California law, it was legal to carry a loaded rifle in public, the Panthers began to do so which escalated the growing tensions between the party and hostile local, state, and, ultimately, federal law enforcement agencies. The situation remained mostly a local phenomenon until March 2, 1967, when approximately thirty Panthers marched on the California legislature in Sacramento brandishing their weapons and their rhetoric. This brought them national attention from other black communities—and from the FBI.

The Panthers would very quickly begin to advocate a revolutionary doctrine relative to the black community. In June 1969, Newton argued, "A people who have suffered so much for so long at the hands of a racist society, must draw the line somewhere. We believe that the Black communities of America must rise up as one man to halt the progression of a trend that leads inevitably to their total destruction." [73]

By 1968, the Panthers were already being targeted for elimination by local and federal authorities. FBI Director J. Edgar Hoover, as paranoid and anti-democratic as they come, called the Panthers "the greatest threat to the internal security of the United States," and the Party, as well as many other black and progressive groups, became the target of the government's deadly counter-intelligence program (COINTELPRO). One of the objectives of the program, as outlined in a FBI memo by Hoover was to "prevent the coalition of militant black nationalist groups." Soon, a series of violent confrontations between the police and the Panthers happened in a number of cities including the Bay Area. On April 6, 1968, an Oakland Police-initiated altercation occured and 17-year-old party member Bobby Hutton was shot and killed by the police and Cleaver was wounded.

Two days earlier, on April 4, Martin Luther King Jr. had been assassinated in Memphis, Tennessee. In response to his murder, uprisings erupted in Washington, DC, Baltimore, Chicago, Kansas, and other cities and campuses around the nation, but not in Oakland. Civil rights leaders had little sway over angry black communities, particularly youth outraged by the killings. For some, groups that advocated a revolutionary solution to the problems of racism, poverty, war, and other concerns appeared to be offer a constructive response to the state terrorist actions that were unfolding against black communities and their leaders. Socialist-advocating organizations, such as the Revolutionary Action Movement and League of Revolutionary Black Workers; and black nationalist groups, such as the Nation of Islam and United Slaves (US)—which was based in Los Angeles and an eventual rival to the Black Panthers—surged.[74] Prior to going to prison on drug and rape charges and while in prison, Cleaver had moved in most of these circles coming to the conclusion that only an armed struggle and violent overthrow of the U.S. state would bring black freedom. Like a number of the organic intellectuals of the period who were never formally trained in political philosophy or theory but managed to forged strong ideological frames that spoke to the political concerns, feelings, and experiences of millions, he developed a passionate following.

It was in this context that Cleaver was chosen by the Peace and Freedom Party to be their candidate in 1968. In a letter to the *New York Times*, the Eldridge Cleaver for President Fund wrote:

> Eldridge Cleaver can present the only electoral challenge to the discreditable politics of Nixon, Humphrey, and Wallace. We see the value of a Cleaver campaign as manifold. A well funded and well publicized campaign will illuminate the inadequacy of establishment politics. It will articulate demands that scarcely have an opportunity to arise within the establishment arena. It will build both critique and demands into a firm, broad, and permanent political formation.[75]

Although Cleaver and the Peace and Freedom Party would win a few votes, he spent most of his time addressing his legal issues before fleeing the country toward the end of the year. He first went to Cuba and finally settled in Algeria. Although he started a Panther chapter there and continued to speak on behalf of the Panther Party, differences over strategy between him and Newton-Seale that had emerged in Oakland were growing and an antagonistic break erupted.

Cleaver, over time, would travel from the extremes of the left to the extremes of the right. While in exile, he disavowed his previous revolutionary leftist ideas and embraced far-right conservative views.[76] "After he returned to the United States in 1975," writes John Kifner in the *New York Times*,

> Mr. Cleaver metamorphosed into variously a born-again Christian, a follower of the Rev. Sun Myung

> Moon, a Mormon, a crack cocaine addict, a designer of men's trousers featuring a codpiece and even, finally, a Republican. . . . His political turnabout was such that, in the 1980's, he demanded that the Berkeley City Council begin its meetings with the Pledge of Allegiance, a practice they had abandoned years before. "Shut up, Eldridge," Mayor Gus Newport told the man who had once been the fiercest emblem of 1960's radicalism. "Shut up or we'll have you removed."[77]

When Cleaver passed on May Day in 1998, he was little remembered or embraced.

Dick Gregory

In the early 1960s, Dick Gregory had emerged as one of the nation's top comedians after a triumphant stint at Chicago's Playboy Club. Although it took him and other black comics years to break the color barrier at the major clubs and hotels, as the *New York Times* noted, he became a major headliner in the New York, San Francisco, and Las Vegas clubs, at one point earning $12,000 a week, and had been one of the first black guests on the Jack Parr show.[78] His comedy was racially edgy without being overly polemical or panicky, and he came across more as a satirical commentator than a traditional comedian. He did not use profanity. He did not dance, sing, or clown around. In 1963, long before academics and rappers re-appropriated the controversy surrounding the word in the contemporary era, Gregory wrote a bestselling autobiography titled, *Nigger*. "I told my mama," stated Gregory, "if she hears anybody shout 'nigger,' they're just advertising my book."[79] Reportedly, the book sold seven million copies.[80]

Gregory used his popularity and talents to help advance

the struggle for civil rights. He befriended Martin Luther King Jr., SNCC, NAACP, and other leaders and organizations, and soon was on the frontlines and at the fundraisers with them in the struggle for political and equal rights. His activism went beyond civil rights and addressed issues ranging from peace, Native American rights, foreign policy, and health. Gregory was always outspoken and passionate.

Prior to his run for the president, Gregory ran against Richard Daley for mayor of Chicago. Daley's hardline approach to dissent and those who spoke out against the brutal Chicago police department earned him the ire of the black community. Gregory lost but got a taste of the platform that one is given when running for political office. He ran as a write-in on the Freedom and Peace Party ticket and received 1.5 million votes, thirty times more than Eldridge Cleaver. In his 1968 book, *Write Me In*, he wrote, "I refuse to be the victim of having to choose between two lesser evils."[81] He outlined his platform in a wide range of areas. He argued that the U.S. Constitution should be amended to include as a qualification for president "a sensitivity to human need"[82] Understandably, given the growing opposition to the Vietnam War, he addressed the issue of war stating, "America speaks with pride of the fruits of democracy and advocates democracy for the rest of the world. Yet we go all over the world trying to force democracy upon people at gunpoint."[83] And, as president, he would propose "legislation to allow American taxpayers to bring suit against the federal government challenging the spending of a sizable portion of the national budget for a possibly illegal war."[84] He questioned the United States' definition of itself as a democratic and inclusive nation writing, "I have a dream and a vision of seeing the Constitution of the United States implemented in full for the first time in American history."[85] In 1977, with researcher

Mark Lane, he wrote a book about the Kennedy assassination, and later developed a number of conspiracy theories concerning the deaths of King, Robert Kennedy, and Michael Jackson, and controversies ranging from Michael Tyson and September 11, to other politicians, celebrities, and news events.[86] His wide range of interests also included health products specifically aimed at addressing some of the obesity and related health issues that disproportionately impact the black community.

Dennis Serrette

The election of Ronald Reagan as the fortieth president of the United States immediately sent alarms through the black community. Reagan opened his campaign after receiving the Republican nomination August 3, 1980 at the Neshoba Country Fair in Mississippi, just down the road from the town of Philadelphia infamous for its role in the 1964 murder of three civil rights workers, James Chaney, Andrew Goodman, and Michael Schwerner. In his remarks, Reagan stated that he believed in "states' rights" and basically promised that he would attack and reverse the gains of the previous twenty years by the civil rights, black power, and peace and social justice movements. Uncomfortable with the response of the Democratic Party and passive resistance to accommodation, radical black voices called for an independent move away from the two parties. One non-black group that had the resources to put forth a black candidate was the New Alliance Party (NAP).

Led by an obscure philosopher and psychotherapist, Fred Newman, the New Alliance Party worked hard to position itself to influence or dominate a number of grassroots movements since its formal inception in 1979. However, it quickly generated criticism from a wide range of progressive activists for its tactics and deceptions. One of the groups that it created was something called the Rainbow Alliance. On more than one occasion it was confused with Jackson's Rainbow Coalition with which it did not have a relationship.

The New York-based party ran labor activist Dennis Serrette as its presidential candidate in 1984. Serrette was a founding member of the Coalition of Black Trade Unionists and a vice president of a local of the Communication Workers of America. In a very muted campaign, Serrette was able to gain only about 35,000 votes on 33 ballots with little visibility. Serrette left the New Alliance Party after the election with some bitter memories contending that the party was not progressive and had cult-like tendencies.

Lenora Fulani

In 1988 and 1992, the New Alliance Party ran Lenora Fulani as its presidential candidate. She had previously run under the NAP banner in New York for lt. governor (1982), New York City mayor (1985), and governor (1986). By 1988, the New Alliance Party had become very skilled at raising funds and ballot access. In 1988, the Fulani/NAP campaign raised $2.6 million with $922,106.34 in matching funds. For a candidate to qualify for matching funds, the campaign must raise at least $5,000.00 in individual contributions from at least twenty states. By April 1992, she had secured over $1,033,000 in federal matching funds.[87] Through a complex but legal process where campaign funds were spent with businesses affiliated or owned by NAP and then whose employees made donations to the campaign, the Fulani campaign was awash in cash.

At the same time, Fulani made history in 1988 by being the first African American to be on the ballot in all fifty states and the District of Columbia. This was a remarkable achievement that few third parties or independents had ever accomplished.

However, it reflected the technical and legal acumen of NAP's lawyers rather than popular support for the candidate or her agenda. In 1988, she received 211,742 votes from across the country.[88] Given the popularity of Jackson's second run, Fulani ran under the theme "two roads are better than one" implying that she and Jackson were going to the same place but using different paths, and that if Jackson failed to win the Democratic Party nomination, then his supporters could vote for her in the general election.

Fulani dropped out of the 1992 race after receiving only 402 votes in New Hampshire despite spending over $140,000.[89] Fulani left the primaries because if she fell below a certain threshold in terms of votes received, she would become ineligible for matching funds in the general election, something she and the campaign were not willing to risk. In that election, she was on the ballot in thirty-two states and the District of Columbia. She sought to get on the party ticket of a number of third parties including California's Peace and Freedom Party, Vermont's Liberty Union Party, South Carolina's United Citizens Party, and Illinois Solidarity Party. Cite. In the end, she received somewhere between 73,707 (*New York Times* figure) and 80,411 (NAP figure).[90] In other words, although Fulani was better known in 1992, and had more financial resources, she received less than half of what she won in 1988.[91]

Between 1992 and 2000, NAP sought to regroup after receiving much criticism from progressives about its problematic behavior. Somewhere along the way, NAP was disbanded, likely due to state and federal investigations tied to its fundraising schemes. It was still stunning to many, however, when Fulani and Newman came out in 2000 and endorsed well-known conservative and former Richard Nixon speechwriter Pat Buchanan who was seeking the Reform Party's nomination for president.

Fulani and Newman argued that they were building a left-center-right coalition. They had given up the fiction that she was leading a black-led movement to empower people of color, women, workers, and other marginalized communities. The Reform Party, which grew out of Ross Perot's 1992 presidential campaign, was their new political home. The battle for a progressive independent black politics would be left to others.

Ron Daniels

One of the most important gatherings in black politics occurred in March 1972, in Gary, Indiana. The National Black Political Convention was the most significant effort to bring together the disparate elements of the post-civil rights black political community. The tent cast was very wide. The Convention included every ideological position active in the black community, including nationalists, socialists, elected officials, Pan Africanists, and others.

The central objective of the meeting was to forge an independent politics that was not tied or beholden to either of the major parities or any of the third parties. This goal was reflected in the leadership of the National Black Political Assembly (NBPA) that included Gary Mayor Richard Hatcher, black radical Amiri Baraka, and Rep. Charles Diggs. More than 12,000 attended the Assembly. The politics of the gathering, captured in the "Gary Declaration," were ideologically to the left. The Declaration stated, "A Black political convention, indeed all truly Black politics, must begin from this truth: The American system does not work for the masses of our people, and it cannot be made to work without radical, fundamental changes. . . . The challenge is thrown to us here in Gary. It is the challenge to consolidate and organize our own Black role as the vanguard in the struggle for a new society."[92]

Two issues that were raised that would manifest a number of years later were the call for a black independent political party, and the suggestion of a black candidate for the presidency. Although he had little intention of really supporting the idea in practice, Jesse Jackson stated, "Without the option of a black political party, we are doomed to remain in the hip pocket of the Democratic Party and the rumble seat of the Republican Party."[93] Although the idea of a future black presidential run was floated, the assemblage ignored and dismissed the black candidate who was running at that moment: Rep. Shirley Chisholm.

The thrust for unity, however, was more or less undermined even before the assembly began. A number of elected officials had already or were about to make commitments to one or other of the Democratic candidates for president. There were also political differences over issues such as busing and international support for the Palestinians. Despite the defection of many of the black elected officials, the NBPA would continue for the next eight years under the leadership of Ohio activist Ron Daniels. Daniels would also play a decisive role in the formation of the National Black Independent Political Party (NBIPP). At the 1980 New Orleans meeting of the NBPA, a resolution to launch an independent black party within 100 days was passed and the NBPA more or less faded into the effort to build NBIPP. The politics of NBIPP were even more chaotic than those of the organization that spawned it. NBIPP struggled over issues of who was qualified to be a member to how to resolve the lack of support by the black community for independent campaigns. The party faced its biggest dilemma in 1984 when Jackson decided to run for president within the Democratic Party and generated overwhelming support from African Americans.

Though still an unyielding advocate for independent politics, by 1988, Daniels had become Executive Director for the

National Rainbow Coalition. His main objective in that position was to keep the NRC alive and not subsumed into the Jackson campaign for the presidency. Unsuccessful in that aim given the decisions made by Jackson to tie his political future to the Democratic Party, he left the NRC after the 1988 race. Emulating somewhat the NRC-Jackson Campaign model, Daniels started another organization, the Campaign for a New Tomorrow, and began to contemplate his own run as an independent candidate for president in the 1992 elections. On October 14, 1991, he announced his candidacy and that of his vice presidential running mate Native American activist Asiba Tupahache. In his statement, he said:

> While this nation prepares to settle in for yet another season of politics as usual, I believe that the progressive movement should launch a massive human rights crusade to place America's injustices against African people, Native Americans, Latinos, Asian Americans, and poor and working people before the world. As part of that crusade, an Independent presidential campaign should be seen as a vehicle to intensify the fight for power. Those who have been the historical victims of a racist and exploitative system must amass the power to govern and create a new society.[94]

Daniels received widespread support from many on the left as well as from long-time activists in the independent politics movement. However, he was unable to generate the resources necessary to really run a nationwide campaign with a paid staff and advertising in big media. As a result, he lacked the reach to bring out voters in his behalf. With Bill Clinton as the Democratic Party's standard bearer in that election, the centrist thrust of the party's politics created some political space for Daniels' progress platform of cuts in the defense budget, a quality education for all, a peace driven foreign policy, a socially-responsible economy with sustainable development, enactment of a domestic Marshall Plan, and elimination of racism and all forms of discrimination. Despite the fact that many progressives agreed with Daniels' politics, few felt that the risk of another four years of Bush was worth it, even if that meant getting Clinton.

Cynthia McKinley

In addition to Keyes and Obama, there was another black candidate for the presidency in the 2008 elections: former U.S. Representative Cynthia McKinley. She first came to Congress in 1992 from Georgia as a member of the group of blacks elected to Congress from the South who benefited from the 1990 redrawing of congressional districts. She early on distinguished herself as a radical and became a leader of the Congressional Progressive Caucus. She lost her seat in 2002 after she and other black Southern representatives were targeted for defeat by conservative forces in Georgia. She won her seat back in 2004, but then lost it again in 2006, in part due to a widely publicized confrontation with a Capitol Hill police officer. As was the experience of other black representatives, a white police officer did not recognize her as a member of Congress. The officer accused her of hitting him. The controversy gave ammunition to her opponents who argued that her politics and demeanor did not represent her constituents.

McKinley was one of the early advocates for an alternative commission to investigate the September 11 attacks. She argued that a cover-up was taking place and the American public was not being told the truth about what happened. While in Congress, she also called for the impeachment of President Bush, Vice President Dick Cheney, and Secretary of State Condoleezza Rice.

After leaving Congress, she also left the Democratic Party. She joined the Green Party and became their candidate for president in the 2008 elections. The party had attempted to recruit her in 2000 and 2004 but she declined their earlier overtures. Her running mate was Latino hip-hop artist and activist, Rosa Clemente. Theirs was the first women-of-color presidential and vice presidential ticket in U.S. history. Their platform included calling for an end to the wars in Iraq and Afghanistan, protection of civil liberties, impeachment of Bush and Cheney, creating a Department of Peace, releasing currently classified information on the Kennedy and King assassinations and September 11, and redirecting the national budget to address social needs.

Her critique was of both major parties. As she stated in her acceptance speech, "In 2008, after two stolen Presidential elections and eight years of George W. Bush, and at least two years of Democratic Party complicity, the racket is about war crimes, torture, crimes against the peace; the racket is about crimes against the Constitution, crimes against the American people, and crimes against the global community." In that same speech, without speaking his name, she also took a swipe at then-candidate Obama stating, "The Democratic presumptive nominee wants to increase the size of the overused military and the budget for an already-bloated and wasteful Pentagon. I am the only candidate who has consistently voted against the Pentagon budget, voted against the war in Iraq, and I voted against the bills that funded it."[95] For a party that has been mostly white, the selection of McKinley and Clemente was a breakthrough in terms of race. Unfortunately, it happened in a year when black votes and two-thirds of Latino voters were supporting an African American candidate who genuinely had a chance of winning the presidency. Green Party members of all colors were flocking to the Obama camp. Unlike some of her supporters, McKinley was careful to frame her critique of Obama as an overall criticism of Democratic Party politics.

One of the key goals of the campaign was to win five percent of the total vote which would allow the Green Party a number of benefits in terms of ballot and federal matching-funds. The Greens have around 200 elected officials around the country, mostly elected at the local level such as school boards and city councils, but like all third parties have an extremely difficult time getting on the ballot in many states. In the 2008 elections, the party did not achieve its goal. On November 4, McKinney received 161,603 votes, about 1 percent of the total.

Two who should have run: King and Powell

Finally, it is relevant to mention two individuals who were promoted and would have presented serious campaigns if they had run for president. In 1968, there were calls for Martin Luther King Jr. to run for president. King's leadership of the Civil Rights Movement and his April 4, 1967 speech opposing the Vietnam War made him an attractive potential candidate for progressives. His sharp rebuke of the war was a political earthquake given the prevailing view at the time that civil rights leaders should stay out of foreign affairs. King demanded that President Johnson halt the bombings, declare a unilateral ceasefire, get out of Laos and Thailand, bring the North Vietnamese into the peace negotiations, and set a deadline for the removal of all foreign troops out of Vietnam.[96] That speech got the attention of many in the peace and anti-war movement. On April 15, King spoke at an anti-war rally at the United Nations that brought out over 125,000. In addition to King, other speakers included pediatrician and activist Dr. Benjamin Spock, singer-activist Harry Belafonte, former SNCC leader Stokely Carmichael, CORE leader Floyd McKissick, and William Pepper of the National Conference for New Politics. In his remarks, after King had spoken and chanted "stop the bombing, stop the bombing," Pepper suggested that the civil rights leader become a candidate for president in 1968. Spock and other peace leaders joined the effort to get King to run. *The Nation* magazine and Socialist Party leader Norman Thomas were among those who urged King to run as a third party candidate. According to Peter John Ling, King seriously considered running.[97]

Speculation about a King candidacy was a nightmare for the Johnson administration and J. Edgar Hoover's FBI who were tracking his every personal and political move. Such a step by King would bring together the civil rights and anti-war movements. FBI wiretaps kept the agency and a worried administration informed about King's deliberations.

However, King demurred almost from the first suggestion that he run. He told one of his assistants, "I need to be in the position of being my own man," and a Boston crowd, "I have never had any political ambitions, and it is strange territory for me to consider. I have never thought of myself moving into the presidential arena."[98] As the days passed, King became more resolute in his decision not to join the race. On April 25, he met with reporters and read a statement, "I have come to think of my role as one which operates outside the realm of partisan politics. I have no interest in any political candidacy and I am issuing this statement to remove doubts about my position on this subject."[99]

In an intriguing take on King's presidential possibility, in 1997 the *Discovery Channel* produced a fictional documentary that elaborated on the notion that King had not been assassinated and went on to become president. In the film, King was able to push through what is termed "the most radical legislation since Roosevelt's 'New Deal' program," NASA selected black astronauts to travel into space, and the doll Barbie had black friends. Racial tensions eased around the nation and a new era of progressivism was begun.[100]

Colin Powell

In the early 1990s, there were efforts to draft Colin Powell to run for president. The popular ex-general was courted by both Democratic and Republican leaders. He had worked in the administrations of both parties but was mostly associated with the Republican Party. He made his affiliation clear when on November 8, 1995, he announced both that he would not run for the presidency and that he had joined the Republican Party.[101]

There was an assumption that Powell's popularity across party and racial lines would translate into electability. In reality, he would have faced difficulty finding support from both the black community and the more conservative wing of the Republican Party. Though frustration with the Democratic Party was high and growing among many blacks, it was due to what many felt was the party's drift to the political right. It was likely that whatever racial pride may have surfaced with a credible run by Powell, his Republican affiliation was certain to lose him a substantial amount of black votes unless he qualitatively broke from the Republican agenda.

Powell's views on race were shaped by his experiences as a second-generation Jamaican-immigrant child in New York City in the 1940s and 1950s. In his mixed raced, multi-national neighborhood, he states that he had "no such sense" of a black racial identity.[102] While many blacks from the Caribbean and Africa identify with the struggles and goals of black Americans, many do not. While Powell grew to become more appreciative of the black American effort for equality, inclusion, and justice, his views on race issues have been mostly moderate. He supported affirmative action but tended to reject black-only approaches to addressing black community issues. He recognized the need for government intervention but leans much more toward self-help solutions. This posture would have made it very difficult for him to receive support from most black leaders and many others in the black community.[103]

His other problem was that many within the Republican Party, particularly as it migrated further and further to the right, viewed Powell as too moderate. His support for affirmative action, a woman's right to choose, and diplomacy along with force in international relations made him suspect in the increasingly neoconservative climate. There were those who blamed him for President H. W. Bush's decision to not go after Saddam Hussein in the first Gulf war. All of these criticisms surfaced when Powell was put forward as George W. Bush's Secretary of State. His conflicts with Vice President Dick Cheney, long running from when they were both in the Reagan administration, arose almost immediately and he barely made it through Bush's first term before being asked to tender his resignation. Although Powell represented the only voice of moderation in the administration and mitigated the global animosity toward Bush, he had few friends in the president's inner circle or party and he had to go. Unsurprisingly, although he remains a Republican, he endorsed Obama for president over Republican candidate John McCain. And while Republicans on and off Capitol Hill are steadfast in their effort to destroy the Obama, Powell serves as one of his most trusted shadow advisors.

Black Presidents in Popular Imagination

While Obama may actually be the first real black American to win the White House, popular culture has produced black presidents for many years. In novels, films, and television, a black president has presided over and usually overcome all manners of crises dealing with racial and non-racial affairs. There are similar themes in nearly all of the fictional accounts of a black presidency. First, the gender politics are pretty consistent. All of the presidents have been male. Second, the presidents are politically liberal to moderate in their domestic policies, including even those relative to race. Early expressions of black presidents' foreign policy, except for references to Africa, were generally missing. This coincided with long-held views by many whites and some blacks that African Americans should stay out of foreign affairs except for Africa and maybe the Caribbean. In other words, it appears that issues such as national security, the Cold War, relations with the United Nations or the European Union, or Asia were beyond the intellectual scope of these writers. Third, black opposition to the president was generally portrayed as muted or, if expressed at all, extremist or black nationalist, a position the president could not take. Fourth, all of the presidents (eventually) demonstrated the highest moral and ethical code to which one could aspire. These are no prevaricating Richard Nixons, George Bushes, Bill Clintons, or Lyndon Johnsons. Fifth, in most of the twentieth century versions of the black president, race was central to the narrative, but not so much for twenty-first century iterations.

One of the first novels about a U.S. black president was actually published in Brazil in 1926. Writer Monteiro Lobato's *O Presidente Negro* tells the science fiction story of how James Roy "Jim" Wilde, an African American, became president in the year 2228. Wilde's elevation, as envisioned by Lobato, is a consequence of the apartheid-like state of U.S. society. Extreme racial and gender segregation have resulted in a triadic political split between Wilde's Black Association, the all white female Sabinas and the all white male Homo Party. The Sabinas' candidate, Evelyn Astor, is running against the Homo Party's Kerlog, who is the current president. Astor and Kerlog command about 51 million votes each as whites split close to evenly down the gender line. At the same time, Wilde controls about 54 million votes since black men and black women decide to vote along racial lines. Kerlog cuts a deal with Wilde whereby he will ease the enforcement of the *Codigo Raca* (Race Code) in exchange for black votes. However, black voters support Wilde regardless and he is elected president. Kerlog then forms a white alliance with Astor and they threaten to never let Wilde assume office. On the morning that he is to officially take over, he is discovered dead in office. Kerlog is then re-elected and, along with Astor, began their final solution of ridding the country of blacks.

While the story concerns Lobato's view of race relations in a distance American future, in many ways it is about his view of race in contemporary Brazil and his embrace of eugenics. In Brazil in the 1920s, eugenics was offered as a solution to the "problem" of race mixing. Brazil, like many Latin American countries, attempted unsuccessfully to whiten their populations in the post-slavery period through strategic racial mixing as a way of avoiding apartheid policies. Those efforts only achieved a browning of the populace. Similar to the Nazis in the 1930s, there were those who desired a more effective eugenic solution such as sterilization, or a ban on mixed marriages and relationships—strategies that are employed in *O Presidente Negro*. Lobato's real politics are spoken by the book's Miss Jane. She is the daughter of the Brazilian scientist who invents the "*porviroscopio*" ("Future Scope), a kind of crystal ball, which allows her to see the hyper-segregated American future. She says regretfully, "Our solution [in Brazil] was mediocre. It spoiled the two races, by fusing them. The Negro lost his admirable physical qualities of the jungle and the white man suffered an inevitable depression of character."

Like many white Americans, Lobato could not see a future United States that was not segregated. Although Lobato had not visited the United States before he wrote the book, segregation in the U.S. South was well known and served as a model for the Hilter regime, the Apartheid government of South Africa, and other racists around the world. Interest in the long forgotten and somewhat embarrassing book, of course, was sparked by the surge of Barack Obama in the Democratic primaries and caucuses. As it became clear that he could possibly win, the book was rushed into re-publication. The book has now been translated and published in Italy with plans underway for Spanish and English versions.

In the United States, Irving Wallace's 1964 novel *The Man* was one of the first works of literature to address the possibility of a black commander-in-chief. In the novel, which was also made into a film staring James Earl Jones in 1972, the president and the speaker of the house are accidently killed when a ceiling in a 600-year-old Frankfurt palace collapses on them during a visit. At the same time, the vice president is unable to assume the office because he is ill. That sends the president pro-tempore of the U.S. Senate to the White House—Douglass Dilman, a black man.

The accidental president is a moderate who must deal with his black militant daughter, racist southern politicians, and backstabbing Cabinet officials. He overcomes all of these issues and, and brimming with newfound confidence, plans to run for the office in the next election cycle. The novel and the film only superficially address the complications of race and politics. While it attempts to be comprehensive, it comes across more as scattered.

Other presidents in film have ranged from the comedic (Chris Rock in *Head of State*) to the deadly serious (Morgan

Freeman in *Deep Impact*). Rock plays dedicated Washington, DC alderman, Mays Gilliam. Similar to *The Man*, the Democratic president and the vice president are killed in a freak airplane accident in which their two planes collide in midair. Gilliam becomes a candidate when the party, figuring it had nothing to lose and seeking black votes, deceptively asks him to run. Not sure if he is qualified, advice from his brother Mitch (Bernie Mac) to speak the truth leads him to rise in the polls and best the Republican candidate, sitting Vice President Brian Lewis (Nick Searcy). In the general election, implausibly, Mays is elected president. The film is a throwaway in most aspects.

But underneath the silliness, stereotypes, and predictability is a rather sharp critique of the manipulative nature of American politics. Both parties are only interested in winning and are willing to sacrifice principles for potential votes. Once Mays discovers why he was chosen and then believes that he has no chance of winning, he is unrestrained in terms of telling the truth. Rock, who wrote and directed the film, is also raising the issue of African American politicians buying into this corruption. As one of the contemporary young black comics who has a vast crossover audience, Rock consistently addresses topical issues in his standup in order to expose hypocrisy, dishonestly, and social inequality. As with his comedy, Rock's solution to the sorry state of U.S. politics is populism, which can lead to a variety of outcomes, from the banalities of Sarah Palin to the inspiring rhetoric of Jesse Jackson.

In the disaster film *Deep Impact*, Freeman brings his legendary gravitas to the role of President Beck. Upon realizing the inevitability of a destructive comet hitting the United States and potentially destroying all life on earth, what the film calls an "Extinction-Level Event," Beck develops a dual response to the crisis. One plan is to send a crew into space to destroy or split the comet in two to minimize the destruction. The other plan is to save one million Americans in caves, 800,000 of whom will be chosen by a lottery.

Beck's race is a non-issue for the entire movie. There is no discussion about how Beck became president. Neither is his politics or ideological bent clear. It can be assumed, however, from his impressive and creative response to the crisis and his soothing but strong demeanor in sharing it with the public that he is imminently qualified for the office.

Perhaps the most skillfully handled and most long-term depiction of a black president has been on the television series *24*. For the first five seasons, Dennis Haysbert played President David Palmer who was a target of assassination as a candidate, pursued for impeachment by his cabinet, and faced with multiple crises while fighting terrorist attacks. His personal life was dominated by a psychotically ambitious wife who would stop at nothing to obliterate her enemies, including Palmer after he divorces her. At the beginning of the fifth season of the show, the retired Palmer was really assassinated. And then in the sixth season, his brother Wayne, played by D. B. Woodside, and who had been David's chief of staff, becomes president. He is eventually stricken with a debilitating illness after a failed assassination attack and mysteriously disappears from the story.

David Palmer is a liberal Democrat who must confront the fundamental thesis of the show that extreme and illegal measures, most notably torture and racial profiling, are undesirable but necessary methods in the fight against imminent acts of terrorism. The show preceded September 11—it first aired two months after that on November 6, 2001 but was filmed much earlier in the year—and benefited from the fear-mongering tactics of the Bush administration. The show's co-creator and producer, Joel Surnow, embraces some of the conservative wing of the Republican Party's most cherished beliefs. Referring to *24* as a "patriotic show" and arguing that conservatives "are the new oppressed class," Surnow not only admires George W. Bush and Ronald Reagan but wants to resurrect anti-communist Senator Joseph McCarthy as an "American hero." Surnow really does pal around with the nation's right-wing elite including friends such as radio host Rush Limbaugh, Supreme Court Justice Clarence Thomas, and pro-McCarthy writer Ann Coulter.[104]

The show has been harshly criticized by human rights, civil libertarians groups, the FBI, and even the U.S. military for its distortions about the benefits of torture. On *24* torture always reaps life-saving information. According to most experts in the field of interrogation, legal issues notwithstanding, it rarely, if ever, does. They universally agree that physically and psychological coercive methods—what the Bush administration termed (and promoted) "enhanced interrogation"—are unreliable and unnecessary. Nevertheless, *24* relentlessly applies these tactics and it is a signature of the popular show. According to Human Rights First, prior to September 11 and *24*, there was an average of four torture scenes a year on prime-time television; by 2007, there were over 100 a year. In its first five years, *24* alone displayed 67 scenes of torture according to research by the Parents' Television Council.[105]

President David Palmer, noted for his integrity and honesty, must decide repeatedly whether to accept this ethos in order to stop terrorist attacks, or uphold the law. Sometimes he succumbs to the argument that only torture will work such as when he orders such methods to be used on his National Security Advisor who he suspected, correctly, was involved with terrorists. Of course, this illegal action comes back to haunt him. Mostly, David Palmer is reluctant to order torture and sees it as a last resort.

Throughout all of this drama, except for the first season, the White House is the space in which nearly all of the activities of the president occur. This is due in part to the narrative structure where an entire season takes place during a 24-hour period. Thus, both Palmers are seen in the Oval Office, the East Wing, giving national addresses, and generally being presidential with race a very muted element in this public life as the drama of preventing a national calamity dominates all activity.

But race never completely escapes as background to the high drama and tensions. Racial justice, rioting, bigotry, crime and profiling are woven in an out of the narrative and its subplots. Haysbert, who voted for Obama, believed that his and Woodside's portrayals helped to ease the path for an Obama victory. He felt that the image of a strong, intelligent, articulate, and moral black commander-in-chief in charge of a White House facing a national crisis coming into the homes of millions weekly negated the idea that a black person could not be president.[106]

It is impossible to say with certainty whether the portrayals of a black president by Haysbert, Woodside, Rock, and Freeman, or its depiction in literature, or the previous efforts by candidates of color contributed cultural prerequisites for Barack Obama's stunning victory and America's first black White House. But it is clear that the idea of a black commander-in-chief running the White House has a long and varied history, and it speaks of a willingness to challenge the notion that the highest political office in the country is for whites only. From Oney Judge's escape from the White House in 1796 to the entry of the Obamas as the First Family in 2009 was by any measure a historic, seemingly impossible, but finally exultant sojourn.

Name	Party/Indep.	Year	Votes Won	Notes
Dizzy Gillespie	Independent	1964	Write-ins	Not on ballots
Dick Gregory	Freedom and Peace	1968	1,500,000	General
Eldrige Cleaver	Peace and Freedom	1968	36,563	General
Shirley Chilsom	Democratic	1972	430,703	Primaries
Jesse Jackson	Democratic	1984	3,500,000	Primaries
Dennis Serette	New Alliance	1984	50,000	General
Jesse Jackson	Democratic	1988	6,900,000	Primaries
Lenora Fulani	New Alliance	1988	211,742	General
Lenora Fulani	New Alliance	1992	73,707- 80,411	General
Ron Daniels	Independent	1992	28,000	General
L. Douglas Wilder	Democratic	1992		Primaries
Alan Keyes	Republican	1996	471,716	Primaries
Monica Moorehead	Workers World	1996	29,083	General
Monica Moorehead	Workers World	2000	4,795	General
Al Sharpton	Democratic	2004	384,766	Primaries
Carol M. Braun	Democratic	2008	0	Quit before primaries
Barack Obama	Democratic	2008	66,882,230	General
Alan Keyes	Republican	2008	47,694	Primaries
Cynthia McKinney	Green Party	2008	161,603	General

CHAPTER 9

The Lastest Political Milestone: The Obamas' White House Story

I am married to a black American who carries within her the blood of slaves and slaveowners.—Barack Obama, March 18, 2008, Philadelphia

Prelude: Michelle Obama's White House Story

The legislation that brought California into the nation as a free state and New Mexico and Utah as slave territories, also created the Fugitive Slave Act of 1850. In the previous decade, abolitionist influence had grown and the movement's activism was successfully weakening enforcement of the 1793 Fugitive Slave law. Local officials were refusing to arrest or return individuals who were accused of being runaways. The "personal liberty laws" that existed in fourteen states found a variety of ways to confound Southern efforts to capture those who had escaped. In particular, Pennsylvania, New York, Massachusetts, Ohio, and Wisconsin passed laws that required a jury trial for anyone accused of being an escapee, forbade the use of local jails to hold those accused, put restrictions on bounty hunters, and allowed local officials to go unpunished for not helping slave catchers. States' rights advocate John Calhoun called the laws "one of the most fatal blows ever received by the South or the Union."[1] In

First Lady Michelle Obama in the White House,
February 18, 2009

1842, the Supreme Court had ruled in *Prigg v. Pennsylvania* that states could refuse to assist in the hunting of escapees.

The 1850 Act was an attempt by the South to strengthen the recapture laws and undermine the gathering storm of abolition. The Act created a $1,000 fine to be levied on federal marshals who did not arrest accused individuals, allowed for arrests without warrants, and eliminated jury trials related to the charge. Individual citizens could also be fined $1,000 and punished with six months in jail for aiding or abetting someone's escape. In their effort to further nationalize the reach of slavery, Southern slaveholders intensified polarization over the issue, which pushed the country that much closer to the edge of civil war.

In that same year, six-year-old Melvinia, an enslaved child of unrecorded parentage, was sent from Spartanburg, South Carolina, to Georgia to continue her life in bondage after David Patterson, her white enslaver, died.[2] Property records indicated that she was valued at $475.00, approximately $12,500.00 in 2010 dollars. Patterson had written in his will that Melvinia would be bequeathed to his wife, Ruth, who would inherit "the use and service of the negro [*sic*] girl, her issue and increase, if any." Doubtless, he believed he was being benevolent when he also wrote in the will that his slave families "be kept together as far as possible," making it clear to his heirs that they were under no obligation to do so. However, it appears that Ruth died before David did, and therefore Melvinia was passed along to Patterson's daughter and son-in-law in Georgia. Christianne and Henry Shields became her new enslavers on a 200-acre farm where Melvinia would eventually toil as a farm laborer, washerwoman, and maid. According to research by the *New York Times*, the farm grew "wheat, corn, sweet potatoes, and cotton" in an area near Atlanta. On this land, she would continue the lineage that would eventually produce the great-great-great-granddaughter who became the nation's first African American First Lady.

While still a child in her teens, Melvina was impregnated by a white man. At the time of this writing, nothing further is known regarding circumstances under which the relations took place. In either 1859 or 1861, Melvina gave birth to a boy and named him Dolphus. He was the first of her three children who would be listed as mulatto, all of whom would be given the last name Shields rather than McGruder, the surname she later adopted. A fourth child was listed as black. Dolphus's father would never be listed in any of the records of his life, nor on his death certificate.

Whether Melvinia was raped by the white man or not, her impregnation took place in a context and era in which black women had little capacity to repel sexual attacks by white men. The slave era was perpetuated by white Americans' violent domination of every aspect of the black women, men, and children that they enslaved. In the hierarchy of ownership and power, black women's bodies were completely at the mercy of whites and, for that matter, of black men. Forced into the dual role of worker and breeder, black women routinely experienced forced sex, as it profited white enslavers to breed more slaves. In *Black Reconstruction*, W. E. B. Du Bois quotes from a letter:

> A Southerner wrote to Olmsted: "In the states of Maryland, Virginia, North Carolina, Kentucky, Tennessee and Missouri, as much attention is paid to the breeding and growth of Negroes as to that of horses and mules. Further south, we raise them both for use and for market. Planters command their girls and women (married or unmarried) to have children; and

I have known a great many Negro girls to be sold off because they did not have children."[3]

White men frequently had sex with the black women they enslaved. The pervasiveness of this practice was such that more than half of those in the contemporary United States who claim African American heritage have documentable white ancestors. Black leaders such as Frederick Douglass, W. E. B. Du Bois, Malcolm X, and many others were of mixed-race heritage. According to scholar Henry Louis Gates, "fully 58 percent of African Americans have at least 12.5 percent European ancestry."[4] At the time of this writing Melvinia is Michelle Obama's most distant ancestor about whom anything is known. Further research may uncover more mixture in her heritage, as would be the case for most blacks whose ancestry in North America dates back to the beginnings of the slave era in the 1600s.

Struggling to raise her children, Melvinia slaved as a farm laborer and was perhaps ordered to do other jobs as well. According to her death certificate, which listed her profession as "domestic," she lived into her early nineties and died on June 4, 1938. While there is ongoing research on her, little is known about her life. It appears that after slavery ended she worked extremely hard to make ends meet. Like most people enslaved at the time, she was illiterate, but she somehow was able to have her son Dolphus educated. Not only could he read and write, but by his late twenties, according to 1888 census records, he owned his own home in Birmingham, Alabama, and had apparently become a successful carpenter. Some years later, he would open his own carpentry and tool-sharpening business, by which time he was married to a woman named Lucy, the last of his wives. Deeply religious, he helped to found two churches.

Dolphus Shields was married four times. His first marriage was with Alice Easley sometime in the early 1880s. Alice was the daughter of Bolus and Mariah Easley, who, along with Melvinia, were also at one time enslaved to David Patterson. The Easleys eventually ended up in Georgia before moving to Birmingham and reuniting with Melvinia. It is possible that, in fact, a community of former slaves from South Carolina was being built based on their common history. The marriage between Dolphus and Alice appeared to have lasted a number of years but had come to an end by 1900 at the latest. By that time Dolphus is listed as having remarried. The *New York Times* reports that after the divorce, Easley moved around and "worked as a seamstress, a washerwoman and a maid." She died in 1915, most likely while living with her daughter, Pearl. Dolphus lived to be ninety-one and died of pneumonia on June 3, 1950. Together, Dolphus and Easley produced at least four children, two girls and two boys, one of whom was Robert, born in 1885 or 1886.

On June 27, 1906, Robert Shields married Annie Estelle Laws (or Lawson), and they had two sons Robert (b. 1909) and Purnell (b. 1910). By 1920, Annie and Robert were no longer together. Annie lived in Birmingham for a while with Robert Jr. and Purnell, and later relocated to Chicago, where she was listed as a seamstress. Purnell worked at a syrup factory and eventually married a woman named Rebecca, whose last name was either Jumper or Coleman. She worked as a nurse, at one point, at Chicago's Grant Hospital. Purnell and Rebecca Shields had eight children. In 1937, their daughter Marian Lois was born.

Purnell Shields, Michelle Obama's maternal grandfather, was a carpenter who attempted to join Chicago's carpenters' union but was denied admission because he was African American, even though the union, unlike some national and Chicago-based skilled unions in the pre–civil rights era, did not have a formal policy barring black carpenters.[5] This meant that Purnell and other qualified black carpenters were generally unable to get the highest-paying construction jobs in the city. Even when they were hired, African American carpenters experienced racism. Many complained that they were "often shunned on the job by their white co-workers and given the most disagreeable work by the foreman."[6] As late as 1980, blacks accounted for only 6.9 percent of working carpenters in the city, 1,705 in all.[7] Purnell's experience was passed down to his children and grandchildren as a story to inspire them to overcome and fight rather than succumb to despair because of racism. It was a lesson that black parents all over the city taught their children.

Chicago was a cauldron of black politics with a wide range of tendencies. It became the headquarters for the Nation of Islam. Founded in Detroit in 1930, the black nationalist religious organization that advocated racial separatism and black self-help would later move to Chicago under the leadership of Elijah Muhammad. From that time until Muhammad's death in 1975, Chicago served as the main office and home of the Nation of Islam, although its most famous disciple and subsequent critic, Malcolm X, emerged out of the Harlem branch of the group. In 1975, there was a split in the organization when Muhammad's son, Warith Deen Muhammad, who had taken over the group after his father died, changed the ideological nature of the group by opening the membership to whites and others, and shifting to a more mainstream Muslim posture. He also changed the name of the organization to the World Community of Al-Islam in the West, a name later replaced by yet another, the American Society of Muslims. These changes were rejected by many of the members, and a significant number of them quit. Three years later, Louis Farrakhan, a key figure under Elijah Muhammad's reign, reconstituted a parallel organization under the old name,

Nation of Islam, bringing along other members who had left or were dissatisfied with the new direction of the American Society of Muslims. Farrakhan also established headquarters in Chicago and positioned the NOI to remain an important element in local and national black politics. Its high-water mark was the Million Man March event in Washington, D.C., in 1995.[8] Since then, in part due to Farrakhan's failing health and its inability to capitalize on the spike in popularity it achieved among some black Americans as a result of the march, the organization's influence in black politics has receded considerably.

The city was also the home of one of the most active chapters of the Black Panther Party. It would become renowned after a deadly police raid on December 4, 1969, in which Panther leader Fred Hampton and party member Mark Clark were killed and several others seriously wounded in a joint operation by the Chicago police, Illinois state law enforcement, and the FBI. Hampton was shot while sleeping in his bed, drugged by barbiturates slipped into his food earlier in the evening by a police informant. The Chicago chapter of the Panthers had been one of the key targets of the FBI's COINTELPRO war under J. Edgar Hoover against black activists and leaders. In spite of the effort to destroy the Chicago branch, one of its members, Bobby Rush, would later be elected in 1992 to the U.S. House of Representatives. In 2000, Barack Obama challenged Rush in the Democratic primary losing badly by a margin of two to one—which turned out to be fortunate for him, as it is highly unlikely that he would have been able to mount a winning campaign for the presidency from a seat in the relatively low-profile U.S. House of Representatives.

Somewhere between the militants and the mainstream was Operation Breadbasket, the organization launched by the Martin Luther King's Southern Christian Leadership Council in

1962. Its Chicago office would eventually be run by Reverend Jesse Jackson, who later left the organization and in 1971 started Operation PUSH (People United to Save Humanity). PUSH would lead numerous boycotts and protests against corporations, pressuring them to hire blacks and buy advertisements in black newspapers. It also became active around the issue of education. After his presidential runs in the 1980s, Jackson would merge Operation PUSH with his National Rainbow Coalition, the organization he started to bring together progressive activists from around the country. At the time of this writing, the Rainbow PUSH Coalition remains based in Chicago.

African Americans were involved in mainstream city politics as well. Chicago produced the first African American to return to the U.S. Congress in the twentieth century, Representative Oscar De Priest, elected in 1928. The number of black congressmembers from Chicago would grow and, strikingly, include three of the four blacks—Carol Moseley Braun (1993–1999), Barack Obama (2005–2008), and Roland Burris (2009–2011)—elected or selected to the U.S. Senate in the twentieth and twenty-first centuries.[9] Beyond the excitement generated by Chicago-based activist Jesse Jackson's presidential runs in 1984 and 1988, progressives around the nation gave enthusiastic support to the historic mayoral campaign that elected Harold Washington (1984–1987). Nearly all these political activities would occur within the orbit of the Democratic Party, which has dominated city politics for decades. The Democratic Party in Chicago, as in other Northern cities, recruited blacks not only to be candidates but also to perform the nitty-gritty, street-level party work, many serving as precinct captains. Their role was essential to the maintenance of Democrat authority, as they were directly responsible for turning out the vote in exchange for favors, funds, and other benefits.

One of those precinct captains was Fraser Robinson III. His grandfather, Jim Robinson, had been born enslaved in Georgetown, South Carolina, around 1850, the same year that Melvina was sold and sent to Georgia. Jim and his wife Louisa had at least two children, Gabriel, who was born around 1877, and Fraser, born in 1884. Fraser married Rose Ella Cohen and their son, Fraser Jr., would be among the millions of African Americans who left the South between World War I and World War II to seek a better life in Northern cities. In Chicago, Fraser Jr. met and married Illinois-born LaVaughn Delores Johnson, who may have been a descendant of blacks who had been free since before the Civil War. Life would be hard for the couple, and there was a period when Fraser abandoned the family, later to return. In 1935, the couple gave birth to Fraser III. LaVaughn and Fraser Jr. would return to Georgetown, South Carolina, after their retirement.[10]

Given the difficult personal times and the Depression era, Chicago-born Fraser III grew up poor, and the family spent some time on welfare during his childhood. As a result he began working on a milk truck at the age of eleven. As an adult, Fraser worked at the Chicago Water Department tending boilers as a pump operator despite being physically challenged by multiple sclerosis, which he had developed when he was young. He walked with crutches but still managed to be an outstanding employee who rarely missed a day of work.

At one point, Marian Lois Shields and Fraser Robinson III met, fell in love, and married. They would occupy a one-bedroom apartment in a brick bungalow in an essentially all-black neighborhood. Marian worked as a secretary but left the job to start a family. She and Fraser had two children Craig (April 21, 1962) and Michelle (January 17, 1964). Fraser would play a key role in the achievements of his children, but he died in 1991 before he could witness the heights of their success. Marian and Fraser had always emphasized the importance of education, and both children were extremely bright. They excelled academically, both learning to read at age four. According to Craig, in 1979, when he was indecisive about whether he should go to Princeton University or the less prestigious but more affordable University of Washington or Purdue University, he turned to his father for counsel. His father stated, "If you pick your school based on how much you have to pay, I'll be very disappointed."[11]

Craig went to Princeton. He later became a successful businessman and then a winning basketball coach at Brown University and Oregon State University.[12] His younger sister, Michelle, followed him to Princeton two years later. Thus began the path that would eventually lead to her meeting a young black lawyer named Barack Obama.

Michelle became very conscious about issues of discrimination and prejudice while studying at Princeton, a time she describes as difficult for her and the other few black students on campus. Her senior thesis was titled, "Princeton-Educated Blacks and the Black Community," where she wrote that her experiences at the school made her more aware of her "blackness" than ever before and that, "I sometimes feel like a visitor on campus, as if I really don't belong."[13] Despite these feelings, she dug in and graduated cum laude with a Bachelor of Arts in sociology. Three years later she earned a Juris Doctor degree from Harvard Law School, graduating only months before Obama started working toward his law degree at the same school. Michelle went to work for the Sidley Austin law firm in Chicago in 1988, and the following year she met Obama, who was a summer intern assigned to the firm. On October 18, 1992, the couple married at Trinity United Church; Michelle's childhood friend Santita Jackson, Jesse Jackson's daughter, sang at the ceremony.

Michelle's life was changing dramatically during this time. Her father died the year before her marriage, and she decided to leave the corporate world for more public service–oriented work. She took a job as an assistant to Mayor Richard Daley Jr., became Chicago's Assistant Commissioner of Planning and Development, and then developed community outreach programs for the University of Chicago, University of Chicago Hospitals, and University of Chicago Medical Center. This work would place her in a position to meet and work with people, organizations, and institutions all across the city. She clearly had the capacity, skill, talent, and connections to be a successful politician, if she so desired. That role, however, would be played by her husband. It is likely that Michelle's father Fraser, the former precinct captain, would have relished his son-in-law's interest, involvement, and success in Chicago politics.

This was the historical environment and context—a trajectory through the slave plantations of South Carolina, tenant farms of Georgia, and black working-class neighborhoods of Chicago—that produced Michelle LaVaughn Robinson Obama, a gifted, sophisticated, intelligent, committed, forthright, and physically stunning woman who has brought a superb dignity to the White House. She has been steadfast in the face of racist attacks on her, her husband, and even her family, as well as sexist attacks on herself, always responding, when response was called for, in an appropriate and measured manner.

During Obama's run for the White House, most critics viewed her articulate, poised, and dignified presence as a valuable asset to the campaign. There was an effort by some conservatives—including Cindy McCain, John McCain's wife—to portray her as anti-American after she stated at a February 18,

President Barack Obama, First Lady Michelle Obama, and their daughters, Malia and Sasha, in the Green Room of the White House, September 1, 2009.

2008, rally in Madison, Wisconsin, "For the first time in my adult lifetime, I'm really proud of my country, and not just because Barack has done well, but because I think people are hungry for change." The charge did not stick. Most people of color rejected the accusation that Michelle was "anti-American." For many African Americans, Latinos, Asians, Native Americans, and others, the country's long violent history of racist exclusion has never been a source of pride. For communities of color, who have been marginalized for generations, endured segregation, and survived the era of lynching, it has been the nation's progressive steps—such as ending legal discrimination or long-standing racial, gender, or class barriers—that have inspired a sense of pride, patriotism, and national community.

On January 20, 2009, the Obama family—Michelle, Barack, their daughters Malia Ann and Natasha (Sasha), and

Michelle's mother Marian—officially moved into the White House. The long saga of African Americans and the White House that began with enslavement, followed by a century of legal segregation and racist terrorism, and continuing with present-day racial disparities, had finally culminated in changing the color of the residents of the most famous address in the nation, 1600 Pennsylvania Avenue, Washington, D.C. For the first time in U.S. history, the First Family in the White House was African American.

Becoming the First Black President of the United States of America

> *I've seen levels of compliance with the civil rights bill and changes that have been most surprising. So, on the basis of this, I think we may be able to get a Negro president in less than 40 years. I would think that this could come in 25 years or less.*[14]—Martin Luther King Jr. in an interview with the BBC, on his way to Oslo, Norway, to receive the Nobel Peace Prize in 1964.

When Martin Luther King Jr. made his prediction about when a black presidency might be possible, he was responding to a question from a BBC interviewer. King began his response by stating, "Well let me say first that I think it is necessary to make it clear there are Negroes who are presently qualified to be president of the United States. There are many who are qualified in terms of integrity, in terms of vision, in terms of leadership ability."[15] King's assertion about black leaders' integrity, vision, and leadership capabilities was one that most whites—even the most liberal—would have rejected at the time. King is also, of course, astute enough to identify the barriers to such an event. He goes on to add, "But we do know there are certain problems and prejudices and mores in our society that make it difficult now."[16] Clearly King is being diplomatic and calculated in his words: at that point he had been the target of assassination attempts, and the body count of murdered civil rights organizers was growing. In many ways, a second Civil War was under way, as White Citizens Councils, the Ku Klux Klan, law enforcement, elected officials, and others with a vested interest in the system of segregation were armed and ready for a fight to the death.

All that said, King still painted a hopeful picture of the years ahead, stating, "I'm very optimistic about the future. Frankly, I have seen certain changes in the United States over the last two years that have surprised me."[17] King is speaking in late 1964, a few months after the Civil Rights Act had been signed into law by President Lyndon Johnson, before the battle over the Voting Rights Act of 1965 and the horrific attacks by police officers, state troopers, and local thugs on civil rights activists, notably on that last great march of the era, over the Pettus Bridge near Selma, Alabama.[18]

The journalist's question had been inspired by an earlier quote from then attorney general Robert Kennedy, who stated in May 1961, "There's no question that in the next thirty or forty years, a Negro can also achieve the same position that my brother has as President of the United States, certainly within that period of time."[19] Given the toxic racial divisions at the time, including legal segregation, Kennedy was speaking very optimistically, perhaps assuming a much greater capacity and willingness on the part of his newly elected brother John to move a civil rights agenda, tone down the vitriolic rage spewing out of the South, and deal with a Congress dominated by Southern Dixiecrats. Both King and Kennedy would come up slightly short in their prediction of when the first black president of the United States would be elected.

Race, Racism, and Obama's White House

> *I chose to run for the presidency at this moment in history because I believe deeply that we cannot solve the challenges of our time unless we solve them together—unless we perfect our union by understanding that we may have different stories, but we hold common hopes; that we may not look the same and we may not have come from the same place, but we all want to move in the same direction—towards a better future for of children and our grandchildren.*—Barack Obama

How long does it take to become president of the United States? By one measure, it took Barack Obama 1,638 days, from July 27, 2004, when he gave the celebrated speech at the Democratic National Convention that introduced him and his message of unity to the nation, to January 20, 2009, when he took the oath of office. His meteoric political ascent to command the highest office in the land was driven, of course, by all that came before him, a long preparatory period for the nation's racial politics and much more. Paradoxically, Obama won because of race and in spite of it.

The images of the Obama family entering the White House transfixed the world. Aware of the long history of white enslavement and racial segregation of blacks, millions across the globe sensed that they were witnessing a barrier of immense importance being broken, and the image of the White House and of the United States itself would be forever transformed. The worldwide celebration of Obama's electoral triumph and subsequent inauguration bespoke an identification on the part of billions and their hope that social marginalization, discrimination, and oppression could be overcome.

Scholars will be analyzing and reinterpreting the Obamas

for a long time to come. That it took the nation and world by surprise and by storm is an understatement. Despite King's optimism, seen in the epigraph above, perhaps only the most imaginative science fiction writer could have predicted in 2001 that in less than ten years the United States would have its first black commander in chief and that that individual would be an unknown junior senator from Illinois with the unusual Middle Eastern–sounding name: Barack Hussein Obama.

One question will vex traditional Democratic and Republican strategists for the rest of their lives: How was Obama able to defeat both the powerful Clinton political machine and the entire Republican Party operation? Obama won for three reasons: he had a compelling message, he had a compelling strategy, and he had a compelling personal narrative. None of these variables by themselves would have sufficed, but their confluence proved victorious in the atmospherics of 2008.

A Compelling Message: Change People Wanted to Believe In

Throughout his fight for the White House, Obama's strategic brilliance was to turn his principal negative into his most expressed positive. There was simply no way he could compare his experience and political history with that of his main Democratic or Republican rivals (not counting the ill-chosen, ignorant, shallow, and untested Sarah Palin). He had been in the U.S. Senate less than three years before jumping into the race. However, his timing was fortunate. as the country became increasingly irritated with both Republican and Democratic leaders. Thus, he used their experience against them. His call for change was in sync with the mood of the nation. His straightforward message became a pledge for "a change you can believe in."

In one sense, George W. Bush, Dick Cheney, and the excesses of their administration prepared the way for Obama's victory.

In the days following September 11, 2001, Bush achieved the highest rating for a president since such data has been recorded. By the time he left office, he had fallen to one of the lowest levels of popularity in U.S. history. On nearly every possible issue, the American public gave the Bush White House failing grades. Bush had started two wars, both of which spiraled out of U.S. control, killed untold thousands, and became vastly unpopular. While the nation and the international community had supported the response of the United States to attack al Qaeda and the Taliban regime in Afghanistan that supported it, the war was deprioritized and lost focus after the December 2001 Battle of Tora Bora failed to capture or kill Osama bin Laden and his top leadership.

Bush and Cheney then focused on Iraq and built a case to invade based upon alleged intelligence that Saddam Hussein possessed weapons of mass destruction. The Iraq War quickly evolved into a deadly affair with mounting Iraqi and U.S. deaths despite global opposition and the revelation that the premises for going to war were false. Iraq had no weapons of mass destruction. Long a foe of the United States, Saddam Hussein had been contained by a wide range of international and U.S.-led political, economic and military punishments. While he periodically rattled his saber, his rash and murderous behavior was reduced to the harm he brought to the people of his own country. Nevertheless, despite public protest, the Bush administration invaded Iraq in February 2003.

Obama had been part of a handful of Democratic leaders who spoke out against the war. On September 15, 2001, in the ultra-paranoid days immediately following the attacks on the Pentagon and World Trade Center, Representative Barbara Lee, an African American legislator from the Bay Area in northern California, was the only member of Congress to vote no on

Bush's war powers measure. The motion she voted against gave the president virtually unlimited license to exercise "all necessary and appropriate force" on anyone associated with the terrorist attacks, authority the administration would exploit to the fullest. The resolution passed 98-0 in the Senate and 420-1 in the House of Representatives.

By 2002, when Obama began thinking about running for the U.S. Senate in Illinois, the Bush administration's fear-mongering PR machine pushed the notion that links existed between Iraq and al Qaeda in order to drum up public support for launching a second war. Obama, however, embraced the opposition and gave a speech at an antiwar rally in Chicago on October 2, declaring, "I don't oppose all wars. What I am opposed to is a dumb war. What I am opposed to is a rash war. What I am opposed to is the cynical attempt by Richard Perle and Paul Wolfowitz and other armchair, weekend warriors in this administration to shove their own ideological agendas down our throats, irrespective of the costs in lives lost and in hardships borne."[20]

Although his position was deemed risky politically at the time, it would be the votes cast in support of the invasion by Senator Hilary Clinton and Obama's other Democratic presidential opponents (excluding Rep. Dennis Kucinich) that would become liabilities. By the beginning of 2008, despite the military escalation known as the "surge" that desperately tried to halt and reverse its losing trend, popular opinion had turned against the war and, to a degree, against Democrats and Republicans who had supported it.

Obama's clarion call for change resonated on many other fronts as well. Bush and Cheney's record of unresponsiveness to the economic and social calamities faced by millions of Americans also undermined support for their administration. The ineffective, insensitive, and inadequate response to the devastation wrought in New Orleans and elsewhere in the aftermath of Hurricane Katrina was symptomatic of his administration's real and perceived callousness. The image released by the White House of Bush flying over the devastated areas was meant to show his concern, but the photo op only cemented the perception that he cared little about low-income and working-class people across racial lines.

A third decisive issue was the economic collapse that Bush policies facilitated and then ineptly addressed in a belated and controversial manner. He pushed through tax cuts while not only fighting two wars but also creating the largest government agency in U.S. history—The Department of Homeland Security. When Bush won the White House in 2000, Clinton was overseeing a budget surplus of $236 billion. Bush inherited a surplus of $128 billion. In his first year, Bush doled out $630 billion in tax cuts to the richest 1 percent of Americans and the transition to a spiraling deficit began. By July 2008, he was projecting a budget deficit of $482 billion.[21]

While Obama's Republican rival, John McCain, engaged in unproductive stunts such as dramatically suspending his campaign to fly back to D.C. in superhero mode to rescue the economy, or stating one day that the economy was fine and the next that it was not, or being unaware of how many houses he owned, Obama appeared steady, rational, deliberate, and presidential. It was impossible not to blame the Republicans for the state of the economy, given Bush's eight years in office and his party's control of Congress for six of those years. In the final months of the campaign, McCain desperately and unsuccessfully attempted to distance himself from Bush.

Hillary Clinton finally realized in the primary campaigns, and McCain in the general election, that a message of change carried a lot more credibility than declaring one's long experience within a political system widely viewed as corrupted, mismanaged, and illegitimate, but their tardy embrace of a rhetoric of change was too little, too late.[22] The eight years of Bush and Cheney's political perfidy, economic mutilations, cowboy foreign policy, and social divisiveness opened the door for an outsider.

A Compelling Strategy: States of All Colors

Although Jesse Jackson and Barack Obama became rivals during the 2008 campaign and since, the latter arguably owes his electoral success to the former. As noted in Chapter 8, Jackson's effort to make the Democratic Party more democratic after his 1984 campaign had created a critical rule change that would be a decisive element for Obama's campaign 24 years later.

Just as he was forced to choose a message that drew a clear distinction between himself and his rivals, Obama also needed a strategy that could beat the Clinton political juggernaut and all that the Republican Party would throw at him. For nearly twenty years, the Clintons had controlled much of the Democratic Party machinery. The conventional wisdom in 2007 was that Clinton, with overwhelming support from blacks and women, would win the nomination with relatively little difficulty. The primaries and caucuses were merely the rituals by which she would be anointed the candidate. As writers Chuck Todd and Sheldon Gawiser point out, the Clinton camp was so confident of her eventual nomination that she never made a formal announcement of her entrance in the race or gave a clear reason why she was running.[23]

Clinton opted to run a traditional strategy of campaigning in the primaries in the large states and paying scant attention to the small states and caucuses. Her campaign also felt there was little to gain by campaigning in states where the Democrats were likely or sure to lose in the November election. To some degree, Clinton's approach was driven by limited resources, as the campaign ran into financial troubles at critical stages in the race and was forced to streamline. In an ordinary year against an ordinary candidate, it was probably would have been a winning strategy.

Obama evolved two-prong tactics: put energy and resources into winning the smaller and Republican Party-oriented states in the primaries and caucuses, and make a competitive showing in the larger states that were going to be difficult if not impossible for him to win. Since the advent of the modern system of primaries and caucuses as the main means by which the major parities select their candidates for the presidency, with the convention serving as a crowning more than anything else, strategies for winning have followed the Electoral College math. Serious Democratic candidates tend to focus their energies on a few swing states, giving token appearances in states the party is likely to win in the fall campaign and completely ignoring states they are likely to lose. Republicans follow a similar path. What this means is that much of the country is marginalized and the sense of political polarization deepens.

Obama stated from the beginning that he wanted to run in all fifty states plus the District of Columbia. While his team's fund-raising proficiency gave him the resources to carry out his pledge, it was the underlying philosophy underneath that was emphasized publicly. Consistent with his message of one nation was the idea of taking his campaign to every community. While the Iowa caucus win was a decisive step in giving his campaign leverage and momentum, it was just the beginning. Obama won all the caucus states and accumulated a strategic reserve of delegates.

While Hillary Clinton's name was on the ballot in every state, her campaign clearly gave priority to the larger states that would figure significantly in the general election. By getting ahead of herself, she got behind. The problem she faced was that her strategy worked. She did win nearly all the big important Democratic and swing states. She won California, New Jersey, New York, Ohio, and Pennsylvania, among others. And she lost many small states that Democrats were unlikely to win that November, which also turned out to be correct. Unfortunately, that strategy misread the mathematics and technical rules of first winning the Democratic nomination.

In the 1980s, in a crucial rule change, the Democratic Party instituted proportional delegate distribution. With a threshold of 15 percent, candidates would receive delegates based on the percentage of the vote they won. If a candidate won 40 percent of the vote in a state, he or she would get roughly 40 percent of the delegates, even if they lost the state. While the media and the Clinton campaign focused on who "won" the big states, they initially paid little attention to the delegate accumulation numbers until Obama had built an insurmountable edge.

In the general campaign, Obama's strategy to some degree reverted to a traditional swing-state focus, but not totally. He had campaign offices across the country, and their activism, even in states where Obama could not win, benefited other Democrats who were on the ticket. Having those offices also forced the McCain campaign to play defense, to some degree. In the end, Obama won a number of states that Bush had carried in 2004, including Colorado, Florida, Indiana, North Carolina, and Virginia.

Much was made of the fact that the map of states that voted for John McCain fit neatly over the map of Confederate states that attempted to secede from the United States in 1861. While the map shows the general racial voting patterns of the South, there is much it does not show. There is no question that the region was the least supportive of Obama, even among Democrats and independents. In nearly every Southern state covered by the Voting Rights Act, with the exception of North Carolina, South Carolina, and Virginia, Obama fared worse than or the same as John Kerry had with white voters. (See Table 1.)

Table 1
States covered by the VRA

	Percent of White Voters for Obama (2008)	Percent of White Voters for Kerry (2004)	Difference
Alabama	10	19	-10
Arkansas	30	36	-6
Florida	42	42	0
Georgia	23	23	0
Louisiana	14	24	-10
Mississippi	11	14	-3
North Carolina	35	27	+8
South Carolina	26	22	+4
Tennessee	34	34	0
Texas	26	25	+1
Virginia	39	32	+7

However, as researcher Chris Kromm notes, when broken down by age, the white voting pattern was inconsistent and broke stereotypes. Older white voters in the region, who have been voting Republican for generations, strongly supported McCain. Yet, Kromm points out, "In six Southern states, 40% of whites under the age of thirty voted for Obama."[24] In fact, only in South Carolina and Georgia did white voters under thirty vote in a lower percentage than the overall white vote. (See Table 2.) In other words, the trend among young white voters in the region is more liberal, in some instances significantly so, than the overall election result indicates.

Table 2
Southern States with the Biggest White Voter Generation Gap for Obama

State	Percent of White Vote Under 30 for Obama	Percent of Overall White Vote for Obama	White Voter "Generation Gap"
North Carolina	56	35	+21
Tennessee	45	34	+11
Mississippi	18	11	+7
Kentucky	42	35	+6
West Virginia	45	41	+4
Arkansas	34	30	+4
Texas	30	26	+4
Virginia	42	39	+3
Louisiana	17	14	+3
Alabama	13	10	+3
Florida	44	42	+2
South Carolina	24	26	–2
Georgia	20	23	–3

Upon examination, the voting patterns were much more complicated than is revealed by a simple framework of blue and red states. In many ways, the national political divide is not so much between red states and blue states but between red states and blue cities. While Republicans are strong in a number of Southern and Western states where there are few African Americans, and depending upon the state, few other racial or ethnic minorities, the nation's urban areas swing Democratic. In virtually every state, the vote was relatively close. Only a few states had a wide gap.

Although Obama won 95 percent of the black vote, 43 percent of the white vote, and 67 percent of the Latino vote, his overall voting constituency was very diverse, especially when compared to McCain's. Broken down by race, 61 percent of Obama's voters were white, 23 percent were black, and 11 percent were Latino. McCain's voting bloc was about 90 percent white, 4 percent black, and 6 percent Latino. (See Table 3.)

Table 3
2008 Vote by Race

Racial Group	% Voting for Obama Vote	% Voting for McCain Vote	Other
Asian	62	35	3
Black	95	4	1
Latino	67	31	2
White	43	55	2
Other	66	31	3

A Compelling Narrative

In addition to his brilliant campaign strategy and a political message that resonated with an America in crisis, Obama had a unique personal story that helped galvanize millions of citizens to volunteer. A perfect storm of factors coalesced in Obama's favor. The country wanted a change in direction and Obama's personal narrative supported his message and resonated with voters. The incumbent's image as a white, spoiled, inarticulate, ne'er-do-well son of a wealthy U.S. president could not have been further from that of the mixed-raced son of a single mother. Clinton and McCain's political longevity, ultimately viewed in a negative light, and their sense of entitlement to the position were also rejected by voters.

Obama's life story is well known due to his best-selling memoir, *Dreams from My Father: A Story of Race and Inheritance*, and the stories he told during the campaign[25] about his childhood as the son of a white mother from Kansas and a black father from

Kenya. Mainstream America viewed Obama's childhood spent in Hawaii and Indonesia as unique, exotic and perhaps, to some, threatening. After Barack Obama Sr. abandoned the family, his mother, Stanley Ann Dunham, remarried and moved with her son to Indonesia for four years. Critics have seized on his time in Indonesia to make the false assertions that he converted to Islam, attended a fundamentalist Wahhabi Muslim school, and took his Senate oath by swearing on a Koran. The Web site for *Insight* magazine posted a piece asking, "Are the American people ready for an elected president who was educated in a Madrassa as a young boy and has not been forthcoming about his Muslim heritage?"[26] The article was immediately picked up and spread by Fox News, then debunked as baseless by CNN, the *Washington Post*, and other news sources.[27]

He later returned to the United States to live with his grandparents in Hawaii, a state as culturally remote to most Americans as Alaska. His mother was a social anthropologist and his father an economist, so education was highly stressed for both Barack and his sister, Maya Soetoro-Ng, who would later earn a Ph.D. in international comparative education. Barack went to Columbia University to finish his undergraduate degree, then went on to Harvard Law School, where he was elected over eighteen others to become the first black president of the *Harvard Law Review*. As the *New York Times* reported it:

> *The Harvard Law Review*, generally considered the most prestigious in the country, elected the first black president in its 104-year history today. The job is considered the highest student position at Harvard Law School.
>
> The new president of the Review is Barack Obama, a 28-year-old graduate of Columbia Univer-

> sity who spent four years heading a community development program for poor blacks on Chicago's South Side before enrolling in law school. . . .
>
> "The fact that I've been elected shows a lot of progress," Mr. Obama said today in an interview. "It's encouraging.
>
> "But it's important that stories like mine aren't used to say that everything is O.K. for blacks. You have to remember that for every one of me, there are hundreds or thousands of black students with at least equal talent who don't get a chance," he said, alluding to poverty or growing up in a drug environment.[28]

Doors were opening for Obama in all directions, and the path he chose to take led to electoral politics. Eager to make a difference in public policy, in 1996 he ran for and won a seat in the Illinois State Senate. When the opportunity presented itself in 2004, he ran for a U.S. Senate seat for Illinois and, due to the misfortunes of his strongest Democratic and Republican challengers, easily defeated the fanatical, hapless Maryland transplant Alan Keyes.

Obama's storybook life was well exposed by the time he actually joined the race for the presidency. Some observers speculated that perhaps one factor that made Obama attractive to whites was that he did not have the lineage of slavery, often perceived as a defining characteristic of being black in American. In fact, research has documented that while some of his mother's ancestors fought for the Union during the Civil War, others were enslavers. According to research by William Addams Reitwiesner and the *Baltimore Sun*, "One of Obama's great-great-great-great-grandfathers, George Washington Overall, owned two slaves who were recorded in the 1850 census in Nelson County, Ky. . . . [and] one of Obama's great-great-great-great-great-grandmothers, Mary Duvall, also owned two slaves" according to that same 1850 census.[29] Overall enslaved a fifteen-year-old black girl and a twenty-five-year-old black man; and Duvall enslaved a sixty-year-old black man and a fifty-eight-year-old black woman.

Obama's nontraditional black history led some in the black community to raise the question of whether he was "black enough."[30] Stanley Crouch, in a *Daily News* article titled "What Obama Isn't: Black Like Me," wrote: "So when black Americans refer to Obama as 'one of us,' I do not know what they are talking about. . . . Obama makes it clear that, while he has experienced some light versions of typical racial stereotypes, he cannot claim those problems as his own—nor has he lived the life of a black American."[31] This view is echoed by writer Debra Dickerson in an article titled, "Colorblind: Barack Obama would be the great black hope in the next presidential race—if he were actually black." She states bluntly that "Obama isn't black," arguing that "'Black,' in our political and social reality, means those descended from West African slaves."[32]

Despite the vigorous debate in some quarters, the issue was settled at the polls when he won well over 90 percent of the black vote in most primary and caucus contests, and over 95 percent in the general election.

There was also an effort to paint Obama as "too black" on the part of conservatives who equated his liberal voting record with his race. However, the same factors that led some to question Obama's blackness also made it difficult to place him in the same box as traditional civil rights leaders or contemporary black elected officials.

Perhaps Pollster Cornell Belcher best articulated the sentiment of Obama's white voters. He stated, "It would be difficult for an African-American to be elected president in this country. However, it is not difficult for an *extraordinary* individual who happens to be African-American to be elected president."[33] (Emphasis in original.)

Race and the Race for the White House

> *I have never been so naïve as to believe that we can get beyond our racial divisions in a single election cycle, or with a single candidacy—particularly a candidacy as imperfect as my own.*—Barack Obama

Although he openly identifies with being black[34] and has never shied away from addressing racial concerns—politically, he shrewdly played them down while campaigning. His core policy focus was on the economy, the wars in Iraq and Afghanistan (issues on which Clinton and McCain were highly vulnerable), health care, and a new energy policy. But the issue of race would not go away.

Prior to winning the White House, Obama constructed a black and multiracial identity forged through the prism of his travels and travails through Hawaii, Indonesia, Los Angeles, New York, Chicago, and Boston, the imaginings passed on from his black immigrant Kenyan father, and the love and ambition given by his white Kansan mother.[35] In *Dreams from My Father*, he discusses his long journey of awareness of the consequences of both social and personal racialization. The book recounts, often painfully, his realization of his complex personal history, and matrix of multiple racial and national identities it created, and the saga of how he comes to clearly identify himself as a black man:

> Yes, I'd seen weakness in other men—Gramps and his

> disappointments, Lolo and his compromise. But these men had become object lessons for me, men I might love but never emulate, white men and brown men whose fates didn't speak to my own. It was into my father's image, the black man, son of Africa, that I'd packed all the attributes I sought in myself, the attributes of Martin and Malcolm, Du Bois and Mandela.[36]

As he notes, the book had a cathartic purpose that had to be expressed before he could actually evolve to the next stage in his life, a public career. Race and a critique of racism have always been salient to the public and personal Obama. How could they not be?

More often than not, however, when discussing race Obama has sought to present a more united and conciliatory tone in his political persona. In his 2004 speech at the Democratic National Convention, which first brought him into the national spotlight for most Americans and set him on the path to the White House, other than his very presence, race is secondary to his chief objective: to quilt a broad picture and projection of an America with minimum racial division. His only references in the speech to race are in his allusion to the interracial marriage of his parents, and his call for national unity, i.e., "There is not a Black America and a White America and Latino America and Asian America—there's the United States of America."[37] At that point, Obama was running for the U.S. Senate in Illinois.

As a politician in Illinois and in the U.S. Senate, when Obama did address race, he tended to use a broad frame that embraced a harsh rebuke of historical U.S. structural and institutional racism, praise for the black struggle for freedom—often with admonishments implying a behaviorist critique of the black community—and a call to acknowledge the significant progress that has been made in race relations. He then would add that there is still work to be done to end discrimination. Thus in one politically brilliant (though not necessarily theoretically coherent) stroke he managed to incorporate mainstream liberal, conservative, and centrist critiques of racism in the United States. During the 2008 campaign, he strategically avoided directly discussing race until the Reverend Jeremiah Wright controversy forced the issue onto the table.

The controversy began when it was first publicized by *ABC News* on March 13, 2008, that Obama's longtime minister, Reverend Jeremiah Wright of Trinity United Church of Christ, had made a number of inflammatory statements in some of his sermons.[38] Criticisms of Wright's sermons, however, had been circulating on right-wing Web sites for months, as soon as it became clear that Obama was a serious candidate, according to writers Adia Wingfield and Joe Feagin.[39] Once the sermons, or rather the most incendiary snippets of them, were aired, both Democratic and Republican opponents would use them to attack Obama. Echoing Malcolm X's response to the assassination of President Kennedy,[40] in a sermon following the September 11, 2001 attacks, Wright said "America's chickens are coming home to roost," and in 2003, he stated in another address from the pulpit, "No, no, no. Not God bless America; God damn America!"[41]

Taken out of context, these phrases painted the ex-military Wright as an unpatriotic, vitriolic, anti-American zealot. Obama was thus guilty by association. The fact that he spoke in the vernacular of black liberation theology, prevalent among many black ministers, was irrelevant to the mainstream media and to Obama's rival candidates for the presidency. Although much of what Wright had to say was not that different from sermons given in thousands of black churches every Sunday attended by local and national black leaders and elected officials, for much of white America those words came across as anti-American or even worse, anti-white. Obama's opponents attempted to link him to those statements and to Wright, who became more defiant as the controversy unfolded. Ultimately, Obama responded by publicly criticizing Wright and leaving Wright's congregation altogether. Media reports of the Philadelphia speech tended to focus on his denunciation of Wright but missed the more substantive and telling elements, and the complicated thesis that Obama is forwarding regarding race in the United States.

When former vice-presidential candidate John Edwards dropped out of the race for the Democratic nomination on January 30, he insured that the 2008 election was going to make history. His departure left only Obama and Clinton, guaranteeing that either a black man or a white woman would head the Democratic ticket. Although Clinton had some black supporters and Obama had some prominent women supporters, the historic nature of the situation created a rift between some white feminists and some activists and scholars in the black community.[42] Denied the black vote, the Clinton campaign sought to appeal to white working-class voters, especially in Ohio and Pennsylvania, and the record shows that a disproportionate amount of Obama's white vote came from college-educated whites. Clinton's statements about "hard-working Americans" were seen, whether intended to be or not, as thinly veiled racial coding that catered to notions of the United States as a white country.

However, the Clinton campaign's tepid efforts to play the race card would pale in comparison to the racial hype and rhetoric that would come from the Republican Party, the McCain-Palin campaign, and the conservative media. During the campaign, racially coded language was used to great effect by McCain and Palin to tap into the racial prejudices of white voters. They played not only the anti-black card but the anti-Muslim one as well. From references to Obama's middle name, Hussein, to accusing him of "palling around with terrorists," the McCain campaign consistently sought to inject racially loaded questions about Obama's character into the campaign.

At a McCain rally in Minnesota, McCain supporter Gayle Quinnell shouted to the crowd that "Obama is an Arab." McCain took away the microphone from her and weakly stated, "No ma'am. He's a decent family man, citizen, that I just happen to have disagreements with on fundamental issues." Quinnell was no ordinary run-of-the-mill angry couch potato stewing in her rage against Obama and Arabs—presumably she meant *Muslim*, making the erroneous leap that all Arabs are Muslim, and vice versa. She actively distributed her inaccurate beliefs as broadly as she could. She claimed that she got the information from a volunteer at the local McCain campaign office and then decided to copy the pamphlet and distribute it widely, including to 400 addresses she randomly pulled from a phone book.[43]

At Palin's rallies, participants screamed, "*Kill him*" and hurled accusations about Obama's "links to terrorists." At an October 11, 2008, rally in Pennsylvania, a participant showed up with a monkey doll made to look like Obama and there were shouts that he should go back to Kenya.[44] In Clearwater, Florida, at another Palin rally, a racial epithet was shouted at a black sound man by a Palin supporter, according to the *Washington Post*.[45] At another October rally in Bethlehem, Pennsylvania, Lehigh County Republican Chairman Bill Platt told the crowd, "Think about how you'll feel on November 5 if you wake up in the morning and see the news, that Barack Obama—that Barack Hussein Obama—is the president-elect of the United

States," emphasizing Obama's middle name.[46] All this was not just tolerated but encouraged by Sarah Palin. Going beyond the parameters set by McCain, Palin sought to incite her crowds by questioning Obama's patriotism, mischaracterizing his relationship with former 1960s radical Bill Ayers, and emphasizing his foreign-sounding middle name, Hussein. It got to the point that the Secret Service had to intervene on behalf of security and directed the campaign to tone down the rhetoric because of the spike in death threats from white supremacists and others to Obama and his family following these events.[47]

This egregious behavior was not limited to the Republican base. Incidents involving Republican officials and activists occurred both before and after the election. The examples seem endless. In October 2008, Buchanan County, Virginia McCain campaign official and local Republican Party treasurer Bobby May wrote a column stating that Obama, if elected, would paint the White House black, change the national anthem to the "Negro National Anthem," and send more aid to Africa so the "Obama family there can skim enough to allow them to free their goats and live the American Dream." Also in October 2008, San Bernardino Republican Women's Club president Diane Fedele, who was later forced to resign, mailed out a newsletter with a cartoon of Obama on a fake food stamp coupon. On the drawing he was surrounded by ribs, watermelons, and fried chicken. In June 2009, longtime South Carolina Republican Party activist Rusty DePass compared Michelle Obama to an escaped gorilla on his Facebook page: "I'm sure it's just one of (First Lady) Michelle's ancestors—probably harmless." In February 2009, Republican mayor Dean Grose of Los Alamitos, California, sent around a photo by email showing the White House in the middle of a watermelon patch, with a caption that read, "No Easter egg hunt this year." He later resigned over the scandal.[48] Unfortunately, many more examples could be cited.

More than just racist newsletters and cyberspace rants, real-world reactions erupted against Obama's election. Within hours of his victory, some students on the North Carolina State University campus spray-painted the words "Let's shoot that Nigger in the head" and "Hang Obama by a noose." That same night, four white men from Staten Island decided to "go after black people" in response to the election and before being apprehended they assaulted two people of color and a white person they believed to be black. Also on election night, a black family in South Ogden, Utah, came home to find that their American flag had been burned. And on that same night, a black church in Springfield, Massachusetts, was set on fire. According to the Southern Poverty Law Center and research by authors John Amato and David Neiwert, more than 200 "hate-related" incidents and actions were documented within the first few weeks of America's election of Obama, a number that would double by late spring 2009 although the data is not exact. [49]

Is the U.S. a "Postracial" Society? The Debate

Within days of the Obama's victory, radically different interpretations of its meaning and significance for American race relations began surfacing. Almost immediately, conservative and some mainstream pundits began to declare the end of racism in the United States. How could a nation be racist any longer if it had just elected someone from a segment of the population that had endured legal segregation within living memory? With not only a black president but two sitting black governors, two recent black secretaries of state, two black Supreme Court justices, one past and one present, and the largest minority bloc in the U.S. House of Representatives, surely African Americans could no longer complain about social exclusion, discrimination, or white bigotry. Race, it was now claimed, was over as a determining force in the lives of black Americans and, presumably, other people of color as well. Americans had grown beyond their racial past and were judging individuals, as Martin Luther King Jr. had dreamed, "not by the color of their skin but by the content of their character." The evidence—the American people's election of Barack Hussein Obama to serve as the forty-fourth president of the United States of America—was clear and irrefutable, the contention went. Racism was no longer an issue because the nation had become colorblind. Well, at least white people had. At the core of the postracial argument is the unspoken but nonetheless clear assumption that it is people of color, especially black Americans, who are obsessed with race, not white Americans. In the wake of the election, conservative black commentator Juan Williams wrote in the *Wall Street Journal*, "Barack Obama's election is both an astounding political victory—and the end of an era for black politics."[50] After citing Colin Powell, Condoleezza Rice, and Clarence Thomas as examples of black achievement, he goes on to contend that the "extortion-like" politics of the Reverends Jesse Jackson, Al Sharpton, and Jeremiah Wright will become a "form of nostalgia." Racial problems from now on, according to Williams, will center on being responsible regarding family obligations, overthrowing gangster cultures, and finding pragmatic, race-neutral solutions to social problems.

Williams's fallacious assumptions are many, but two stand out. One is that the election of one black person to the White House sweeps away hundreds of years of accumulated social and economic underdevelopment and institutions distorted by racism. As even Obama states in the epigraph noted earlier, such thinking is pitifully naïve. Vast and persistent racial disparities in criminal justice, incarceration, education, health care, housing, and environmental hazards, to name a few, did not disappear on election night. The second issue is the assumption that a majority of whites voted for Obama and for a new era of racial harmony. The facts tell a different and more complicated story. According to exit polls, as noted in Table 3, page 434, Obama won 43 percent of the white vote, an increase of two percentage points over what Kerry won in 2004, and about the same percentage Clinton won in 1996. In effect, the white vote for Democrats has not shifted in many years and has not been a majority in over forty years. Obama won primarily by building a coalition of black voters, Latino voters, and young voters of all colors. Project Vote, which has done a comparative analysis of the 2008 turnout, documents a large surge of minority voters, an increase of 21 percent compared to 2004. At the same time, white votes cast actually dropped. And the youth vote (ages eighteen to twenty-nine), which overwhelmingly went to Obama, grew by 9 percent from 2004.[51]

In a defining piece for the postracial thesis, published in the *New York Times* just prior to the election, Matt Bai put forth the proposition that Obama's rise signaled the end of black politics altogether.[52] According to Bai, a new generation of black politicians, from Newark mayor Cory Booker to Massachusetts governor Deval Patrick and others, represented a paradigm shift in African American politics wherein race has been neutralized as the most effective means of mobilization on issues facing low-income black communities. To make his case, Bai constructs two straw men—an undifferentiated, protest-driven, black, civil rights mafia on the one hand, and a young, enlightened, modernist talented tenth on the other—locked in mortal combat for the political soul of black, and white, America. The head of the latter group, symbolically and through voter legitimation, is Obama. Bai, like Williams, displays a gender bias that erases black women from both groups.

The ideological and political aim of this argument is to marginalize the confrontational politics of the militant wing of the Civil Rights Movement and traditional black nationalists—conveniently ignoring, of course, their nearly universal support of Obama. It is also aimed at undermining legislative and policy initiatives on the part of the states and the federal government as ameliorative actions to end racial disparities and discrimination. There is little danger that the majority of black Americans, who will continue to live in the world of gross racial disparities, police profiling, and institutional racism, will buy this. The argument's real targets are policy makers, the mass media, and those who genuinely or disingenuously want to get past the racial discord that has long defined the nation. The notion of a postracial world is not only factually wrong, but profoundly hazardous as well.

After Obama's win, conservative foundations and legal groups almost immediately attempted to use his election as a justification for ending affirmative action and other race-conscious programs. As the *Los Angeles Times* noted, "Obama's success has emerged as a central argument from conservatives who say his victory proves that some of the nation's most protective civil rights laws can be erased from the books."[53] In a case before the Supreme Court in 2009, *Northwest Austin Municipal Utility District No. 1 v. Holder*, involving a utility board election process in Austin, Texas, plaintiffs sought to eliminate their Voting Rights Act requirement of Justice Department preclearance. A brief filed in support of the plaintiffs by conservative foundations cited Obama's election as a reason why the Voting Rights Act should be scrapped. The brief stated that Obama's win "stands as a remarkable testament to the tremendous progress this country has made in terms of racial equality and voting rights."[54] While some involved with the brief claimed that they did not want to see an end to the Voting Rights Act, others, such as the ultraconservative Pacific Legal Foundation and Southeastern Legal Foundation, clearly do. In the end, the Court refused to rule on the constitutionality of the case and sent it back to the lower courts.

Proponents of postracial policy celebrate the willingness of a growing number of whites, disproportionately young, to vote for black candidates, but fail to explain why. There are at least three reasons. First, black civil rights activists and other black leaders have been successful in exposing the lingering and persistent nature of racism and racial disparities. Clearly, many whites become antiracist because they are open to this information. Second, the Obama–Democratic Party win was the fulcrum with which the nation repudiated conservatism and Republican Party politics. Obama, for many, was the vehicle for the solid rejection of more than a decade of the most regressive government in recent memory. The wretched campaign of John McCain embodied the deadly combination of contradictions that Bush-era Republicans face: a base split between competing cultural, social and economic constituencies; an economic collapse popularly linked to the failed tenets of neoliberalism; unnecessary wars of choice whose cost in lives and resources is too high to tolerate even for many patriotic Republicans; and party demographics that are going in the opposite direction of a more diversifying nation.

And third, the unacceptability of overt racism in the public sphere crosses party lines, and at least some conservatives reject such tactics. This made Palin's venture into these waters problematic for John McCain. Despite a hard-core racist, anti-immigrant, Islamophobic wing in the party, most Republicans know that they actually turn off voters when they go too far in that direction. At least this appeared to be the case until the possibility, and then the reality, of Obama's election ignited a firestorm of public racial rage not seen in the United States in decades. As former President Jimmy Carter so inconveniently opined, the wrath and animosity aimed at Obama is "based on the fact that he is a black man."[55]

At one level, the public sphere has become replete with references to Obama as Hitler, a witch doctor, a socialist/communist/Marxist, and a Muslim. These references surfaced at rallies of groups like the "birthers," who believe he was not born in the United States and has illegally assumed the presidency. These views also arise among the so-called "tea partiers" who promote states' rights and limited federal government authority. Both birthers and tea partiers include a mixed bag of libertarians, genuine conservatives, and racists. The tea party movement, championed by Sarah Palin and most national Republican Party officials and leaders, has generally ignored, if not supported, racists in its midst, such as Houston-based *teaparty.com* founder and tea party leader Dale Robertson, who was caught in a photo carrying a sign using the (misspelled) word "niggar" and who sent out a fundraising letter with an image of Obama manipulated to look like a pimp.[56]

Bigoted tirades against legislation for health care reform from white reactionaries like Rush Limbaugh were thoroughly racialized, as when he referred to the legislation as a "reparations" bill.[57] Despite the claim that opposition to Obama is based on his politics, these virtually all-white movements, with a few notable exceptions, have been driven by political extremists who are informed by neoconservative leaders and hate media. Republicans such as Palin, Representative Michelle Bachman, and Representative Joe Wilson—who lowered himself to shout

"You lie!" while the president was addressing a joint session of Congress—are stoking the flames rather than attempting to douse them with reason and reality. During his first two years in office, the entire Republican membership in both the House of Representatives and the Senate marched lock-step in opposition to everything Obama did, signaling to their constituencies that compromise, negotiation, and civility were not options for dealing with this president.

All of this has been aided and abetted by right-wing talk radio and Fox TV News. Just as Wilson's "You lie" can be seen as an attempt to sow public uncertainty and antipathy toward the president, so too can the punditry of Fox News' Glenn Beck, who tries to stoke fear and paranoia with accusations that Obama has a "deep-seated hatred for white people."[58] It is nearly impossible to imagine a black (or white) media personality on the traditional networks, CNN, or MSNBC making a similar statement about a white political leader, let alone the president of the United States, and not being removed from the air immediately and denounced in a rapid-fire press release. Far from being regretful, Beck, Wilson, and others have used these controversies to raise funds and deepen their ties to the most reactionary elements of the far right.[59]

With each milestone in racial life in the United States, the trope of "postraciality" is dusted off and used by its proponents to call for an end to real, substantive progress in achieving social equality. Indeed, advocacy of postraciality has emerged from prominent people of color, such as Republican National Committee chairman Michael Steele, who is African American, and Louisiana Gov. Bobby Jindal, who is of South Asian descent. However, the impulse to close the door on race must be resisted. Well-documented and persistent forms of inequality, driven by institutional racism, inadequate public policy, and racial blinders, remind us on a daily basis of the unfinished agenda of equal rights. So does the daily venom on the right that is thoroughly racialized. The journey has never been to achieve benefits for a few at the top, but for the advancement of all, beginning with the many at the bottom.

Race Neutral or Race Conscious?: Obama's Dilemma

> *This is one of those singular moments that nations ignore at their peril. . . . There have been a few prescient leaders in our past, but you are the man for this time.*[60]—Toni Morrison, endorsement of Obama

It would be a mistake to reduce Obama's election as primarily a victory for black America. His triumph is a collective one that highlights the persistence of the long struggle for democracy by a wide range of communities and constituencies. In this light, his win is a benefit for the nation and the world as a whole. And when we elected Obama to lead the nation at home and represent us abroad, for once, at least in this era, nearly the entire world rejoiced with us. In villages, towns, cities, favelas, barrios, prisons, army bases, cafés, and public spaces around the globe, people celebrated. In some neighborhoods people stopped traffic to dance in the streets.

Obama's win—our victory—is also a repudiation of the conservatism that has dominated American politics for forty or more years. Manipulating racial fear, class prejudices, imperial global relations, and deregulated markets, conservative Republicans and opportunistic Democratic administrations in the 1980s and 1990s attempted to roll back the social and legislative advances of the Great Depression and the Great Society. But especially under the George W. Bush administration and the hyper-reactionary Republican Congress of 1995–2007, the nation and the world experienced the most radical retreat on political and human rights imaginable. All the while, transnational corporations, disproportionately U.S.-based, pillaged the nation and the world with the full assistance of the antigovernment Bush administration.

Obama has called for, and he should receive, fierce support for the progressive dimensions of his agenda: ending the war in Iraq, building a green capitalist economy, reining in constitutional abuses, reforming the health care system, focusing on job creation, closing foreign prisons where torture has occurred, and so on. He should also receive fierce opposition to his more conservative proposals and any stalling or rollback on campaign promises, like ending the Iraq War, closing Guantánamo Bay prison, and prohibiting torture. The Obama administration must also be pushed to fulfill its promise to address the urban issues that have been left to fester for decades. He must overcome fears of being called a "racial hostage" i.e., appearing to be obligated to addressing racial concerns, and a real—rather than imagined—effort to ensure equality for all must continue to forge ahead.

Obama seems to get it. In his July 2009 speech before the NAACP he stated:

> I understand there may be a temptation among some to think that discrimination is no longer a problem in 2009. And I believe that overall, there probably has never been less discrimination in America than there is today. I think we can say that. But make no mistake: The pain of discrimination is still felt in America. . . . But we also know that prejudice and discrimination—at least the most blatant types of prejudice and discrimination—are not even the steepest barriers to

> opportunity today. The most difficult barriers include structural inequalities that our nation's legacy of discrimination has left behind; inequalities still plaguing too many communities and too often the object of national neglect.[61]

The "some" he cites at the outset are the proponents of "postracialism," who contend that only an individual's personal shortcomings hold them back in today's post–Civil Rights era. The reference to "structural inequalities" is significant because it implies the need for programmatic remedies that address institutional change. President Obama's speech was well received by an audience that longed to hear the country's leader speak in such clear terms.

Many supporters believe—or want to believe—that Obama will be a transformative political leader in a transformative time. They eagerly await the flowering of peace and social justice policies that will open a new chapter in the abatement of "the structural inequalities that our nation's legacy of discrimination has left behind." Whether Obama, carrying the weight of race on his shoulders in a manner that no other United States president ever has, will provide leadership and initiative on these issues is yet to be seen. At every opportunity, we should remind him to try.

Several ironies have already emerged. One, the race-based backlash against Obama might actually generate the type of crisis that will open up space for policy reforms relevant to the ongoing crisis in communities of color that has been ignored for decades. Such backlash could prompt a discussion that Obama's White House feels it cannot otherwise initiate. An honest and frank discussion from a thoughtful and articulate president in the effort to resolve a crisis might be on the horizon. Then again, it might not.

Another striking irony is that, left to race-neutral strategies, the main beneficiaries of Obama's progressive policies will be the very working-class whites who are mobilizing to oppose him. Obama's White House might just be the best development in U.S. politics for generations for low-income and working-class white Americans. While certainly black, Latino, and Native Americans suffer disproportionately from the wrecked state of the U.S. health care system, in terms of raw numbers it is overwhelmingly whites who are being harmed and exploited by the current state of affairs. As has nearly always been the case, the spread of democracy and inclusiveness to the nation's communities of color reaps benefits for white people as well.

For the millions of Americans who drove his campaign and voted for him, Obama's victory was a collective and transcendent historic moment one rarely experiences in a lifetime. The country can retreat on the extension of civil and political rights to blacks—as it did after Reconstruction and during the Reagan era. Conservative administrations and movements can abandon or outlaw affirmative action—as happened in California, Washington, and Florida, and was unsuccessfully attempted in the 2008 election in Colorado. But none can undo Obama's victory and the fact that it forever changes the image of the White House and who has legitimate claim on it. And this is the feeling that Obama supporters, across all the boundaries and dividing lines, have embraced. The notion that a black man has the right to govern the country—and that a family of color runs the White House—counters centuries-old views of exclusive white entitlement to power. Except for those who believe Obama has no legal right to be in the White House, itself a reflection of some whites' extreme racial reaction to his victory, even his conservative opponents concede the historic change that has occurred. This transformed view of the White House was celebrated and acknowledged not only in the United States but around the world, as captured in the jubilant response broadcast on election night and the thousands of newspaper and magazine covers that followed.

However, redefining the symbolism of the White House is not the same as changing its racial politics. Obama will not, in fact, cannot, govern as a "black" president who mainly addresses the concerns of people of color, even though those concerns are real, serious, and national in scale. Beyond the fact that such a governing model is not Obama's style or sentiment, the checks and balances of the U.S. political system and the deep-rooted racial suspicion that has animated a significant segment of his opposition will resist all efforts in that direction. As was seen in the first year and a half of his administration, issues of race, no matter how seemingly small, will take on an especially significant tone during his command in the White House. There was a remarkably large number of prominent race-related controversies during the first eighteen months of Obama's presidency, including:

- The revival of "Confederate History Month" in Virginia by Governor Bob McDonnell who initially did not even include a mention of slavery in his original press statement; Georgia and Mississippi governors, Sonny Perdue and Haley Barbour respectfully, also declared "Confederate History" months and neither mentioned slavery in their official proclamations. All three neglected the interests, sensitivities, and history of their black constituents. [62]
- Fierce anti-Muslim opposition to the building of an Islamic Center that would include a mosque two blocks from the "ground zero" site in New York City. Nearly all national Republican leaders, from former Alaska Gover-

nor Sarah Palin to former House Speaker Newt Gingrich, joined the hysteria against the mosque, thereby fueling an atmosphere of religious intolerance. Even Senate Majority leader Harry Reid also came out against the mosque saying through a spokesman that he thought "the mosque should be built somewhere else." President Obama eventually made a strong statement defending the legality and right of the Center, "As a citizen and as president, I believe that Muslims have the same right to practice their religion as anyone else in this country." However, after coming under fire from the Republicans and the conservative right, he demurred on whether that right should be exercised in this particular case. Obama has also made no public comment on the racist nature of much of the opposition to the Center. [63]

- The Obama administration's refusal to attend or participate in the Durban Review Conference (aka Durban II) in Geneva, an international conference to assess the follow-up and legacy of the 2001 UN World Conference Against Racism endorsed by civil rights activists and members of the Congressional Black Caucus. Although Obama signaled before the election that he was interested in his administration attending the conference, under pressure from the right and Israel, the administration ultimately decided not to attend. The decision to boycott the conference occurred after the organizers made changes in key documents demanded as a condition for its attendance. While the Obama White House could not argue that the current documents contained objectionable language, it maintained that the documents stilled supported the original conference which was unacceptable.[64]
- Passage and then judicial suspension of an Arizona law

(SB 1070) that would have forced police officers to check the citizenship status of anyone they "reasonably suspected" of being undocumented, i.e., an official obligation of the police to racially profile Latinos. On July 6, 2010, the U.S. Justice Department filed a lawsuit against arguing that it is unconstitutional for states to make immigration laws. The Justice Department did not tie its opposition to the law to racial profiling. On July 28, 2010, U.S. District Court Judge Susan Bolton issued an injunction against key provisions of SB 1070 preventing its implementation.[65]

- Resistance to the nomination of Sonia Sotomayor, the first Latina and the first Latino, to the U.S. Supreme Court; Conservatives attacked Sotomayor as a bigot when it was discovered that in a 2001 University of California speech she had stated, "I would hope that a wise Latina woman with the richness of her experiences would more often than not reach a better conclusion than a white male who hasn't lived that life." Talk show host Rush Limbaugh and former House speaker Newt Gingrich referred to her as a "racist" but she was ultimately confirmed by the U.S. Senate in a 68-31 vote. [66]
- Accusations that Obama's Justice Department had a double standard for not harshly prosecuting members of the New Black Panther Party for an incident that had occurred outside of a voting site during the 2008 presidential election. The incident involved two members of the New Black Panther Party, Jerry Jackson and King Samir Shabazz, who on election day, November 4, 2008, stood outside a polling site in Philadelphia and engaged in verbal insults against whites who came to vote. The case had actually been reviewed by the Bush administration

> which decided to only seek an injunction against the men and their leader, Malik Zulu Shabazz. In April 2009, the Obama Justice Department dropped charges against everyone except King Samir Shabazz, thereby winning an injunction against him. In 2009 and 2010, conservatives cited the case as evidence that the administration tolerates racism perpetrated by blacks against whites.[67]

For the most part, the Obama White House exhibited restraint on these controversies and either intervened legally or spokeout without addressing the underlying racial dimensions. Many of these issues were used by conservatives to booster their case that the Obama administration is "anti-white" and, as right-wing Fox News talk show host Glenn Beck infamously stated, that Obama himself has a "deep-seated hatred for white people."[68] However, two incidents stand out where Obama and key members of his administration actually allowed the right-wing media and politicos to dictate their response, leaving many inside and outside the black community unsatisfied and agitated. The July 16, 2009, incident involving Harvard professor Henry Louis Gates, who is African American, and James Crowley, a white police officer for the city of Cambridge, Massachusettes, symbolizes the racial minefield that lies before Obama and the country. When Gates and his black driver arrived at his house, they found the front door jammed and Gates had to enter by the back door. Gates and his driver then attempted to force the front door open, an action that promoted a call to the police, though the caller did not identify the men as black nor claim that there was a crime being committed. After the police arrived, a confrontation ensued that led to some back-and-forth between Gates and Crowley, who decided to arrest the Harvard professor on the charge of disorderly conduct, a charge that was later dropped. A national controversy exploded over whether Crowley went overboard in making the arrest, given that in spite of the heat of the moment Gates was in his home and no crime had been committed. In response to a reporter's question about the incident, Obama stated the police "acted stupidly."[69] His words were immediately pounced upon by conservatives. Writing in the *Wall Street Journal*, conservative Shelby Steele, who wrote a book in 2007 outlining why Obama could not win the presidency, opined, "Mr. Obama's 'postracialism' was a promise to operate outside of tired cultural narratives. But he has a demon arm of reflexive racialism—identity politics, Rev. Jeremiah Wright, and now Skip Gates."[70]

Much of the black media and black public opinion, carrying two and half centuries of police abuse and ongoing experiences with racial profiling, sided with Obama.[71] Eventually, the controversy was defused when Obama invited Gates, Crowley, and Vice President Joe Biden to the White House to have a beer and discuss the matter. The "beer summit" was probably the first of its kind at the White House and was the most notable White House meal, outside of an official state dinner, since the Roosevelt-Washington supper more than 100 years earlier.

While the media focused on the short phrase "acted stupidly," the whole of Obama's remarks addressed not only the Gates incident but the larger context of racial profiling. He also noted that "race remains a factor in this society," words rarely spoken by any white political leaders. His whole response was:

> Well, I should say at the outset that Skip Gates is a friend, so I may be a little biased here. I don't know all the facts. What's been reported, though, is that the guy forgot his keys. He jimmied his way to get into the house. There was a report called into the police

station that there might be a burglary taking place. So far so good. Right? I mean, if I was trying to jigger in—well, I guess this is my house now so it probably wouldn't happen. Let's say my old house in Chicago. Here I'd get shot. But so far so good. They're reporting, the police are doing what they should. There's a call. They go investigate what happens. My understanding is at that point Professor Gates is already in his house. The police officer comes in. I'm sure there's some exchange of words, but my understanding is that Professor Gates then shows his I.D. to show that this is his house. And at that point he gets arrested for disorderly conduct, charges which are later dropped. Now, I don't know, not having been there and not seeing all the facts, what role race played in that, but I think it's fair to say, number one, any of us would be pretty angry. Number two, that the Cambridge police acted stupidly in arresting somebody when there was already proof that they were in their own home, and number three, what I think we know separate and apart from this incident is that there is a long history in this country of African Americans and Latinos being stopped by law enforcement disproportionately. And that's just a fact.

As you know, Lynn, when I was in the state legislature in Illinois we worked on a racial profiling bill because there was indisputable evidence that blacks and Hispanics were being stopped disproportionately. And that is a sign, an example of how, you know, race remains a factor in this society. That doesn't lessen the incredible progress that has been made. I am standing here as testimony to the progress that's been made.

> And yet, the fact of the matter is that, you know, this still haunts us. And even when there are honest misunderstandings, the fact that blacks and Hispanics are picked up more frequently and oftentime for no cause casts suspicion even when there is good cause, and that's why I think the more that we're working with local law enforcement to improve policing techniques so that we're eliminating potential bias, the safer everybody's going to be.[72]

The Gates incident, minor in many respects, underscores the inescapable challenge of race that the administration will have to address whether it wants to or not. It also shows that Obama's reflex on race, in an unguarded moment, reflects the temperament and understandings of most African Americans. Fortunately, Obama has demonstrated that when he does take on the issue, his intellect, sentiments, and politics are generally progressive in direction. The struggle will be to get him to take up these concerns despite the political costs and the tendency of some of his advisers to move cautiously, if at all.

The Gates controversy revolved around Obama's use of a loaded word whose racial dimensions were seized upon by the conservative press and opportunistic politicians. The situation's ultimate resolution by the "beer summit" evaded the larger issue of racism in the criminal justice system. However, it would be the actions of his administration in another incident that revealed the power of the right-wing media to strike fear throughout his government when it comes to racial matters. On July 19, 2010, conservative blogger Andrew Breitbart, who has a long history of producing carefully doctored videos, posted a video clip on his Web site, *Biggovernment.org*, a clip that had already been circulating on two other rightwing Web sites, *Hotair.com* and *USActionNews.com.* It reportedly showed a black U.S. Department of Agriculture (USDA) employee stating that she had discriminated against a white farmer because he was white and arrogant. The employee, Shirley Sherrod, says in the two-and-a-half-minute clip that she did not give "the full force of what [she] could do" to help a white farmer who came to her for assistance.[73] Her remarks were given at an event held by the NAACP in Douglas, Georgia. On Monday morning, July 19, the story was picked up by Fox News and began to rapidly spread to other news organizations and throughout the Internet.

Racial tensions were in the air, because the previous week had witnessed a public scuffle between the NAACP and the tea party movement. On July 14, 2010, the NAACP passed a resolution at its annual convention that called for tea party leaders to denounce the racist behavior that had been manifest at some of its events.[74] The response of some tea party leaders and activists was to incorrectly accuse the NAACP of calling the entire tea party movement racist. The controversy was furthered intensified when one tea party leader, Mark Williams of the Tea Party Express, wrote a supposedly satirical letter from an enslaved black individual to President Lincoln using racist imagery and language. He wrote, "We Coloreds have taken a vote and decided that we don't cotton to that whole emancipation thing. Freedom means having to work for real, think for ourselves, and take consequences along with the rewards. That is just far too much to ask of us Colored People and we demand that it stop."[75] He and the Tea Party Express were subsequently booted out of the National Tea Party Federation, an organization with dozens of member organizations and affiliates. Tea party leaders from Sarah Palin to Michelle Bachman defended the virtually all-white movement against the NAACP, mostly by not addressing the issue that had been raised but simply accusing the NAACP of being racial hustlers or worse.

When the Sherrod story first broke, officials at the USDA panicked, believing that the administration was about to be attacked for sanctioning "reverse racism." Reportedly, some unnamed sources within the White House raised concerns that all the facts were not known, but no one there intervened to prevent what occurred next.[76] Within hours, Sherrod came under intense pressure from high officials in the department, including Secretary of Agriculture Tom Vilsack, who, solely based on news reports, wanted to put her on immediate suspension. Sherrod had been appointed in August 2009 as the first black director of the USDA's Rural Development in Georgia. At one point, on Monday evening, Undersecretary Cheryl Cook caught up with Sherrod as she was driving. Sherrod stated that while she was attempting to explain her side of the story, she was asked to pull over to the side of the road and immediately submit her resignation via text message, because the issue was "going to be on *Glenn Beck*" that evening.[77] In fact, she had tried days earlier to warn Vilsack and other USDA officials that a bogus clip was circulating, but information she sent via email either went to addresses that were no longer in use, rarely checked, or were sat on by a mid-level official.[78] Sherrod was pressured to resign, but she did not go down passively. Meanwhile, the NAACP issued a statement denouncing Sherrod and applauding her resignation. Officials with the organization had addressed the issue earlier with the White House Office of Public Engagement, an office run by Obama's highest ranking black staffer, Valarie Jarrett.[79] The NAACP wrote in its condemnation, "We concur with U.S. Agriculture Secretary Vilsack in accepting the resignation of Shirley Sherrod for her remarks at a local NAACP Freedom Fund banquet. Racism is about the abuse of power. Sherrod had it in her position at USDA. According to her remarks, she mistreated a white farmer in need of assistance because of his race. We are appalled by her actions, just as we are with abuses of power against farmers of color and female farmers."[80]

Suspicious of the source, some news organizations, in particular MSNBC's *Rachel Maddow Show*, the *Atlanta Journal-Constitution*, and CNN, raised questions about the legitimacy of the tape and tried to locate Sherrod to interview her. As it turned out, by Tuesday morning the clip was exposed to be entirely misleading—in fact, Sherrod had been using the story to tell how she overcame whatever prejudicial feelings she had had, realizing that people of all races needed help. The incident had occurred twenty-four years earlier in 1985 when she worked for a local nonprofit, the Federation of Southern Cooperatives/Black Land Fund (FSC), not while she was an employee of the U.S. government. In the full version of the speech, she states, "God helped me to see that it's not just about black people—it's about poor people."[81] In speaking about her work helping the farmer in question, she stated, "Well, working with him made me see that it's really about those who have versus those who don't, you know. And they could be black; they could be white; they could be Hispanic."[82] She ended up playing a decisive role in helping the farmer, Roger Spooner, save his farm, a fact that he and his wife, Eloise, testified to in subsequent media interviews.[83] Calls and emails began to flood into the White House and Agriculture Department demanding Sherrod's reinstatement.

The cruel irony of the situation, in which a black USDA employee is accused of racism against a white farmer and is forced to resign, was that in the long history of struggle around black land ownership and fairness for black farmers, the USDA had never fired a single white employee for the virulent, overt, and persistent racism in its ranks against blacks and other people of color. That the USDA has a dishonorable record of racial discrimination is indisputable. In its history of documented racism the USDA has denied loans to black and minority farmers, given loans that were too late in the farming cycle, conducted excessive supervisions of loans that white farmers did not have to endure, ignored black famers' claims of discrimination, disrespected individuals, and had a mostly whites-only hiring policy.[84] In 1983, President Reagan eliminated the USDA Office of Civil Rights, which would not be reopened until 1996, but even then did little to address the concerns of farmers of color.[85] Indeed, the USDA's own National Commission on Small Farmers—which itself was created as a result of black farmer's complaints about discrimination—declared in 1998 it was disturbed by "the indifference and blatant discrimination experienced by minority farmers in their interactions with USDA programs and staff. . . . Discrimination has been a contributing factor in the dramatic decline of Black farmers over the last several decades."[86]

Sherrod herself had been a victim of USDA discrimination. In 1969, the Sherrods founded the New Communities Land Trust, a black farm cooperative in Lee County, Georgia. Suffering from the same drought that struck much of the South in the mid-to-late 1970s, New Communities applied for and was promised an emergency loan by federal authorities in1982. However, the distribution of the money was controlled by state officials then under the governorship of stern segregationist Lester Maddox of pickaxe fame. The "emergency loan" came three years too late and the farm was forced to close in 1985. A Sherrod family farm faced a similar fate, which is why she was included in the subsequent lawsuit filed by black farmers against USDA.[87]

More generally, the racism that denied assistance to black farmers continually for more than 100 years has been a central factor in shaping the economic fortune of millions of African Americans, resonating in the disproportionate levels of poverty that exist in the black community today. On January 16, 1865, General William Tecumseh Sherman issued Field Order 15, which promised forty acres off the South Carolina Sea Islands and plantations from Charleston to Jacksonville, South Carolina, and a federal mule to those who had left slavery and were working with the Union army.[88] This pledge was given further legal support on March 3, 1865, when Lincoln signed the Freedmen's Bureau Act, which assigned "not more than 40 acres" to the freed to rent with an option to purchase after three years.[89] Lincoln also had created the USDA in 1862 referring to it as the "people's department."[90] Indeed, more than 40,000 African Americans had settled on confiscated land by June 1865.[91] However, after Lincoln's assassination April 14, President Andrew Johnson rescinded the order in his effort to reintegrate southern rebels into the nation. At the expense of African Americans, Johnson issued an amnesty order that included property restoration, and blacks were subsequently forced off these lands. Despite the broken promise of the U.S. government, by 1900, African Americans owned 15 million acres of land mostly in the South. By 1910 this would grow to 16 million, with a peak of 925,000 black farmers in 1920. This would represent a high point as discrimination and racism including by the USDA would reduce significantly this ownership over the next 100 years. By 2000, according to a statement made by Judge Paul Freidman in the successful lawsuit against the USDA by black farmers, there were only about 18,000 black farmers left on less than three million acres.[92]

A number of black farm organizations would rise over the years to fight back against the unjust and racist policies of local, state, and federal officials. This would include the Colored

Farmers National Alliance and Cooperative Union, National Black Farmer's Association, Black Farmers and Agriculturalists Association (BFAA), and Federation of Southern Cooperatives/ Black Land Fund (FSC), with whom Sherrod had once worked as a staff member. In 1997, black farmers filed a lawsuit, *Pigford v. Glickman*, against the USDA for discrimination. In 1999, the black farmers won over $2.3 billion in what has been called "the largest civil rights settlement in history."[93] However, many black farmers were left out of the suit, because it only covered those who had been discriminated against between 1981 and 1996. And some estimate that even among this restricted group, close to 90 percent of farmers were denied when they applied for restitution.[94] That figure is probably accurate given that the Bush administration spent more than 56,000 office hours and $12 million fighting the claims made by black farmers.[95] A suit dubbed *Pigford II*, initiated by members of Congress and carried through by the Obama administration, won an agreement that included an additional payout to more than 65,000 black farmers who were excluded from the original suit.

Indeed, Vilsack himself stated soon after coming to office, "Civil rights is one of my top priorities," and "I intend to take definitive action to improve USDA's record on civil rights."[96] Obama proposed $1.25 billion in his 2010 budget to pay what is owed to the black farmers, a proposal that Republicans in Congress have repeatedly blocked as of August 2010.[97]

It is also notable that Sherrod herself has been a critical actor in this history. When she was seventeen-years-old, her father was murdered by a white man in Baker County, Georgia. There were three witnesses, but the grand jury refused to indict the person responsible. [98] Months later, a cross was burned in front of the Miller home in an effort to intimidate the family. Outraged by the injustice, Miller's widow and Shirley's mother became a local civil rights leader in Baker County, Georgia where they lived, and later became the county's first black elected official, a position she still holds.[99] As noted by researcher and former Boston judge Margaret Burnham, Baker County had a long and notorious record of lynching blacks, often with the complicity and leadership of the local law enforcement.[100] Rather than leave the South, Shirley Sherrod decided to stay and try to bring about much needed social and racial justice. Her activism was enhanced when she married Charles Sherrod, a founder and leader of the Student Nonviolent Coordinating Committee (SNCC) in Albany, Georgia. They both remained activists on issues of fairness and antipoverty. She worked for a number of organizations and movements, earning a stellar reputation as a strong, reliable, articulate, and committed leader to the region's poor, traits that were revealed in her media interviews as the controversy unfolded.

Given this history and Breitbart's discredited record, both the administration and the NAACP should have acted more cautiously before going after Sherrod. Vilsack and USDA officials clearly violated her right to due process, not to mention the simple protocol of giving her the benefit of the doubt until she could reply to her accusers. At a minimum, they had the responsibility to perform an investigation prior to initiating such strong action against her. So did the NAACP. The incident in question took place at a meeting of one of their chapters, allowing the organization immediate access to witnesses of the speech as well as videos of the event. In fact, once the leadership did look at the entire speech, the NAACP immediately issued an apology, stating that it had been "snookered" by Breitbart and calling for her reinstatement.[101]

Strong letters of support were sent from the FSC and BFAA. In a blistering letter, FSC Executive Director Ralph

Paige charged the USDA with failing to review the facts before it acted and, noting Sherrod's "remarkable career," argued that she deserved "to be honored" rather than persecuted.[102] BFAA President Gary Grant also called Sherrod "honorable and hard working" and Vilsack's statement that the USDA does not tolerate racism "a complete lie."[103] Singer Willie Nelson, who is president of Farm Aid, called her "a great friend" to himself and the Farm Aid, and noted that "advocates like Ms. Sherrod have moved mountains to ensure that families can remain in their homes and on their farms."[104] Sherrod would later state, "It hurts me that they didn't even try to attempt to see what is happening here, they didn't care."[105]

Meanwhile, on Tuesday July 20, 2010, USDA officials vacillated even as the evidence mounted that Sherrod had been framed. Vilsack stated that regardless of the context, her comments—or, more honestly, the right-wing hysteria about them—"compromise the director's ability to do her job."[106] In other words, conservative accusations of "reverse racism," whether true or not, were enough to have someone dismissed from the employ of the Obama administration. However, Sherrod's powerful interviews in the media, letters and emails from around the nation, and even a retreat by Breitbart himself, disingenuously claiming that he did not know the clip was incomplete, forced the administration to change its position. On Wednesday, July 21, apologies were issued by both White House Press Secretary Robert Gibbs and Vilsack. Gibbs stated, "On behalf of our administration, I offer an apology."[107] Vilsack remarked, "This is a good woman. She's been put through hell. She was put through hell, and I could have done and should have done a better job," and even offered Sherrod a new position at USDA focused on civil rights.[108] On July 22, 2010 President Obama called Sherrod to apologize as well. According to the *Washington Times*, he expressed his regrets about the whole situation and told her that "this misfortune can present an opportunity for her to continue her hard work on behalf of those in need, and he hopes that she will do so."[109] Sherrod accepted Obama's apology, but also invited him to come to the South to witness the ongoing struggles of black farmers and other poor working people in the region. She volunteered to guide him on the tour. There was also a reconciliation between her and the NAACP. In an open letter she wrote to the NAACP "You and I Can't Yield—Not Now, Not Ever," she stated that she did not want the incident to be used against the organization and she supported their work.[110] Above all, Sherrod demonstrates the type of powerful leadership that is needed to overcome current efforts by conservatives to rollback the gains of people of color, working people, and others who must continue to fight for inclusion and equality.

While Vilsack took personal responsibility for what occurred, Obama and the White House blamed the media environment for the rapid spread of the story and the reactions of his administration. There is no argument that some in the media played a harmful role in the controversy, Fox News and other conservative media outlets in particular. But many believe that the fear of right-wing media has created a milieu encouraging knee-jerk reactions to even the slightest threat of bad news, particularly on the issue of race, and that it is this fear that drives the administration's actions. As some noted, it is hard to imagine that the Bush administration would have fired a staffer because an unsubstantiated (or even substantiated) report was going to be discussed on the left-leaning *The Keith Olberman Show* or Amy Goodman's *Democracy Now!* The incident revealed that the Obama administration gave undue power and influence to the likes of Glenn Beck and Rush Limbaugh to shape its agenda.

The embarrassing fact that the president himself had to express his regrets to Sherrod made it more likely that those in his administration who believe any discussion about race should be taboo will continue to hold sway against those who argue that proactive words and deeds are needed more than ever. It is possible, however, that the Sherrod incident represents a turning point, making it clear to the Obama White House that it must stand on principle and fight for racial justice and fairness regardless of the rantings of its opponents or even the political costs at stake.

As president of the United States, Obama confronts a confluence of unique challenges unlike any his predecessors ever faced. He won the White House in a period of transition, when U.S. political, economic, military, and cultural power was being resisted on numerous fronts. The effective dissolution of the G-7, the outdated coalition of finance ministers of dominant Western nations—Canada, France, Germany, Italy, Japan, United Kingdom, and United States—who set much of the world's economic and political agenda, represents the collapse of one model of hegemonic global governance that has been replaced by the G-20.[111] The rise of the G-20, incorporating states from the global North and global South, reflects the early twenty-first-century change in the balance of power worldwide, with the United States (and other Western powers) holding diminished authority and no longer able to dictate the world's agenda.[112] Although in most ways, the formation of the G-20 represents a change in form more than a true seizure of power, it foreshadows a trend with the potential to bring about such a transformation. In the immediate, the so-called BRIC nations (Brazil, Russia, India, and China) and the European Union provide substantive oppositional politics and a growing economic threat to U.S. hegemony.

This coalition, albeit unstable, and the rise of non-state

actors—from human rights organizations to terrorist networks—have placed limits on the politics of force that characterized the Bush administration and the neoliberal wing of U.S. strategists. The adventurism of the latter, of course, generated conflicts that have become untenable and from which Obama desperately seeks extrication. The U.S. military is bogged down in wars in Iraq and Afghanistan, neither of which will produce a decisive victory, nor can the U.S. agenda of political dominance impose the fiction of a stable democratization (or perhaps any democratization at all). More critically, although the U.S. military possesses a preponderance of hard power compared to other major states, it is shamelessly bloated, perpetually demoralized, politically curtailed, and financially unviable; no competitor nation incurs expenditures and debt even remotely approaching those of the United States.

Regional mobilization by social democratic forces in Latin America and aspiring democratic movements in Africa and Asia have also reduced the U.S. footprint in those areas. Given BRIC efforts to increase its economic influence and positioning in Latin America and Africa, and the eager receptivity of a number of states, the United States must scramble to maintain, let alone expand, its current geostrategic posture. Some U.S. political and military leaders, including Obama, recognize that the future will witness a reconfigured global balance in those areas. Middle East politics are no less complicated, as allies in the region and contiguous South Asia, such as Egypt, Israel, Pakistan, and Saudi Arabia, exhibit little ability to act as legitimate surrogates for policies that are anathema to political leaders and popular opinion on nearly all of the key debates.

Domestically, Obama confronts a unified opposition that is willing to harm the nation's interests in order to bring down his presidency. During his first two years in office, Obama has received near zero support by the Republicans in Congress for any of his major initiatives. Opposition is based on the cynical and irresponsible notion that defeating Obama's agenda, regardless of its merits, is the only path back to congressional and perhaps presidential power. Anger at the state of the nation, coupled with real and constructed fears, has given rise to a broad antigovernment social movement composed of a wide range of social and ideological forces, including the disjointed tea party network that in itself is politically diverse. Within this movement, forms of mild to virulent racism have emerged that some in the movement have denounced but most national tea party leaders have ignored, been defensive about, or winked at. A major dynamic targets Obama personally and (racialized) immigrants and black and Hispanic communities in general. It is difficult for the conservative movement to divorce itself from these elements, because it has cultivated racist stereotypes from the days of the "Southern strategy," Willie Horton, and "white hands" advertisements up to the fictions about welfare queens and Obama's birth certificate.

Obama must also operate within the confines of a federal political system that places severe restraints on his ability to generate or implement progressive public policy, a circumstance that perhaps many of his supporters from 2008 do not necessarily understand. Congress, the U.S. Senate in particular, exercises a check on presidential power—normally—and can become an obstacle to White House ambitions even when it is the president's party in charge. Republicans in Congress, though in the minority have been able to employ legal, though undemocratic, tactics such as the filibuster and "secret holds" that frustrate Obama's agenda. After the death of Senator Edward Kennedy (D-MA) and his seat being won by Republican Scott Brown, Senate Democrats lacked the 60 votes needed to stop a filibuster. This is an arcane rule that allows any senator to give an endless speech on the floor of the U.S. Senate that can only be cutoff by a vote of 60 members. Also, under Senate rules, any senator can anonymously hold up presidential nominations to federal jobs. Using this rule, Republicans held up hundreds of Obama's nominations purely for partisan reasons.

While the Obama administration struggles to find its footing, the black community is also addressing a new political landscape. Historically, both internally and internationally, black politics has been theorized as oppositional and liberation-oriented, an alternative ideological and mobilizing force to the historically white, racist, profit-obsessed, corporate constellation of elites that have dominated U.S. politics. Yet the increasing incorporation of black Americans into the centers of U.S. political power—most notably in the pre-Obama period with the conservative elevation of Clarence Thomas, Colin Powell, and Condoleezza Rice—reached a new milestone with the election of Obama and fundamentally challenges that framework. A new paradigm of black politics is required to address the denser, more complicated matrix of intersecting, often contradictory and ideologically tangled issues confronting the U.S. state and its engagement with local and global communities, including African and African American ones.

We need a progressive black social movement for the twenty-first century, one that theorizes beyond the demand for racial equality and reparations to a broader demand for society-wide social and economic justice, participatory democracy, and a decisive role in governance. Institutional injustice continues to perpetuate inequalities, particularly in low-income and impoverished communities that remain underserved or ignored. The positioning of African Americans (as well as other people of color and women) should neither be dismissed as irrelevant nor

The First Family visiting Ghana, Africa, July 11, 2009

celebrated as the end of racism. We need a crisp political framework that strikes the precise balance between rigorous criticism and tactical and political support. Its manner of addressing the persistent and well-documented disparities between blacks and whites in economic, education, health care, and criminal justice matters will be a measure of the administration's racial and national politics, but just as important to the nation's direction will be the intensity, nature, strategies, and dimension of the response from black civil society.

Like the tea party movement, black Americans today are angry at the misplaced priorities of the corporate-dominated, militarized, unaccountable administrations that have governed U.S. society for generations. Unlike the tea party movement—significantly mobilized by the politics of resentment, fear, and false nostalgia—a broad-based national movement for social justice does not call for less government but rather the construction of a government—and governing theory and practice—that is accountable, democratic, inclusive, and able to inspire hope.

Meanwhile, Obama's leadership from the White House is not a negation of black politics, but represents its extension into the realm of presidential governance. Whether Obama turns out to be one of America's greatest presidents or something less, his tenure will nevertheless represent one nexus where black politics and American politics meet. At this writing, they both live and lead from 1600 Pennsylvania Avenue. Given the confluence of circumstances he faced in winning the White House, along with unknown events to come, it certainly will not be an uneventful presidency.

Inevitably, there will be some disappointments. In a nation as race conscious as the United States, not only will blacks view Obama's policies, politics, and behavior through the prism of race, but other groups will do the same. For some observers, every utterance, every move will be interpreted in terms of race. It will be impossible to satisfy all the social justice interests that will look to the White House for transformation and resolution of issues that have been centuries in the making.

But there will also be some breakthroughs. The Obama White House changes the game in many respects. Not only is Obama one of the smartest individuals to ever command the presidency, but he brings rich life experiences that few American political leaders can come close to matching. It is not a stretch to say that more than any other president, he is conscious of the historic and contemporary role that race and social standing play in shaping the destiny of millions of his fellow citizens. Removing "whites-only" signs did not in and of itself end racism in either the United States or South Africa, but the action was the result of a sustained and determined strategy of mobilization and resistance. The sign has been removed from the White House. A black family running the White House tells the nation and the world that the struggle for equality, inclusion, and freedom has moved a bit further down the road.

NOTES

Introduction

1. Throughout this work, the terms "enslaved person" and "slave" are used interchangeably. They are not quite equivalent. The term "slave," arguably, generates a more emotive response and connotes a personal status of being that resonates with popular understandings of the word. "Enslaved person" implies the process and context by which an individual ends up in a specific condition of oppression and maintains the humanity of that individual. In this work, however, both interpretations seem warranted and I make use of both terms, privileging breadth over consistency.
2. By comparison, Ronald Reagan drew 500,000, Bill Clinton 800,000, and George W. Bush 300,000. See "Strollers, umbrellas forbidden at Obama inauguration," AFP, December 21, 2008. www.google.com/hostednews/afp/article/ALeqM5jAxfsUb6KLjwIDSt0zMbKoKfqncA.
3. George Santayana, *The Life of Reason*, Volumes 4 and 5 (Charleston, SC: BiblioBazaar, 2009), p. 208.
4. Quoted in Andy Barr, "Arizona Bans 'Ethnic Studies,' " *Politico*, May 12, 2010.
5. Gerald F. Seib, "In Crisis, Opportunity for Obama," *Wall Street Journal*, November 21, 2008.
6. It is important to note that "free" is not the same as "equal." While a small percentage of African Americans were not held in chattel slavery and are commonly referred to as having been free, they did not enjoy the same rights and privileges whites had. Restrictions were placed on votings rights, business and property ownership, marriage, legal rights, education, and other areas of life and livelihood, such that the distinction between being enslaved and being free was not as broad as it may appear. And there was always the omnipresent threat of being kidnapped and openly sold into slavery, an atrocity no white American has ever suffered. This is not to diminish the qualitative difference between being held in slavery and not, but to demythologize exactly how "free" free blacks really were.
7. U.S. Supreme Court, *Dred Scott v. Sandford*, 60 U.S. 393 (1856), 60 U.S. 393 (How.) *dred scott, plaintiff in error, v. john f. a. sandford*. December Term, 1857. See http://caselaw.lp.findlaw.com/scripts/getcase.pl?court=US&vol=60&invol=393.
8. W. E. B. Du Bois, *Black Reconstruction in America, 1860–1880* (New York: Free Press, 1998).
9. See James M. McPherson, *Abraham Lincoln* (Oxford[* Or New York? Some of the earlier Oxford Univ. Press references have given New York as the locale.]New York: Oxford Univ. Press, 2009); and Lerone Bennett, *Forced Into Glory: Abraham Lincoln's White Dream* (Chicago: Johnson Publishing, 2007).
10. Christian Saint-Etienne, *The Great Depression, 1929–1938: Lessons for the 1980s* (Stanford, CA: Hoover Press, 1984), p. 10; and "Farming in the 1930s." See Living History Farm Web site: www.livinghistoryfarm.org/farminginthe30s/money_08.html.
11. Ira Katznelson, *When Affirmative Action Was White: An Untold History of Racial Inequality in Twentieth-Century America* (New York: W. W. Norton and Company, 2005), p. 17.

12. Barack Obama, "A More Perfect Union" speech, Philadelphia, March 18, 2008. See Barack Obama "Organizing for America" Web site: http://my.barackobama.com/page/community/post/stateupdates/gGBbTW.

Chapter 1

1. George Washington's Mount Vernon Web site: www.mountvernon.org/learn/meet_george/index.cfm/ss/101/. See also Fritz Hirschfeld, *George Washington and Slavery: A Documentary Portrayal* (Univ. of Missouri Press, 1997); and Henry Wiencek, *An Imperfect God: George Washington, His Slaves, and the Creation of America* (New York: Macmillan, 2004).
2. Edward Lawler Jr., "Oney Judge." www.ushistory.org/presidentshouse/slaves/oney.htm.
3. T.H. Adams, "Washington's Runaway Slave, and How Portsmouth Freed Her," *The Granite Freeman*, Concord, New Hampshire, May 22, 1845.
4. Helen Bryan, *Martha Washington: First Lady of Liberty* (Hoboken, NJ: John Wiley and Sons Inc., 2002), p. 341.
5. Ibid., p. 242.
6. See Stanley W. Campbell, *The Slave Catchers: Enforcement of the Fugitive Slave Law, 1850–1860* (New York: W. W. Norton & Company, 1972).
7. Slavery in the North, Web site: www.slavenorth.com/newhampshire.htm.
8. See Paul Finkelman, *An Imperfect Union: Slavery, Federalism, and Comity* (Buffalo, NY: Wm. S. Hein Publishing, 2000).
9. Albert P. Blaustein and Robert L. Zangrando, eds., *Civil Rights and African Americans: A Documentary History* (Evanston, IL: Northwestern Univ. Press, 1968), p. 52.
10. "1780 Act for the Gradual Abolition of Slavery," afrolumens project Web site: www.afrolumens.org/slavery/gradual.html.
11. Ibid.
12. Edward Lawler Jr., "Washington, the Enslaved, and the 1780 Law," www.ushistory.org/presidentshouse/slaves/washingtonand8.htm.
13. Hirschfeld, *George Washington and Slavery*, p. 28.
14. Ibid., pp. 186–187.
15. John C. Fitzpatrick, ed., *The Writings of George Washington*, Vol. 36 (Washington, DC: United States Government Printing Office, 1933), p.2.
16. Bryan, *First Lady of Liberty*, p. 342.
17. Ibid., p. 344.
18. George Washington letter to Oliver Wipple, September 1, 1796. www.weekslibrary.org/ona_maria_judge.htm.
19. Ibid.
20. Ibid.
21. Adams, "Washington's Runaway Slave."
22. The legal issues were even more complicated. Under the law, the legal status of slaves was determined by the mother's history. If the mother was a dower, then all of her children were dowers. In a marriage between a dower and a slave who was owned outright, the children of that marriage would or would not be dowers depending on the status of the mother.

23. Richard Beeman, *Plain, Honest Men: The Making of the American Constitution* (New York: Random House, 2009), p. 35.
24. Donald R. Egerton, *Death or Liberty: African Americans and Revolutionary America* (New York: Oxford Univ. Press, 2009), p. 46.
25. Ibid.
26. Ibid., p. 55; and Peter Linebaugh and Marcus Rediker, *The Many-Headed Hydra: Sailors, Slaves, Commoners and the Hidden History of the Atlantic* (Boston: Beacon Press, 2001), p. 240.
27. Egerton, *Death or Liberty*, pp. 55–56. Also, see William Wemms and John Hodgson, *The Trial of the British Soldiers, of the 29th Regiment of Foot, for the Murder of Crispus Attucks, Samuel Gray, Samuel Maverick, James Caldwell, and Patrick Carr, on Monday Evening, March 5, 1770* (Boston: Belcher and Armstrong, 1807).
28. Alfred W. Blumrosen and Ruth G. Blumrosen, *Slave Nation: How Slavery United the Colonies & Sparked the American Revolution* (Naperville, IL: Sourcebooks Inc., 2005), p. 25.
29. See Charles Stuart, *A Memoir of Granville Sharp* (Whitefish, MT: Kessinger Publishing, 2008); Adam Hochschild, *Bury the Chains: Prophets and Rebels in the Fight to Free an Empire's Slaves* (Boston: Houghton Mifflin, 2005); and Simon Schama, *Rough Crossings: The Slaves, the British, and the American Revolution* (London: Oberon Books, 2007).
30. Blumrosen and Blumrosen, p. 11. See James Oldham, "New Light on Mansfield and Slavery," *The Journal of British Studies*, Vol. 27, No. 1, January 1988.
31. Egerton, *Death of Liberty*, pp. 51–52.
32. Albert P. Blaustein and Robert L. Zangrando, eds., *Civil Rights and African Americans: A Documentary History* (Evanston, IL: Northwestern Univ. Press, 1968), p. 36; and Blumrosen and Blumrosen, *Slave Nation*, p. 35.
33. Blumrosen and Blumrosen, *Slave Nation*, pp. 24–25.
34. John Hope Franklin, *From Slavery to Freedom* (New York: Vintage Books, 1969), p. 346.
35. Virginia's Declaration of Rights, June 12, 1776. See www.constitution.org/bcp/virg_dor.htm.
36. Blumrosen and Blumrosen, *Slave Nation*, p. 127.
37. Egerton, *Death of Liberty*, pp. 41–43.
38. See "Declaration of the Rights of Man and the Citizen," adopted by the French National Constituent Assembly August 1789; and H⊠ Chí Minh, "Proclamation of Independence," September 2, 1945.

39 In the infamous *Dred Scott* case of 1857, Chief Justice Roger Taney referred to the Declaration of Independence to argue that "slaves, nor their descendants, whether they had become free or not, were then acknowledged as a part of the people." See *Dred Scott v. Sanford* (60 U.S. 19 How. 393,1857).

40. Paul Leicester Ford, ed., *Works of Thomas Jefferson*, Vol. 1 (New York: G. P. Putnam's Sons, 1904), p. 28.
41. Blumrosen and Blumrosen, *Slave Nation*, p. 141.
42. Gary Wills, *"Negro President": Jefferson and the Slave Power* (Boston: Houghton Mifflin Company, 2003), p. 121.
43. Egerton, pp. 62–63.

44. Herbert Aptheker, *American Negro Slave Revolts*, Chapter VIII: Early Plots and Rebellions (Columbia Univ. Press, 1943; International Publishers, 1993), pp. 162–208; Lerone Bennett Jr., *Before the Mayflower: A History of Black America* (New York: Penguin, 1988), pp. 444–446, and C. L. R. James, *A History of Pan-African Revolt* (Washington: Drum and Spear Press, 1969), pp. 21-22.
45. Aptheker, *American Negro Slave Revolts*, p. 19, citing Verner W. Crane, *The Southern Frontier, 1670–1732*, pp. 184, 247.
46. Aptheker, p. 163, citing Woodbury Lowry, *The Spanish Settlements Within the Present Limits of the United States, 1513–1561*, pp. 165–67.
47. Joseph Cephas Carroll, *Slave Insurrections in the United States, 1800–1865* (New York: New American Library, 1969), p. 13.
48. Aptheker, *American Negro Slave Revolts*, p. 163.
49. Terry Jordan, *The U.S. Constitution and Fascinating Facts About It* (Naperville, IL: Oak Hill Publishing, 2007), p. 16.
50. Frederick Douglass speech, July 5, 1852, Rochester, NY, Corinthian Hall. http://teachingamericanhistory.org/library/index.asp?document=162
51. Aptheker, *American Negro Slave Revolts*, p. 372
52. George Rogers Jr. and David R. Chestnutt, eds., *The Papers of Henry Laurens*, Vol. 1(Columbia, SC: Univ. of South Carolina, 1979), pp. 99–100.
53. Blumrosen and Blumrosen, *Slave Nation*, p. 148.
54. Martin Luther King Jr., "I Have a Dream" speech, Washington, DC, August 28, 1963.
55. Wynton Marsalis, *Moving to a Higher Ground: How Jazz Can Change Your Life* (New York: Random House, 2008), pp. 88–89.
56. Condoleezza Rice, "Dr. Condoleezza Rice Discusses Foreign Policy," speech, Annual Convention of the National Association of Black Journalists, Dallas, TX, August 7, 2003.
57. Howard Zinn, *A People's History of the United States: 1492–Present* (New York: Harper Collins, 2005 edition) pp. 92–95.
58. See David Szatmary, *Shays' Rebellion: The Making of an Agrarian Insurrection* (Amherst: Univ. of Massachusetts Press, 1980). For an oppositional view that challenges the idea that the rebellion was rooted in the working class, see Leonard Richards, *Shays's Rebellion: The American Revolution's Final Battle* (Philadelphia: Univ. of Pennsylvania Press, 2002).
59. George Livermore, *An Historical Research: Opinions of the Founders of the Republic on Negroes as Slaves, as Citizens, and as Soldiers* (New York: Augustus M. Kelley Publishers, 1970), p. 71.
60. Derrick Bell, *And We Are Not Saved: The Elusive Quest for Racial Justice* (New York: Basic Books, 1987), p. 34. For a conservative interpretation of the role of slavery in the Constitution, see Robert A. Goldwin and Art Kaufman, *Slavery and Its Consequences: The Constitution, Equality, and Race* (Washington, DC: American Enterprise Institute for Public Policy Research, 1988), p. 32.
61. Beeman, *Plain, Honest Men*, p. 333.
62. The Federalist Papers. http://www.foundingfathers.info/federalistpapers/fed54.htm.
63. Beeman, *Plain, Honest Men*, p. 319.
64. Livermore, *Opinions of the Founders*, p. 73.

65. See Angela Lakwete, *Inventing the Cotton Gin: Machine and Myth in Antebellum America* (Baltimore: Johns Hopkins Univ. Press, 2003).
66. Beeman, *Plain, Honest Men*, p. 330.
67. Stanley W. Campbell, *The Slave Catchers: Enforcement of the Fugitive Slave Law, 1850–1860* (Univ. of North Carolina Press, 1970), p. 236.

Chapter 2

1. Edward Lawler Jr., "Hercules." www.ushistory.org/presidentshouse/slaves/hercules.htm.
2. Ibid.
3. Ibid.
4. Ibid.
5. Donald Egerton, *Death or Liberty: African Americans and Revolutionary America* (New York: Oxford Univ. Press, 2009), p. 4.
6. Fritz Hirschfeld, *George Washington and Slavery: A Documentary Portrayal* (Univ. of Missouri Press, 1997), P. 98.
7. Egerton, *Death or Liberty*, p. 10.
8. "The Papers of George Washington" Web site: http://gwpapers.virginia.edu/documents/will/index.html.
9. See William Loren Katz, *Black Pioneers: An Untold Story* (Taylor & Francis US, 1999); and John W. Ravage, *Black Pioneers: Images of the Black Experience on the North American Frontier* (Univ. of Utah Press, 1997).
10. See Mary Louise Clifford, *From Slavery to Freetown: Black Loyalists After the American Revolution* (Jefferson, NC: McFarland, 1999); and John W. Pulis, ed., *Moving On: Black Loyalists in the Afro-Atlantic World* (New York: Garland Publishing, 1999). See also Nova Scotia Museum Web site: *Remembering Black Loyalists; Black Loyalists in Nova Scotia,* http://museum.gov.ns.ca/blackloyalists/who.htm.
11. See A. P. Kup, *Sierra Leone: A Concise History* (New York: St. Martin's Press, 1975); J. Peter Pham, *The Sierra Leonean Tragedy: History and Global Dimensions* (New York: Nova Science Publishers, 2006); and John Peterson, *Province of Freedom: A History of Sierra Leone, 1787-1870* (Evanston, IL: Northwestern Univ. Press, 1969).
12. Jill Lepore, "Goodbye, Columbus: When America Won Its Independence, What Became of the Slaves Who Fled for Theirs?," *The New Yorker*, May 8, 2006. www.newyorker.com/archive/2006/05/08/060508crat_atlarge.
13. Egerton, *Death or Liberty*, p. 4.
14. Jack D. Warren Jr., "Uncle George's Cabin," *Free Lance-Star*, Fredericksburg, VA, February 22, 2003.
15. Ibid.
16. Hirschfeld, *George Washington and Slavery*, p. 70.
17. Sharron E. Wilkins, "The President's Kitchen," *American Visions*, Feb.-March, 1995.
18. For the most detailed and objective accounting of the relationship between Hemings and Jefferson, see Annette Gordon-Reed, *Thomas Jefferson and Sally Hemings: An American Controversy* (Charlottesville, VA: Univ. Press of Virginia, 1997). For a defense of Jefferson regarding the relationship, see William G. Hyland Jr., *In Defense of Thomas Jefferson: The Sally Hemings Sex Scandal* (New York: Thomas Dunne Books, 2009).
19. Ibid., Wills, p. 210.

20. Wilkins. "The President's Kitchen."
21. Hirschfeld, *George Washington and Slavery*, p. 70.
22. Ibid.
23. Ibid.
24. According to Edward Lawler Jr.: "Hercules had been married to a dower slave named Lame Alice, a seamstress at Mount Vernon, and they had three children, Richmond (born 1777), Evey (born 1782), and Delia (born 1785). Alice died in 1787, leaving Hercules to raise the children. When he learned that he was to be transferred to Philadelphia, he asked Washington's permission to bring his son with him to the President's House. It is likely that Hercules, Richmond and Christopher shared a divided room on the fourth floor of the main house." See www.ushistory.org/presidentshouse/slaves/hercules.htm
25. Louis Philippe, *Diary of My Travels in America* (New York: Delacorte Press, 1976), p. 32.
26. Edward Lawler Jr., "The President's House in Philadelphia: The Rediscovery of a Lost Landmark," *The Pennsylvania Magazine of History and Biography*, January 2002. The President's House in Philadelphia Web site: www.ushistory.org/presidentshouse/plans/pmhb/index.htm.
27. The Residence Act of 1790. Library of Congress Web site: http://memory.loc.gov/cgi-bin/ampage?collId=llsl&fileName=001/llsl001.db&recNum=253.
28. Ibid, Wills, 205.
29. U.S. Census 1790. The other three were Connecticut, New Hampshire, and Vermont.
30. Edward Lawler Jr., "A Brief History of the President's House in Philadelphia." See U.S. History Web site: www.ushistory.org/presidentshouse/history/briefhistory.htm.
31. Thomas Edward Drake, *Quakers and Slavery in America* (New Haven, CT: Yale University Press, 1950), p. 11.
32. Maurice Jackson, *Let This Voice Be Heard: Anthony Benezet, Father of Atlantic Abolitionism* (Philadelphia: Univ. of Pennsylvania Press, 2009), pp. 33–34.
33. "Washington's Letter to Robert Morris," Public Broadcasting System: www.pbs.org/wgbh/aia/part2/2h66t.html. Also, see Gary B. Nash and Jean R. Soderlund, *Freedom by Degrees: Emancipation in Pennsylvania and Its Aftermath* (New York: Oxford Univ. Press, 1991).
34. For more on Benezet, see Jackson, *Let This Voice Be Heard.*
35. Richard Newman, "The Pennsylvania Abolition Society: Restoring a Group to Glory," *Pennsylvania LEGACIES*, November 2005, p. 7.
36. Ibid., p. 9.
37. Sidney Kaplan, *The Black Presence in the Era of the American Revolution 1770–1800* (Washington, DC: Smithsonian Institution Press, 1975), pp. 84–85.
38. Exploring Pennsylvanian History Web site: http://explorepahistory.com/hmarker.php?markerId=280.
39. Lerone Bennett, *Before the Mayflower: A History of Black America* (Chicago, IL: Johnson Publishing, 1987), p. 82.
40. Hirschfeld, *George Washington and Slavery*, pp. 199–204.
41. Jackson, *Let This Voice Be Heard*, p. 252.
42. Blondell Reynolds Brown, "Full Story Must Be Told at New Bell Site," *Philadelphia Inquirer*, October 25, 2002.

43. President Adams did not have any slaves in Philadelphia or in Washington, D.C., where he relocated in the last months of his term in 1800. It was later discovered that Washington had at least nine slaves over time who were at the house during his two terms in office.
44. Charles Blockson, *The Liberty Bell Era: the African American Story* (Harrisburg, PA: RB Books, 2003), p. 56.
45. Linn Washington Jr., "Park Service Compromises Black Rights," *Philadelphia Inquirer*, May 7, 2002.
46. Edward Lawler Jr., "The President's House in Philadelphia: The Rediscovery of a Lost Landmark," *The Pennsylvania Magazine of History and Biography*, January 2002. The President's House in Philadelphia Web site: www.ushistory.org/presidentshouse/plans/pmhb/index.htm.
47. The Liberty Bell Web site: www.ushistory.org/libertybell/.
48. Lawler, "The President's House in Philadelphia."
49. Linn Washington Jr., "Park Service Compromises Black Rights,"
50. Acel Moore, "As Liberty Bell Flap Continues, a Slave Memorial Is Suggested," *Philadelphia Inquirer*, June 2, 2002.
51. Ibid.
52. Ad-Hoc Historians, "Summary of Ad-Hoc Historians group position," press release, September 2003. www.ushistory.org/presidentshouse/adhoc/position.htm.
53. Stephan Salisbury, "Panel Calls for Slave Commemoration," *Philadelphia Inquirer*, July 10, 2002.
54. Ibid.
55. Stephan Salisbury, "Committee is Put in Place to Guide Slavery Memorial," *Philadelphia Inquirer*, September 23, 2005.
56. Ibid. And Joseph A. Slobodzian, "Independence Mall slavery memorial gets federal funding," *Philadelphia Inquirer*, September 6, 2005.
57. Ibid.
58. Avenging The Ancestors Coalition Web site: http://avengingtheancestors.com/index.htm.
59. Edward Lawler, "Letter: Historic Accuracy Should Not Be Ignored," *Philadelphia Inquirer*, August 25, 2009; and Stephan Salisbury, "Despite Criticism, President's House Project Advances," *Philadelphia Inquirer*, October 10, 2009.
60. Michael Coard, "President's House Must Be Practical, Too," *Philadelphia Inquirer*, August 31, 2009.
61. Ibid.

Chapter 3

1. Phillis Wheatley, Julian Dewey Mason, ed., *The Poems of Phillis Wheatley* (Chapel Hill: Univ. of North Carolina Press, 1989), p. 53. Phillis Wheatley was abducted in Africa when she was seven years old and eventually sold to a wealthy Boston family. Unlike most enslaved, she was taught to read and demonstrated a propensity for letters and literature. She was first published at twelve years of age, and a book of her poems was published six years later. She was the first African American to publish a book of poems. *See* also Henry Louis Gates, *The Trials of Phillis Wheatley: America's First Black Poet and Her Encounters With the Founding Fathers* (New York: Basic Civitas Books, 2003).

2. Bob Arnebeck, "The Use of Slaves to Build and [*sic*] Capitol and White House 1791-1801." *See* Bob Arnebeck Web site: http://bobarnebeck.com/slaves.html. Much of the information and data included here, if not otherwise noted, comes from Arnebeck's extensive research.
3. William C. Allen, *History of Slave Laborers in the Construction of the U.S. Capitol* (Washington, DC: U.S. House of Representatives, Office of the Architect of the Capitol, June 1, 2005), p. 6.
4. Walter C. Clephane, "The Local Aspect of Slavery in the District of Columbia," *Records of the Columbia Historical Society*, Washington, DC, Vol. 3,1900, p. 235.
5. G. Franklin Edwards and Michael R. Winston, "Commentary: The Washington of Paul Jennings—White House Slave, Free Man, and Conspirator for Freedom," White House Historical Association, http://www.whitehousehistory.org/whha_publications/publications_documents/whitehousehistory_01-jennings.pdf; Citing Letitia Woods Brown, *Free Negroes in the District of Columbia, 1790–1846.* New York: Oxford Univ. Press, 1972.
6. Ibid, p. 239.
7. Ibid, Arnebeck, "The Use of Slaves."
8. Bob Arnebeck, *Through A Fiery Trial: Building Washington 1790-1800* (Lanham, MD: Madison Books, 1991), p. 456.
9. Charles A. Cerami, *Benjamin Benneker: Surveyor, Astronomer, Publisher, Patriot* (Hoboken, NJ: John Wiley and Sons, 2002), p. 122.
10. The "triangular slave trade" is a reference to the trade link between Europe, Africa, and the Americas during the slave era. Ships would leave Europe and sail to Africa, where they would trade manufactured goods such as rum for captured Africans. Those ships would then carry the newly enslaved people to the Americas and sell or trade them for raw goods or cash crops. Finally, the ships would return to Europe with cotton, sugar, tobacco, and other products produced from slave labor and sell them at great profit.
11. Roger Wilkins, *Jefferson's Pillow: The Founding Fathers and the Dilemma of Black Patriotism* (Boston: Beacon Press, 2001), p. 11.
12. Allen, *History of Slave Laborers*, p. 4; and Arnebeck, "The Use of Slaves."
13. All three were slave owners. They were replaced in 1794 by Gustavus Scott, William Thornton, and Alexander White. Scott and Thornton were slave owners as well.
14. See Cerami, op. cit.; and Silvio A. Bedini, *The Life of Benjamin Banneker: the First African-American Man of Science* (Baltimore, MD: Maryland Historical Society, 1999).
15. Ibid, Arnebeck, "The Use of Slaves."
16. Ibid.
17. Ibid., Allen, *History of Slave Laborers*, p. 10.
18. Ibid., p. 8.
19. Arnebeck, "The Use of Slaves."
20. Ibid.
21. Ibid.
22. Ibid.
23. Ibid.

24. Ibid.
25. Ibid.
26. Ibid., p. 205; and Jesse J. Holland, *Black Men Built the Capitol: Discovering African-American History In and Around Washington* (Guilford, CT: Globe Pequot, 2007), p. 4.
27. Arnebeck, "The Use of Slaves."
28. Ibid.
29. Ibid. Research on the census records of the time was inconclusive in determining LeClair's race.
30. Ibid.
31. Myra Weatherly, *Benjamin Banneker: American Scientific Pioneer* (Mankato, MN: Compass Point Books, 2006), p. 75.
32. *The Georgetown Weekly Record*, March 12, 1791, cited in Cerami, op. cit, p. 136.
33. Thomas Jefferson, *Notes on the State of Virginia*, Query XIV. See also Conor Cruise O'Brien, "Thomas Jefferson: Radical and Racist," *The Atlantic Monthly*, October 1996, pp. 53–74.
34. Ibid, Cerami, p. 164.
35. Since 1978, the United States Postal Service has released the following Black Heritage stamps: Harriet Tubman (1978), Martin Luther King (1979), Benjamin Banneker (1980), Whitney Moore Young (1981), Jackie Robinson (1982), Scott Joplin (1983), Carter G. Woodson (1984), Mary McLeod Bethune (1985), Sojourner Truth (1986), Jean Baptiste DuSable (1987), James Weldon Johnson (1988), A. Phillip Randolph (1989), Ida B. Wells (1990), Jan E. Matzeliger (1991), W.E.B. Du Bois (1992), Percy Lavon Julian (1993), Dr. Allison Davis (1994), Bessie Coleman (1995), Ernest E. Just (1996), Benjamin O. Davis, Sr. (1997), Benjamin O. Davis, Sr. (1997), Madam C. J. Walker (1998), Madam C. J. Walker (1998), Madam C. J. Walker (1998), Malcolm X (El-Hajj Malik El-Shabazz) (1999), Patricia Roberts Harris (2000), Roy Wilkins (2001), Langston Hughes (2002), Thurgood Marshall (2003), Paul Robeson (2004), Marian Anderson (2005), Hattie McDaniel (2006), Ella Fitzgerald (2007), Charles Chesnutt (2008), Anna Julia Cooper (2009) . *See*: /www.usps.com/communications/news/stamps/2005/sr05_016.htm
36. Jefferson Morley, "The Snow Riot," *Washington Post*, Sunday, February 6, 2005. Also: www.washingtonpost.com/wp-dyn/articles/A55082-2005Feb1_2.html
37. Ibid.
38. *Records of the Columbia Historical Society of Washington*, Volumes 3–4 (Washington, DC: Columbia Historical Society, 1900), p. 245.
39. Ibid, Morley.
40. Ibid.
41. Karolyn Smardz Frost, *I've Got a Home in Glory Land: A Lost Tale of the Underground Railroad* (New York: Macmillan, 2008), p. 271.
42. "The Statue of Freedom." See Architect of the Capitol Web site: www.aoc.gov/cc/art/freedom.cfm.
43. Megan Smolenyak Smolenyak, "Philip Reed, the Slave Who Rescued Freedom, *Ancestry*, May–June 2009, p. 55. See Mary Jordan, "Tiny Irish Village Is Latest Place to Claim Obama as Its Own," *Washington Post*, May 13, 2007, and Megan Smolenyak Smolenyak, "The Quest for Obama's Irish Roots," December 3, 2008.

Ancestry.com Web site: www.ancestrymagazine.com/2008/12/found/the-quest-for-obama%25E2%2580%2599s-irish-roots/.

44. Holland, p. 5.
45. Smolenyak, "Philip Reed," p. 54.
46. Holland, p. 6–7.
47. William Seale, *The President's House: A History* (Washington, D.C.: White House Historical Association, 1986), p. 81.

Chapter 4

1. Paul Jennings, *A Colored Man's Reminiscences of James Madison: Electronic Edition* (Chapel Hill, Univ. of North Carolina), 1865.
2. Ibid., p. iii.
3. Ibid., pp. 5–6.
4. Ibid., p. 19.
5. Rachell Swarns, "Madison and the White House, Through the Memoir of a Slave," *New York Times*, August 16, 2009.
6. Jennings, *Reminiscences*, p. 13.
7. Ibid., p. 13.
8. Ibid., p. 14.
9. Ibid., p. 11.
10. "Research in Progress: Paul Jennings Marries Fanny Gordon." http://Montpelier.org/blog/?cat=8.
11. Swarns, "Madison and the White House."
12. Beth Taylor, "Paul Jennings—Enamoured with Freedom," www.montpelier.org/explore/community/paul_jennings.php.
13. Ibid., Jennings, p. 12.
14. Mary Kay Ricks, *Escape on the Pearl: The Heroic Bid for Freedom on the Underground Railroad* (New York: William Morrow, 2007), pp. 42–43; and Jennings, *Reminiscences*, p. v.
15. Jennings, *Reminiscences*, pp. 14–15.
16. Ibid., p. 12.
17. Ricks, *Escape on the Pearl*, p. 38.
18. Ibid., p. 40.
19. Henry Chase, "Plotting a Course for Freedom; Paul Jennings: White House Memoirist," *American Visions*, Feb.–March, 1995.
20. G. Franklin Edwards and Michel R. Winston, "Commentary: The Washington of Paul Jennings—White House Slave, Free Man, and Conspirator for Freedom," The White House Historical Society. http://www.whitehousehistory.org/whha_publications/publications_documents/whitehousehistory_01-jennings.pdf
21. Karl Marx and Shelia Rowbotham, *The Revolutions of 1848: Political Writings* (London: Verso Books, 2010); Priscilla Smith Robertson, *Revolutions of 1848: A Social History* (Princeton, NJ: Princeton Univ. Press, 1968); and Roger Price, *The Revolutions of 1848* (Oxford: Macmillan Education, 1968).
22. Ricks, *Escape on the Pearl*, p. 57.
23. John Paynter, "The Fugitives of the *Pearl*," *Journal of Negro History*, Washington, DC, July 1916, p. 246.

24. Ibid., pp. 247–248; and Ricks, *Escape on the Pearl*, p. 75.
25. G. Franklin Edwards and Michel R. Winston, "Commentary: The Washington of Paul Jennings—White House Slave, Free Man, and Conspirator for Freedom," The White House Historical Society. http://www.whitehousehistory.org/whha_publications/publications_documents/whitehousehistory_01-jennings.pdf
26. Ricks, *Escape on the Pearl*, pp. 122–123.
27. Taylor, "Enamoured with Freedom."
28. Ibid., and Ricks, *Escape on the Pearl*, pp. 243–244.
29. Daniel Drayton and American and Foreign Anti-Slavery Society, *Personal Memoir of Daniel Drayton: For Four Years and Four Months a Prisoner (For Charity's Sake) in Washington Jail: Including a Narrative of the Voyage and Capture of the Schooner Pearl* (New York: B. Marsh, 1855), p. 121.
30. Ricks, *Escape on the Pearl*, p. 44.
31. Ibid., p. 181.
32. The Obamas were not present at the reunion—they were vacationing on Martha's Vineyard at the time. David Montgomery, "For D.C. Family, a Distinguished, If Little-Known Ancestor," *Washington Post*, August 25, 2009.
33. William Seale, *The President's House: A History* (Washington, D.C.: White House Historical Association, 1986), p. 136.
34. Ibid., pp. 142–143.
35. Ibid., p. 143.
36. Ibid., p. 147.
37. Henry Chase, "Black Life in the Capital," *American Visions*, February–March, 1995, p. 14.
38. Thomas Jefferson, *Memoirs, Correspondence, and Private Papers of Thomas Jefferson*, Vol. 4, (London: H. Colburn and R. Bentley, 1829), pp. 323–333.
39. Glover Moore, *The Missouri Controversy, 1819–1821*, (Lexington, KY: Univ. of Kentucky Press, 1953), p. 46.
40. Kenneth C. Barnes, *Journey of Hope: The Back-to-Africa Movement in Arkansas in the Late 1800s* (Chapel Hill: Univ. of North Carolina Press, 2004), p. 3.
41. See Eric Burin, *Slavery and the Peculiar Solution: A History of the American Colonization Society* (Gainsville: Univ. Press of Florida, 2008); Early Lee Fox, *The American Colonization Society: 1817–1840* (New York: AMS Press, 1971); and Allan Yarema, *The American Colonization Society: An Avenue to Freedom?* (Lanham, MD: Univ. Press of America, 2006).
42. Winthrop D. Jordan, *White Over Black: American Attitudes toward the Negro, 1550–1812* (Chapel Hill, NC: 1968), p. 394.
43. Herbert, Aptheker, *American Negro Slave Revolts* (New York: International Publishers, 1943, 1993), p. 368; citing Calvin Jones to Governor John Owen, Wake Forest, North Carolina, December 28, 1830, in MS. Governor's Papers, no. 60, Historical Commission, Raleigh.
44. Charles Sellers, *James K. Polk: Jacksonian, 1795–1843* (Princeton, NJ: Princeton Univ. Press, 1957), p. 422.
45. Howard Zinn, *A People's History of the United States, 1492–Present* (New York: HarperPerennial, 1980, 2003), p. 127.
46. Kenneth O'Reilly, *Nixon's Piano: Presidents and Racial Politics from Washington to Clinton* (New York: The Free Press, 1995), p. 32.

47. Ibid., p. 33.
48. Ibid., and Christopher Booker, African-Americans & the Presidency: A History of Broken Promises (New York: Franklin Watts, 2000), pp. 40–41.
49. Aptheker, *Slave Revolts*, p. 259; and Robert Vincent Remini, *The Life of Andrew Jackson* (New York: HarperCollins, 2001), p. 239.
50. Russel B. Nye, *Fettered Freedoms: Civil Liberties and the Slavery Controversy, 1830–1860* (Lansing, MI: Michigan State College Press, 1949), p. 34.
51. Garry Wills, *Negro President*, p. 218.
52. Ibid., p. 219.
53. *Argument of John Quincy Adams Before the Supreme Court of the United States in the case of the United States, Appellants, vs. Cinque, and others, Africans, captured in the schooner Amistad, by Lieut. Gedney, Delivered on the 24th of February and 1st of March 1841*. The complete text of this document is available electronically from History Central: www.historycentral.com/amistad/amistad.html.
54. Denise M. Henderson, "John Quincy Adams, the Amistad Case, and the Idea of the Inalienable Rights of Man," *American Almanac*, August, 1998. http://american_almanac.tripod.com/amistad.htm.
55. Exploring Amistad Web site: http://academic.sun.ac.za/forlang/bergman/real/amistad/history/msp/main_wel.htm
56. www.whitehouse.gov/about/history
57. The three surnames reflected various stages of the slave status and ownership of Thomas and his family. James Wiggins claimed ownership of Thomas's mother, Charity, at one point; and Myles Greene claimed ownership of his father, Mingo, when he was born. Gen. James Neil Bethune would purchase the entire family about six months after Thomas's birth. For most of his performing years, Thomas would use the surname Bethune, but in his final years, he generally went by Wiggins.
58. Afri-Classical.com Web site: http://chevalierdesaintgeorges.homestead.com/JohnsonF.html.
59. On July 22, 1992, the 200th anniversary of his birth, Johnson was honored by the U.S. Senate. "Commemoration of A Musical Master," *Congressional Record*, U.S. Senate, July 22, 1992, p. S10152. See Library of Congress: http://rs9.loc.gov/cgi-bin/query/D?r102:72:./temp/~r1021MHOhw
60. Ibid.
61. See Barbara Clemenson, "Justin Holland: Black Guitarist in the Western Reserve," *Western Reserve Studies Symposium*: The Western Reserve Historical Society, Cleveland, OH, 1989; and Douglas Back, *American Pioneers of the Classical Guitar*, liner notes, Mento Music Press SMM 3023, 1994.
62. See Philip S. Foner and George E. Walker, eds., *Proceedings of the Black State Conventions, 1840–1855* (Philadelphia: Temple Univ. Press, 1980); and Philip S. Foner and George E. Walker, eds., *Proceedings of the Black State Conventions, 1865–1900* (Philadelphia: Temple Univ. Press, 1986).
63. Howard H. Bell, "Negro Nationalism: A Factor in Emigration Projects, 1858–1861," *The Journal of Negro History*, January 1962), p. 48; and Robert L. Harris Jr., "H. Ford Douglas: Afro-American Antislavery Emigrationist," *The Journal of Negro History*, July 1977), p. 224.

64. Deirdre O'Connell, *The Ballad of Blind Tom: Slave Pianist, America's Lost Musical Genius* (New York: Overlook Duckworth, 2009), p. 32.
65. O'Connell, *Ballad of Blind Tom*, p. 29.
66. Deirdre O'Connell, "Who Was Blind Tom," BlindTom.org Web site: www.blindtom.org/who_was_blind_tom.html.
67. Geneva H. Southall, *Blind Tom: The Post–Civil War Enslavement of a Black Musical Genius* (Minneapolis: Challenge Books, 1979); Geneva H. Southall, *The Continuing Enslavement of Blind Tom, the Black Pianist-Composer (1865–1887)* (Minneapolis: Challenge Books, 1983); and Geneva H. Southall, *Blind Tom, the Black Pianist-Composer (1849–1908)* (Lanham, MD: The Scarecrow Press, Inc., 1999).
68. See O'Connell, *Ballad of Blind Tom*, p. 132; and Geneva H. Southall, "Blind Tom: A Misrepresented and Neglected Composer-Pianist," *The Black Perspective in Music*, May, 1975, p. 145.
69. O'Connell, *Ballad of Blind Tom*, p. 74; and Southall, "A Misrepresented and Neglected Composer-Pianist," p. 90.
70. O'Reilly, *Nixon's Piano*, p. 41; and Booker, 54–55.
71. See Paul Finkelman, *Dred Scott v. Sandford: A Brief History With Documents* (London: Palgrave Macmillan, 1997); Don Edward Fehrenbacher, *Slavery, Law, and Politics: The Dred Scott Case in Historical Perspective* (New York: Oxford Univ. Press US, 1981); and Andrew P. Napolitano, *Dred Scott's Revenge: A Legal History of Race and Freedom in America* (Nashville, TN: Thomas Nelson Inc, 2009).
72. Elise K. Kirk, *Music at the White House: A History of the American Spirit* (Urbana, IL: Univ. of Illinois Press, 1986), p. 72.
73. Virginia Clay-Clopton and Ada Sterling, *A Belle of the Fifties: Memoirs of Mrs. Clay of Alabama, Covering Social and Political Life in Washington and the South, 1853–66* (New York: Doubleday, 1905), pp. 104–105.
74. Kirk, *Music at the White House*, pp. 75–76; and O'Connell, *Ballad of Blind Tom*, p. 105.
75. O'Connell, *Ballad of Blind Tom*, p. 115.
76. Ibid, *Blind Tom: The Post–Civil War Enslavement of a Black Musical Genius,* p. 9.
77. Following South Carolina, and before Lincoln took office on March 4, 1861, six other states voted for secession: Mississippi (January 9, 1861), Florida (January 10, 1861), Alabama (January 11, 1861), Georgia (January 19, 1861), Louisiana (January 26, 1861), and Texas (February 1, 1861). They would be joined by four other states after the war started with an attack on Fort Sumter in North Carolina on April 12, 1861. These were Virginia (April 17, 1861), Arkansas (May 6, 1861), Tennessee (May 7, 1861), and North Carolina (May 20, 1861).

Chapter 5

1. Jennifer Fleischner, *Mrs. Lincoln and Mrs. Keckly: The Remarkable Story of the Friendship Between a First Lady and a Former Slave* (New York: Broadway Books, 2003), pp. 285–287.
2. See Elizabeth Keckley, *Behind the Scenes or Thirty Years a Slave and Four Years in the White House* (New York: The New York Printing Company, 1868). The book was published with the author's name spelled "Keckley," rather than the correct "Keckly."
3. Ibid., pp. 20–21.

4. Ibid., pp. 31–39.
5. Fleischner, *Mrs. Lincoln and Mrs. Keckly*, p. 140.
6. In 1848, Emerson had transferred the advocacy of the case to her brother, John Sanford. The Supreme Court reporter who registered the case, however, misspelled his name so the case has officially been registered as Dred Scott v. Sandford. See Paul Finkelman, *Dred Scott v. Sandford: A Brief History with Documents* (Boston: Bedford Books, 1997); and Mark A. Graber, *Dred Scott and the Problem of Constitutional Evil* (Cambridge Univ. Press, 2006).
7. Keckley, *Behind the Scenes*, p. 49.
8. Ibid., pp. 63–64.
9. Ibid., pp. 69–73.
10. Fleischner, *Mrs. Lincoln and Mrs. Keckly*, p. 200.
11. Keckley, *Behind the Scenes*, pp. 84–85.
12. Ibid., p. 127.
13. Ibid., p. 105.
14. Ibid., pp. 112–116.
15. Fleischner, *Mrs. Lincoln and Mrs. Keckly*, p. 317.
16. Stunningly, in his massive work on Lincoln focusing on the president's racial views, Lerone Bennett does not mention Keckly at all. He is not alone. See Lerone Bennett Jr., *Forced Into Glory: Abraham Lincoln's White Dream* (Chicago: Johnson Publishing Company, 2007)
17. Bennett, *Forced Into Glory*, p. 531.
18. Ibid., p. 532.
19. Doris Kearns Goodwin, "Introduction," in Philip B. Kunhardt III, Peter W. Kunhardt, and Peter W. Kunhardt Jr., *Looking for Lincoln: The Making of an American Icon* (New York: Alfred A. Knopf, 2008), p. ix.
20. See Michael K. Fauntroy, *Republicans and the Black Vote* (Boulder, CO: Lynne Rienner Publishers, Inc., 2007).
21. Roy P. Basler, ed., Marion Dolores Pratt and Lloyd A. Dunlap, asst. eds., *The Collected Works of Abraham Lincoln*, Vol. 3 (New Brunswick, NJ: Rutgers Univ. Press, 1955), p. 264.
22. Abraham Lincoln, Roy Prentice Basler, and Carl Sandburg, *Abraham Lincoln: His Speeches and Writings* (Cambridge, MA: Da Capo Press, 2001), p. 404.
23. Lincoln (Basler, ed.), *Collected Works*, 9 vols., 2:132
24. Bennett, *Forced Into Glory*, pp. 464–465.
25. See Robert Morgan, "The 'Great Emancipator' and the Issue of Race: Abraham Lincoln's Program of Black Resettlement." Institute for Historical Review Web site: www.ihr.com; and Allan Nevins, *The War For The Union*, Vol. 2, "War Becomes Revolution, 1862–1863" (New York: C. Scribner's Sons, 1960), p. 10.
26. See Michael Vorenberg, "Abraham Lincoln and the Politics of Black Colonization," *Journal of Abraham Lincoln Association*, Vol. 14, Issue 2, pp. 24–45; Charles H. Wesley, "Lincoln's Plan for Colonizing the Emancipated Negroes," *Journal of Negro History* 4 (1919), pp. 7–21; and Don E. Fehrenbacher, "Only His Stepchildren: Lincoln and the Negro," *Civil War History* 20 (1974), pp. 307–8.
27. Mitchell, a white minister, had written Lincoln earlier in the year, "Our republican system was meant for a homogeneous people. As long as blacks continue to live with

the whites they constitute a threat to the national life. Family life may also collapse and the increase of mixed breed bastards may some day challenge the supremacy of the white man." Impressed with this rhetoric, Lincoln made the special appointment. See "James Mitchell to A. Lincoln," May 18, 1862, *Lincoln Collection*, Vol. 76, f. 16044.; and P. J. Scheips, "Lincoln and the Chiriqui Colonization Project," *Journal of Negro History*, Vol. 37, No. 4 (1952), pp. 426–427.

28. "The Colonization of People of African Descent," *New York Tribune*, August 15, 1862.
29. Ibid.
30. Lincoln (Basler, ed.), *Collected Works*, Vol. 5, p. 371.
31. Henry Jarvis Raymond, *History of the Administration of President Lincoln: Including His Speeches, Letters, Addresses, Proclamations, and Messages. With a Preliminary Sketch of His Life* (New York: J. C. Derby & N. C. Miller, 1864), p. 469.
32. Ibid., p. 469.
33. Ibid., p. 471.
34. Ibid., p. 374.
35. Ibid., p. 373.
36. See Sheldon H. Harris, *Paul Cuffee: Black America and the African Return* (New York: Simon & Schuster, 1972).
37. See Stephen Ward Angell, *Bishop Henry McNeal Turner and African-American Religion in the South* (Knoxville: Univ. of Tennessee Press, 1992).
38. Kenneth C. Barnes, *Journey of Hope: The Back-to-Africa Movement in Arkansas in the Late 1800s* (Chapel Hill: Univ. of North Carolina Press, 2004), pp. 1–2.
39. Thomas F. Schwartz, *For a Vast Future Also: Essays from the Journal of the Abraham Lincoln Association* (Bronx, NY: Fordham Univ. Press, 1999), p. 42.
40. Edwin [*sic*] M. Thomas to A. Lincoln, August 16, 1862, *Lincoln Collection*, Vol. 84, ff. 17718–17719.
41. Bennett, *Forced Into Glory*, p. 464.
42. Isaiah C. Wears, "Lincoln's Colonization Proposal Is Anti-Christian," in Foner and Walker, *Proceedings, 1865–1900,* p. 260.
43. Ibid., p. 261.
44. Frederick Douglass, "The President and His Speeches," *Douglass Monthly*, September 1862.
45. Ibid.
46. Eric Foner, *Reconstruction: America's Unfinished Revolution, 1863–1877* (New York: Perennial Classics, 2002), p. 6; Benjamin P. Thomas and Michael Burlingame, *Abraham Lincoln: A Biography* (Carbondale, IL: Southern Illinois Univ. Press, 2008), p. 363; and Ellis Paxson Oberholtzer, *A History of the United States Since the Civil War* (New York: The Macmillan Company, 1917), p. 78.
47. "General Fremont's Proclamation," See John Charles Frémont Web site: www.longcamp.com/proc4.html.
48. Allan Nevins, *Fremont: Pathmarker of the West* (Lincoln: Univ. of Nebraska Press, 1992).
49. Horace Greeley, *The American Conflict: A History of the Great Rebellion in the United States, 1860–1864* (Oxford Univ. Press, 1867), p. 246.
50. Abraham Lincoln, "The President on the Negro Question, Executive Mansion,

Washington, August, 22, 1862," letter to editor, *Harper's Weekly*, September 6, 1862, p. 563.

51. Lincoln (Basler, ed.), *Collected Works*, Vol. 8, p. 403.
52. Ibid., p. 404.
53. James M. McPherson, *Abraham Lincoln* (New York: Oxford Univ. Press, 2009), p. 61.
54. Henry Highland Garnet, "An Address to the Slaves of the United States," in Philip S. Foner, ed., *The Voice of Black America: Major Speeches by Negroes in the United States, 1791–1971* (New York: Simon & Schuster, 1972), p. 89.
55. The pamphlet's full title was *Walker's Appeal, in Four Articles; Together with a Preamble, to the Coloured Citizens of the World, but in Particular, and Very Expressly, to Those of the United States of America.*
56. See David Walker, *David Walker's Appeal: to the Coloured Citizens of the World, But in Particular, and Very Expressly, to Those of the United States of America* (Baltimore: Black Classic Press, 1993).
57. Ibid., p. 73.
58. Frederick Douglass, "The Meaning of the Fourth of July for the Negro," in P. Foner, *Voice of Black America*, p. 117. See also James A. Colaiaco, *Frederick Douglass and the Fourth of July* (New York: Macmillan, 2007); and Bernard W. Bell, "The African-American Jeremiad and Frederick Douglass' Fourth of July 1852 Speech," in Paul Goetsch and Gerd Hurm, eds., *The Fourth of July: Political Oratory and Literary Reactions, 1776–1876* (Tübingen, Germany: Gunter Narr Verlag, 1992), pp. 139–154.
59. Douglass, "Meaning of the Fourth," p. 114.
60. Ibid., p. 115.
61. Ibid., p. 126.
62. Ibid., p. 128.
63. Frederick Douglass, *Life and Times of Frederick Douglass* (New York: Collier Books, 1962), p. 336.
64. Philip S. Foner, ed., *The Life and Writings of Frederick Douglass*, Vol. 3 (New York: International Publishers, 1975), p. 268.
65. Ibid., p. 342.
66. Benjamin Quarles, *The Negro in the Civil War* (Boston: Little, Brown Publishers, 1969), p. 117.
67. Clinton, Catherine, *Harriet Tubman: The Road to Freedom* (Back Bay Books, Little, Brown and Company, 2004), p. 184
68. Ibid.
69. Ibid., p. 348.
70. James W. Loewen, *Lies Across America: What Our Historical Sites Get Wrong* (New York: Touchstone–Simon & Schuster, 2000), p. 255.
71. Ibid. Also, see John Cimprich, *Fort Pillow, A Civil War Massacre, and Public Memory* (Baton Rouge, LA: LSU Press, 2005); and John Cimprich and Robert C. Mainfort Jr., "The Fort Pillow Massacre: A Statistical Note," *Journal of American History*, November 1989, pp. 832–837.
72. Quarles, *Negro in the Civil War*, pp. 347–349.
73. Don E. Fehrenbacher and Virginia Fehrenbacher, eds., *Recollected Words of Abraham Lincoln* (Palo Alto, CA: Stanford Univ. Press, 1996), p. 145.

74. Douglass, *Life and Times*, p. 358.
75. Ibid, 435.
76. Keckley, *Behind the Scenes*, p. 158; and Douglass, *Life and Times*, p. 366.
77. Allen Thorndike Rice, ed., *Reminiscences of Abraham Lincoln by Distinguished Men of His Time* (New York: North American Review, 1888), pp. 191–193.
78. Bennett, *Forced Into Glory*, pp. 33–34.
79. Douglass, *Life and Times*, pp. 370–372.
80. P. Foner, *Life and Writings of Frederick Douglass*, Vol. 3, p. 314.
81. Sojourner Truth, "Ain't I A Woman?" speech delivered at Women's Convention, Akron, Ohio, 1851. Historian Nell Painter points out, significantly, that it is not altogether clear what Truth said at the convention. There were various reports issued claiming to present the speech verbatim but many were in racist black dialect and reflected the opposition that some women had at the gathering to Truth speaking and linking the feminist cause with abolition. See Nell Painter, *Sojourner Truth: A Life, A Symbol* (New York: W. W. Norton & Company, 1997), pp. 164–175.
82. Carleton Mabee and Susan Mabee, *Sojourner Truth: Slave, Prophet, Legend* (New York Univ. Press, 1995), pp. 121–122.
83. Ibid., Mabee and Mabee, p. 121.
84. Ibid, p. 1,256.
85. Bennett, *Forced Into Glory*, pp. 109–110.
86. Carleton Mabee, "The Demise of Slavery," in Martin H. Greenberg and Charles G. Waugh, eds., *The Price of Freedom, Slavery and the Civil War*, Vol. 1 (Naperville, IL: Cumberland House, 2000), p. 353.
87. See Sarah H. Bradford, *Scenes in the Life of Harriet Tubman* (Auburn, NY: W.J. Moses, 1869); Sarah H. Bradford, *Harriet, The Moses of Her People* (NY: Geo. R. Lockwood & Son, 1886); and Kate Clifford Larson, *Bound for the Promised Land: Harriet Tubman, Portrait of an American Hero* (NY: Ballantine Books, December 2003).
88. Catherine Clinton, Harriet Tubman: The Road to Freedom (Back Bay Books, Little, Brown and Company, 2004), p. 147.
89. William Friedheim, *Freedom's Unfinished Revolution, American Social History Project* (New York: The New Press, 1996), p. 62.
90. At this writing, Congress has introduced legislation (S. 227, Harriet Tubman National Historical Park and Harriet Tubman Underground Railroad National Historical Park Act; and H.R. 1078, Harriet Tubman National Historical Park and Harriet Tubman Underground Railroad National Historical Park Act) to honor Tubman.
91. See W. E. B. Du Bois, *Black Reconstruction: An Essay Toward a History of the Part Which Black Folk Played in the Attempt to Reconstruct Democracy in America, 1860–1880* (New York: Oxford Univ. Press, 2007); and Eric Foner, *A Short History of Reconstruction* (New York: Harper & Row, 1990).
92. See Paul A. Cimbala and Randall M. Miller, eds., *The Freedmen's Bureau and Reconstruction: Reconsiderations* (New York: Fordham Univ. Press, 1999); and Paul A. Cimbala, *The Freedmen's Bureau: Reconstructing the American South After the Civil War* (Malabar, FL: Krieger Pub., 2005).
93. Ira Berlin, *The Wartime Genesis of Free Labor: the Lower South* (Cambridge Univ. Press, 1990), pp. 338–40.

94. See Doris Kearns Goodwin, *Team of Rivals: The Political Genius of Abraham Lincoln* (New York: Simon & Schuster, 2005).
95. Douglass, *Life and Times*, p. 364.
96. James E. Sefton, *Andrew Johnson and the Uses of Constitutional Power* (Boston: Little, Brown, 1980), p. 50.
97. "The Late Convention of Colored Men," *New York Times*, August 13, 1865.
98. Albert Castel, *The Presidency of Andrew Johnson* (Lawrence: Regents Press of Kansas, 1979), p. 64.

Chapter 6

1. "McCain Delivers Concession Speech," *Washington Post*, November 4, 2008.
2. Lena Doolin Mason, "A Negro In It," in Daniel Wallace Culp, ed., *Twentieth Century Negro Literature: or, A Cyclopedia of Thought on the Vital Topics Relating to the American Negro* (Naperville, IL: J. L. Nichols & Co., 1902), pp. 447–448.
3. Marshall Everett, *Complete Life of William McKinley and Story of His Assassination* (Whitefish, MT: Kessinger Publishing, 2003), pp. 33–40.
4. A sampling of the articles include "The Case of Jim Parker," *Atlanta Constitution*, September 26, 1901; "Editorial and Publishers' Announcements," *Colored American Magazine*, October 190; "Editorial Mention," *Zion's Herald*, September 11, 1901; "Hanna Thanks 'Big Jim,' " *Chicago Daily Tribune*, September 10, 1901; and "Savannah Remembers Him," *News and Courier*, September 10, 1901.
5. "Tells His Story in a Modest Way," *Afro-American-Ledger*, September 28, 1901.
6. Daryl Rasuli, "James B. Parker Revisited," University of Buffalo Library Web site: http://library.buffalo.edu/exhibits/panam/essays/rasuli/rasuli.html.
7. Czolgosz was convicted and sentenced to death on September 23, 1901 and executed in the electric chair on October 29, 1901.
8. "Editorial Mention," *Zion's Herald*, September 11, 1901.
9. Rasuli, "Parker Revisited."
10. "The Case of Jim Parker," *Atlanta Constitution,* September 26, 1901.
11. "Negroes Applaud Parker," *Atlanta Constitution*, September 13, 1901.
12. Booker T. Washington, "Atlanta Exposition Address," in Philip S. Foner, *The Voice of Black America: Major Speeches by Negroes in the United States, 1797–1971* (New York: Simon & Schuster, 1972), p. 581.
13. Ibid., pp. 580–581.
14. W. E. B. Du Bois, *Souls of Black Folks* (New York: Signet Classic, 1995), pp. 80, 87.
15. William Seale, *The President's House: A History* (Washington, DC: White House Historical Association, 1986), p. 652.
16. Kenneth O'Reilly, *Nixon's Piano: Presidents and Racial Politics From Washington to Clinton* (New York: The Free Press, 1995), p. 66.
17. Ibid., p. 67.
18. Ibid., p. 65; Michael Chapman, "TR: No Friend of the Constitution," *Cato Policy Report*, November/December 2002, p. 6; David Levering Lewis, *W. E. B. Du Bois: Biography of a Race, 1868–1919* (New York: Henry Holt and Company, 1993), p. 276.
19. Theodore Roosevelt, *A Compilation of the Messages and Speeches of Theodore Roosevelt, 1901–1905* (New York: Bureau of National Literature and Art, 1906), p. 564.
20. Seale, *The President's House*, p. 652.

21. Garry Wills, *Negro President: Jefferson and the Slave Owner* (New York: Houghton Mifflin Harcourt, 2005), p. 38. Also, see James P. P. Horn, Jan Lewis, and Peter S. Onuf, *The Revolution of 1800: Democracy, Race, and the New Republic* (Charlottesville: Univ. of Virginia Press, 2002), p. 314; David McCullough, *John Adams* (New York: Simon & Schuster, 2008), p. 519; and Tim Matthewson, *A Proslavery Foreign Policy: Haitian-American Relations During the Early Republic* (Santa Barbara, CA: Greenwood Publishing Group, 2003), p. 67.
22. O'Reilly, *Nixon's Piano*, p. 68.
23. Quoted in Gardiner Harris, "The Underside of the Welcome Mat," *New York Times*, November 8, 2008.
24. Louis Harlan, *Booker T. Washington: The Wizard of Tuskegee, 1901–1915* (New York: Oxford Univ. Press, 1983), p. 4.
25. Ibid., p. 5
26. Ibid., p. 5.
27. Ibid., p. 67.
28. See John Riley, "White House Tea and No Sympathy: The DePriest Incident," in *National History Day 2006 Curriculum Book* (Washington, DC: White House Historical Association, 2006); White House Historical Association Web site: www.whitehousehistory.org/04/subs/images_subs/primary_1929.pdf; John Hope Franklin, *From Slavery to Freedom* (New York: Vintage Books, 1969), p. 526.
29. White House Historical Association, email to the author, October 15, 2010: According to the records at the White House curator's office, President Roosevelt had the name officially changed from Executive Mansion to White House, but did not issue an executive order to make the changes. They have a letter dated October 17, 1901, from the president's secretary to the Secretary of State which reads: My dear Sir, I am directed by the President to bring to your attention his desire To change the headings, or date lines, of all official papers and Documents requiring his signature from "Executive Mansion" to "White House." In view of the approaching session of Congress, it will become necessary in preparing nominations for the Senate, as well as messages for either House of Congress, to observe the above change.
30. Ronald W. Walters, *Black Presidential Politics: A Strategic Approach* (Albany, NY: State Univ. of New York Press, 1988), p. 21.
31. See Edward Cary Royce, *The Origins of Southern Sharecropping* (Philadelphia: Temple Univ. Press, 1993).
32. Douglas A. Blackmon, *Slavery By Another Name, The Re-Enslavement of Black Americans from the Civil War to World War II*, (New York, Anchor Books, Random House: 2008) pp. 8–9.
33. W. E. B. Du Bois, "The Spawn of Slavery: The Convict-Lease System in the South," in Shaun L. Gabbidon and Helen Taylor Greene, *Race, Crime, and Justice: A Reader* (New York: Routledge, 2005), p. 3.
34. Ibid., p. 4.
35. Ibid., pp. 4–5.
36. For a detailed discussion of the controversy, see Paul Leland Haworth, *The Hayes-Tilden Disputed Presidential Election of 1876* (Cleveland: Burrows Brothers Company, 1906).
37. Robert Vincent Remini, *Fellow Citizens: The Penguin Book of U.S. Presidential Addresses* (New York: Penguin Group, 2008), pp. 206–208.
38. W. E. B. Du Bois, *Black Reconstruction in America, 1860-1880* (New York: Free Press, 1998), p. 637, citing J.J. Alvord in *Report of Joint Committee on Reconstruction*, Part II, p. 247.
39. Justus D. Doenecke, *The Presidencies of James A. Garfield & Chester A. Arthur* (Lawrence: Regents Press of Kansas, 1981), p. 48.
40. Douglass, *Life and Times*, p. 522.

41. Zachary Karabell, *Chester Alan Arthur* (New York: Macmillan, 2004), p. 127.
42. Rayford Whittingham Logan, *The Betrayal of the Negro, From Rutherford B. Hayes to Woodrow Wilson* (New York: Da Capo Press, 1997), p. 83.
43. Ibid., p. 82.
44. U.S. Senate: Hiram Rhodes Revels (MS, 1870–71); Blanche Kelso Bruce (MS, 1875–81); and U.S. House of Representatives: Joseph Hayne Rainey (SC, 1870–1879), Jefferson Franklin Long (GA, 1871), Benjamin Sterling Turner (AL, 1871–73), Robert Carlos De Large (SC, 1871–73), Robert Brown Elliott (SC, 1871–1874), Josiah Thomas Walls (FL, 1871–76), Richard Harvey Cain (SC, 1873–75, 1877–79), Alonzo Jacob Ransier (SC, 1873–75), James Thomas Rapier (AL, 1873–75), John Roy Lynch (MS, 1873–77, 1882–83), Jeremiah Haralson (AL, 1875–77), John Adams Hyman (NC, 1875–1877), Charles Edmund Nash (LA, 1875–77), Robert Smalls (SC, 1875–79, 1882–87), James Edward O'Hara (NC, 1883–87), Henry Plummer Cheatham (NC, 1889–93), Thomas Ezekiel Miller (SC, 1890–91), John Mercer Langston (VA, 1890–91), George Washington Murray (SC, 1893–95, 1896–97), and George Henry White (NC, 1897–01). William L. Clay, *Just Permanent Interests: Black Americans in Congress, 1870–1991* (New York: Amistad Press, 1992), pp. 355–356.
45. Clay, *Just Permanent Interests*, p. 13.
46. Ibid., p. 42.
47. In 1900 White proposed one of the first anti-lynching bills in Congress, which would have made lynching a federal crime. It was ignored and died in the Judiciary Committee. See "George Henry White," Black Americans in Congress Web site: http://baic.house.gov/member-profiles/profile.html?intID=22.
48. Thomas Walker Page, "The Real Judge Lynch," *Atlantic Monthly*, December 1901, pp. 731–743.
49. See "Photographs and Postcards of Lynching in America," Without Sanctuary Web site: www.withoutsanctuary.org/main.html.
50. Ida B. Wells, "Lynch Law," in Ida B. Wells, Frederick Douglass, Irvine Garland Penn, and Ferdinand L. Barnett (Robert W. Rydell, ed.), *The Reason Why the Colored American Is Not in the World's Columbian Exposition* (Urbana, IL: Univ. of Illinois Press, 1999), p. 32.
51. See Catherine Welch, *Ida B. Wells-Barnett: Powerhouse With a Pen* (Minneapolis: Carolrhoda Books, 2000), p. 71; Mia Bay, *To Tell the Truth Freely: The Life of Ida B. Wells* (New York: Macmillan, 2009), pp. 236–238; and Suzanne Freedman, *Ida B. Wells-Barnett and the Antilynching Crusade* (Minneapolis: Millbrook Press, 1994), p. 21.
52. See Tom Henderson Wells, "The Phoenix Election Riot," Phylon, 1st Quarter, 1970, pp. 58–69; Daniel Levinson Wilk, "The Phoenix Riot and the Memories of Greenwood County," *Southern Cultures*, Vol. 8, 2002, pp. 29–55; David S. Cecelski, *Democracy Betrayed: The Wilmington Race Riot of 1898 and Its Legacy* (Chapel Hill, NC: University of North Carolina Press Books, 1998).
53. Eric Foner, John Arthur Garraty, and Society of American Historians, *The Reader's Companion to American History* (Orlando, FL: Houghton Mifflin Harcourt, 1991), p. 685.
54. Walter White, *Rope and Faggot: A Biography of Judge Lynch* (Notre Dame, IN: Univ. of Notre Dame Press, 2001), p. 97.

55. Herbert Shapirio, *White Violence and Black Response: From Reconstruction to Montgomery* (Amherst, MA: Univ. of Massachusetts Press, 1988), pp. 142–143.
56. Theodore Roosevelt, IV, *State of the Union Addresses of Theodore Roosevelt* (London: Echo Library, 2007), p. 165.
57. "Taft Condemns Lynching: President Says Man That Pulls the Rope Should Hang by the Rope," *New York Times*, April 10, 1912; and "Taft Deplores Lynching: The Remedy, He Tells The Times, Is Better Enforcement of the Law," *New York Times*, June 27, 1912.
58. O'Reilly, *Nixon's Piano*, p. 78.
59. Germany would also raise the issue again during the Nazi era. Ernest Allen Jr., "'Close Ranks': Major Joel E. Spingarn and the Two Souls of Dr. W. E. B. Du Bois," Contributions in Black Studies, Vol. 3, 1979, p. 6.
60. See "Warren G. Harding," Marion County Historical Society Web site: http://marionhistory.com/wgharding/harding-2.htm.
61. "Harding for Kellogg Bill; President Prefers It to Dyer Anti-Lynching Measure," *New York Times*, August 28, 1922.
62. Melvyn Stokes, *D. W. Griffith's The Birth of a Nation: A History of "The Most Controversial Motion Picture of All Time"* (New York: Oxford Univ. Press, 2007), p. 111.
63. John T. Woolley and Gerhard Peters, "J. Edgar Hoover Message Condemning Lynching," American Presidency Project Web site: www.presidency.ucsb.edu/ws/?pid=22360.
64. Franklin, p. 526.
65. Richard Polenberg, *The Era of Franklin D. Roosevelt, 1933–1945: A Brief History with Documents* (New York: Palgrave Macmillan, 2000), p. 30.
66. Donald Grant, *The Way It Was in the South: The Black Experience in Georgia* (Athens, GA: Univ. of Georgia Press, 2001), p. 331; and Garth E. Pauley, *The Modern Presidency & Civil Rights: Rhetoric on Race from Roosevelt to Nixon* (College Station, TX: Texas A&M Univ. Press, 2001), pp. 26–27.
67. Ira Katznelson. *When Affirmative Action Was White: An Untold History of Racial Inequality in Twentieth-Century America* (New York: W. W. Norton & Company, 2005), p. 17.
68. It should be noted here that during the nineteenth century, until the Thirteenth, Fourteenth, and Fifteenth Amendments, Southern legislators received an advantage because of the three-fifths clause in the Constitution. For the purposes of House representation, 60 percent of their black populations was counted as part of the overall state population, even though black people themselves were denied the right to vote. After the amendments and the reinstitution of black disenfranchisement, the entire black population was included in Southern population totals, although nearly all were denied the right to vote. The larger numbers increased Southern membership in Congress still further.
69. Katznelson, *An Untold Story*, p. 22.
70. Ibid., p. 32.
71. Richard Sterner, *The Negro's Share: A Study of Income, Consumption, Housing, and Public Assistance* (New York: Harper & Brothers, 1943), p. 214.
72. Alferdteen Harrison, *Black Exodus: The Great Migration from the American South* (Jackson: Univ. Press of Mississippi, 1992), pp. 10–11.
73. David Bositis, *Blacks and the 1992 Democratic National Convention* (Washington,

DC: Joint Center for Political and Economic Studies, 1992), p. 29; and David Greenberg, "The Party of Lincoln . . . But not of Hayes, Harrison, Hoover, Eisenhower, Nixon, Reagan, or Bush," *Slate*, August 10, 2000, *Slate* Web site: www.slate.com/id/87868.

74. Bositis, *Blacks and the 1992 Democratic National Convention*, p. 29.
75. Paul Robeson, *Paul Robeson Speaks: Writings, Speeches, Interviews, 1918–1974* (New York: Citadel Press, 1978), p. 173.
76. For more information on lynchings and the anti-lynching campaigns, see James E. Cutler, *Lynch-Law: An Investigation into the History of Lynching in the United States* (New York: Negro Universities Press, 1969); Walter F. White, *The Fire in the Flint* (New York: Negro Universities Press, 1969); Walter F. White, *Rope and Faggot: A Biography of Judge Lynch* (Notre Dame, IN: University of Notre Dame Press, 2001); Ralph Ginsburg, *100 Years of Lynchings* (Baltimore: Black Classic Press, 1996); Ida B. Wells, *On Lynching; Southern Horrors; A Red Record; Mob Rule in New Orleans* (New York: Arno Press, 1969); James R. McGovern, *Anatomy of a Lynching* (Baton Rouge, LA: Louisiana State University Press, 1982); and Trudier Harris, *Exorcising Blackness: Historical and Literary Lynching and Burning Rituals* (Bloomington, IN: Indiana University Press, 1984.
77. Sheryl Gay Stolberg, "Senate Issues Apology Over Failure on Lynching Law," *New York Times*, June 14, 2005.
78. Daniel B. Wood, "Racist Acts at UC San Diego Underscore Deeper Tension on Campus," *Christian Science Monitor*, March 2, 2010.
79. Philip Dray, "Noose: The True History of a Resurgent Symbol of Hate," *Boston Globe*, December 2, 2007.
80. See Fisk Jubilee Singers Web site: www.fiskjubileesingers.org/music.html.
81. Dominique-René de Lerma, "The Violin in Black Music History," December 31, 2008, Myrtle Hart Society Web site: http://myrtlehart.org/content/view/275/5/
82. James Oliver Horton, Landmarks of African American History (New York: Oxford Univ. Press US, 2005), p. 99.
83. Email correspondence between Kenneth B. Morris, Jr. and author, September 30, 2010.
84. Walter Christmas, Negroes in Public Affairs and Government Educational Heritage, 1966 p. 306.
84. Reid Badger, A Life in Ragtime: A Biography of James Reese Europe (New York: Oxford Univ. Press, 1995), p. 24.
85. Ibid.
86. Ibid.
87. "This Week in Black History," Jet, July 4, 1983, p. 23; Negro Year Book and Annual Encyclopedia of the Negro (Tuskegee, AL: Negro Year Book Publishing Co., 1916), p. 288; and C. Edward Spann and Michael Edward Williams, Presidential Praise: Our Presidents and Their Hymns (Macon, GA: Mercer Univ. Press, 2008), p. 165.
88. "This Week in Black History," *Jet*, July 4, 1983, p. 23; *Negro Year Book and Annual Encyclopedia of the Negro* (Tuskegee, AL: Negro Year Book Publishing Co., 1916), p. 288; and C. Edward Spann and Michael Edward Williams, *Presidential Praise: Our Presidents and Their Hymns* (Macon, GA: Mercer Univ. Press, 2008), p. 165.
89. Kenneth B. Morris Jr., "New Shoes," public talk, Frederick Douglass Memorial and Historical Association Public Meeting, Washington, DC, September 15, 2007.

90. Kirk, *Music at the White House*, p. 365.
91. Deborah McNally, "Marie Selika," Blackpast.org Web site: www.blackpast.org/?q=aah/williams-marie-selika-c-1849-1937.
92. "Madame Marie Selika: First African American to Perform at the White House." See Ohio's Yesterdays Web site: http://ohiosyesterdays.blogspot.com/2009/01/madame-marie-selika-first-african.html.
93. Kirk, *Music at the White House*, p. 365.
94. Ibid., pp. 151–152; and African American Registry Web site: www.aaregistry.com/detail.php?id=1232.
95. Kirk, *Music at the White House*, p. 229. See also Marian Anderson, *My Lord, What a Morning; an Autobiography* (New York: Viking Press, 1956); Jerri Ferris, *What I Had Was Singing: The Story of Marian Anderson* (Minneapolis: Carolrhoda Books, 1994); and Allan Keiler, *Marian Anderson: A Singer's Journey* (New York: Lisa Drew/Scribner, 2000).
96. Kirk, *Music at the White House*, p. 230.
97. Ibid., p. 308.
98. Ibid., p. 342.
99. "Biography of Grace Bumbry." Kennedy Center Web site: www.kennedy-center.org/calendar/index.cfm?fuseaction=showIndividual&entity_id=56004&source_type=A.
100. Ibid.
101. Anne Midgette, " 'Always in Ccharacter Onstage,' " *Washington Post*, December 6, 2009.
102. Alonzo Fields, *My 21 Years at the White House* (New Castle, DE: Coward-McCann, 1961).
103. "White House Staff: Then & Now. Alonzo Fields." See Harry S. Truman Library and Museum Web site: www.trumanlibrary.org/educ/fields1.htm.
104. Ibid.
105. "21 Years in the White House," *Ebony*, October 1982, p. 62.
106. Fields, *My 21 Years*, p. 14.
107. "Alonzo Fields," Truman Library and Museum Web site.
108. "21 Years in the White House" (*Ebony*), p. 66.
109. Ibid., p. 64.
110. Ibid, p. 62.
111. Ibid.
112. "Maitre d' to Presidents John Ficklin Retires; Guest At White House," *Jet*, August 15, 1983, p. 24.
113. Bob Dart, "Ex–White House Butler Takes Seat as Honored Guest," *Sunday Star News* (Wilmington, DE), July 24, 1983.
114. "The Working White House," White House Historical Association Web site: www.whitehousehistory.org/whha_exhibits/working_whitehouse/d3_working-family_c.html.
115. Lillian Rogers Parks, *My Thirty Years Backstairs at the White House* (Mountain View, CA: Ishi Press, 2008)
116. Robert Thomas, "Lillian Parks, 100, Dies; Had 'Backstairs' White House View," *New York Times*, November 12, 1997.
117. Milton S. Katz, "E. Frederick [*sic*] Morrow and Civil Rights in the Eisenhower Administration," *Phylon*, Vol. 42, No. 2, 2nd Quarter, 1981), p. 133.
118. O'Reilly, *Nixon's Piano*, p. 167; Katz, "Morrow and Civil Rights," p. 133.
119. Katz, "Morrow and Civil Rights," p. 134.

120. Ibid, pp. 134–135.
121. Ibid, pp. 136–137.
122. Ibid., p. 137.
123. Ibid., p. 141.
124. Katz, p. 143.

Chapter 7

1. Stokely Carmichael, "What We Want," in Jonathan Birnbaum and Clarence Taylor, *Civil Rights Since 1787: A Reader on the Black Struggle* (New York: New York Univ. Press, 2000), p. 612.
2. Abraham Bolden, *The Echo From Dealey Plaza: The True Story of the First African American on the White House Secret Service Detail and His Quest for Justice After the Assassination of JFK* (New York: Harmony Books, 2008), p. 26.
3. See House Select Committee on Assassinations (HSCA) Vol. X, pp. 161, 172–175, 193; HSCA 180-10070–10273; HSCA 180-10070–10276; HSCA 180-10080–10154; Warren Commission internal memo dated 4-30-64; Warren Commission document 117; and Warren Commission, Vol. XXV.
4. The Kennedy Records Act mandated that that all assassination-related material be housed in a single collection in the National Archives and Records Administration. See President John F. Kennedy Assassination Records Collections Act. Access Reports Web site: www.accessreports.com/statutes/JFK.ACT.htm; Lamar Waldron, *Ultimate Sacrifice: John and Robert Kennedy, the Plan for a Coup in Cuba, and the Murder of JFK* (New York: Carroll & Graf Publishers, 2005), pp. 258–259, 620–621, 632–633; and Lamar Waldron and Thom Hartmann, "After 45 Years, a Civil Rights Hero Waits for Justice," June 12, 2009, Huffington Post Web site: www.huffingtonpost.com/thom-hartmann/after-45-years-a-civil-ri_b_213834.html.
5. Philip H. Melanson, *The Secret Service: The Hidden History of an Enigmatic Agency* (New York: Carroll & Graf Publishers, 2005), p. 10.
6. See Ronald Kessler, *In the President's Secret Service: Behind the Scenes with Agents in the Line of Fire and the Presidents They Protect* (New York: Crown, 2009).
7. See James Farmer, *Lay Bare the Heart: An Autobiography of the Civil Rights Movement* (New York: Arbor House, 1985).
8. Taylor Branch, *Parting the Waters: America in the King Years, 1954–63* (New York: Simon and Schuster, 1988), p. 470.
9. Bolden, *Echo From Dealey Plaza*, p. 17.
10. Ibid., p. 16.
11. Ibid., p. 5.
12. Ibid., p. 37.
13. Ibid., pp. 23–24.
14. Ibid., 19.
15. Ibid., pp. 34–35.
16. See Wilson Fallin, *The African American Church in Birmingham, Alabama, 1815–1963: A Shelter in the Storm* (New York: Taylor & Francis, 1997).
17. United Press International, "Six Dead After Church Bombing," September 16, 1963, Washington Post Web site: www.washingtonpost.com/wp-srv/national/longterm/churches/archives1.htm.

18. Ibid., Waldron, *Ultimate Sacrifice*, pp. 595–651.
19. Ibid., pp. 652–665.
20. Bolden, *Echo From Dealey Plaza*, p. 161.
21. Ibid., pp. 194–200.
22. Waldron, *Ultimate Sacrifice*, pp. 4, 795–796; and Waldron and Hartmann, "A Civil Rights Hero Waits."
23. Waldron, *Ultimate Sacrifice*, p. 2.
24. Lamar Waldron and Thom Hartmann, "After 40 Years, the First National Security Whistleblower Still Seeks Justice," Common Dreams, *February 17, 2006, http://www.commondreams.org/views06/0217-20.htm.*
25. Ibid.
26. "Secret Service agents claim White House turning blind eye to racism," October 26, 2004. See Narcosphere Web site: http://narcosphere.narconews.com/notebook/bill-conroy/2004/10/secret-service-agents-claim-white-house-turning-blind-eye-racism.
27. "Black Agents of the Secret Service Demand Attention to Still-Unaddressed Class Action Discrimination Suit Filed in 2000," *Business Wire*, October 22, 2004.
28. Conroy, "White House turning blind eye to racism."
29. Moore was one of the agents called by Kenneth Starr to testify in the Monica Lewinsky case.
30. Mark Hosenball and Eve Conant, "A Secret Side to the Secret Service," *Newsweek*, June 2, 2008.
31. Conroy, "White House turning blind eye to racism."
32. Ibid.
33. Ibid.
34. David Johnston, "E-Mail Shows Racial Jokes by Secret Service Supervisors," *New York Times*, May 10, 2008.
35. Ibid.
36. Jim Spellman and Jeanne Meserve, "Secret Service Probes Alleged Noose Incident," CNN, May 2, 2008.
37. Ibid.
38. Ibid., Hosenball and Conant, "Secret Side."
39. Amy Argetsinger and Roxanne Roberts, "Secret Service Confirms Third Crasher at White House State Dinner, *Washington Post*, January 5, 2010.
40. C. Vann Woodward, "The Political Legacy of Reconstruction," *Journal of Negro Education* 26, Summer 1957, pp. 231–240. See also Gary Donaldson, *The Second Reconstruction: A History of the Modern Civil Rights Movement* (Malabar, FL: Kreiger, 2000); and Manning Marable, *Race, Reform, and Rebellion: The Second Reconstruction in Black America, 1945–1990* (Jackson, MS: Univ. Press of Mississippi, 1991).
41. Christopher Booker, *African Americans and the Presidency* (New York: Franklin Watts, 2000), p. 122.
42. Branch, *Parting the Waters*, p. 837.
43. Kenneth O'Reilly, *Black Americans: The FBI Files* (New York: Carroll & Graf Publishers, 1994), p. 28.
44. Thomas C. Reeves, *A Question of Character: A Life of John F. Kennedy* (New York: The Free Press, 1991), p. 359.

45. Clayborne Carson, David J. Garrow, Vincent Harding, and Darlene Clark Hine, eds., *Eyes on the Prize: America's Civil Rights Years* (New York: Penguin, 1987).
46. "SNCC Position Paper: Vietnam," in Judith Clavir Albert and Steward Edward Albert, *The Sixties Papers: Documents of a Rebellious Decade* (New York: Praeger, 1984), p. 118.
47. Martin Luther King Jr., "A Time to Break Silence," in Philip S. Foner, ed., *The Voice of Black America: Major Speeches by Negroes in the United States, 1797–1971* (New York: Simon & Schuster, 1972), p. 1051.
48. James Boggs, *Racism and the Class Struggle: Further Pages From a Black Worker's Notebook* (New York: Monthly Review Press, 1970), pp. 39–45.
49. Stephen G. Spottwood, "The Nixon Administration's Anti-Negro Policy" in Philip S. Foner, ed., *The Voice of Black America: Major Speeches by Negroes in the United States, 1797–1973* (New York: Capricorn Books, 1975), p. 560.
50. Booker, *African Americans and the Presidency*, p. 141.
51. Cited in Ward Churchill and Jim Vander Wall, *The COINTELPRO Papers: Documents From the FBI's Secret Wars Against Dissent in the United States* (Boston: South End Press, 1990), p. 92.
52. Ibid., pp. 303–328.
53. William L. Clay, *Just Permanent Interests: Black Americans in Congress, 1870–1991* (New York: Amistad Press, 1992), pp. 139–157.
54. Bob Herbert, "Impossible, Ridiculous, Repugnant," *New York Times*, October 6, 2005.
55. Kevin Phillips, *The Emerging Republican Majority* (New York: Arlington House, 1969).
56. James Boyd, "Nixon's Southern strategy: 'It's All In the Charts,' " *New York Times*, May 17, 1970.
57. Mike Allen, "RNC Chief to Say It Was 'Wrong' to Exploit Racial Conflict for Votes," *Washington Post*, July 14, 2005.
58. Ronnie Bernard Tucker, *Affirmative Action, the Supreme Court, and Political Power in the Old Confederacy* (Lanham, MD: University Press of America, 2000), pp. 80–82.
59. Leon Newton, "The Role of Black Neo-Conservatives During President Ronald Reagan's Administration," in Anthony J. Eksterowicz and Glenn P. Hastedt, eds., *White House Studies Compendium*, Vol. 6 (New York: Nova Science Publishers, Inc., 2008), p. 10.
60. Manning Marable, *Blackwater: Historical Studies in Race, Class Consciousness, and Revolution* (Dayton, OH: Black Praxis Press, 1981), p. 160–161.
61. See Jane Mayer and Jill Abramson, *Strange Justice: The Selling of Clarence Thomas* (Orlando, FL: Houghton Mifflin, 1994).
62. See Clarence Lusane, *Pipe Dream Blues: Racism and the War on Drugs* (Boston: South End Press, 1991).
63. James Fellner, *Decades of Disparity: Drug Arrests and Race in the United States* (New York: Human Rights Watch, March 2009), p. 16.
64. William Sabol and Heather Couture, *Prison Inmates at Midyear 2007* (Washington, DC: U.S. Department of Justice, Bureau of Justice Statistics, June 2008), p. 7.
65. Toni Morrison, "Talk of the Town: Comment," *The New Yorker*, October 5, 1998. See *New Yorker* Web site: www.newyorker.com/archive/1998/10/05/1998_10_05_031_TNY_LIBRY_000016504?currentPage=all.

66. See Gary Webb, *Dark Alliance: the CIA, the Contras, and the Crack Cocaine Explosion* (New York: Seven Stories Press, 1998).
67. For a timeline of the events, see Seven Stories Press Web site: www.sevenstories.com/closeup/index.cfm?page=Webb_timeline_1.html%22.
68. David Bositis, *Blacks and the 1992 National Democratic Convention* (Washington, DC: Joint Center for Political and Economic Studies, 1992), p. 29.
69. Laura Kipnis, "Condi's Inner Life: What Freudian slips do—or don't—tell us about politicians," April 26, 2004. See *Slate* Web site: www.slate.com/id/2099516.
70. "Sec. of State Rice: U.S. Has 'Birth Defect, About Race," The NPR News Blog, March 28, 2008. http://www.npr.org/blogs/news/2008/03/sec_of_state_rice_us_has_birth_1.html
71. "Interview with Editors," March 11, 2005. See *Washington Times* Web site: www.washingtontimes.com/news/2005/mar/11/20050311-102521-9024r/.
72. Dan Duray, "Rice Congratulates Obama Tearfully, Says She Is 'Especially Proud' of Obama," November 5, 2008. See *Huffington Post* Web site: www.huffingtonpost.com/2008/11/05/rice-congratulates-obama_n_141414.html.
73. Kathy Matheson, "Aretha Franklin, Condoleezza Rice Perform Duet For Charity," July 28, 2010 (Huffington Post Web site: www.huffingtonpost.com/2010/07/28/aretha-franklin-condoleez_n_662347.html); and Anne Midgette, "Condoleezza Rice, Aretha Franklin: A Philadelphia Show of a Little R-E-S-P-E-C-T," *Washington Post*, July 29, 2010.
74. Michael D. Shear, " 'Conservative Values' Guide Court Appointee," *Washington Post*, May 5, 2003; Ernesto Londoño, "Admission Attributed to Bush's Ex-Aide," *Washington Post*, March 14, 2006; "Domestic Policy Advisor Quits, White House Says," *Los Angeles Times*, February 10, 2006; and Faiz Shakir, "Friday Night Surprise: White House Aide Caught in Shoplifting Scheme," March 10, 2006, Think Progress Web site: http://thinkprogress.org/2006/03/10/claude-allen.
75. Dan Froomkin, "A Polling Free-Fall Among Blacks," *Washington Post*, October 13, 2005.
76. Matt Schudel, "Top Jazz Students Play Big Number: 1600 Penn.," *Washington Post*, June 16, 2009.
77. Stanley Dance, *The World of Duke Ellington* (Cambridge, MA: Da Capo Press, 2000), p. 283.
78. John Edward Hasse, *Beyond Category: The Life and Genius of Duke Ellington* (Da Capo Press, 1995), p. 374.
79. Elise K. Kirk, *Music at the White House: A History of the American Spirit* (Urbana, IL: Univ. of Illinois Press, 1986), p. 227.
80. Ibid., p. 264.
81. Ibid., p. 297.
82. Gary Giddens, *Satchmo* (New York: Doubleday, 1988), pp. 160–165.
83. Stephen R. Weissman, "Opening the Secret Files on Lumumba's Murder," *Washington Post*, July 21, 2002.
84. Kirk, *Music at the White House*, p. 315.
85. For an extended discussion of "jazz as democracy," see Kabir Sehgal, *Jazzocracy: Jazz, Democracy, and the Creation of a New American Mythology* (Mishawaka, IN: Better World Books, 2008).

86. See Michael H. Kater, *Different Drummers: Jazz in the Culture of Nazi Germany* (New York: Oxford Univ. Press, 1992); Gwen Ansell, *Soweto Blues: Jazz, Popular Music & Politics in South Africa* (New York: Continuum, 2004); Chris McGowan, *The Brazilian Sound: Samba, Bossa Nova, and the Popular Music of Brazil* (Philadelphia: Temple Univ. Press, 2009); Leonardo Acosta, *Cubano Be, Cubano Bop: One Hundred Years of Jazz in Cuba* (Washington, DC: Smithsonian Books, 2003); and Warren Pinckney Jr., "Jazz in India: Perspectives on Historical Development and Musical Acculturation," *Asian Music*, Autumn 1989–Winter 1990), pp. 35–77.
87. Robert McG. Thomas Jr., "Willis Conover Is Dead at 75; Aimed Jazz at the Soviet Bloc," *New York Times*, May 19, 1996.
88. Penny Marie Von Eschen, *Satchmo Blows Up the World: Jazz Ambassadors Play the Cold War* (Cambridge, MA: Harvard Univ. Press, 2004), p. 17.
89. Thomas, "Willis Conover Is Dead."
90. Joseph S. Nye, "Public Diplomacy and Soft Power," *The Annals of the American Academy of Political and Social Science*, Vol. 616, No. 1, 2008, p. 94.
91. Penny Von Eschen, *Race Against Empire: Black Americans and Anti-colonialism, 1937–1957* (Ithaca, NY: Cornell Univ. Press, 1997), p. 178).
92. Von Eschen, *Satchmo Blows Up the World.*
93. Ibid., p. 123.
94. Eric Porter, *What Is This Thing Called Jazz?: African American Musicians as Artists, Critics, and Activists* (Berkeley, CA: Univ. of California Press, 2002); Scott Saul, *Freedom Is, Freedom Ain't: Jazz and the Making of the Sixties* (Cambridge, MA: Harvard Univ. Press, 2003); John Litweiler, *The Freedom Principle: Jazz After 1958* (New York: Da Capo Press, 1984); John D. Baskerville, *The impact of Black Nationalist Ideology on American Jazz Music of the 1960s and 1970s* (Lewiston, NY: E. Mellen Press, c2003); and Frank Kofsky, *Black Nationalism and the Revolution in Music* (New York: Pathfinder Press, 1970).
95. Arguably, jazz or at least a precursor to it was heard at the White House when Scott Joplin's "Maple Leaf Rag" was performed by the Marine Band at the request of President Theodore Roosevelt's daughter Alice. Kirk, *Music at the White House*, p. 365.
96. "6 Jazzmen Play at White House; Young People's Program of First Lady Sets a Precedent," Top of Form*Bottom of FormNew York Times*, November 20, 1962.
97. Gardiner Harris, "The Underside of the Welcome Mat," *New York Times*, November 8, 2008.
98. Kirk, *Music at the White House*, p. 307.
99. Constance McLaughlin Green, *Washington: Capital City, 1879–1950* (Princeton, NJ: Princeton Univ. Press, 1963), vii–viii.
100. Mark Tucker, *Ellington: The Early Years* (Urbana, IL: Univ. of Illinois Press, 1995), p. 17.
101. Ibid., pp. 17–18; and Mercer Ellington, *Duke Ellington in Person: An Intimate Memoir* (Boston: Houghton Mifflin Company, 1978), pp. 7–8; and John Edward Hasse, *Beyond Category: The Life and Genius of Duke Ellington* (Boston: Da Capo Press, 1993), p. 23.
102. Richard Nixon, "Toast of the President at a Dinner Honoring Duke Ellington," White House, Washington, DC, April 29, 1969, American Presidency Project Web site: www.presidency.ucsb.edu/ws/index.php?pid=2025.

103. Bositis, *Blacks and the 1992 National Democratic Convention*, p. 29.
104. A. H. Lawrence, *Duke Ellington and His World: A Biography* (New York: Routledge, 2001), p. 377; and Leonard Garment, *Crazy Rhythm: My Journey From Brooklyn, Jazz, and Wall Street to Nixon's White House, Watergate, and beyond....* (New York: Times Books, 1997), p. 172.
105. Hasse, *Beyond Category*, p. 373.
106. Ibid.
107. Kirk, *Music at the White House*, p. 322.
108. Ibid., p. 343.
109. Ibid.
110. Richard Harrington, "Lionel Hampton's South Lawn Serenade," *Washington Post*, September 11, 1981.
111. William H. Honan, "Book Discloses That Reagan Planned to Kill National Endowment for Arts," *New York Times*, May 15, 1988.
112. Text of H.CON.RES 57:

Whereas, jazz has achieved preeminence throughout the world as an indigenous American music and art form, bringing to this country and the world a uniquely American musical synthesis and culture through the African-American experience and

1. makes evident to the world an outstanding artistic model of individual expression and democratic cooperation within the creative process, thus fulfilling the highest ideals and aspirations of our republic,
2. is a unifying force, bridging cultural, religious, ethnic and age differences in our diverse society,
3. is a true music of the people, finding its inspiration in the cultures and most personal experiences of the diverse peoples that constitute our Nation,
4. has evolved into a multifaceted art form which continues to birth and nurture new stylistic idioms and cultural fusions,
5. has had an historic, pervasive and continuing influence on other genres of music both here and abroad, and
6. has become a true international language adopted by musicians around the world as a music best able to express contemporary realities from a personal perspective;

Whereas, this great American musical art form has not yet been properly recognized nor accorded the institutional status commensurate with its value and importance;

Whereas, it is important for the youth of America to recognize and understand jazz as a significant part of their cultural and intellectual heritage;

Whereas, in as much as there exists no effective national infrastructure to support and preserve jazz;

Whereas, documentation and archival support required by such a great art form has yet to be systematically applied to the jazz field; and

Whereas, it is now in the best interest of the national welfare and all of our citizens to preserve and celebrate this unique art form;

Now, therefore be it Resolved by the House of Representatives (the Senate concurring), that it is the sense of the Congress that jazz is hereby designated as a rare and valuable national American treasure to which we should devote our attention, support and resources to make certain it is preserved, understood and promulgated.

113. Howard Reich, "Jazz at the White House Newport Stars, The Clintons And WTTW Celebrate America's Music," *Chicago Tribune*, September 12, 1993.
114. Peter Watrous, "Jazz at the White House: A Metaphor for Democracy (and a Help to the Boss)," *New York Times*, September 21, 1998.
115. Ibid.
116. "NEA Jazz Masters Honored At White House Event: A Salute to NEA Jazz Masters Celebrates Black Music Month," National Endowment for the Arts press release, Washington, DC, June 22, 2004.
117. Public Law 108-72. SEC. 6. Sense of Congress Regarding Jazz Appreciation Month.
    (a) FINDINGS- Congress finds the following:
    (1) On December 4, 1987, Congress approved House Concurrent Resolution 57, designating jazz as 'a rare and valuable national American treasure'.
    (2) Jazz has inspired some of the Nation's leading creative artists and ranks as one of the greatest cultural exports of the United States.
    (3) Jazz is an original American art form which has inspired dancers, choreographers, poets, novelists, filmmakers, classical composers, and musicians in many other kinds of music.
    (4) Jazz has become an international language that bridges cultural differences and brings people of all races, ages, and backgrounds together.
    (5) The jazz heritage of the United States should be appreciated as broadly as possible and should be part of the educational curriculum for children in the United States.
    (6) The Smithsonian Institution has played a vital role in the preservation of American culture, including art and music.
    (7) The Smithsonian Institution's National Museum of American History has established April as Jazz Appreciation Month to pay tribute to jazz as both a historic and living American art form.
    (8) The Smithsonian Institution's National Museum of American History has received great contributions toward this effort from other governmental agencies and cultural organizations.
    (b) SENSE OF CONGRESS It is the sense of Congress that—
    (1) the Smithsonian Institution's National Museum of American History should be commended for establishing a Jazz Appreciation Month; and
    (2) musicians, schools, colleges, libraries, concert halls, museums, radio and television stations, and other organizations should develop programs to explore, perpetuate, and honor jazz as a national and world treasure.
118. "Remarks by the First Lady at the White House Music Series: The Jazz Studio," Office of the First Lady, The White House, June 15, 2009.
119. Schudel, "Top Jazz Students.
120. "Remarks by the First Lady at the White House Music Series: The Jazz Studio," White House press release, Office of the First Lady, Washington, DC, June 15, 2009.

Chapter 8

1. "Declaration of the Rights of the Negro Race." See Universal Negro Improvement Association and African Communities League: http://www.unia-acl.org/archive/declare.htm.

2. Ibid, http://www.unia-acl.org/archive/anthem.htm.
3. "'Black House' for Capitol, [*sic*]" *New York Times*, August 18, 1920.
4. John Hope Franklin, *From Slavery to Freedom: A History of Negro Americans* (New York: Vintage Books, 1969), pp. 481–483. In a parallel development, race riots also broke out in the United Kingdom in Liverpool, London, and Cardiff during this same summer. In Cardiff, lynch mobs raided the black community and at least three people were killed and dozens were injured. http://www.nationalarchives.gov.uk/pathways/firstworldwar/spotlights/demobilisation.htm.
5. For a listing of all the cities where riots occurred, see "For Action on Race Riot Peril," *New York Times*, October 5, 1919.
6. David M. Kennedy, *Over Here: The First World War and American Society (NY: Oxford University Press, 2004),* 279, 281–2.
7. Mark I. Solomon, *The Cry Was Unity: Communists and African Americans, 1917-1936* (Jackson: University Press of Mississippi, 1998), pp. 3–21.
8. Garvey would later name of one of the ships he planned to use to ferry blacks to Africa the *Booker T. Washington.*
9. "Meeting Of The Universal Negro Improvement Association," http://www.initheba-beandsuckling.com/GARVEY.html.
10. Ibid.
11. Ibid.
12. Ibid.
13. Robert Hill, *The Marcus Garvey and Universal Improvement Association Papers: 27 August 1919 - 31 August 1920* (Berkeley: University of California Press, 1983), p. 35.
14. Ibid, p. 36.
15. Ibid, p. 38.
16. Ibid, p. 39. Robert Moten was Booker T. Washington's successor at the Tuskegee Institute.
17. Letter to Harry M. Daugherty, United States Attorney-General from Harry H. Pace and et al. Undated. Cited in Marcus Garvey and Amy Jacques Garvey, *Philosophy and Opinions of Marcus Garvey: or Africa for the Africans, Vol. 3* (New York: Routledge, 1967), pp. 294-300.
18. Ibid, Hill, p. 25; and "Report by Special Agent Mortimer J. Davis, January 6, 1923. Marcus Garvey website: http://www.marcusgarvey.com/wmview.php?ArtID=423.
19. The only major work on Callie House and the National Ex-Slave Mutual Relief, Bounty, and Pension Association has been done by civil rights activist and legal scholar Mary Frances Berry. *See* Mary Frances Berry, *My Face is Black is True: Callie House and the Struggle for Ex-Slave Reparation* (New York: Vintage Books, 2005).
20. Individuals over 70 years of age would get a lump sum of $500 and a monthly pension of $15. Those between 60 and 70 would receive a $300 lump sum and $12 monthly. Those between 50 and 60 would receive a $100 lump sum and $8 monthly. And finally, those under 50 would receive $4 monthly. As they aged, they would receive a corresponding increase in monthly pension. Ibid, p. 34.
21. Callie House letter to membership, undated. Cited in Mary Francis Berry, p. 78.
22. Ibid, Berry, p. 84.
23. For a discussion of the abuses of the Post Office, see Dorothy Garfield Fowler, *Unmailable: Congress and the Post Office* (Athens, GA: University of Georgia Press, 1977).

24. Ibid, Berry, p. 83.
25. Ibid, Kornweibel, p. 104.
26. Theodore Kornweibel Jr., *"Seeing Red": Federal Campaigns Against Black Militancy, 1919-1925* (Bloomington, IN: Indiana University Press, 1998), pp. 20–21, 46–47.
27. Ibid, p. 102.
28. BBC, "Interview with Martin Luther King, http://news.bbc.co.uk/2/hi/programmes/world_news_america/7838851.stm. Accessed July 26, 2009.
29. Shirley Chisholm, "It is Time for a Change," in Philip S. Foner, ed., *The Voice of Black America: Major Speeches by Negroes in the United States, 1797-1971* (New York: Simon and Schuster, 1972), p. 1153.
30. Ibid, 1156.
31. John Nichols, "Shirley Chisholm's Legacy," *The Nation*, January 3, 2005. See *The Nation* website: http://www.thenation.com/blogs/thebeat/2098.
32. Ibid, Nichols; and Peniel Joseph, *Dark Days, Bright Nights: From Black Power to Barack Obama* (New York: Basic Civitas Books, 2010), p. 188.
33. Ibid, Nichols. The first African American to receive votes for the presidential nomination at a major party convention was Frederick Douglass at the 1888 Republican National Convention. Rev. Channing Philips, a Washington, DC-based minister who led the DC delegation to the 1968 Democratic National Convention, had his name put in for the nomination and received 68 votes, thus becoming the first African American at the DNC to receive votes for nomination for the president.
34. James Haskins, *Fighting Shirley Chisholm* (New York: The Dial Press, 1975), pp. 167, 173.
35. Shirley Chisholm, *The Good Fight* (New York: Harper & Row, 1973), p. 3.
36. *See* Shirley Chisholm, *Unbought and Unbossed* (Orlando, FL: Houghton Mifflin, 1970).
37. Jesse Jackson, "A Chance to Serve," in *Jesse Jackson and Frank Clemente, Keep Hope Alive: Jesse Jackson's 1988 Presidential Campaign* (Boston: South End Press, 1989), p. 32.
38. For a critique of the rise and fall of the National Rainbow Coalition, see Sheila Collins, *The Rainbow Challenge: The Jackson Campaign and the Future of U.S. Politics* (New York: Monthly Review Press, 1987).
39. R.H. Melton and Richard Morin, "Wilder Taking Command in Va. Race, Polls Show," *Washington Post*, October 29, 1989.
40. Scott Keeter and Nilanthi Samaranayake, *Can You Trust What Polls Say about Obama's Electoral Prospects?*, Pew Research Center, 2007. See Pew Research Center website: http://pewresearch.org.
41. http://www.4president.org/speeches/dougwilder1992announcement.htm.
42. Dwayne Yancey, *When Hell Froze Over: The Untold Story of Doug Wilder, A Black Politician's Rise to Power in the South* (Dallas: Taylor Publishing, 1988), p. 34.
43. Robert Jordan, "Is the Jackson Political Era Ending?," *Boston Globe*, December 3, 1989.
44. Juan Williams, "One-Man Show," *Washington Post*, June 9, 1991.
45. David Mills, "Sister Souljah's Call to Arms," *Washington Post*, May 13, 1992.
46. Clinton also allowed the execution of a mentally retarded black man, Ricky Ray, on January 24, 1992, to burnish, many felt, his credentials with the law-and-order

crowd. Despite pleadings to commute his sentence to life in prison without the possibility of parole from Jackson, Rep. Charles Rangel (D-NY), the National Coalition Against the Death Penalty, the NAACP Legal Defense Fund and others, Clinton refused. Nat Hentoff, "Hard Line on the Death Penalty," *Washington Post*, March 21, 1992; and "Reverend Jesse Jackson and Rainbow Coalition Ask Clinton to Spare Rector," press release, National Rainbow Coalition, Chicago, January 24, 1993.

47. "Preacher ends another electoral bid," on CNN website: http://us.cnn.com/ELECTION/2004/special/president/candidates/sharpton.html.
48. Peter Wallsten, "Obama's New Partner: Al Sharpton," *Wall Street Journal*, March 17, 2010.
49. Ibid.
50. Sally Cragin, "Black Leaders Press Obama on Economic Help for African-Americans," *Boston Globe*, February 11, 2010.
51. Maureen O'Donnell, Panel Criticizes Obama's Handling of Black Agenda," *Chicago Sun-Times*, March 21, 2010.
52. Brigid Schulte, "Gingrich, Sharpton Finally Teammates: Close Education Gap," *Washington Post*, May 17, 2009.
53. David C. Ruffin, "Moseley Braun & Sharpton Eye Presidential Nominations; Funding is Likely to Be a Big Challenge for Both Campaigns, *Black Enterprise*, June 1, 2003, pp. 31-2.
54. For a listing of Helms most outrageous statements and behavior, see John Nichols, "Jesse Helms, John McCain and the Mark of the White Hands," *The Nation*, July 4, 2008. http://www.thenation.com/blogs/thebeat/334586.
55. See Karen L. Cox, *Dixie's Daughters: The United Daughters of the Confederacy and the Preservation of the Confederacy and the Preservation of Confederate Culture* (Gainsville: University of Florida, 2003).
56. All quotes are from Marc Fisher, "When Sexuality Undercuts a Family's Ties," *Washington Post*, February 13, 2005.
57. "Obama Wins Senate Race to Become 5th Black U.S. Senator in History," *USA Today*, November 2, 2004.
58. Ibid, Fisher.
59. Alan Keyes, "Obama's on the Verge of Outright Dictatorship. Loyal to Liberty: http://loyaltoliberty.com/.
60. Dizzy Gillespie, *Dizzy To Be Or Not To Bop: The Autobiography of Dizzy Gillespie* (London: Quartet Books Limited, 1982), p. 456.
61. Ibid, p. 453.
62. Ibid, p. 453.
63. Ibid, p. 454.
64. Ibid, pp. 454–457.
65. Ibid, p. 456.
66. See Kay Mills, *This Little Light of Mine: The Life of Fannie Lou Hamer* (New York: Dutton, 1993).
67. Fannie Lou Hamer, "Testimony Before the 1964 DNC Credentials Committee," in Jonathan Birnbaum and Clarence Taylor, eds, *Civil Rights Since 1787: A Reader on the Black Struggle* (New York: New York University Press, 2000), p. 522.
68. Ibid, pp. 522–523

69. John Dittmer, *Local People: The Struggle for Civil Rights in Mississippi* (Champaign, IL: University of Illinois Press, 1995).
70. John Fordham, "Dizzy for President," *Guardian*, October 20, 2004.
71. Ibid, Gillespie, p. 460.
72. Eldridge Cleaver, "Revolution in the White Mother Country and National Liberation in the Black Colony," in Philip S. Foner, ed., *The Voice of Black America: Major Speeches by Negroes in the United States, 1797-1971* (New York: Simon and Schuster, 1972), pp. 1104-1105.
73. Huey Newton, "In Defense of Self-Defense: Exeuctive Mandate Number One," in Philip Sheldon Foner and Clayborne Carson, eds., *The Black Panthers Speak* (New York: Da Capo Press, 2002), p. 41.
74. See Dan Georgakas and Marvin Surkin, Detroit: I Do Mind Dying: A Study in Urban Revolution (Cambridge, MA: South End Press, 1998); and Peniel E. Joseph, *Waiting 'til the Midnight Hour: A Narrative History of Black Power in America* (New York: Henry Holt and Co., 2006).
75. Eldridge Cleaver for President Fund, "Cleaver for President," *New York Times*, November 7, 1968.
76. See Eldridge Cleaver, *Soul on Fire* (New York: McGraw-Hill, 1968); Eldridge Cleaver, *Soul on Fire* (Waco, TX: Word Books, 1978); and; Robert Scheer, ed., *Eldridge Cleaver: Post-Prison Writings and Speeches*, (New York: Vintage Books, 1969).
77. John Kifner, "Eldridge Cleaver, Black Panther Who Became G.O.P. Conservative, Is Dead at 62," *New York Times*, May 2, 1998.
78. Bruce Headlam, "For Him, the Political Has Always Been Comical," *New York Times*, March 13, 2009.
79. Paul Krassner, *Who's to Say What's Obscene? Politics, Culture and Comedy in America Today* (San Francisco: City Lights Books, 2009), p. 35.
80. "Dick Gregory Biography." See AEI Speakers Bureau website: http://www.aeispeakers.com/print.php?SpeakerID=461.
81. Dick Gregory, *Write Me In!* (New York: Bantam Books, 1968), p. 24.
82. Ibid, p. 18.
83. Ibid, p. 49.
84. Ibid, p. 104.
85. Ibid, p. 58.
86. See Mark Lane and Dick Gregory, *Code Name "Zorro": The Murder of Martin Luther King, Jr.* (Englewood Cliffs, NJ: Prentice-Hall, 1977).
87. George E. Jordan, "Fulani Party Raises Funds Creatively," *New York Newsday*, April 6, 1992.
88. Marina Ortiz, "The New Alliance Party: Parasites in Drag," *The NY Planet,* March 31, 1993. The Public Eye website: http://www.publiceye.org/newman/critics/NY-Planet-1993.html.
89. Ibid, Jordan.
90. Ibid, Oritz.
91. For Fulani's own assessment of her campaigns, see Lenora B. Fulani, *The Making of a Fringe Candidate, 1992* (New York: Castillo International, 1992.)
92. Michael T. Martin and Marilyn Yaquinto, *Redress for Historical Injustices in the*

United States: On Reparations for Slavery, Jim Crow, and Their Legacies (Durham, NC: Duke University Press, 2007), pp. 602, 604.
93. Paulette Pierce, "The Roots of the Rainbow Coalition," *The Black Scholar*, March/April 1988, p. 9.
94. Ron Daniels, announce speech, October 14, 1991, Washington, DC.
95. Cynthia McKinney, "Acceptance Remarks," Green Party Convention, Chicago, Illinois, July 12, 2008. See Independent Political Report website: http://www.independentpoliticalreport.com/2008/07/mckinneys-acceptance-speech/.
96. David Garrow, *Bearing the Cross: Martin Luther King, Jr. and the Southern Christian Leadership Conference* (New York: Vintage Books, 1988), p. 553.
97. Peter John Ling, *Martin Luther King, Jr.* (New York: Routledge, 2002), 270.
98. Ibid, Garrow, p.558.
99. Ibid, p. 559.
100. http://www.yourdiscovery.com/top-20-ultimate-discovery/martin-luther-king-what-if/index.shtml.
101. See Colin Powell, *My American Journey: An Autobiography* (New York: Random House, 1995); and Clarence Lusane, *Colin Powell and Condoleezza Rice: Foreign Policy, Race and the New American Century* (Westport, CT: Praeger, 2006).
102. Colin Powell, *My American Journey* (New York: Ballentine, 1995), p. 19.
103. For more on the racial views of Powell and Condoleezza Rice, see Clarence Lusane, *Colin Powell and Condoleezza Rice: Foreign Policy, Race, and the New American Century* (Westport, CT: Prager, 2006).
104. Jane Mayer, "Whatever It Takes: The Politics of the Man Behind '24,'" *The New Yorker*, February 19, 2007. See *The New Yorker* website: http://www.newyorker.com/reporting/2007/02/19/070219fa_fact_mayer?printable=true#ixzz0f914fO1F.
105. Ibid, Mayer; and Human Rights Watch "Primetime Torture" project http://www.humanrightsfirst.org/us_law/etn/primetime/index.asp.
106. Scott Sonner, "Dennis Haysbert: I Helped Pave Obama's Way," Huffington Post, July 1, 2008. See Huffington Post website: http://www.huffingtonpost.com/2008/07/01/dennis-haysbert-i-paved-o_n_110359.html.

Chapter 9

1. Thomas D. Morris, *Free Men All: The Personal Liberty Laws of the North: 1780–1861* (Baltimore: The Johns Hopkins Univ. Press, 1974), pp. 5, 130.
2. Most of the ancestral data cited here regarding Michelle Obama comes from research by genealogist Megan Smolenyak Smolenyak and researchers at the *New York Times*. Data cited here comes from that research unless otherwise cited. See Rachel L. Swarns and Jodi Kantor, "In First Lady's Roots, a Complex Path From Slavery," *New York Times*, October 7, 2009.
3. W. E. B. Du Bois, *Black Reconstruction: An Essay Toward a History of the Part Which Black Folk Played in the Attempt to Reconstruct Democracy in America, 1860–1880* (New York: Oxford Univ. Press, 2007) p. 44.
4. Henry Louis Gates, "Shared Ancestries Revealed," *New York Times*, October 8, 2009.
5. Richard Schneirov and Thomas J. Suhrbur, *Union Brotherhood, Union Town: The History of the Carpenters' Union of Chicago, 1863–1987* (Carbondale, IL: Southern Illinois Univ. Press, 1988), p. 156.

6. Ibid., p. 157.
7. Ibid., p. 158.
8. See Mattias Gardell, *In the Name of Elijah Muhammad: Louis Farrakhan and the Nation of Islam* Durham, NC: Duke Univ. Press, 1996).
9. The other individual was Republican senator Edward Brooke of Massachusetts (1967–1979).
10. Shailagh Murray, "A Family Tree Rooted in American Soil: Michelle Obama Learns About Her Slave Ancestors, Herself and Her Country," *Washington Post*, October 2, 2008.
11. Pete Thamel, "Coach With a Link to Obama Has Hope for Brown's Future," *New York Times*, February 16, 2007.
12. For more on Craig Robinson, see Craig Robinson, *A Game of Character: A Family Journey From Chicago's Southside to the Ivy League and Beyond* (New York: Penguin, 2010).
13. Michelle LaVaughn Robinson, "Princeton Educated Blacks and the Black Community," B.A. thesis, Princeton University, Princeton, New Jersey, 1985, pp. 12–13.
14. BBC, "Interview with Martin Luther King, http://news.bbc.co.uk/2/hi/programmes/world_news_america/7838851.stm. Accessed July 26, 2009.
15. Ibid.
16. Ibid.
17. Ibid.
18. See David Garrow, *Bearing the Cross: Martin Luther King, Jr., and the Southern Christian Leadership Conference* (New York: Harper, 2004); and Charles E. Fager, *Selma 1965: The March That Changed the South* (Boston: Beacon Press, 1985).
19. Joseph Loftus, "U.S. Tells World of Rights Strife," *New York Times*, May 27, 1961.
20. Barack Obama, "Remarks of Illinois State Sen. Barack Obama Against Going to War with Iraq," speech at Chicago Anti-War Rally, October 2, 2002. See Organizing for America Web site: http://www.barackobama.com/2002/10/02/remarks_of_illinois_state_sen.php
21. Robert Freeman, "The Bush Budget Deficit Death Spiral," Common Dreams, October 22, 2004. See commondreams.org: http://www.commondreams.org/views04/1022-26.htm; and "White House Projects Record Deficit for 2009," CNN, July 28, 2009. See CNN.com http://edition.cnn.com/2008/POLITICS/07/28/2009.deficit/index.html.
22. During the long campaign, Clinton's changing slogans of change included "Working for Change, Working for You," "The Strength and Experience to Make Change Happen," "The Change We Need," and "Ready for Change, Ready to Lead." R. Sebastian Gibson, "The Marketing Of Presidential Candidates Using Trademarks and Campaign Slogans," October 24, 2008, HG.org Web site: www.hg.org/article.asp?id=5600.
23. Chuck Todd and Sheldon Gawiser, *How Barack Obama Won: A State-By-State Guide to the Historic 2008 Presidential Election* (New York: Vintage Books, 2009), p. 10.
24. Chris Kromm, "Analysis: A New South Rising," *Facing South*, November 23, 2008; and Chris Kromm, "Election 2008: The Generation Gap: Young white voters in the South," *Facing South*, November 12, 2008.
25. Barack Obama, *Dreams from My Father: A Story of Race and Inheritance* (New York: Three Rivers Press, 2004).

26. "Hillary's Team Has Questions About Obama's Muslim Background," *Insight*, January 17, 2007. Republished on WorldTribune.com.
27. "CNN debunks false report about Obama," CNN, January 23, 2007; and editorial, "Sticks, Stones and Mr. Obama," *Washington Post*, January 28, 2007.
28. Fox Butterfield, "First Black Elected to Head Harvard's Law Review," *New York Times*, February 6, 1990. www.nytimes.com/1990/02/06/us/first-black-elected-to-head-harvard-s-law-review.html.
29. David Nitkin and Harry Merritt, "A New Twist to an Intriguing Family History: Census Records, Genealogical Research Show Forebears of Obama's Mother Had Slaves," *Baltimore Sun*, March 2, 2007.
30. See Ta-Nehisi Paul Coates, "Is Obama Black Enough?," *Time*, February 1, 2007; Gary Younge, "Is Obama black enough?," *The Guardian*, March 1, 2007; and Satta Sarmah, "Is Obama Black Enough?," *Columbia Journalism Review*, February 15, 2007.
31. Stanely Crouch, "What Obama Isn't: Black Like Me," *Daily News*, November 2, 2006.
32. Debra J. Dickerson, "Colorblind: Barack Obama would be the great black hope in the next presidential race—if he were actually black," *Salon*, January 22, 2007. See Salon Web site: www.salon.com/news/opinion/feature/2007/01/22/obama.
33. Eugene Robinson, "An Inarticulate Kickoff," *Washington Post*, February 2, 2007.
34. While serving as president of the United States, Obama declared he was "black" in the 2010 U.S. Census. On April 2, 2010, the *New York Times* published an article about this, saying: "It is official: Barack Obama is the nation's first black president. A White House spokesman confirmed that Mr. Obama, the son of a black father from Kenya and a white mother from Kansas, checked African-American on the 2010 census questionnaire.

    "The president, who was born in Hawaii and raised there and in Indonesia, had more than a dozen options in responding to Question 9, about race. He chose 'Black, African Am., or Negro.' (The anachronistic 'Negro' was retained on the 2010 form because the Census Bureau believes that some older blacks still refer to themselves that way.)

    "Mr. Obama could have checked white, checked both black and white, or checked the last category on the form, 'some other race,' which he would then have been asked to identify in writing.

    "There is no category specifically for mixed race or biracial." Sam Roberts and Peter Baker, "Asked to Declare His Race, Obama Checks 'Black,' " *New York Times*, April 2, 2010. See www.nytimes.com/2010/04/03/us/politics/03census.html.
35. In the kind of biographical racial twist that could perhaps only be produced in the United States, the future first black president is related both to former vice president Dick Cheney and to former president Harry Truman. See Bob Neer, *Barack Obama for Beginners: An Essential Guide* (Hanover, NH: Steerforth Press, 2008), p. 3.
36. Barack Obama, *Dreams from My Father: A Story of Race and Inheritance*, (New York: Times Books, 1995), p. 44.
37. The speech was titled "Audacity of Hope," which became the title of his second best-selling book. Barack Obama, "Audacity of Hope," Democratic National Convention,

Boston, July 27, 2004. See Barack Obama, *The Audacity of Hope: Thoughts on Reclaiming the American Dream* (New York: Three Rivers Press, 2006).

38. Brian Ross and Rehab El-Buri, "Obama's Pastor: God Damn America, U.S. to Blame for 9/11," ABC News, March 13, 2008: http://abcnews.go.com/Blotter/DemocraticDebate/story?id=4443788&page=1.
39. Adia Harvey Wingfield and Joe R. Feagin, *Yes We Can?: White Racial Framing and the 2008 Presidential Campaign* (New York: Routledge, 2010), p. 130.
40. Speech by Malcolm X, December 4, 1963. See http://www.malcolm-x.org/speeches/spc_120463.htm
41. Ross and El-Buri,"Obama's Pastor."
42. For a glimpse of the lines of the debate, see Ishmael Reed, "Going Old South on Obama: Ma and Pa Clinton Flog Uppity Black Man," *Counterpunch*, January 14, 2008: www.counterpunch.org/reed01142008.html; and Gloria Steinhem, "Women Are Never Front-Runners," *New York Times*, January 8, 2008.
43. "McCain Responds to 'Arab' Epithet at Rally: 'Obama a Decent Family Man,' " October 10, 2008. See Huffington Post: www.huffingtonpost.com/the-uptake/mccain-responds-to-arab-a_b_133820.html.
44. "Racism and Vitriol at Palin Rally in Jonestown, PA," *Salon*, October 13, 2008. See Opensalon.com: http://open.salon.com/blog/keystone_progress/2008/10/13/racism_and_vitriol_at_palin_rally_in_johnstown_pa.
45. Dana Milbank, "Unleashed, Palin Makes a Pit Bull Look Tame," *Washington Post*, October 7, 2008.
46. Dana Milbank, "Rage in the Town of Bethlehem," *Washington Post*, October 9, 2008.
47. Tim Shipman, "Sarah Palin Blamed by the US Secret Service Over Death Threats Against Barack Obama," *The Telegraph* (UK), November 8, 2008.
48. The following articles are sources for all the quotes in this paragraph. Peter Wallsten, "Frank Talk of Obama and Race in Virginia," *Los Angeles Times*, October 05, 2008; "GOP Club Offers 'Obama Bucks' While Democrats Rib Palin," *Los Angeles Times*, October 17, 2008; Helen Kennedy, "GOP Activist DePass Apologizes After Joking on Facebook That Gorilla Is Related to Michelle Obama," *New York Daily News*, June 15, 2009; Tony Barboza, "Dean Grose to Quit as Los Alamitos Mayor Over Racial Cartoon," *Los Angeles Times*, February 28, 2009.
49. John Amato and David Neiwet, "How Obama's Election Drove the American Right Insane," *Alternet*, May 27, 2010. See Alternet Web site: www.alternet.org/story/146963. Also, John Amato and David Neiwet, *Over the Cliff: How Obama's Election Drove the American Right Insane* (Sausalito, CA: Polipoint Press, 2010).
50. Juan Williams, "What Obama's Victory Means for Racial Politics," *Wall Street Journal*, November 10, 2008.
51. Jody Herman and Lorraine Minnite, "The Demographics of Voters in America's 2008 General Election: A Preliminary Assessment," Research Memo, Project Vote, November 18, 2008: www.projectvote.org.
52. Matt Bai, "Is Obama the End of Black Politics?," *New York Times*, August 6, 2008.
53. Peter Wallsten and David G. Savage, "Conservatives invoke Obama in Voting Rights Act challenge," *Los Angeles Times*, March 18, 2009.

54. Robert Barnes, "High Court to Weigh Relevance of Voting Law in Obama Era," *Washington Post*, April 1, 2009.
55. Ewen MacAskill, "Jimmy Carter: Animosity towards Barack Obama is due to racism," *The Guardian*, September 16, 2009.
56. Zachary Roth, "Tea Party Fundraising Email Shows Obama as Pimp," TPM-Muckraker.com, January 28, 2010. See Talking Points Memo Web site: http://tpmmuckraker.talkingpointsmemo.com/2010/01/tea_party_fundraising_email_shows_obama_as_pimp.php?ref=fpb.
57. Ezra Klein, "Rush Limbaugh: Health-care Reform is 'Reparations,' a 'Civil Rights Act,' " *Washington Post*, February 22, 2010.
58. *Fox & Friends*, Fox News, July 28, 2009.
59. Paul Kane, "S.C.'s Wilson Rakes In $750,000 in Less Than 48 Hours; Opponent Tops $1 Million," *Washington Post*, September 11, 2009.
60. Tom McGeveran, "Toni Morrison's Letter to Obama," *The New York Observer*, January 28, 2008.
61. Barack Obama, speech, NAACP Annual Convention, New York, July 16, 2009.
62. See Frank Rich, "Welcome to Confederate History Month," *New York Times*, April 17, 2010; and Eugene Robinson, "Haley Barbour's 'diddly' Sense of Slavery's History," *Washington Post*, April 13, 2010.
63. Karen Tumulty and Michael D. Shear, "Obama: Backing Muslims Right to Build NYC Mosque is Not an Endorsement," *Washington Post*, August 15, 2010; Chris Cillizza, "Democrats Divided Over Proposed New York City Mosque, *Washington Post*, August 17, 2010; and Erica Werner, "Obama Defends Ground Zero Mosque Plans in Ramadan Dinner," August 13, 2010. See Huffington Post website: http://www.huffingtonpost.com/2010/08/13/obama-defends-ground-zero-mosque_n_682064.html.
64. See Naomi Klein, "Minority Death Match: Jews, Blacks, and the 'Post-racial' Presidency," *Harper's Magazine*, September 2009.
65. Daisy Hernandez, "Don't Call Me Racist, and Other Arizona Lies," *Colorlines*, April 27, 2010. See Colorlines website: http://colorlines.com/archives/2010/04/dont_call_me_racist_and_other_arizona_lies.html; and Randal C. Archibold, "Judge Blocks Arizona's Immigration Law," *New York Times*, July 28 2010.
66. "Lecture: 'A Latina Judge's Voice,'" *New York Times*, May 14, 2009; and "Sotomayor's 'wise Latina' Comment a Staple of Her Speeches," CNN, June 8, 2009. See CNN website: http://www.cnn.com/2009/POLITICS/06/05/sotomayor.speeches/.
67. "New Black Panther Hysteria," *Think Progress*, July 8, 2010. See Think Progress website: http://thinkprogress.org/search/search.php?q=new+black+panther+hysteria.
68. "Fox & Friends," Fox News, July 28, 2009.
69. CNN, "Obama: Police who arrested professor 'acted stupidly,' " July 23, 2009, www.cnn.com/2009/US/07/22/harvard.gates.interview/index.html.
70. Shelby Steele, "From Emmett Till to Skip Gates," *Wall Street Journal*, August 1, 2009. Also see Shelby Steele, *A Bound Man: Why We Are Excited About Obama and Why He Can't Win* (New York: Free Press, 2007).
71. For the most detailed assessment of the event and its racial, legal, and political implications, see Charles Ogletree, *The Presumption of Guilt: The Arrest of Henry Louis Gates, Jr. and Race, Class and Crime in America* (New York: Palgrave Macmillan, 2010).

72. Nicholas Graham, "Obama on Skip Gates Arrest: Police Acted 'Stupidly,' " Huffington Post, July 22, 2009. See Huffington Post Web site: www.huffingtonpost.com/2009/07/22/obama-on-skip-gates-arres_n_243250.html.
73. Patrik Jonsson, "Shirley Sherrod: Casualty of Escalating 'Tea Party'-NAACP Race Spat?," *Christian Science Monitor*, July 20, 2010.
74. Reportedly, the initial proposal had condemned the tea party movement itself as racist but then was watered down. The full text of the resolution was not revealed to the public because it required approval by the NAACP National Board of Directors that was scheduled to meet in October 2010.
75. Clarence Page, "Tea Party Owes NAACP a Big Thank You," *Los Angeles Times*, July 26, 2010.
76. Julie Pace, "AP Exclusive: USDA Racial Flap Reconstructed," Associated Press, August 4, 2010. See NPR Web site: http://www.npr.org/templates/story/story.php?storyId=128969052
77. David Corn, "The Sad Tale of Shirley Sherrod: Vilsack Is the Villain," *PoliticsDaily*, July 21, 2010. See PoliticsDaily Web site: www.politicsdaily.com/2010/07/21/the-sad-tale-of-shirley-sherrod-vilsack-is-the-villain.
78. Ibid, Pace.
79. Ibid.
80. NAACP, "NAACP Statement on Shirley Sherrod Resignation," press release, July 20, 2010.
81. See "Shirley Sherrod: the FULL video" at NAACP Web site: www.naacp.org/news/entry/video_sherrod.
82. Ibid.
83. Marcus K. Garner and Christian Boone, "USDA Reconsiders Firing of Ga. Official Over Speech on Race, *Atlanta Journal-Constitution*, July 21, 2010.
84. Chris Kromm, "The Real Story of Racism at the USDA," Institute of Southern Studies, July 22, 2010. See Institute of Southern Studies Web site: www.southernstudies.org/2010/07/the-real-story-of-racism-at-usda.html.
85. Ibid., Kromm.
86. *A Time to Act: A Report of the USDA National Commission on Small Farms* (Washington, DC: U.S. Department of Agriculture, National Commission on Small Farms, 1998), unnumbered. See USDA Web site: http://www.csrees.usda.gov/nea/ag_systems/pdfs/time_to_act_1998.pdf.
87. Jim Kavanagh, "Sherrod's Steadfast Motto: 'Let's Work Together,'" CNN, July 22, 2010. See CNN website: http://ac360.blogs.cnn.com/2010/07/21/sherrods-steadfast-motto-lets-work-together/.
88. Mary Frances Berry, *My Face Is Black Is True* (New York: Vintage Books, 2005), p. 11.
89. Ibid., p. 12.
90. Kromm, "The Real Story."
91. Berry, *My Face Is Black*, p. 12.
92. Ibid.
93. Kromm, "The Real Story."
94. Ibid.
95. Ibid.

96. Thomas J. Vilsack, "A New Civil Rights Era for USDA," Memo to All USDA Employees, Office of the Secretary, United States Department of Agriculture, April 21, 2009.
97. Ben Evans, "Obama to Propose $1.25B for Black Farmers," *Associated Press*, May 6, 2009.
98. "Open Letter From Shirely Sherrod: You and I Can't Yield –Not Now, Not Ever," NAACP, Web site, undated. See NAACP Web site: http://www.naacp.org/news/entry/you-and-i-cant-yield-not-now-not-ever/; and Terrance Heath, "Dear Obama, Learn From Shirley Sherrod and Stop Letting the Right-Wing Propaganda Machine Win," *AlterNet*, July 22, 2010. See AlterNet Web site: www.alternet.org/story/147607.
99. Ibid, "Open Letter From Shirley Sherrod;" and Will Bunch, "The Story Behind the 1965 Killing of Sherrod's Dad," HuffingtonPost.com, July 21, 2010. See Huffington Post Web site: http://www.huffingtonpost.com/will-bunch/the-story-behind-the-1965_b_655218.html.
100. Margaret Burnham, "Sherrod's Father Still Needs Justice," *Atlanta Journal-Constitution*, August 3, 2010.
101. "NAACP Statement on the Resignation of Shirley Sherrod," press release, NAACP, July 20, 2010. See NAACP Web site: www.naacp.org/press/entry/naacp-statement-on-the-resignation-of-shirley-sherrod1.
102. Ralph Paige, "The Federation Sends Letter to USDA Secretary Vilsack," press release, Federation of Southern Cooperatives, July 21, 2010.
103. Gary Grant, "Shirley Sherrod and USDA Discrimination," press release, Black Farmers and Agriculturalists Association and the Land Loss Fund, Tillery, NC, July 21, 2010.
104. Willie Nelson, "Shirley Sherrod, A Family Farmer's Friend," Huffington Post, July 21, 2010. See Huffington Post Web site: http://www.huffingtonpost.com/willie-nelson/shirley-sherrod-a-family_b_654824.html
105. Heath, "Dear Obama."
106. Corn, "Sad Tale."
107. Sam Stein, "White House Apologizes to Shirley Sherrod," *Huffington Post*, July 21, 2010. See HuffingtonPost.com Web site: www.huffingtonpost.com/2010/07/21/gibbs-apologizes-to-shirl_n_654623.html.
108. Ibid.
109. Kara Rowland, "Obama Apologizes to Sherrod," *Washington Times*, July 22, 2010.
110. Ibid, "Open Letter From Shirley Sherrod."
111. Larry Elliott, "G7 Elite Group Makes Way for G20 and Emerging Nations," *The Guardian* (UK), October 4, 2009.
112. In addition to the states that comprised the G-7, the other thirteen powers are South Africa, Mexico, Argentina, Brazil, China, Japan, South Korea, India, Indonesia, Saudi Arabia, Russia, Turkey, and the European Union.

BIBLIOGRAPHY

Books

Acosta, Leonardo. *Cubano Be, Cubano Bop: One Hundred Years of Jazz in Cuba.* Washington, DC: Smithsonian Books, 2003.

Allen, William C. *History of Slave Laborers in the Construction of the U.S. Capitol.* Washington, DC: U.S. House of Representatives, Office of the Architect of the Capitol, 2005.

Anderson, Marian. *My Lord, What a Morning: An Autobiography.* New York: Viking Press, 1956.

Ansell, Gwen. *Soweto Blues: Jazz, Popular Music & Politics in South Africa.* New York: Continuum, 2004.

Aptheker, Herbert. *American Negro Slave Revolts.* New York: Columbia University Press, 1943; International Publishers, 1993.

Arnebeck, Bob. *Through a Fiery Trial: Building Washington 1790–1800.* Lanham, MD: Madison Books, 1991.

Badger, Reid. *A Life in Ragtime: A Biography of James Reese Europe.* New York: Oxford University Press, 1995.

Banat, Gabriel. *The Chevalier de Saint-Georges: Virtuoso of the Sword and the Bow.* Hillsdale, NY: Pendragon Press, 2006.

Barnes, Kenneth C. *Journey of Hope: The Back-to-Africa Movement in Arkansas in the Late 1800s.* Chapel Hill: University of North Carolina Press, 2004.

Baskerville, John D. *The Impact of Black Nationalist Ideology on American Jazz Music of the 1960s and 1970s.* Lewiston, NY: E. Mellen Press, 2003.

Basler, Roy P., ed. *The Collected Works of Abraham Lincoln*, 9 Volumes. New Brunswick, NJ: Rutgers University Press, 1953–55.

Basler, Roy Prentice and Carl Sandburg, eds. *Abraham Lincoln: His Speeches and Writings.* Cambridge, MA: Da Capo Press, 2001.

Bay, Mia. *To Tell the Truth Freely: The Life of Ida B. Wells.* New York: Macmillan, 2009.

Berlin, Ira. *The Wartime Genesis of Free Labor: The Lower South.* Cambridge, MA: Cambridge University Press, 1990.

Beeman, Richard. *Plain, Honest Men: The Making of the American Constitution.* New York: Random House, 2009.

Bell, Derrick. *And We Are Not Saved: The Elusive Quest for Racial Justice.* New York: Basic Books, 1987.

Bennett, Lerone Jr. *Before the Mayflower: A History of Black America.* Chicago: Johnson Publishing, 1987.

———. *Forced Into Glory: Abraham Lincoln's White Dream.* Chicago: Johnson, 2007.

Blackmon, Douglas A. *Slavery By Another Name, The Re-Enslavement of Black Americans from the Civil War to World War II.* New York: Anchor Books, Random House, 2008.

Blaustein, Albert P., and Robert L. Zangrando, eds. *Civil Rights and African Americans: A Documentary History/* Evanston, IL: Northwestern University Press, 1968.

Blockson, Charles. *The Liberty Bell Era: the African American Story*. Harrisburg, PA: RB Books, 2003.

Blumrosen, Alfred W. and Ruth G.Blumrosen. *Slave Nation: How Slavery United the Colonies & Sparked the American Revolution*. Naperville, IL: Sourcebooks, 2005.

Boggs, James. *Racism and the Class Struggle: Further Pages From a Black Worker's Notebook*. New York: Monthly Review Press, 1970.

Bolden, Abraham. *The Echo From Dealey Plaza: The True Story of the First African American on the White House Secret Service Detail and His Quest for Justice After the Assassination of JFK*. New York: Harmony Books, 2008.

Booker, Christopher. *African Americans and the Presidency*. New York: Franklin Watts, 2000.

Bradford, Sarah H. *Scenes in the Life of Harriet Tubman*. Auburn, NY: W. J. Moses, 1869.

———. *Harriet, The Moses of Her People*. New York: Geo. R. Lockwood & Son, 1886.

Branch, Taylor. *Parting the Waters: America in the King Years, 1954–63*. New York: Simon & Schuster, 1988.

Bryan, Helen. *Martha Washington: First Lady of Liberty*. (Hoboken, NJ: John Wiley, 2002).

Burin, Eric. *Slavery and the Peculiar Solution: A History of the American Colonization Society*. Gainsville: University Press of Florida, 2008.

Campbell, Stanley W. *The Slave Catchers: Enforcement of the Fugitive Slave Law, 1850–1860*. New York: W. W. Norton, 1972.

Carroll, Joseph Cephas. *Slave Insurrections in the United States, 1800–1865*. New York: New American Library, 1969.

Carson, Clayborne, David J. Garrow, Vincent Harding, and Darlene Clark Hine. eds. *Eyes on the Prize: America's Civil Rights Years*, New York: Penguin, 1987.

Castel, Albert. *The Presidency of Andrew Johnson*. Lawrence, KS: Regents Press of Kansas, 1979.

Cerami, Charles A. *Benjamin Benneker: Surveyor, Astronomer, Publisher, Patriot*. Hoboken, NJ: John Wiley, 2002.

Chisholm, Shirley. *Unbought and Unbossed*. Orlando, FL: Houghton Mifflin, 1970.

Christmas, Walter. *Negroes in Public Affairs and Government Educational Heritage*. Yonker, NY: Educational Heritage, 1966.

Cimbala, Paul A. *The Freedmen's Bureau: Reconstructing the American South After the Civil War*. Malabar, FL: Krieger Pub., 2005.

Cimbala, Paul A. and Randall M. Miller, eds.*The Freedmen's Bureau and Reconstruction: Reconsiderations*. New York: Fordham University Press, 1999.

Clay, William L. *Just Permanent Interests: Black Americans in Congress, 1870–1991*. New York: Amistad Press, 1992.

Clay-Clopton, Virginia and Ada Sterling. *A Belle of the Fifties: Memoirs of Mrs. Clay of Alabama, Covering Social and Political Life in Washington and the South, 1853–66*. New York: Doubleday, 1905.

Cleaver, Eldridge. *Soul on Ice*. New York: McGraw-Hill, 1968.

———. *Soul on Fire*. Waco, TX: Word Books, 1978.

Clifford, Mary Louise. *From Slavery to Freetown: Black Loyalists After the American Revolution*. Jefferson, NC: McFarland, 1999.

Collins, Sheila. *The Rainbow Challenge: The Jackson Campaign and the Future of U.S. Politics*. New York: Monthly Review Press, 1987.

Cox, Karen L. *Dixie's Daughters:The United Daughters of the Confederacy and the Preservation of Confederate Culture*. Gainesville: University of Florida, 2003.

Cutler, James E. *Lynch-Law: An Investigation into the History of Lynching in the United States*. New York: Negro Universities Press. 1969.

Dance, Stanley. *The World of Duke Ellington*. Cambridge, MA: Da Capo Press, 2000.

Dittmer, John. *Local People: The Struggle for Civil Rights in Mississippi*. Champaign: University of Illinois Press, 1995.

Doenecke, Justus D. *The Presidencies of James A. Garfield & Chester A. Arthur*. Lawrence, KS: Regents Press of Kansas, 1981.

Douglass, Frederick. *Life and Times of Frederick Douglass*. New York: Collier Books, 1962.

Dove, Rita. *Sonata Mulattica: A Life in Five Movements and a Short Play. New York: W. W. Norton, 2009.*

Du Bois, W. E. B. *Black Reconstruction: An Essay Toward a History of the Part Which Black Folk Played in the Attempt to Reconstruct Democracy in America, 1860–1880*. New York: Oxford University Press, 2007.

———. *Souls of Black Folks*. New York: Signet Classic, 1995.

Egerton, Donald. *Death or Liberty: African Americans and Revolutionary America*. New York: Oxford University Press, 2009.

Ellington, Mercer. *Duke Ellington in Person: An Intimate Memoir*. Boston: Houghton Mifflin, 1978.

Everett, Marshall. *Complete Life of William McKinley and Story of His Assassination*. Whitefish, MT: Kessinger, 2003.

Fager, Charles E. *Selma 1965: The March That Changed the South*. Boston: Beacon Press, 1985.

Fallin, Wilson. *The African American Church in Birmingham, Alabama, 1815–1963: A Shelter in the Storm*. New York: Taylor & Francis, 1997.

Farmer, James. *Lay Bare the Heart: An Autobiography of the Civil Rights Movement*. New York: Arbor House, 1985.

Fauntroy, Michael K. *Republicans and the Black Vote*. Boulder, CO: Lynne Rienner, 2007.

Fehrenbacher, Don Edward. *Slavery, Law, and Politics: The Dred Scott Case in Historical Perspective*. New York: Oxford University Press, 1981.

Fehrenbacher, Don E. and Virginia Fehrenbacher. Eds. *Recollected Words of Abraham Lincoln*, Palo Alto, CA: Stanford University Press, 1996.

Ferris, Jerri. *What I Had Was Singing: The Story of Marian Anderson*. Minneapolis: Carolrhoda Books, 1994.

Fields, Alonzo. *My 21 Years at the White House*. New Castle, DE: Coward-McCann, 1961.

Finkelman, Paul. *Dred Scott v. Sandford: A Brief History with Documents*. Boston: Bedford Books, 1997.

Finkelman, Paul. *An Imperfect Union: Slavery, Federalism, and Comity*. Buffalo, NY: Wm. S. Hein, 2000.

Fitzpatrick, John C., ed. *The Writings of George Washington*, Vol. 36. Washington, DC: United States Government Printing Office, 1933.

Fleischner, Jennifer. *Mrs. Lincoln and Mrs. Keckly: The Remarkable Story of the Friendship Between a First Lady and a Former Slave*. New York: Broadway Books, 2003.

Foner, Eric. *A Short History of Reconstruction*. New York: Harper & Row, 1990.

Foner, Eric, John Arthur Garraty, and Society of American Historians, eds. *The Reader's Companion to American History*. Orlando, FL: Houghton Mifflin Harcourt, 1991.

Foner, Philip S. *The Civil War, 1861–1865* (Vol. III of *The Life and Writings of Frederick Douglass*). New York: International Publishers, 1952.

Foner, Philip S. and George E. Walker, eds. *Proceedings of the Black State Conventions, 1840–1855*. Philadelphia: Temple University Press, 1980.

———. *Proceedings of the Black State Conventions, 1865–1900*. Philadelphia: Temple University Press, 1986.

Ford, Paul Leicester, ed. *Works of Thomas Jefferson*, Vol. 1. New York: G. P. Putnam's Sons, 1904.

Fox, Early Lee. *The American Colonization Society: 1817–1840*. New York: AMS Press, 1971.

Franklin, John Hope. *From Slavery to Freedom: A History of Negro Americans*. New York: Vintage Books, 1969.

Freedman, Suzanne. *Ida B. Wells-Barnett and the Antilynching Crusade*. Minneapolis: Millbrook Press, 1994.

Friedheim, William. *Freedom's Unfinished Revolution: An Inquiry into the Civil War and Reconstruction*. New York: New Press, 1996.

Frost, Karolyn Smardz. *I've Got a Home in Glory Land: A Lost Tale of the Underground Railroad*. New York: Macmillan, 2008.

Fulani, Lenora B. *The Making of a Fringe Candidate, 1992*. New York: Castillo International, 1992.

Gardell, Mattias. *In the Name of Elijah Muhammad: Louis Farrakhan and the Nation of Islam*. Raleigh, NC: Duke University Press, 1996.

Garment, Leonard. *Crazy Rhythm: My Journey From Brooklyn, Jazz, and Wall Street to Nixon's White House, Watergate, and Beyond...* New York: Times Books, 1997.

Garrow, David. *Bearing the Cross: Martin Luther King, Jr., and the Southern Christian Leadership Conference*. New York: HarperCollins, 2004.

Garvey, Marcus and Amy Jacques Garvey. *Philosophy and Opinions of Marcus Garvey: or Africa for the Africans*, Vol. 3. New York: Routledge, 1967.

Georgakas, Dan and Marvin Surkin. *Detroit: I Do Mind Dying. A Study in Urban Revolution*. Cambridge, MA: South End Press, 1998.

Giddens, Gary. *Satchmo*. New York: Doubleday, 1988.

Gillespie, Dizzy. *To Be or Not To Bop: The Autobiography of Dizzy Gillespie*. London: Quartet Books Limited, 1982.

Goldwin, Robert A. and Kaufman, Art. *Slavery and Its Consequences: The Constitution, Equality, and Race*. Washington, DC: American Enterprise Institute for Public Policy Research, 1988.

Goodwin, Doris Kearns. *Team of Rivals: The Political Genius of Abraham Lincoln*. New York: Simon & Schuster, 2005.

Gordon-Reed, Annette. *Thomas Jefferson and Sally Hemings: An American Controversy*. Charlottesville: University Press of Virginia, 1997.

Graber, Mark A. *Dred Scott and the Problem of Constitutional Evil*. UK: Cambridge University Press, 2006.

Grant, Donald. *The Way It Was in the South: The Black Experience in Georgia*. Athens: University of Georgia Press, 2001.

Green, Constance McLaughlin. *Washington: Capital City, 1879–1950*. Princeton, NJ: Princeton University Press, 1963.

Harlan, Louis. *Booker T. Washington: The Wizard of Tuskegee, 1901–1915*. New York: Oxford University Press, 1983.

Harris, Sheldon H. *Paul Cuffee: Black America and the African Return*. New York: Simon & Schuster, 1972.

Harris, Trudier. *Exorcising Blackness: Historical and Literary Lynching and Burning Rituals*. Bloomington. Indiana University Press, 1984.

Harrison, Alferdteen. *Black Exodus: The Great Migration from the American South*. Jackson: University Press of Mississippi, 1992.

Hasse, John Edward. *Beyond Category: The Life and Genius of Duke Ellington*. Boston: Da Capo Press, 1995.

Haworth, Paul Leland. *The Hayes-Tilden Disputed Presidential Election of 1876*. Cleveland: Burrows Brothers, 1906.

Hill, Robert. *The Marcus Garvey and Universal Improvement Association Papers: 27 August 1919–31 August 1920*. Berkeley: University of California Press, 1983.

Hirschfeld, Fritz. *George Washington and Slavery: A Documentary Portrayal*. St. Louis: University of Missouri Press, 1997.

Hochschild, Adam. *Bury the Chains: Prophets and Rebels in the Fight to Free an Empire's Slaves*. Boston: Houghton Mifflin, 2005.

Horn, James P. P., Jan Lewis, and Peter S. Onuf. *The Revolution of 1800: Democracy, Race, and the New Republic*. Charlottesville: University of Virginia Press, 2002.

Horton, James Oliver. *Landmarks of African American History*. New York: Oxford University Press, 2005.

Hyland, William G. Jr. *In Defense of Thomas Jefferson: The Sally Hemings Sex Scandal*. New York: Thomas Dunne Books, 2009.

Jackson, Maurice. *Let This Voice Be Heard: Anthony Benezet, Father of Atlantic Abolitionism*. Philadelphia: University of Pennsylvania Press, 2009.

James, C. L. R. *A History of Pan-African Revolt*. Washington, DC: Drum and Spear Press, 1969.

Jefferson, Thomas. *Memoirs, Correspondence, and Private Papers of Thomas Jefferson*, Vol. 4. London: H. Colburn and R. Bentley, 1829.

———. *Notes on the State of Virginia*. New York: Penguin Classics, 1998.

Jennings, Paul. *A Colored Man's Reminiscences of James Madison*, Electronic Edition. Chapel Hill: University of North Carolina, 1865.

Joseph, Peniel. *Dark Days, Bright Nights: From Black Power to Barack Obama.* New York: Basic Civitas Books, 2010.

———. *Waiting 'til the Midnight Hour: A Narrative History of Black Power in America.* New York: Henry Holt, 2006.

Kaplan, Sidney. *The Black Presence in the Era of the American Revolution 1770–1800.* Washington, DC: Smithsonian Institution Press, 1975.

Karabell, Zachary. *Chester Alan Arthur*. New York: Macmillan, 2004.

Kater, Michael H. *Different Drummers: Jazz in the Culture of Nazi Germany*. New York: Oxford University Press, 1992.

Katz, William Loren. *Black Pioneers: An Untold Story*. New York: Atheneum, 1999.

Katznelson, Ira. *When Affirmative Action Was White: An Untold History of Racial Inequality in Twentieth-Century America.* New York: W. W. Norton, 2005.

Keckley, Elizabeth. *Behind the Scenes or, Thirty Years a Slave, and Four Years in the White House*. New York: New York Printing Company, 1868.

Keiler, Allan. *Marian Anderson: A Singer's Journey*. New York: Lisa Drew/Scribner, 2000.

Kennedy, David M. *Over Here: The First World War and American Society*. New York: Oxford University Press, 2004.

Kessler, Ronald. *In the President's Secret Service: Behind the Scenes with Agents in the Line of Fire and the Presidents They Protect*. New York: Crown, 2009.

Kirk, Elise K. *Music at the White House: A History of the American Spirit.* Urbana: University of Illinois Press, 1986.

Kofsky, Frank. *Black Nationalism and the Revolution in Music*. New York: Pathfinder Press, 1970.

Kornweibel, Theodore Jr. *"Seeing Red": Federal Campaigns Against Black Militancy, 1919–1925*. Bloomington: Indiana University Press, 1998.

Kup, A. P. *Sierra Leone: A Concise History*. New York: St. Martin's Press, 1975.

Lane, Mark and Dick Gregory. *Code Name "Zorro": The Murder of Martin Luther King, Jr.* Englewood Cliffs, NJ: Prentice-Hall, 1977.

Lakwete, Angela. *Inventing the Cotton Gin: Machine and Myth in Antebellum America*. Baltimore: Johns Hopkins University Press, 2003.

Larson, Kate Clifford. *Bound for the Promised Land: Harriet Tubman, Portrait of an American Hero*. New York: Ballantine Books, 2003.

Lawrence, A. H. *Duke Ellington and His World: A Biography.* New York: Routledge, 2001.

Levering Lewis, David. *W. E. B. Du Bois: Biography of a Race, 1868–1919*. New York: Henry Holt, 1993.

Linebaugh, Peter and Rediker, Marcus. *The Many-Headed Hydra: Sailors, Slaves, Commoners and the Hidden History of the Atlantic*. Beacon Press, 2001.

Ling, Peter John. *Martin Luther King, Jr.* New York: Routledge, 2002.

Litweiler, John. *The Freedom Principle: Jazz After 1958.* New York: Da Capo Press, 1984.

Livermore, George. *An Historical Research: Opinions of the Founders of the Republic on Negroes as Slaves, as Citizens, and as Soldiers.* New York: Augustus M. Kelley, 1970.

Lusane, Clarence. *Colin Powell and Condoleezza Rice: Foreign Policy, Race and the New American Century.* Westport, CT: Praeger, 2006.

———. *Pipe Dream Blues: Racism and the War on Drugs.* Boston: South End Press, 1991.

Mabee, Carleton and Susan Mabee. *Sojourner Truth: Slave, Prophet, Legend.* New York: New York University Press, 1995.

Marsalis, Wynton. *Moving to a Higher Ground: How Jazz Can Change Your Life.* New York: Random House, 2008.

Marx, Karl and Sheila Rowbotham. *The Revolutions of 1848: Political Writings.* London: Verso Books, 2010.

Mayer, Jane and Jill Abramson. *Strange Justice: The Selling of Clarence Thomas.* Orlando, FL: Houghton Mifflin, 1994.

McGovern, James R. *Anatomy of a Lynching.* Baton Rouge. Louisiana State University, 1982.

McGowan, Chris. *The Brazilian Sound: Samba, Bossa Nova, and the Popular Music of Brazil.* Philadelphia: Temple University Press, 2009.

McPherson, James M. *Abraham Lincoln.* New York: Oxford University Press, 2009.

Melanson, Philip H. *The Secret Service: The Hidden History of an Enigmatic Agency.* New York: Carroll & Graf, 2005.

Mills, Kay. *This Little Light of Mine: The Life of Fannie Lou Hamer.* New York: Dutton, 1993.

Moore, Glover. *The Missouri Controversy, 1819–1821.* Lexington: University of Kentucky Press, 1953.

Morris, Thomas D. *Free Men All: The Personal Liberty Laws of the North: 1780–1861.* Baltimore, MD: Johns Hopkins University Press, 1974.

Napolitano, Andrew P. *Dred Scott's Revenge: A Legal History of Race and Freedom in America.* Nashville, TN: Thomas Nelson, 2009.

Nash, Gary B. and Jean R. Soderland. *Freedom by Degrees: Emancipation in Pennsylvania and Its Aftermath.* New York: Oxford University Press, 1991.

Neer, Bob. *Barack Obama for Beginners: An Essential Guide.* Hanover, NH: Steerforth Press, 2008.

Negro Year Book and Annual Encyclopedia of the Negro. Tuskegee, AL: Negro Year Book Publishing Co., 1916.

Nevins, Allan. *Fremont: Pathmarker of the West.* Lincoln: University of Nebraska Press, 1992.

Nevins, Allan. *War Becomes Revolution, 1862–1863: The War For the Union,* Vol. II. New York: Scribner, 1960.

Nye, Russel B.. *Fettered Freedoms: Civil Liberties and the Slavery Controversy, 1830–1860.* Lansing: Michigan State College Press, 1949.

Obama, Barack. *Audacity of Hope: Thoughts on Reclaiming the American Dream*. New York: Three Rivers Press, 2006.

———. *Dreams from My Father: A Story of Race and Inheritance*. New York: Three Rivers Press, 2004.

O'Connell, Deirdre. *The Ballad of Blind Tom: Slave Pianist, America's Lost Musical Genius*. New York: Overlook Duckworth, 2009.

O'Reilly, Kenneth. *Black Americans: The FBI Files*. New York: Carroll & Graf, 1994.

———. *Nixon's Piano: Presidents and Racial Politics from Washington to Clinton*. New York: Free Press, 1995.

Painter, Nell. *Sojourner Truth: A Life, a Symbol*. New York: W. W. Norton, 1997.

Parks, Lillian Rogers. *My Thirty Years at the White House*. Mountain View, CA: Ishi Press, 2008.

Pauley, Garth E. *The Modern Presidency & Civil Rights: Rhetoric On Race from Roosevelt to Nixon*. College Station: Texas A&M University Press, 2001.

Peterson, John. *Province of Freedom: A History of Sierra Leone, 1787–1870*. Evanston, IL: Northwestern University Press, 1969.

Pham, J. Peter. *The Sierra Leonean Tragedy: History and Global Dimensions*. New York: Nova Science Publishers, 2006.

Philippe, Louis. *Diary of My Travels in America*. New York: Delacorte Press, 1976.

Phillips, Kevin. *The Emerging Republican Majority*. New York: Arlington House, 1969.

Polenberg, Richard. *The Era of Franklin D. Roosevelt, 1933–1945: A Brief History with Documents*. New York: Palgrave Macmillan, 2000.

Porter, Eric. *What Is This Thing Called Jazz?: African American Musicians as Artists, Critics, and Activists*. Berkeley: University of California Press, 2002.

Powell, Colin. *My American Journey: An Autobiography*. New York: Random House, 1995.

Price, Roger. *The Revolutions of 1848*. Oxford: Macmillan Education, 1968.

Pulis, John W., ed. *Moving On: Black loyalists in the Afro-Atlantic World*. New York: Garland Publishing, 1999.

Quarles, Benjamin. *The Negro in the Civil War*. Boston: Little, Brown, 1969.

Ravage, John W. *Black Pioneers: Images of the Black Experience on the North American Frontier*. Salt Lake City: University of Utah Press, 1997.

Records of the Columbia Historical Society of Washington, Vol. 3–4. Washington, DC: Columbia Historical Society, 1900.

Reeves, Thomas C. *A Question of Character: A Life of John F. Kennedy*. New York: Free Press, 1991.

Remini, Robert Vincent. *Fellow Citizens: The Penguin Book of U.S. Presidential Addresses*. New York: Penguin Group, 2008.

Rice, Allen Thorndike, ed. *Reminiscences of Abraham Lincoln by Distinguished Men of His Time*. New York: Harper & Brothers, 1907.

Richards, Leonard. *Shays' Rebellion: The American Revolution's Final Battle*. Philadelphia: University of Pennsylvania Press, 2002.

Ricks, Mary Kay. *Escape on the Pearl: The Heroic Bid for Freedom on the Underground Railroad.* New York: William Morrow, 2007.

Robertson, Priscilla Smith. *Revolutions of 1848: A Social History.* Princeton, NJ: Princeton University Press, 1968.

Rogers, George Jr. and David R. Chestnutt, eds. *The Papers of Henry Laurens*, Vol. 1. Columbia: University of South Carolina, 1979.

Roosevelt, Theodore. *A Compilation of the Messages and Speeches of Theodore Roosevelt, 1901–1905.* New York: Bureau of National Literature and Art, 1906.

———. *State of the Union Addresses of Theodore Roosevelt.* London: Echo Library, 2007.

Sacks, Oliver W. *An Anthropologist on Mars: Seven Paradoxical Tales.* New York: Vintage Books, 1995.

Saul, Scott. *Freedom Is, Freedom Ain't: Jazz and the Making of the Sixties.* Cambridge, MA: Harvard University Press, 2003.

Schama, Simon. *Rough Crossings: The Slaves, the British, and the American Revolution.* London: Oberon Books, 2007.

Scheer, Robert, ed. *Eldridge Cleaver: Post-Prison Writings and Speeches.* New York: Vintage Books, 1969.

Schneirov, Richard and Thomas J. Suhrbur. *Union Brotherhood, Union Town: the History of the Carpenters' Union of Chicago, 1863–1987.* Carbondale: Southern Illinois University Press, 1988.

Schwartz, Thomas F. *For a Vast Future Also: Essays from the Journal of the Abraham Lincoln Association.* Bronx, NY: Fordham University Press, 1999.

Seale, William. *The President's House: A History.* Washington, DC: White House Historical Association, 1986.

Sefton, James E. *Andrew Johnson and the Uses of Constitutional Power.* Boston: Little, Brown, 1980.

Sehgal, Kabir. *Jazzocracy: Jazz, Democracy, and the Creation of a New American Mythology.* Mishawakak, IN: Better World Books, 2008.

Sellers, Charles. *James K. Polk: Jacksonian, 1795–1843.* Princeton, NJ: Princeton University Press, 1957.

Solomon, Mark I. *The Cry Was Unity: Communists and African Americans, 1917–1936.* Jackson: University Press of Mississippi, 1998.

Southall, Geneva H. *Blind Tom, the Black Pianist-Composer (1849–1908).* Lanham, MD: Scarecrow Press, 1999.

———. *Blind Tom: The Post–Civil War Enslavement of a Black Musical Genius.* Minneapolis: Challenge Books, 1979.

———. *The Continuing Enslavement of Blind Tom, the Black Pianist-Composer (1865–1887).* Minneapolis: Challenge Books, 1983.

Southern, Eileen. *The Music of Black Americans: A History.* New York: W. W. Norton, 1997.

Spann, C. Edward and Michael Edward Williams. *Presidential Praise: Our Presidents and Their Hymns.* Macon, GA: Mercer University Press, 2008.

Sterner, Richard. *The Negro's Share: A Study of Income, Consumption, Housing, and Public Assistance*. New York: Harper & Brothers, 1943.

Stokes, Melvyn. *D. W. Griffith's The Birth of a Nation: A History of "The Most Controversial Motion Picture of All Time."* New York: Oxford University Press, 2007.

Stuart, Charles. *A Memoir of Granville Sharp*. Whitefish, MT: Kessinger, 2008.

Szatmary, David. *Shays' Rebellion: The Making of an Agrarian Insurrection*. Amherst: University of Massachusetts Press, 1980.

Terry, Jordan. *The U.S. Constitution and Fascinating Facts About It*. Naperville, IL: Oak Hill Publishing, 2007.

Thayer, Alexander Wheelock and Elliot Forbes Thayer, eds. *Thayer's Life of Beethoven*, Princeton, NJ: Princeton University Press, 1993.

Todd, Chuck and Sheldon Gawiser. *How Barack Obama Won: A State-by-State Guide to the Historic 2008 Presidential Election*. New York: Vintage, 2009.

Tucker, Mark. *Ellington: The Early Years*. Urbana: University of Illinois Press, 1995.

Tucker, Ronnie Bernard. *Affirmative Action, the Supreme Court, and Political Power in the Old Confederacy*. Lanham, MD: University Press of America, 2000.

Von Eschen, Penny M. *Satchmo Blows Up the World: Jazz Ambassadors Play the Cold War.* Cambridge, MA: Harvard University Press, 2004.

———. *Race Against Empire: Black Americans and Anti-Colonialism, 1937–1957*. Ithaca, NY: Cornell University Press, 1997.

Waldron, Lamar. *Ultimate Sacrifice: John and Robert Kennedy, the Plan for a Coup in Cuba, and the Murder of JFK*. New York: Carroll & Graf, 2005.

Walters, Ronald W. *Black Presidential Politics: A Strategic Approach*. Albany: State University of New York Press, 1988.

Ward Angell, Stephen. *Bishop Henry McNeal Turner and African-American Religion in the South*. Knoxville: University of Tennessee Press, 1992.

Weatherly, Myra. *Benjamin Banneker: American Scientific Pioneer*. Mankato, MN: Compass Point Books, 2006.

Webb, Gary. *Dark Alliance: the CIA, the Contras, and the Crack Cocaine Explosion*. New York: Seven Stories Press, 1998.

Welch, Catherine. *Ida B. Wells-Barnett: Powerhouse With a Pen*. Minneapolis, MN: Carolrhoda Books, 2000.

Wells, Ida B. *On Lynching; Southern Horrors; A Red Record; Mob Rule in New Orleans*. New York: Arno Press. 1969.

Wemms, William and John Hodgson. *The Trial of the British Soldiers, of the 29th Regiment of Foot, for the Murder of Crispus Attucks, Samuel Gray, Samuel Maverick, James Caldwell, and Patrick Carr, on Monday Evening, March 5, 1770*. Boston: Belcher and Armstrong, 1807.

White, Walter. *Rope and Faggot: A Biography of Judge Lynch*. Notre Dame, IN: University of Notre Dame Press, 2001.

White, Walter F. *The Fire in the Flint*. New York: Negro Universities Press. 1969.

Whittingham Logan, Rayford. *The Betrayal of the Negro, From Rutherford B. Hayes to Woodrow Wilson*. New York Da Capo Press, 1997.

Wilkins, Roger. *Jefferson's Pillow: The Founding Fathers and the Dilemma of Black Patriotism*. Boston: Beacon Press, 2001.

Wills, Garry. *"Negro President": Jefferson and the Slave Power*. Boston: Houghton Mifflin, 2003.

Yarema, Allan. *The American Colonization Society: An Avenue to Freedom?* Lanham, MD: University Press of America, 2006.

Yancey, Dwayne. *When Hell Froze Over: The Untold Story of Doug Wilder, A Black Politician's Rise to Power in the South*. Dallas: Taylor Publishing, 1988.

Zinn, Howard. *A People's History of the United States, 1492–Present*. New York: HarperPerennial, 1980, 2003.

Articles

"21 Years in the White House." *Ebony.* October 1982.

"Open Letter From Shirely Sherrod: You and I Can't Yield—Not Now, Not Ever," NAACP, Web site, undated: www.naacp.org/news/entry/you-and-i-cant-yield-not-now-not-ever.

Adams, T. H. "Washington's Runaway Slave, and How Portsmouth Freed Her." *The Granite Freeman* (Concord, NH). 22 May 1845.

Allen, Mike."RNC Chief to Say It Was 'Wrong' to Exploit Racial Conflict for Votes." *Washington Post.* 14 July 2005.

Argetsinger, Amy and Roxanne Roberts. "Secret Service Confirms Third Crasher at White House State Dinner," *Washington Post.* 5 January 2010.

Bai, Matt. "Is Obama the End of Black Politics?." *New York Times.* 6 August 2008.

Barnes, Robert. "High Court to Weigh Relevance of Voting Law in Obama Era." *Washington Post.* 1 April 2009.

Barboza, Tony. "Dean Grose to Quit as Los Alamitos Mayor Over Racial Cartoon." *Los Angeles Times.* 28 February 2009.

Bell, Howard H. "Negro Nationalism: A Factor in Emigration Projects, 1858–1861." *The Journal of Negro History.* January 1962.

"Black Agents of the Secret Service Demand Attention to Still-Unaddressed Class Action Discrimination Suit Filed in 2000," *Business Wire.* 22 October 2004.

" 'Black House' for Capitol [sic]." *New York Times.* 18 August 1920.

Bositis, David. *Blacks and the 1992 Democratic National Convention.* Washington, DC: Joint Center for Political and Economic Studies, 1992.

Boyd, James. "Nixon's Southern Strategy 'It's All In the Charts.' " *New York Times.* 17 May 1970.

Brown, Blondell Reynolds. "Full Story Must Be Told at New Bell Site." *Philadelphia Inquirer.* 25 October 2002.

"The Case of Jim Parker." *Atlanta Constitution.* 26 September 1901.

Chase, Henry. "Black Life in the Capital." *American Visions*. February–March, 1995.

Chase, Henry. "Plotting a Course for Freedom. Paul Jennings: White House Memoirist." *American Visions*. February–March, 1995.

Chisholm, Shirley. "It Is Time for a Change." In *The Voice of Black America: Major Speeches by Negroes in the United States, 1797–1971*, Philip S. Foner, ed. New York: Simon & Schuster, 1972.

Clemenson, Barbara. "Justin Holland: Black Guitarist in the Western Reserve." Paper presented at the Western Reserve Studies Symposium. Western Reserve Historical Society, Cleveland, 1989.

Clephane, Walter C. "The Local Aspect of Slavery in the District of Columbia." *Records of the Columbia Historical Society*, Vol. 3 (Washington, D.C.). 1900.

Coard, Michael. "President's House Must Be Practical, Too." *Philadelphia Inquirer*. 31 August 2009.

Coates, Ta-Nehisi Paul. "Is Obama Black Enough?" *Time*. 1 February 2007.

"The Colonization of People of African Descent." *New York Tribune*. 15 August 1862.

Dart, Bob. "Ex–White House Butler Takes Seat as Honored Guest." *Sunday Star News* (Wilmington). 24 July 1983.

Doolin Mason, Lena. "A Negro In It." In *Twentieth Century Negro Literature: or, A Cyclopedia of Thought on the Vital Topics Relating to the American Negro*, Daniel Wallace Culp, ed. Naperville, IL: J. L. Nichols & Co., 1902.

"Domestic Policy Advisor Quits, White House Says." *Los Angeles Times*. 10 February 2006.

Douglass, Frederick. ⊠The President and His Speeches.⊠ *Douglass Monthly*. September 1862.

"Editorial and Publishers' Announcements." *Colored American Magazine*. October 1901: 478–79.

"Editorial Mention." *Zion's Herald*. 11 September 1901.

Eldridge Cleaver for President Fund. "Cleaver for President." Letter to the editor, *New York Review of Books*. 7 November 1968.

Fehrenbacher, Don E. "Only His Stepchildren: Lincoln and the Negro." *Civil War History* 20. 1974.

Fisher, Marc. "When Sexuality Undercuts a Family's Ties." *Washington Post*. 13 February 2005.

"For Action on Race Riot Peril." *New York Times*. 5 October 1919.

Fordham, John. "Dizzy for President." *Guardian*. 20 October 2004.

Garnet, Henry Highland. "An Address to the Slaves of the United States." In *The Voice of Black America: Major Speeches by Negroes in the United States, 1791–1971*, Philip S. Foner, ed. New York: Simon & Schuster, 1972.

Gates, Henry Louis. "Shared Ancestries Revealed." *New York Times*. 8 October 2009.

Georgetown Weekly Record. 12 March 1791.

Goodwin, Doris Kearns. Introduction to Philip B. Kunhardt III, Peter W. Kunhardt, and

Peter W. Kunhardt Jr. *Looking for Lincoln: The Making of An American Icon.* New York: Alfred A. Knopf, 2008.

"GOP Club Offers 'Obama Bucks' While Democrats Rib Palin." *Los Angeles Times.* 17 October 2008.

"Hanna Thanks 'Big Jim.'" *Chicago Daily Tribune.* 10 September 1901.

"Harding for Kellogg Bill; President Prefers It to Dyer Anti-Lynching Measure." *New York Times.* 28 August 1922.

Harrington, Richard. "Lionel Hampton's South Lawn Serenade." *Washington Post.* 11 September 1981.

Harris, Gardiner. "The Underside of the Welcome Mat." *New York Times.* 8 November 2008.

Harris, Robert L. Jr. "H. Ford Douglas: Afro-American Antislavery Emigrationist." *Journal of Negro History.* July 1977.

Headlam, Bruce. "For Him, the Political Has Always Been Comical." *New York Times.* 13 March 2009.

Hentoff, Nat. "Hard Line on the Death Penalty." *Washington Post.* 21 March 1992.

Herbert, Bob. "Impossible, Ridiculous, Repugnant." *New York Times.* 6 October 2005.

Honan, William H. "Book Discloses That Reagan Planned To Kill National Endowment for Arts." *New York Times.* 15 May 1988.

Hosenball, Mark and Eve Conant. "A Secret Side to the Secret Service." *Newsweek.* 2 June 2008.

"Jazzmen Play at White House; Young People's Program of First Lady Sets a Precedent." *New York Times.* 20 November 1962.

Johnston, David. "E-Mail Shows Racial Jokes by Secret Service Supervisors." *New York Times.* 10 May 2008.

Jordan, George E. "Fulani Party Raises Funds Creatively." *New York Newsday.* 6 April 1992.

Jordan, Mary. "Tiny Irish Village Is Latest Place to Claim Obama as Its Own." *Washington Post.* 13 May 2007.

Jordan, Robert. "Is the Jackson Political Era Ending?" *Boston Globe.* 3 December 1989.

Kane, Paul. "S.C.'s Wilson Rakes In $750,000 in Less Than 48 Hours: Opponent Tops $1 Million." *Washington Post.* 11 September 2009.

Katz, Milton S. "E. Frederick [sic] Morrow and Civil Rights in the Eisenhower Administration." *Phylon* 42, June 1981.

Kennedy, Helen. "GOP Activist DePass Apologizes After Joking on Facebook That Gorilla Is Related to Michelle Obama." *New York Daily News.* 15 June 2009.

King, Martin Luther Jr. "A Time to Break Silence." In *The Voice of Black America: Major Speeches by Negroes in the United States, 1797–1971.* Philip S. Foner, ed. New York: Simon & Schuster, 1972.

Klein, Ezra. "Rush Limbaugh: Health-care Reform Is 'Reparations,' a 'Civil Rights Act.' " *Washington Post.* 22 February 2010.

Kromm, Chris. "Analysis: A New South Rising" *Facing South.* 23 November 2008.

———. "Election 2008: The Generation Gap: Young White Voters in the South." *Facing South*. 12 November 2008.

"The Late Convention of Colored Men." *New York Times.* 13 August 1865.

Lawler, Edward. "Letter: Historic Accuracy Should Not Be Ignored." *Philadelphia Inquirer.* 25 August 2009.

Lincoln, Abraham. "Letter to the Editor: The President on the Negro Question, Executive Mansion, Washington, Aug, 22, 1862." *Harper's Weekly*. 6 September 1862.

Loftus, Joseph. "U.S. Tells World of Rights Strife." *New York Times.* 27 May 1961.

Londoño, Ernesto. "Admission Attributed To Bush's Ex-Aide." *Washington Post.* 14 March 2006.

Mabee, Carleton. "The Demise of Slavery," in *The Price of Freedom, Slavery and the Civil War*, Vol. One, Martin H. Greenberg and Charles G. Waugh, eds. Naperville, IL: Cumberland House, 2000.

MacAskill, Ewen. "Jimmy Carter: Animosity towards Barack Obama Is Due to Racism." *Guardian*. 16 September 2009.

"McCain Delivers Concession Speech." *Washington Post*. 4 November 2008.

Melton, R.H. and Richard Morin. "Wilder Taking Command in Va. Race, Polls Show." *Washington Post*. 29 October 1989.

Midgette, Anne. "Always in Character Onstage." *Washington Post*. 6 December 2009.

Mitchell, James. "James Mitchell to A. Lincoln, May 18, 1862." *Lincoln Collection*, Vol. 76.

Mills, David. "Sister Souljah's Call to Arms." *Washington Post*. 13 May 1992.

Montgomery, David. "For D.C. Family, a Distinguished, If Little-Known Ancestor." *Washington Post*. 25 August 2009.

Moore, Acel. "As Liberty Bell Flap Continues, a Slave Memorial Is Suggested." *Philadelphia Inquirer*. 2 June 2002.

Morley, Jefferson. "The Snow Riot," *Washington Post.* 6 February 2005.

Morris, Kenneth B. Jr. "New Shoes." Frederick Douglass Memorial and Historical Association Public Meeting (Washington, DC). 15 September 2007.

Morrison, Toni."Letter to Obama Campaign." Undated.

Murray, Shailagh. "A Family Tree Rooted in American Soil: Michelle Obama Learns About Her Slave Ancestors, Herself and Her Country." *Washington Post*. 2 October 2008.

"NEA Jazz Masters Honored at White House Event: A Salute to NEA Jazz Masters Celebrates Black Music Month." Press Release. National Endowment for the Arts, Washington, DC. 22 June 2004.

"Negroes Applaud Parker." *Atlanta Constitution*. 13 September 1901.

Newman, Richard. "The Pennsylvania Abolition Society: Restoring a Group to Glory." *Pennsylvania LEGACIES*. November 2005.

Newton, Leon. "The Role of Black Neo-Conservatives During President Ronald Reagan's Administration." In *White House Studies Compendium*, Vol. 6. Anthony J. Eksterowicz and Glenn P. Hastedt, eds. New York: Nova Science Publishers, Inc., 2008.

Nitkin, David and Harry Merritt. "A New Twist to an Intriguing Family History: Census

Records, Genealogical Research Show Forebears of Obama's Mother Had Slaves." *Baltimore Sun*. 2 March 2007.

Nye, Joseph S. "Public Diplomacy and Soft Power." *The ANNALS of the American Academy of Political and Social Science,* Vol. 616, No. 1. 2008.

"Obama Wins Senate Race to Become 5th Black U.S. Senator in History." *USA Today*. 2 November 2004.

O'Brien, Conor Cruise. "Thomas Jefferson: Radical and Racist." *Atlantic Monthly*. October 1996.

Oldham, James. "New Light on Mansfield and Slavery." *Journal of British Studies*, Vol. 27, No. 1. January 1988.

Page, Thomas Walker. "The Real Judge Lynch." *Atlantic Monthly*. December 1901.

Paynter, John. "The Fugitives of the *Pearl*." *Journal of Negro History* (Washington, DC). July 1916.

Pierce, Paulette. "The Roots of the Rainbow Coalition." *The Black Scholar*. March/April 1988.

Pinckney, Warren Jr. "Jazz in India: Perspectives on Historical Development and Musical Acculturation." *Asian Music*. Autumn 1989–Winter 1990.

Reich, Howard. "Jazz at the White House Newport Stars, The Clintons And WTTW Celebrate America's Music." *Chicago Tribune.*12 September 1993.

"Reverend Jesse Jackson and Rainbow Coalition Ask Clinton to Spare Rector." Press Release, National Rainbow Coalition (Chicago). 24 January 1993.

Riley, John. "White House Tea and No Sympathy: The DePriest Incident." In *National History Day 2006 Curriculum Book*. Washington, DC: White House Historical Association, 2006.

Robinson, Eugene. "An Inarticulate Kickoff." *Washington Post*. 2 February 2007.

Salisbury, Stephan. "Committee Is Put in Place to Guide Slavery Memorial." *Philadelphia Inquirer*. 23 September 2005.

———. "Despite Criticism, President's House Project Advances." *Philadelphia Inquirer*. 10 October 2009.

———. "Panel Calls for Slave Commemoration." *Philadelphia Inquirer*. 10 July 2002.

Sarmah, Satta. "Is Obama Black Enough?" *Columbia Journalism Review*. 15 February 2007.

"Savannah Remembers Him." *News and Courier* (Charleston, SC). 10 September 1901.

Scheips, P. J. "Lincoln and the Chiriqui Colonization Project." *Journal of Negro History*, Vol. 37, No. 4. 1952.

Schudel, Matt. "Top Jazz Students Play Big Number: 1600 Penn." *Washington Post*. 16 June 2009.

Shear, Michael D. " 'Conservative Values' Guide Court Appointee." *Washington Post*. 5 May 2003.

Shipman, Tim. "Sarah Palin Blamed by the US Secret Service Over Death Threats Against Barack Obama." *The Telegraph* (UK). 8 November 2008.

Slobodzian, Joseph A. "Independence Mall Slavery Memorial Gets Federal Funding." *Philadelphia Inquirer*. 6 September 2005.

Smolenyak Smolenyak, Megan. "Philip Reed, the Slave Who Rescued Freedom." *Ancestry.* May–June 2009.

"SNCC Position Paper: Vietnam." In *The Sixties Papers: Documents of a Rebellious Decade.* Judith Clavir Albert and Steward Edward Albert, eds. New York: Praeger, 1984.

Southall, Geneva Handy. "Blind Tom: A Misrepresented and Neglected Composer-Pianist." *The Black Perspective in Music.* May 1975.

Spellman, Jim and Meserve, Jeanne. "Secret Service Probes Alleged Noose Incident." *CNN.* 2 May 2008.

Spottwood, Stephen G. "The Nixon Administration's Anti-Negro Policy." In *The Voice of Black America: Major Speeches by Negroes in the United States, 1797–1973.* Philip S. Foner, ed. New York: Capricorn Books, 1975.

Steinhem, Gloria. "Women Are Never Front-Runners." *New York Times.* 8 January 2008.

Swarns, Rachel L. "Madison and the White House, Through the Memoir of a Slave." *New York Times.* 16 August 2009.

Swarns, Rachel L. and Jodi Kantor. "In First Lady's Roots, a Complex Path From Slavery," *New York Times.* 7 October 2009.

"Taft Condemns Lynching: President Says Man That Pulls the Rope Should Hang by the Rope." *New York Times.* 10 April 1912.

"Taft Deplores Lynching: The Remedy, He Tells The Times, Is Better Enforcement of the Law." *New York Times.* 27 June 1912.

"Tells His Story in a Modest Way." *Afro-American-Ledger.* 28 September 1901.

Thamel, Pete. "Coach With a Link to Obama Has Hope for Brown's Future." *New York Times.* 16 February 2007.

"This Week in Black History." *Jet.* 4 July 1983.

Thomas, Edward. "Edwin [sic] M. Thomas to A. Lincoln, August 16, 1862." *Lincoln Collection*, Vol. 84. ff. 17718–17719.

Thomas, Robert. "Lillian Parks, 100, Dies; Had 'Backstairs' White House View." *New York Times.* 12 November 1997.

Thomas, Robert McG. Jr. "Willis Conover Is Dead at 75; Aimed Jazz at the Soviet Bloc." *New York Times.* 19 May 1996.

Vittes, Laurence. "The Power and the Passion." *Strings Magazine*, January 2009.

Vorenberg, Michael. "Abraham Lincoln and the Politics of Black Colonization." *Journal of Abraham Lincoln Association*, Vol. 14, Issue 2, Summer 1993.

Wallsten, Peter. "Frank Talk of Obama and Race in Virginia." *Los Angeles Times.* 5 October 2008.

Wallsten, Peter and David G. Savage. "Conservatives Invoke Obama in Voting Rights Act Challenge." *Los Angeles Times.* 18 March 2009.

Warren, Jack D. Jr. "Uncle George's Cabin." *Free Lance-Star* (Fredericksburg, VA). 22 February 2003.

Washington, Linn Jr. "Park Service Compromises Black Rights." *Philadelphia Inquirer.* 7 May 2002.

Watrous, Peter. "Jazz at the White House: A Metaphor for Democracy (and a Help to the Boss)." *New York Times.* 21 September 1998.

Weissman, Stephen R. "Opening the Secret Files on Lumumba's Murder." *Washington Post.* 21 July 2002.

Wells, Ida B. "Lynch Law." In Ida B. Wells, Frederick Douglass, Irvine Garland Penn, and Ferdinand L. Barnett. *The Reason Why the Colored American Is Not in the World's Columbian Exposition.* Robert W. Rydell, ed. Urbana: University of Illinois Press, 1999.

Wesley, Charles H. "Lincoln's Plan for Colonizing the Emancipated Negroes." *Journal of Negro History.* January 1919.

Williams, Juan. "One-Man Show." *Washington Post.* 9 June 1991.

———. "What Obama's Victory Means for Racial Politics." *Wall Street Journal.* 10 November 2008.

Wilkins, Sharron E. "The President's Kitchen." *American Visions.* February–March 1995.

Younge, Gary. "Is Obama Black Enough?" *Guardian.* 1 March 2007.

Zoninsein, Manuela. "The Black President." *Slate.* 30 September 2008.

Studies and Reports

Chapman, Michael. "TR: No Friend of the Constitution." *Cato Policy Report.* November-December 2002.

Public Law 108-72. SEC. 6. Sense of Congress Regarding Jazz Appreciation Month.

Robinson, Michelle LaVaughn. *Princeton Educated Blacks and the Black Community,* B.A. Thesis. Princeton, NJ: Princeton University, 1985.

United States Senate. "Commemoration of A Musical Master." *Congressional Record,* S. 10152. 22 July 1992.

The White House & President's Park: Administrative History, 1781–1983. Washington, DC: United States Department of the Interior, 2001.

Web sites

About Famous People. www.aboutfamouspeople.com.

Ad-Hoc Historians. www.ushistory.org/presidentshouse/adhoc/position.htm.

Afri-Classical.com Web. http://chevalierdesaintgeorges.homestead.com/JohnsonF.html.

African American Registry. www.aaregistry.com/detail.php?id=1232.

Afrolumens Project. www.afrolumens.org/slavery/gradual.html.

American Almanac. http://american_almanac.tripod.com/amistad.htm.

American Entertainment International Speakers Bureau. 2009. www.aeispeakers.com/print.php?SpeakerID=461.

The American Presidency Project. www.presidency.ucsb.edu/ws/?pid=22360.

Ancestry Magazine. www.ancestrymagazine.com.

Architect of the Capitol. www.aoc.gov/cc/art/freedom.cfm.

Autism Research Institute. www.autism.com/families/problems/savant.htm.

Avenging the Ancestors Coalition. http://avengingtheancestors.com/index.htm.

The Black Past. www.blackpast.org.

Bloomberg. www.bloomberg.com.

British Broadcasting Company.http://news.bbc.co.uk.

CNN. http://us.cnn.com .

Common Dreams. www.commondreams.org.

Counterpunch. www.counterpunch.org.

Exploring Pennsylvanian History. http://explorepahistory.com/hmarker.php?markerId=280.

Harry S. Truman Library and Museum. www.trumanlibrary.org.

History Central. www.historycentral.com/amistad/amistad.html.

Huffington Post. www.huffingtonpost.com.

Institute for Historical Review. www.ihr.com.

James Madison's Montpelier. http://Montpelier.org/blog/?cat=8.

Kennedy Center. www.kennedy-center.org.

The Myrtle Hart Society. http://myrtlehart.org/content/view/275/5.

Narcosphere. http://narcosphere.narconews.com.The Nation. www.thenation.com/blogs. The New Yorker. www.newyorker.com.

Pew Research Center. http://pewresearch.org.

Project Vote. Web. www.projectvote.org.

Public Broadcasting Service (PBS). www.pbs.org.

The Public Eye. http://publiceye.org.

Slate. www.slate.com/id/87868.

Slavery in the North. www.slavenorth.com.Talking Points Memo. http://tpmmuckraker.talkingpointsmemo.com.

Think Progress. http://thinkprogress.org/2006/03/10/claude-allen.

U.S. History. www.history.org.

Universal Negro Improvement Association and African Communities League. www.unia-acl.org/archive/declare.htm.

White House Historical Association. www.whitehousehistory.org.

INDEX

Index

ABOUT THE AUTHOR

Dr. Clarence Lusane is an Associate Professor of Political Science in the School of International Service at American University, where he teaches and researches on international human rights, comparative race relations, social movements, and electoral politics.

He is also an author, activist, scholar, lecturer, and journalist. For more than 30 years he has written about and been active in national and international antiracism politics, globalization, U.S. foreign policy, human rights, and social issues such as education and drug policy. He spent two years living in London conducting research on racism and human rights in Europe and working with European institutions and NGOs.

His most recent book is *Colin Powell and Condoleezza Rice: Foreign Policy, Race, and the New American Century*. Other books by Dr. Lusane include *Hitler's Black Victims: The Experiences of Afro-Germans, Africans, Afro-Europeans and African Americans During the Nazi Era*; *Race in the Global Era: African Americans at the Millennium*; *No Easy Victories: A History of Black Elected Officials*; *African Americans at the Crossroads: The Restructuring of Black Leadership and the 1992 Elections*; *The Struggle for Equal Education*; and *Pipe Dream Blues: Racism and the War on Drugs.*

Dr. Lusane is the former editor of the journal *Black Political Agenda* and has edited newsletters for a number of national nonprofit organizations. He is a national columnist for the Black Voices syndicated news network, and his writings have appeared in *The Black Scholar*, *Race and Class*, *Washington Post*, *Covert Action Information Bulletin*, *Z Magazine*, *Radical History*

Journal, Souls, New Political Science, Journal of Popular Film and Television and many other publications. Over the past two decades he has won several research and writing awards. His essay "Rhapsodic Aspirations: Rap, Race, and Power Politics" won the 1993 Larry Neal Writers' Competition Grand Prize for Art Criticism. In 1983, his article "Israeli Arms to Central America" won the prestigious Project Censored Investigative Reporting Award as the most censored story of the year.

He is the former Chairman of the Board of the National Alliance of Third World Journalists. As a journalist he has traveled to numerous countries to investigate their political and social circumstances or crises, including Panama in the aftermath of the U.S. invasion; East Germany during the last months of its existence; and Zimbabwe as a delegate to the Congress of the International Organization of Journalists. Other nations he has visited and reported on include Cuba, Egypt, Mexico, Jamaica, North Korea, South Korea, Italy, Pakistan, and South Africa.

Dr. Lusane has been a political and technical consultant to the World Council of Churches, the Congressional Black Caucus Foundation, and a number of elected officials and nonprofit organizations. He worked for eight years in the U.S. House of Representatives as a staff aide to former D.C. Congressman Walter E. Fauntroy, and then for the former Democratic Study Group that served as the primary source of legislative information and analysis for House Democrats. He has taught and worked at Howard University's Center for Drug Abuse Research and Center for Urban Policy; Medgar Evers College's Du Bois Bunche Center for Public Policy, and Columbia University's Institute for Research in African American Studies. Dr. Lusane received his Ph.D. in Political Science from Howard University in 1997.

In 2001–2002, he received the prestigious British Council Atlantic Fellowship in Public Policy where he investigated the impact of regional antiracism legislation on the antiracist movement in the UK. From 2002 to 2003 he served as Assistant Director of the 1990 Trust, one of the UK's largest and most important antiracist, human rights nongovernmental organizations.

He has lectured and presented scholarly papers at a wide range of colleges and universities including Harvard, Georgetown, George Washington, North Carolina A&T, University of California at Berkeley, University of Chicago, Yale, London School of Economics, and University of Paris among others. He has also lectured on U.S. race relations in numerous foreign nations including Colombia, Cuba, England, France, Germany, Guadeloupe, Haiti, Japan, the Netherlands, Panama, Switzerland, and Zimbabwe, among other countries.

Dr. Lusane has regularly appeared on C-SPAN, PBS, BET, and other local, national, and international television and radio programs, where he has discussed international relations, global black politics, economic globalization and new technologies, cultural issues, and multilateral narcotics policy.

He is the Co-Chair of the Civil Society Committee of the U.S.-Brazil Joint Action Plan to Eliminate Racial & Ethnic Discrimination & Promote Equality (JAPER). The project is an effort to build collaborative anti-racist and anti-discrimination projects in the areas of criminal justice, education, employment, the environment, and health.

RECENT AND FORTHCOMING TITLES IN THE OPEN MEDIA SERIES

Narrative of the Life of Frederick Douglass, an American Slave
A New Critical Edition
by Angela Y. Davis

Colorblind
The Rise of Post-Racial Politics and the Retreat from Racial Equity
by Tim Wise

Between Barack and a Hard Place
Racism and White Denial in the Age of Obama
by Tim Wise

Making the Future
The Unipolar Imperial Moment
By Noam Chomsky

Interventions
By Noam Chomsky

Crossing Zero
The AfPak War at the Turning Point of American Empire
By Paul Fitzgerald, Elizabeth Gould

The Bomb
By Howard Zinn

A Power Governments Cannot Suppress
By Howard Zinn